Worlds Apart

Worlds Apart explores the notions of the 'local' and the 'global', topics which are currently generating a great deal of discussion in many different disciplines. Anthropology has traditionally been concerned with regional traditions, which today appear threatened by the spread of transnational institutions. In this volume, the contributors examine global institutions, ranging from bureaucracy to business and from soap opera to beauty contests, in their specific localised forms. Through detailed ethnographic examples, in regions such as West Africa, Hawaii, Australia, Belize and Egypt, they show precisely how global institutions, including capitalism and mass consumption, are manifested in local contexts. Their work exemplifies the role of anthropologists in this area and provides a model for future anthropological research. It also shows that an ethnographic approach will be invaluable to emerging disciplines such as cultural studies and media studies.

Worlds Apart gives a firm foundation for future debates about local–global relations, and sets a new agenda, demonstrating the continued relevance of anthropology in the contemporary world. It will be stimulating reading for all students of anthropology, cultural studies, media studies, human geography and sociology.

Daniel Miller is Reader in Anthropology at University College London.

ASA Decennial Conference Series
The Uses of Knowledge: Global and Local Relations
Series editor: Marilyn Strathern

Other titles in this series:

Worlds Apart

Modernity through the prism of the local

Edited by Daniel Miller

London and New York

First published 1995
by Routledge
11 New Fetter Lane, London EC4P 4EE

Simultaneously published in the USA and Canada
by Routledge
29 West 35th Street, New York, NY 10001

Typeset in Times 10/12 by
Florencetype Ltd, Stoodleigh, Devon

Printed and bound in Great Britain by
T. J. Press (Padstow) Ltd, Padstow, Cornwall

British Library Cataloguing in Publication Data
A catalogue record for this book is available from the British
Library

Library of Congress Cataloguing in Publication Data
A catalogue record for this book has been requested

ISBN 0–415–10788–1 (hbk)
ISBN 0–415–10789–X (pbk)

Contents

Illustrations

Contributors

Professor Lila Abu-Lughod: Department of Anthropology, New York University, USA.

Dr Karin Barber: Centre of West African Studies, The University of Birmingham, UK.

Professor Veena Das: Department of Sociology, Delhi School of Economics, Delhi University, India.

Professor Jonathan Friedman: Department of Social Anthropology, University of Lund, Sweden.

Dr Kajsa Ekholm Friedman: Research School in Historical Anthropology and Sociology, University of Lund, Sweden.

Dr Caroline Humphrey: Department of Social Anthropology, University of Cambridge, UK.

Professor Bruce Kapferer: Department of Anthropology, University College London, UK.

Dr Daniel Miller: Department of Anthropology, University College London, UK.

Dr Howard Morphy: Pitt Rivers Museum, University of Oxford, UK.

Professor Michael Rowlands: Department of Anthropology, University College London, UK.

Professor Jean-Pierre Warnier: Department of Anthropology, Université René Descartes, Paris, France.

Professor Christopher A. Waterman: School of Music, University of Washington, USA.

Professor Richard Wilk: Department of Anthropology, University of Indiana, USA.

Preface

This book is one of five to have been produced from the Fourth Decennial Conference of the Association of Social Anthropologists of the Commonwealth, held at St Catherine's College, Oxford, in July 1993. Sections were organised by Richard Fardon, Wendy James, Daniel Miller and Henrietta Moore, each of whom has edited their proceedings. In addition Wendy James acted as Oxford Co-ordinator, and it is principally due to her untiring efforts that the conference took place at all. As Convenor, I take the opportunity of acknowledging our debt to her, and of registering gratitude to Priscilla Frost for her organisational assistance and to Jonathan Webber for acting as conference Treasurer.

The Institute of Social and Cultural Anthropology gave material as well as moral support. The following bodies are to be thanked for their generous financial assistance: the Wenner-Gren Foundation for Anthropological Research; the British Council; the Oxford University Hulme Trust Fund; the Royal Anthropological Institute and the Association of Social Anthropologists itself.

To suppose anthropological analysis can shift between global and local perspectives may well imply that the two coexist as broader and narrower horizons or contexts of knowledge. Indeed, the relationship seems familiar from the ethnographic record: in cosmologies that set a transcendent or encompassing realm against the details of everyday life; or in systems of value that aggrandise this feature while trivialising that; or in shifts between what pertains to the general or the particular, the collective or the individual. And if knowledge consists in the awareness of contextual shift, then such scaling may well seem routine. However, this book does not take scale for granted. It examines certain contexts in which people (including anthropologists) make different orders of knowledge for themselves as a prelude to questioning assumptions about the 'size' of knowledge implied in the contrast between global and local perspectives.

Marilyn Strathern
University of Cambridge

Foreword

The overall organiser of the Fourth Decennial conference of the Association of Social Anthropologists was Marilyn Strathern, and it was she who requested my participation alongside the other organisers of the individual days within this conference. This book is one of five being published as a product of that conference and I would like to record my deep gratitude to Professor Strathern not only for entrusting me with this responsibility but more generally for her constant encouragement and support of my academic work over the last few years. The team she selected worked together for some years prior to the conference itself and I gratefully acknowledge the assistance and advice given by Richard Fardon, Wendy James and Henrietta Moore.

The overarching theme selected by Professor Strathern was 'The Uses of Knowledge'. Within this the committee decided to concentrate on the theme of local–global articulations. A further subdivision was then organised with each individual being made responsible for a more specific academic domain. The topic of this volume is constructed in part through its focus on the new technologies of embodiment and objectification as expressing more generally the anthropological contribution to the study of modernity and consumption. But it is also defined by its respect for the areas that were being covered in its sister volumes which are to be published in this series, and subsequently various topics which are not addressed here may be found to be well served in these companion books. The conference itself attracted far more people than any of us had anticipated and I would wish to acknowledge here the hard work that Priscilla Frost, Wendy James and Marilyn Strathern had to put into the logistics of the event. This included preparation of background documents and notes, dealing with the bookings and facilities, the search for funding and assistance to the speakers, requirements for special equipment and the like. I took no part in this work and was merely the happy beneficiary of the high degree of organisational efficiency.

I would next like to record my appreciation to the speakers themselves. The present volume is slightly altered from the actual conference event in as much as the excellent paper given by Nicholas Thomas is not included in this particular publication. On the other hand Caroline Humphrey was an invited participant but unable to attend as she was in the field, but has now contributed a paper to the published volume. I am grateful to both speakers and writers for their forbearance of my organisational and editorial intrusions and panics during this last year. I still feel a sense of neglect in that I was unable to provide the hospitality and support for the individual speakers that I should have liked to have given, owing to the rather frenetic atmosphere of the conference, and for this I apologise. I have received very positive feedback on the papers and discussions that took place on that day. This related not only to the contributions of all the speakers involved but also to the chairing of Sandra Wallman and Anthony Cohen as well as the commentaries given by Alfie Gell and Johannes Fabian. I am very grateful to all four of them for their participation, assistance and advice.

I would normally acknowledge separately all those who commented on the paper I present here as an introduction which is an expansion of that given on the day itself. I must admit, however, that I simply cannot recall all those who offered comments on the earlier draft which I circulated. I do recall the sound advice provided by Henrietta Moore and I believe I received comments from many of the day's speakers. I do not recall which of my departmental colleagues commented on the paper, but I do know that I am highly privileged to be working at the Department of Anthropology at University College London since I cannot imagine receiving greater support and inspiration for my work than I constantly obtain from my colleagues in that department. As one example of this Allen Abramson (not for the first time) provided me with a title for this volume. If I have left out any others who provided comments I ask their forgiveness.

Daniel Miller
University College London

1 Introduction

Anthropology, modernity and consumption[1]

D. Miller

MODERNITY AS CONSUMPTION

The larger framework to the study of anthropology has always been a concern with modern life as an experience of rupture. While the general public continues to perceive anthropology as primarily a discipline which utilises fieldwork in order to identify and characterise a condition opposed to modernity, this has never been a true representation of the actual range of anthropological concerns. Although at times marginal there has always been present a disciplinary interest in describing and understanding the abstractions and reflexivity of modern life. Today, what might once have been peripheral has now become so ubiquitous as to be almost typical of contemporary anthropological work. This development need not, however, be seen as simply a change in focus or interest, since it must also reflect the culmination of a shift in the consciousness of the peoples we study who almost all now view themselves in direct relation to an explicit image of modern life.

With respect to the specific term 'consumption', anthropologists such as Appadurai (1986), Bourdieu (1984) and Douglas (Douglas and Isherwood 1978) have played a conspicuous role in the expansion of this concept from its parochial roots in economics. From economics the term retains as a primary connotation a debate about the role of goods and services. Although there are papers in this book that share this more defined concern, my use of the term in the Introduction will be rather different. In addressing the idea of consumption I want to evoke something more abstract, potentially a philosophical rather than an economic debate. While in economics to be a consumer is to have choice, my emphasis is on quite another aspect. I use the term consumer in opposition to the aesthetic ideal of a creative producer. I want to reflect on a condition in which very little of what we possess is made by us in the first instance. Therefore to be a consumer is to possess consciousness that one is living through objects and images not of one's own creation. It is this which makes the term symptomatic of what some at least have seen as the core meaning of the term modernity (Habermas 1987: 1–44). This sense of consumption as a secondary relationship takes on particular importance within an ideology which espouses not only the aesthetic ideal of authenticity through creation, but its more mundane philosophical counterpart of a notion of natural ownership through labour. Within such a dominant ideology the condition of consumption is always a potential state of rupture. Consumption then may not be about choice, but rather the sense that we have no choice but to attempt to overcome the experience of rupture using those very same goods and images which create for many the sense of modernity as rupture.

I concede immediately that this is only one perspective. Few of the following chapters make particular use of this term. They have their own keywords such as 'authenticity' and 'identity' and their own perspectives, but I do feel we share what is now a common concern in the discipline to address issues of reflexivity, rupture and distance. These were the topics introduced by Marilyn Strathern as the overall theme of the Decennial conference of which this book is one product. My point of departure is the suggestion that the condition of consumption represents, at the very least, one possible idiom for these larger problems of modernity.

A simplifying dualism may assist in drawing out emergent foci of concern. This may be posed between what could be called a priori and a posteriori cultural diversity. Anthropologists have generally had as their subject the observation of differences between peoples. The degree to which it was merely an assumption that these differences originated out of their diverse historical circumstance has been particularly challenged by the Comaroffs (Comaroff and Comaroff 1992: 3–48). Through both the study of the sheer complexity of pre-colonial inter-cultural contacts (e.g. Thomas 1991) and the study of the impact of colonial regimes (e.g. Wolf 1982), it is now recognised that we cannot treat the cultural world as though it were a series of isolated historical trajectories leading to current diversity.

Nevertheless there has remained a sense that even if these 'roots' were thoroughly entangled, the key source of difference remains historical. So, for example, when anthropologists turn their attention to the differential reception and development of capitalism (e.g. Sahlins 1988) the dominant issue is the impact of the prior regional differences upon the subsequent development of this new institution. These 'locals' are held to retain authentic differences at least until they become victims of mass consumption as the latest version of post-colonial influences. Mass consumption goods often come to stand for the new superordinate point of identity that subsumes and suppresses cultural difference and creates drastic global homogenisation. It is as though after anthropologists have documented the resilience of local resistance and the ability to 'tame' imported ideas and traditions, these might finally fall exhausted before the onslaught of imported goods.

By contrast, there is another source of difference, which might be called a posteriori difference, that is more rarely acknowledged or theorised.

This is the sense of quite unprecedented diversity created by the differential consumption of what had once been thought to be global and homogenising institutions. Examples might include the increasingly differentiated forms of modernity, of bureaucracy, of media worlds and of capitalism. It is commonly our relation to these massive institutions which gives us our identity as consumers. The idea of a posteriori diversity allows for the possibility of more radical rupture under conditions of modernity, but does not assume that homogenisation follows. Rather it seeks out new forms of difference, some regional, but increasingly based on social distinctions which may not be easily identified with space. It treats these, not as continuity, or even syncretism with prior traditions, but as quite novel forms, which arise through the contemporary exploration of new possibilities given by the experience of these new institutions.

I am certainly not claiming this is an unprecedented issue. The regional responses to the universalist claims of religion, creating new unpredictable local movements which are not merely continuous with earlier cults, are among the many examples which should have given the lie to the notion of some pure a priori source of difference. There is, however, a danger in the interpretive framework through which these are judged. The problem arises from our willingness to view the bending of forms to local trajectories as creating difference which is respected – that is, granted authenticity. Indeed, anthropologists tend to 'cheer' from the sidelines any sign that the 'local' has fragmented and shifted some larger form to meet its own projects of value. The discipline identifies with this David in its struggle with some monstrous global Goliath. In contrast, however, a posteriori diversity may be condemned precisely because it has no 'roots'. The critique of postmodernism which seems to equate such 'depthlessness' with other pejorative terms such as 'superficiality' has been popular within anthropology perhaps because it appeals to this conservatism which protects diversity with patina attached but may denigrate the '*nouveaux*' or '*parvenu*' locals of the contemporary world, especially when attached to 'inauthentic' social fractions such as the lower-middle classes of the developed world, or the middle classes of the developing world. With a posteriori diversity the myth of the a priori 'original difference' falls away, but there is a danger that a belief in pure authenticity will be replaced by a myth of pure inauthenticity.

Obviously cultural forms do not arise out of the ether, but there may be an argument that, for example, the emergence of a new variety of 'public sphere' through the development of television chat-shows does not necessarily arise out of the historical trajectory documented by Habermas (1991). This would not make it any less important in considering the kind of public sphere which can exist and should be considered in debates about the comparative nature of the public sphere today (e.g. Livingstone and Lunt 1994).

This is the common thread which runs through the chapters of this book. They all deal with social groups who are no longer best understood as self-constructed within the terms of some customary value system. Rather they are constructing themselves through appropriating or rejecting contexts in which they find themselves – or, as the papers reveal, usually through more complex dialectics of identitification. Peoples do not choose for themselves as their 'starting points' the legacy of West African colonialism (Barber and Waterman, Rowlands, Warnier), a collapsed communism (Humphrey), a status as minorities in their own lands (Friedman, Kapferer, Morphy). They may not choose domains such as beauty contests (Wilk), or television programmes (Abu-Lughod, Das) upon which they have to constitute themselves as different. For these reasons it may be best to consider them as the consumers rather than creators of their conditions of culture. Nevertheless in all cases the authors trace negotiations, creative appropriations and the production of strategies which develop the possibilities given by these historical conditions. In some cases these do appear to demonstrate continuities with previous projects of value and struggles over power. In other cases there is the emergence of unprecedented forms of identity which appear as explicit encounters with novel aspects of modernity.

There have been several recent discussions as to whether it is possible to use the term 'modernity' without suggesting a stigma of primitivism, and whether it characterises unprecedented conditions (e.g. Giddens 1991, Lash and Friedman 1992, Miller 1994). But most of the papers in this volume are concerned with the more straightforwardly unprecedented resources provided by the industrial, scientific and most especially the communications revolutions which provide new technologies of objectification. We are responding to the forms of knowledge and doubt that arise with media such as television and the internet, which allow people to reflect on themselves in the light of almost instantaneous knowledge about global events and local consequences.

People are often suspicious of culture defined as a process of consumption, seeing it as somehow less authentic or worthy given its comparative transience and lack of roots. There is still too often a denigration of these novel sources of difference as merely a new superficiality, a pretension to difference in as much as this is granted us by global institutions such as capitalism. By contrast, the following chapters accept the challenge of these new forms of reflexivity and suggest that the social beings who live within complex and diverse worlds, may, as the subjects of ethnography (as Friedman argues), be neither more complex nor less profound. We cannot presume to know how something will be experienced. A novel practice may become an instrument of reflexivity and rupture, but equally it may sink back into the unreflective practical taxonomies of everyday material culture.

Faced with these new technologies of objectification the primary aim of ethnographic study should remain an evocation of ordinary human commensurability. The anthropological task is often to show just how ordinary and mundane Mongolian breakdancing or gatherer-hunters watching soap opera may have become in everyday experience. The mundane requires empathetic understanding, just as much as the traditional anthropological concern to make extraordinary that which has become taken for granted. That is to show how what we took to be the mundane may be the idiom for core cosmological and moral debates in society.

An anthropology which demonstrates how the consumption of global forms is located in ordinary commensurability also creates an equality between the peoples of the world. The rituals of British capitalism are no more nor less bizarre than Nigerian capitalism, world music is evolving in the Balkans as much as in Brazil. Furthermore, as Rowlands, and Barber and Waterman, point out, the supposed characteristics of modernity may be derived from many regional trajectories, Chinese and West African or at least other than a supposed generic Westernisation.

MODERNITY AND CONSUMPTION AS HISTORICAL MOMENTS

The chapters in this book are without exception ethnographically based. The emphasis is upon the detailed elucidation of specific case studies. Though they take note of more general and comparative materials none of them consists primarily of a sustained theoretical discussion. Yet anthropology has been one of the most constant contributors to the development of major theoretical debates in the social sciences. By now it may be conceded that this is because of and not despite its unusual mixture of relativism and a qualitative version of non-naturalistic empiricism. In this Introduction therefore I am concerned to draw out the wider implications of what in themselves are very particular and focused case studies. I will supplement these comments with data from my own research in Trinidad.

The first paper by Rowlands is typical of the anthropological prism that breaks modernity apart in its attention to the specific nuances of the local. In this case through examining first historically and then ethnographically how the interpenetration of a sense of being modern and being traditional is mapped onto a shifting hierarchy and competing claims to legitimation in Cameroon. Yet this relativism is precisely what allows the paper to stand for a much more general concern to document the transition in the world that warrants a change in the discipline's perception of its subject of study. By revealing that there are African roads to modernity Rowlands is able to document the particular manner in which a dialectic of being both traditional and modern (which is common throughout the contemporary world) takes the form of a very specific and nuanced relationship of partial resolutions and subsumptions, both in the lives of individuals and through contrasts between regional groups. It is the insistence upon difference, what he calls 'the instability of temporalities' that makes this safe ground from which to theorise generalities about modernity.

The importance of Rowlands's contribution may be made more evident by its contrast with Trinidad. Rowlands demonstrates the manner by which the growing confrontation with the contradictions of modernity is best understood through the specific history of the region. In Trinidad, as with the Caribbean more generally, although many of the peoples came from West Africa, their history was punctured by a much more radical rupture in the form of the extreme de-humanisation of slavery. This historical experience is then overlaid by that of many other immigrant groups. Here then there is no easy recourse to tradition or roots and the road to modernity is that much more direct. In Trinidad the result is quite distinct from Cameroon and establishes the importance of relativism in this 'consumption' of history. While for Cameroon the core distinction is one of the sense of being modern, which is able to interpenetrate (often without contradiction) the sense of tradition, in Trinidad (Miller 1994) it is the event that is held as contradiction and threat to the sense of the long term. Thus in the latter case an orientation toward plans and strategies for future success goes together with a concern for building respect for the past and the previous generations. Both orientations are contrasted with a radical refusal of either by those absorbed with events as transient states. Because this is completely different from the sense of temporality described by Rowlands it establishes the validity of his point that although a dialectic of modernity and tradition is found in many regions, it cannot be taken for granted and must be related back to the specific experience of history in that locality.

There are several issues in common between Rowlands's and Humphrey's chapter. Both emphasise the ways in which increasingly self-conscious developments of cultural identity evolve out of the desire to retain local visions of what may be ascribed to as global futures. Both contributors (as also several of the later contributors) here, as in their previous work, emphasise the role of material culture. This perspective comes into its own given the increasing need to consider the consequences of the new forms of objectification, whether in shopping or household furnishings. Rowlands, in particular, articulates these with an older Cameroonian trajectory of more literal embodiments through his analysis of the 'bio-politics' by which property and possessions are hierarchically objectified in the potency of persons. This act of taming of the new signs of success is precisely what seems to be no longer an option in contemporary Moscow. These chapters also demonstrate the importance of ethnographic contributions to the process of commodification. This process is easily over-generalised, but localised studies reveal striking contrasts. Working in an area close to Rowlands, Geschiere (1992) has recently noted the surprise of outsiders that it is often intimate and domestic relations which here are easily commoditised although elsewhere these are regarded as bastions against commodification, while aspects of the economy which in Europe were were commoditised early on, may be resistant to such changes in West Africa.

Finally both chapters show the importance of the term 'consumption' as linking questions concerned with the symbolic potential of goods with the more general secondary relationship peoples increasingly take to the forms through which they have to live. In both cases this is represented as a 'burden of history'. Muscovites may be struggling with some version of capitalism or the market, but it is likely to be a good while before they see this as 'their' capitalism. Rather, as with colonialism in Cameroon, these changes highlight the sense that one is consuming in the more abstract sense of dealing with forces which have come from outside and that one does not have the experience or knowledge to properly harness them to one's own historical project. Indeed they are not even able to stabilise the present around some specific 'other' group who can be identified as the instruments of importation.

It is in relation to the title of this section – the experience of 'historical moments' that a contrast between the two papers becomes most evident. In Cameroon one is dealing with longer transformations of colonialism and post-colonial regimes. As a result the dialectic of tradition and modernity provides in some senses a stable structure through which current differences, as between francophiles and anglophiles, find their resonance, even though this experience of coherence may hide a deeper instability and ambivalence which today threatens a more radical rupture. By contrast, what Humphrey points out in the case of Muscovites is the difficulty of establishing the positive use of this historical legacy as against a mere scepticism with regard to whatever opportunity purports to be on offer. This is a result of the bewildering experience of that extreme modernity that arises when the criteria for value are cut from beneath one. Humphrey evokes the suddenness of the transition from the Soviet system, which rendered the skills and resourcefulness of consumption built during that regime suddenly worthless. At the same time, what previously had been regarded as private vices of accumulation suddenly became officially valorised as public virtues.

As a result, 1993 becomes a long time in the history of local consumption, since within the course of the year Muscovites are buffeted between different possibilities for consumer goods and the constant learning and unlearning of consumption strategies. Given this radical 'presentness' there is no simple affirmation of 'tradition' as a resource in confronting modernity. Rather there is a state of rupture which means that people cannot remove the patina of otherness and thus render the purchased object truly their possession. Humphrey thereby makes ethnographically the point argued above with respect to a posteriori diversity. Rather than assuming it is the well-established cosmologies derived from historical experience that will determine the development of consumption,

Humphrey implies that given the present conditions of rupture it is those who experienced the historical moment of recent turbulence who may be best positioned to react appropriately. The past is certainly not irrelevant to the formation of current scepticism but this new anthropology and these new consumers require a different sense of historical consciousness than has hitherto been the norm for the discipline.

THE ANTHROPOLOGY OF GLOBAL INSTITUTIONS

The premise for the position taken in this Introduction is that culture has become increasingly a process of consumption of global forms. But the term 'global' could easily become a lazy cliché and it is to the credit of Chapters 4 and 5 that they attempt to problematise typical examples of what we tend to call 'global'. Fortunately, unlike other forms of analysis which tend to accept the self-representations and legitimations of institutions, ethnography can reveal the internal contradictions and differences which emerge when one insists that the global form is always to be located also in its specific local manifestation. Yet given the long history of anthropological rhetoric about how the next stage would include the ethnographies of the World Health Organisation and the IMF we should be concerned with how few such studies have as yet been carried out.

A future anthropology might well have high on its agenda the study of comparative capitalism, comparative bureaucracy, comparative modernity and comparative consumption. In an absence of anthropology we are left with book stores stuffed with volumes on what is seen as the essential nature of modernity and conditions of postmodernity – debates about space–time compression, materialism, the substitution of the sign, etc. But when Trinidad is used to exemplify modernity instead of Paris or Berlin, these oft-repeated generalities about modernity become suspect. Born as peripheral agro-industry for the European core, it was amongst the most extreme examples of a people shorn of mere custom. Ethnographic study in Trinidad does encounter many of these supposed attributes of modernity, but often in unanticipated configurations. For example, the uses of style as transience, the consequences of reflexivity on self-definition, the forms of individualism. All of these were quite unlike those postulated in these generalised textbooks based mainly upon Western Europe and the United States. For example the relationship between the self and the event in Trinidad bears no relation to Giddens's characterisation of the autobiographical self in his recent book on modernity (Giddens 1991, Miller 1994).

The need for a comparative ethnographic study of capitalism is if anything even stronger than that for comparative modernity. Capitalism has become a lazy word which lends support to this latter-day Wizard of Oz, this mask of the abstract logic of profitability that rules the world, in part because it remains unchallenged in its dominant representation –

as much fostered by socialist stereotyping as generalised by its admirers. By contrast, ethnography has the capacity to go behind the mask and reveal the alternative quarrelsome logics, of which profitability is merely one, which struggle for ascendency within its interior worlds.

Much of my own ethnography was based in the offices of the transnational companies and advertising agencies, where the folly of assuming that these represent merely some project in global homogenising flooding some remnant localism is quickly evident. By ethnography I mean listening in to endless conversations about image construction for a new colour in disinfectant or flavour in soft drinks as firms search endlessly for niches in which to commoditise some tiny prediction amidst the cacophony of transforming cultural worlds. It is here where the structural contradictions in the new articulations between the local and the global are perhaps most evident.

There are, for example, six major advertising agencies in Trinidad including one true transnational – McCann Erickson, though the staff are without exception Trinidadian. From the perspective of transnational companies represented in the island, maximum profitability is to be gained by the use of adverts which are produced in one place and then shown in as many countries as possible. From the point of view of the local agencies, however, the profit made from placing these 'canned' adverts in the local media is a mere percentage. If, however, the local agencies can persuade the transnationals that a product will not sell in Trinidad unless there is local advertising then the agency becomes responsible for actually creating adverts, which means a vastly larger budget and, in turn, much bigger agencies. On the whole Trinidadian agencies have been very effective in promulgating this argument, and the bulk of adverts which are shown on Trinidadian television are in fact made in Trinidad. My study suggested that agencies happily ignore evidence that the more glamorous international adverts might be more effective in actually selling goods. It follows that since the argument for local production of adverts can only ever be based on a claim that Trinidadian consumption is somehow special and different, it is therefore incumbent upon agencies if they want to make big profits to highlight anything which addresses local specificity. The irony is, of course, that because profitability itself has become a contradictory imperative, it is advertising including transnational agencies which have become the major investors in preserving and promoting images of local specificity, retaining if not creating the idea that Trinidad is different, and inculcating this belief within the population at large. Furthermore they need to do so at the expense of their own 'global' profitability' (for details see Miller (in preparation)).

Such ethnographic observations are vital if terms such as 'post-Fordism' are ever to be more than glib generalities. Our micro-studies of consumption are not a retreat from political economy because we are finding that the local has become the commanding heights of the political economy. It is only here that we can relate directly to questions of, for example, the comparative experience of World-Bank-sponsored structural adjustment. I believe the fall of socialist societies has brought into fierce focus the paucity of our attempts towards comparative theories of capitalism.

Both Kapferer and Warnier demonstrate the potential of ethnography in addressing issues of rupture in relation to global institutions. Kapferer articulates the general emergence of the concept of identity out of the rise of bureaucracy with the emotional struggles of Aboriginal and non-Aboriginal Australians for control over their identity against an encompassing state bureaucracy. As in many of these chapters the intention is to force the reader to acknowledge the poignancy of the articulation between the smallest and the most immense facets of social experience. On the one hand there is the event in which the individual mocks and rails against the structures of authority that are represented in the encounter, and thereby appears momentarily to undermine them. But against this is the overarching point of the paper as to the longer historical trajectory which has created a tight relationship between the emergence of bureaucracy and the ideal of identity. It is this that makes the apparent comedy of encounter merely a revelation of the larger tragedy in which it is powerlessness rather than resistance that is revealed (compare Abu-Lughod 1990). Indeed the poignancy renders not only the behaviour of a few Aboriginal people tragic. In the same space Kapferer's paper provides an equal mockery of contemporary social scientists including anthropologists who seem to have treated the issue of 'identity' as a refuge from larger issues of power. Identity has started to attain an aura of self-constructed plurality which escapes the documentation of institutional growth. Instead Kapferer locates at the heart of this enterprise the same bureaucratisation which contemporary academics have used 'identity politics' to try and negate.

The modesty of anthropologists' attempts to deal with radical encounters is equally acknowledged in Warnier's final remarks with respect to his case study of local and global business. This chapter may be read in conjunction with a more general project on comparative capitalism (Bayart 1994). With respect to the larger Decennial theme of 'the uses of knowledge', Warnier demonstrates that for capitalism in Cameroon commensurability between the local and global is achieved as much through encompassable ignorance as through attempted knowledge. The situation Warnier describes is surely an increasingly common one under conditions of modernity. Here we are concerned less with what the social participants know than the need for action in conditions where there are clear limits to the knowledge we might have. While economists seem content to deal with ignorance through the projection of ideal models of the market and to treat the actuality of the world as messy distortions, it is the endeavour of anthropologists to sink themselves into this mire of contradictory realities and reveal the effects of the economists' models as perhaps the true 'distortions' of the contemporary world (see also Gudeman 1991, Dilley 1992).

LOCAL ARTICULATIONS AND DIS-ARTICULATIONS

An approach which emphasises the construction of local culture as a process by which global institutions are consumed and, as it were, regurgitated as locality, does at least have the benefit of concentrating upon the effects of these institutions. Given the decline of Marxism, consumption provides a promising new perspective upon capitalism and bureaucracy precisely because it forces us to view them in terms of their local consequences. But it is not just the institutions themselves that require study but equally the social relations that are constructed and destroyed through their consumption. This suggests comparative capitalist or bureaucratised society as much as comparative bureaucracy. It is the anthropologist, if anyone, who should be able to insist that Norway and Nigeria are allowed to stand for typical capitalist societies just as much as Britain or the United States.

The third section therefore complements the second. Both Chapters 6 and 7 deal with the issues of plural identity and societal self-authentification that result from this consumption of the global. Academics have recently questioned the new stress on consumption where it seems to be some kind of celebration of creative and inevitable appropriation. The point however of focusing upon the struggle for consumption, hopefully its failures as much as its successes, is not that it is good or bad, but merely that it is increasingly the inevitable cultural process in which we find ourselves. As Strathern (1992) and her colleagues have shown with respect to 'new reproductive technologies', the imagination of technologies can swiftly become the actuality of new choices made tragic precisely because they are authenticated in the agonising of those who feel burdened by new responsibilities intrinsic to the idea of choice in an area where none had previously existed.

What is rejected, however, is the idea that this is a fall or degeneration from an earlier state, that either we or the peoples we study are somehow diminished from what we or they have been. Anthropologists cannot regard Amerindians who exploit protectionist legislation to extract maximum profits from gambling in the United States or the Amazonian Kayapo who quickly appropriate the possibilities of video for both self-representation and presenting themselves to the outside world (Turner 1992) as somehow irredeemably less authentic than the historical Nuer or Trobriand Islanders. For a future anthropology the equality we require for comparative studies will no more be achieved by a sense of our inferiority than by an assumption of our superiority to others. There has always been a danger that what should be (and in these chapters hopefully is) a detailed study of differential empowerment and access to resources by the weak might become essentialised in 'us and them' dualisms.

Chapters 6 and 7 demonstrate the necessity for understanding acts of articulation, in Wilk's case within structures of common difference, in Friedman's case as acts of self-conscious rejection, but in both cases as emerging precisely from that state of consumption examined by the previous chapters – that is the potentially oppressive consequences of being labelled by others and having to inhabit these imposed categories and cultural idioms. This is simply because most people are no longer the prime producers of the images they use, because consumption or rejection have become, as it were, the only game in town.

These chapters are, however, both highly original in their response to the documentation of the 'local'. Both provide powerful models for reconceptualising the local–global distinction. Wilk's concept of 'structures of common difference' is applied to beauty contests but the reader will almost certainly think of a dozen other domains which could be viewed in the light shone from this chapter. Again it would be too easy to dismiss such domains of difference simply because they seem to be a form of local culture which is 'permitted' by global consensus. As becomes clear from the paper, to some extent this is merely an artefact of increasingly transnational experience. Peoples choose to compete on the world stage (whether actual or imagined) because their experience is in fact transnational. In the Caribbean, where families even at the nuclear level often unite various countries and where small islands or states have since their inception been bound into larger social, economic and political formations, to consider oneself only in relation to one's home state would itself be an artificial parochialism. The super-ordinate term 'global' as a marker of who one is, complements the sense of being Belizian, just as the term 'Belizian' has been accepted as super-ordinate to some more localised ethnic terminology.

The potential 'pathology' of this relationship is still more evident in the recent study of another Caribbean state, that of Nevis, by Fog-Olwig. This island has reached the point where perhaps the majority of people who would associate their origins with Nevis live abroad. The island's cultural activities and even its economic activities of traditional farming have thereby become largely directed towards the concerns of authentification for the visiting émigrés who want a taste of home. As she puts it 'Home is where you leave it' (1993: 187–98). Yet even in this extreme case, Fog-Olwig retains her regard for the form of local identity being constructed, given the context that most Nevisian families are actually transnational.

The importance of Wilk's and Friedman's contributions is made evident by their juxtaposition here. Wilk analyses certain structures which articulate the local and the global, but we cannot assume that because these are quite understandable all such social groups will necessarily construct them. Friedman's ethnography provides a dramatic example of a social group that, far from exploring this potential articulation and creating new institutions thereby, have chosen simply to reject this possibility. Their project is clearly one of dis-articulation at least in so far as their hold on highly localised power allows them to fulfil this possibility. As Friedman notes, the assumption that society is made necessarily more complex under conditions of modernity is just that – an assumption. Under the prism of the local we see the possibility of something quite different: that societies which were once characterised by anthropologists as 'simple' in terms of their sociality, may defend their rights to simplicity. In an act of what Friedman calls endo-sociality, this particular group amongst the Hawaiian peoples creates barriers to the outside and attempts to preserve the sense of 'community' that might be broken asunder by greater contact.

Such cases are not unusual, though they are more familiar as buttressed by religious persuasion as in Umble's (1992) study of the careful circumscription on the use of the telephone by the contemporary Amish in the United State, or the (perhaps apocryphal) stories of a notice in the area of Jerusalem inhabited by ultra-orthodox Jews: 'We demand our rights to ignorance.' These may be extreme versions of this tendency but echoes of it are strongly felt in the politics of localism in ordinary English villages in the disputes and exclusionary boundaries constructed around the idea of 'real' members of the community and idealised village endogamy (Strathern 1981). Friedman gives us the clarity of an extreme case but the point may help illustrate tensions found at the heart of many modern urban and suburban complexes.

THE NEW MEDIA OF OBJECTIFICATION: WHOSE NARRATIVES?

If Chapters 2 to 7 provide a range of examples as to the consequences of the consumption of images we project as global, the remaining four chapters represent a necessary complement in that they are primarily directed to the opposite trend – revealing how elements of the local are extracted to provide the building blocks of new images of the global, before being in turn localised. In each case they are dealing with the exploitation of new media to exploit this task, or in Morphy's case a transformation of customary practice of such profundity as to render it new.

The reason for introducing these concerns with two papers on soap opera is that this medium may be viewed as a manifest transformation in one of the definitional topics for the discipline, that is kinship and the family, leading to a reflexive reconstruction of families around increasingly global images. The study of these new media should not therefore stand opposed to the traditional study of topics such as the household and kinship. Instead there may be appropriate continuities in analysis between, on the one hand, generic representations of actual and idealised social relations in, for example, folklore or religion and, on other hand, their objectification in television and similar new media. By retaining the focus of attention on soap opera as expressing the same kind of debate about the normative models of social relations as kinship, the assumption that the term 'global' necessarily indicates 'homogenised' can be challenged (as it has been even in areas which most sought to promote this linkage (Mattelart 1991: 48–67)). Most anthropologists refused the biological essentialism of kinship gloriously demonstrating the extraordinarily diverse cultural projects that kinship carried as idiom, and this point may be extended rather than repudiated by the study of commoditised images.

Das, however, forces us to hesitate before merely assuming any simple continuities between the family in kinship and the family in soap opera. She provides a careful analysis of the conventions not only of soap opera but also of tele-documentaries based on real family crises. But she then goes on to describe the conventional forms of many discourses on morality that take place within real families as revealed in letters by viewers of these programmes. This suggests that the ethnography of these new media requires an understanding of the inter-textuality between them and various conventional structures through which 'discussions' take place, seeing both continuities and also important differences from these established forms of performance. She thereby goes beyond some simple notion of 'real-time' or 'real-life' portrayal, to show how spaces for moral discussion may be closed down as well as opened up by these programmes. This is an important corrective to some recent work which takes a more naive stance as to the nature of some new media-based 'public sphere'.

But who controls these generalised images of social relations extracted from soap opera? As Abu-Lughod's paper reveals for Egypt, media producers and equally their critics have tried to make themselves the prism that deflects modernity into what they see as significant cultural differences. They see themselves as the arbiters of what should enlighten, 'protecting' the populace against the 'wrong' political and moral messages that might be carried by television. Similarly, Das reveals the close relation between the intensely domestic concerns of an Indian soap opera and its actual origins in international bureaucratic developments of new forms of social 'paternalism'. The aim is shown to be a collusion in the inculcation of largely conservative but not entirely traditional moral 'norms'.

Faced with this projection of themselves, Abu-Lughod describes how viewers have their own mechanisms of selective focusing and filtering based on a modernity constituted by the changes that they themselves have experienced, such as the advent of television itself. This may make a scene from an American city more relevant to villagers than one based upon a local elites-projected model of village issues. The points of identification, as is often the case in narrative drama, depend more upon character and moral conundrums. Viewers do not have to accept the framing effects of the genre, such as separating the anti-materialism of serials from the adverts that surround them. Similarly for India, Das shows that letter writers may refuse the moral messages of the programme, and direct their messages to the programme makers rather than to their characters. There is a parallel with France where Bourdieu (1984: 397–465) notes that the pressure to have opinions of what are regarded as 'proper politics' may be resisted by the working-class French whose popular press deals instead with the same micro-'politics' of social relations and scandal objectified in the 'news' about individuals.

This work of soap opera adds considerable sophistication to my earlier definition of consumption as a secondary relationship to culture. It reveals more of a dialectic between the derivation of images in life-worlds, their construction in media and their reception. Such analysis clearly requires more complex models of articulation. For example, points of introjection and projective identification (to use the Kleinian terms) seem to be just as important as acts of appropriation and rejection.

THE LOCAL ARTIST IN WORLD ARTS

By placing Morphy's paper directly after Abu-Lughod's the key question posed by Morphy is highlighted. The Egyptian audience is unambiguously the consumer of the television series, though their consumption may be both creative and productive. In the case of the Australian Aboriginal artists, by contrast, we appear to have the opposite condition in as much as they are the producers of the materials on exhibition. However, as Morphy makes clear, there is a possible irony in that the producer artist may have, if anything, less room for creative manoeuvre in the establishment of meaning than the Egyptian audience/consumer.

This is because by entering both the institutions of high art and the market for high art they submit their work to a milieu where power lies at increasing distance. This may have its positive effects, in as much as global connoisseurship may turn out to be more sympathetic than the more parochial Australian art market. As a result, Aboriginal art may now be achieving much greater 'success' than what had been the dominant Australian art production which is of less interest to world markets. But as Morphy shows there is a cost to be paid in terms of control over the objectification of both Aboriginal art and Aboriginal people, which may be used to buttress a generic notion of primitive art which has always been central to modernist high art. By contrast, the Egyptian villagers not only select by interpretation but also through what they choose to focus upon and ignore on the television. They extract those images and issues that they can use to negotiate (in Rowlands's terms) their own dialectic of being modern and being traditional, as has often been noted in the case of locally produced genres (e.g. Peacock 1968 on Indonesian theatre).

The compromises forced upon the Aborigines as producers of art makes Morphy's paper a clear illustration of key points made throughout this volume. By entering the sphere of high art they have in fact submitted themselves to one of Wilk's 'structures of common difference'. After all, what is the market for high art but a 'beauty contest'? Theoretically the Aborigines' alternative would be to refuse such an articulation by following the route of endo-sociality indicated by Friedman. It is, however, highly unlikely that they would be able to do this, even where this is the preferred strategy, for reasons which emerge clearly in Kapferer's account of a very different encounter between Aborigines and dominant white Australia.

There are two reasons for closing the volume with the paper by Barber and Waterman. Firstly a theme running throughout is a consideration of the potential of the super-ordinate term 'global'. In Morphy's paper this becomes a point where local tensions are trumped by an appeal that reaches beyond to a world art market. Not many people yet envisage themselves as world citizens, but the one area where the arts have developed an explicit exploitation of this possibility is in the arena of 'World Music' with which Barber and Waterman are concerned. The second reason for ending with this paper is that it provides a balance to some of the other cases. Barber and Waterman end (if one can excuse the pun) on a rather more up-beat note. While Kapferer reminds us of the anguish of powerlessness in the face of struggles for self-identity in the modern world, there is also the tremendous sense of exhilaration and excitement given by creatively playing with the possibilities of disorder and place-lessness. Here neither their status as producers nor their status as consumers has prevented the emergence of this music as a positive form of objectification for those involved. Although emerging out of the same tensions and contradictions of West African post-colonial politics discussed early on in the volume by Rowlands and then Warnier, this sphere illustrates one more possibility in the encounter with modernity.

Barber and Waterman also provide another perspective on the notion of a posteriori diversity. They are fully conversant with the local histories behind the music they are studying and can easily enumerate the various influences that have helped forge this new form. But they stand clearly against any attempt to reduce the event to its component parts. They reject the notion of hybridisation which might attempt to separate out so-called 'indigenous' and 'imported' aspects. Rather as cuisine transcends mere ingredients, so also this music transcends its sources through a process of intensification in performance, where it achieves its own integrity as a cultural form. Here in the final chapter the prism has been reversed. The local does not disperse light into the myriad colours of Wilk's structures of common difference, but unites them into a clear vision which cannot easily be disaggregated back into some component parts. Of course this is itself only a local possibility. The artists documented by

Morphy may have similar aspirations to the musicians of the Yorùbá but as yet little chance of achieving them.

To conclude – the first section related modernity and consumption to the experience of historical moments, and the sheer transience which speaks equally of exhilaration and fragility is evident throughout this book. It is not just in Humphrey's paper that the debates being documented were unimaginable just a few years ago. Most of the situations being studied are very much of the time, and as a group the volume indicates the contribution anthropologists may still make when exposed to the flux of events. This should help remove the last stains of that veneer of 'timeless tradition' with which some protected themselves during the colonial period. These chapters reveal a world in which we are now all living within the contradictions of modernity. Increasingly we do so as consumers struggling with a secondary relationship to the structures and institutions which we inhabit and constructing ourselves as a posteriori diversity no longer legitimated by some deep tradition of original difference. But these conditions only spell the end of anthropology if we are wedded to a myth of difference as a priori. Otherwise this is precisely where a modern anthropology based on an equality of difference might begin. It is to the future of this disciplinary involvement that the final section of this introduction is directed.

AN ANTHROPOLOGICAL FUTURE

In the previous section I have highlighted the ways in which the contents of this volume illustrate the shift in anthropology towards an explicit encounter with modernity. In all cases they are ethnographic exemplifications of a somewhat traditional form, so that they cannot be held to represent the kind of repudiation of that style of anthropology which the debate on postmodernism threatened. Rather we are edging towards what might be called a 'third way' anthropology. The trends embodied here (but which may also be discerned in leading journals such as *Man* and *American Ethnologist*) lie more in their subject matter than in their methodology. They continue to employ many of the stalwarts of the discipline, not just ethnography, but also kinship studies, symbolic exegesis and the re-deployment of material-culture studies.

The last decade has seen a trenchant critique against what are seen as overly abstract, analytical and objectivising tendencies in the discipline. But anthropology exists as a project within the framework of education, and originated in opposition to the ideologies of individualism fostered by psychology and most humanities. Its foundation is therefore precisely in collectivising terms such as 'society' which in turn promote greater abstraction and reflexivity. I believe such abstractions retain clear progressive consequences. Any recent liberation for women has come not from the individual experience of oppression but from the totalising and abstract concept of feminism. As Bourdieu has argued (1985) it is common for abstract representation to also become colloquial identity – as in the global experience of 'class' consciousness. Any commitment to critical knowledge or a concept of ideology requires such educative abstraction. When anthropology was threatened by science the problem was that it would retain commensurability but lose relativism. The current threat from the debate on postmodernism is that it will retain relativism but lose commensurability. A 'third-way' anthropology needs to insist on the intrinsic link between these two disciplinary projects.

Reflexive abstraction, as its critics have noted, forms part of several modernising processes. But their achievements should not be gainsaid, whether it is the role of rigid positivistic science in combating pain and poverty or of anonymous bureaucrats in achieving complex forms of equality. This perspective must be retained at the same moment that we condemn their frequently oppressive consequences. The dangers of the totalising meta-narratives of human history have been endlessly reiterated over the last decade (though against the occasional spirited defence e.g. Rose 1992). Obviously critical study should retain self-doubt, especially about the status of knowledge. But for anthropologists to wait around until someone gets epistemology right would be like Sisyphus waiting for Godot.

The new technologies of objectification that we are concerned with in this volume create new possibilities of understanding at the same moment that they pose new threats of alienation and rupture. Yet our first concern is not to resolve these contradictions in theory but to observe how peoples sometimes resolve or more commonly live out these contradictions in local practice. For example, I have been working with several colleagues to try and understand why Christmas has managed to expand around the world while so many other festivals have contracted. We noted that this festival is both beloved of folklorists, who constantly find parochial local customs associated with it, and yet has also developed as potentially the first truly global festival encompassing many non-Christian countries. This we would argue is the point. While philosophers struggle with the question of what is called 'being at home in the world' the celebrants of Christmas take this phrase literally. The festival enshrines the home as pure domesticity, the only place one should really be at Christmas time. It then uses the domestic microcosm to encompass the sense of a globe, that is envisaging the peoples of the world all conducting the same rite at the same time, as a global family. As such the festival both symbolically and actually creates commensurability between the largest social (or for the religious – cosmological) universe we are called upon to imagine and the smallest social universe we tend to assume. In some areas, as part of a striving to be 'at home in the world', participants also attempt, through a bout of shopping and gift-giving, to domesticate materialism precisely because materialism has become the key symbol of the potential death of society (Miller 1993).

Anthropology of this kind works as a dialectic between mundane ethnographic observation, such as of shopping as practice, and abstract explanatory conjecture. Like Christmas itself good anthropology vulgarises philosophy and philosophises life. What anthropologists should not become is middle-range theorists who neither attempt the philosophical heights nor the qualitative commitment of complex experience. So much social science works with slightly abstract categories to slightly generalised models. By contrast, anthropology juxtaposes polarities – extensive qualitative experience with philosophical generalities. To achieve this some of these chapters may have to travel extraordinary distances in a short compass as, for example, Kapferer between an analysis of the historical development of the concept of identity *per se*, and the emotions of identity construction for neglected corners of humanity.

The more that academia seems to create rupture and distance the more important the appeal of a discipline that forces its practitioners to spend at least a year within communities and then attempts to write philosophy from everyday life. Anthropology has been a discipline whose practice insists on at least attempting commensurability, observing how people both utilise new technologies of objectification or are oppressed by them. As such it must refuse the appeal to incommensurability posed by its own aestheticised avant-garde. A news bulletin may evoke ordinary human suffering. But because of this combination of abstraction and experience anthropology can remain close enough to what might be called people's colloquial reflexivity and yet distant enough to use this in the project of understanding. It is in understanding (not explaining) the causes of suffering, or for that matter happiness, that comparative anthropology, at the very least, has a potential that will not be found in the journalistic anecdote or image.

What I am suggesting is that a new significance for anthropology may be consequential not upon changes in the discipline so much as changes in the context in which anthropological knowledge is consumed. Quite properly we have become concerned by our possible contribution to a state of rupture. Not that anyone necessarily experiences modernity as rupture, but that in our academic abstractions we might have helped make that more likely. It is, however, precisely this sense of rupture as potential which suggests the positive role of anthropology as against other forms of academic knowledge, which is really all we can fairly compare ourselves with.

I believe anthropology can and should retain claims to authority based upon what Habermas (1972) described as knowledge claims subject to critical and moral evaluation. But this is precisely because our kind of doubt-ridden knowledge is amongst that most clearly distinct from the naturalistic positivism evoked by the term 'science', and because our plural and quarrelsome rationalities are equally distinct from what might be called the bureaucratic lack of imagination. As Warnier notes in his chapter the kind of global knowledge that we produce can and should be juxtaposed with the closed systems that form the ideologies of economists. For this reason we must not collude in attempts to marginalise our forms of knowledge and doubt from positions of authority and responsibility, as advised by some over the last decade. Some anthropologists may enjoy their own sense of marginality, but they take up this position at the expense of their ability to foreground and challenge the situation of peoples whose marginality is not chosen but is a consequence of their oppression.

This is because within the social sciences it has become almost anthropology alone that challenges the idea that there is only one model of knowledge that gives authority and legitimises power. Ethnography is becoming an island of open research in a sea of closed 'hypothesis testing' surveys. Just consider how anthropologists continually provide a troublesome presence within governmental grant-giving agencies, especially those dominated by economists. How much more anomalous this qualitative and comparative discipline becomes at a time when auditing and managerial authorities wish to reduce academic knowledge to standard types. Traditional qualitative anthropology achieves this tremendous significance today because, within this domain of academia, it is becoming amongst the last 'otherness' that, as it were, empowers the otherness of others. It is anthropologists who still insist on highly qualitative and morally infused knowledges, just as we confuse categories with our 'African' bureaucracy and 'Caribbean' capitalisms. We need to remain a model of progressive understanding based on radical doubt.

To conclude, I believe anthropology as exemplified here remains a vision of 'third-way' academia that resists potential rupture through observing and attempting commensurability. It stands for moral and qualified objectivism between narrow positivistic science and self-indulgent aestheticised irrationalism. Within this the chapters in this volume represent one and only one particular concern for the discipline. They were constructed deliberately as part of a larger set of volumes which deal with topics such as poverty and religion (James), inequality, including that between the academic and the informant (Moore), the implications of new critiques of studies of meaning (Fardon) and more generally the uses of knowledge (Strathern). As such, these topics are not dwelt upon within this volume to the degree that will be found in its sister publications. Rather, this volume is directed towards radical change in the world that follows from new technologies of objectification and, in particular, the continued increase in material culture, capitalism and the revolution in communications, all of which increase the tendency towards reflexivity and consumption as modes of life. Of course there are many other equally worthwhile projects for anthropology and one welcomes the potentially quarrelsome variants even within the chapters of this volume. But collectively they are an attempt to construct an agenda for academic enquiry in a qualified version of the enlightenment tradition, for which they must now take responsibility.

NOTES

1. I feel that this Introduction itself requires a short preface to account for its tone and content. I present it in the spirit of the Decennial conference which was concerned with the role of anthropological knowledge. I have therefore taken my stance from the position of the discipline. I should confess that I do so despite some misgivings that I thereby take up a fraudulent posture. My own training is not in anthropology and I more usually define my own academic research as within material-culture studies rather than anthropology *per se*. Nevertheless in this Introduction I attempt to make clear criticisms and recommendations with regard to possible future work by anthropologists. As such to note that I may be regarded as something of an outsider is not meant to suggest that I do not take full responsibility for the opinions expressed.

REFERENCES

Abu-Lughod, L. (1990) The romance of resistance: tracing transformations of power through Bedouin women. *American Ethnologist*, 17 (1): 41–55.

Appadurai, A. (ed.) (1986) *The Social Life of Things: Commodities in Cultural Perspective*. Cambridge: Cambridge University Press.

Bayart, J.-F. (ed.) (1994) *La Réinvention du Capitalisme*. Paris: Karthala.

Bourdieu, P. (1984) *Distinction*. London: Routledge & Kegan Paul.

Bourdieu, P. (1985) The social space and the genesis of groups. *Theory and Society*, 14: 723–44.

Comaroff, J. and Comaroff, J. (1992) *Ethnography and the Historical Imagination*. Boulder: Westview.

Dilley, R. (1992) Contesting markets. In Dilley, R. (ed.) *Contesting Markets*. Edinburgh: Edinburgh University Press. 1–34.

Douglas, M. and Isherwood, B. (1978) *The World of Goods*. London: Allen Lane.

Fog-Olwig, K. (1993) *Global Culture, Island Identity*. London: Harwood Academic Press.

Geschiere, P. (1992) Kinship, witchcraft and 'the market'. In Dilley, R. (ed.) *Contesting Markets*. Edinburgh: Edinburgh University Press.

Giddens, A. (1991) *Modernity and Self-Identity*. Cambridge: Polity.

Gudeman, S. (1991) Re-modelling the house of economics: culture and innovation. *American Ethnologist*, (1): 141–59

Habermas, J. (1972) *Knowledge and Human Interests*. London: Hutchinson.

Habermas, J. (1987) *The Philosophical Discourse of Modernity*. Cambridge, MA: MIT Press.

Habermas, J. (1991) *The Structural Transformation of the Public Sphere*. Cambridge, MA: MIT Press.

Lash, S. and Friedman, J. (eds) (1992) *Modernity and Identity*. Oxford: Blackwell.

Livingstone, S. and Lunt, P. (1994) *Talk on Television*. London: Routledge.

Mattelart, A. (1991) *Advertising International*. London: Routledge.

Miller, D. (1987) *Material Culture and Mass Consumption*. Oxford: Basil Blackwell.

Miller, D. (ed.) (1993) *Unwrapping Christmas*. Oxford: Oxford University Press.

Miller, D. (1994) *Modernity: An Ethnographic Approach*. Oxford: Berg.

Miller, D. (in preparation) *Capitalism: An Ethnographic Approach*

Peacock, J. (1968) *Rites of Modernization* Chicago. Chicago University Press.

Rose, G. (1992) *The Broken Middle*. Oxford. Basil Blackwell.

Sahlins. M. (1988) Cosmologies of capitalism: the trans-Pacific sector of the world system. *Proceedings of the British Academy*, LXXIV: 1–51.

Strathern, M. (1981) *Kinship at the Core*. Cambridge: Cambridge University Press.

Strathern, M. (1992) *Reproducing the Future*. Manchester: Manchester University Press.

Thomas, N. (1991) *Entangled Objects*. Cambridge, MA: Harvard University Press.

Turner, T. (1992) Defiant images: the Kayapo appropriation of video. *Anthropology Today* 8 (6): 5–16.

Umble, D. (1992) The Amish and the telephone, resistance and reconstruction. In Hirsch, E. and Silverstone, R. (eds) *Consuming Technologies*. London: Routledge.

Wolf, E. (1982) *Europe and the People without History*. Berkeley, CA: University of California Press.

2 Inconsistent temporalities in a nation-space

Michael Rowlands

INTRODUCTION

Defined as perhaps the key value of the historical experience of the twentieth century the desire to be modern became for much of the world an aspiration to achieve through emulation rather than the working out of an indigenous history. How to become modern and remain the same became more or less the equivalent of how to develop without becoming dependent.

Writing the future of national cultures since the nineteenth century has described the strategies evolved to achieve this panacea either as roads (the Russian, Chinese, Cuban, Albanian, etc. roads) to mark various interpretations of Marxist-Leninism or as nation building, under the influence of modernisation theory. Whilst academic discourse has moved on through dependency theory, modes of articulation and world systems to cultural globalisation, the residue that something traditional could become modern remained at the gut level of aspiration and desire in many apparently developing countries. There is more than the odd echo of modernisation theory's recognition that progress would not be smooth and the voyage towards the 'modern society' 'entails a sustained commingling of joyous anticipation with lingering anxieties, sensuous euphoria with recurrent shame, guilt and puzzlement' (Lerner 1968: 73).

Another well-established view of modernity also imagines itself defined by a temporal contradiction. On the one hand it opens up future possibilities of freedom and identity to which all can gain access if willing to avoid the conventional and the prescribed (Berman 1983). The European version of this historical transformation has been described by Sennett (1986) and Campbell (1987) as the freedom of individuals to present themselves to others in such a way that self and the representation of self (private/public realms) become very different things. The collapse of ascribed status hierarchies results not only in the autonomy of the self but the internalisation of constraint into the body which becomes a self-managing and self-propelling agency (cf. Friedman 1989). Modernity is also a process which structures identity and prevents the anomie implied by too much freedom by encouraging localised rediscoveries of heritage within a secure sense of cultural space and time (cf. Miller 1994). Commonly experienced as the contradiction between modernity and tradition, nobody is surprised any more by the claim that each dialectically constitutes the other or that the identities formed reveal an ambivalence between the minority voices claiming their own genealogies of 'origin' and the dominant voice of the majority representing the history of national unity. Nor is it surprising that the manifestations of authentic tradition reveal, in Keesing's words, 'structures of thought framed in opposition to subjugation and modelled on the very ideological systems they challenge' (Keesing 1994: 41).

However, for much of this century the dialogue has been held in place through the recognition that every national culture deserves a modernity consistent with its sense of precedent. A Russian or a Chinese road to development required that the claim for one was irreducible to the other precisely because a sense of past was both constitutive of it and constituted by it. The supposed dawn of a new world order no longer provides this constraint. Whether or not one goes along with an 'end of history' philosophy, the expectation that all we can expect now are various culturally constituted forms of capitalism threatens to swing the pole of the dialectic to that of global homogenisation, historical rupture and the commodification of heritage. It has been perhaps easily forgotten that in its origins, the conflict between capitalism, communism and fascism was justified as the right of a national culture to determine its own path to modernity.

Fanon wrote against forms of nationalist historicism that attempted to condense different temporalities into a single and immediately readable future (Fanon 1969). Instead, he argued that the present is a practice that constantly undermines the principles of a national culture that claim to embody unalterable fundamentals and a 'true' or authentic past. In many cases these totalisations were founded on fear of a past that would hold back national cultures from future achievement. The peasantry, according to the scientific marxists in Russia influenced by Marx's analysis of the failure of the 1848 revolution in France, had to be boiled in the industrial boiler to cleanse them of their recalcitrance; tribes in Africa had to assimilated as the chief threat to national unity according to modernisation theorists. The ensuing carnage has borne witness to the fact that national cultures, represented as fixed and stable histories, combine different temporalities articulated in a dialectic of unstable configuration. This point is developed by Bhabha in his claim that the borders of the nation are constantly faced with a double temporality; what he calls the process of identity constituted by historical sedimentation and the loss of identity in the signifying process of cultural identification (Bhabha 1994: 152–3). In this particular instance he proposes that post-colonial time questions 'both the teleological traditions of past and present, and the polarised historicist sensibility of the archaic and the modern' (1994: 152). His fundamental point is to oppose the loss of identity characteristic of the undecidability of the present to the ongoing repetition of the language of national cohesion. The desire for a future in which the possible is extracted from the impossible emerges against a background in which a future is imagined only as a repetition of a past (Bhabha 1994: 156).

It is this instability of temporalities that I wish to explore further in the writings of national history and contemporary debates about postcoloniality in Cameroon. Such notions identify specifically a given historical trajectory, that of societies recently emerging from the experiences of colonialism and of a particular form of violence that was institutionalised within particular forms of bureaucratic practice. In Africa the recent experiences of Angola, Mozambique, Somalia, Liberia and Rwanda bear potent witness to the catastrophic consequences of the advocacy of new forms of multipartyism without any corresponding change in old forms of coercive rule and legitimised by appeals to progress and development. But as Mbembe has remarked, they are also marked by a particular kind of political improvisation and by distinctive ways in which identities are multiplied, transformed and put into circulation (Mbembe 1992: 3). Such a mixture of pluralism and drive for internal coherence produces a symbolic history of the nation as an 'imagined community' that would be realised in the fullness of time but in the meanwhile was always teetering on the edge of crisis and chaos. A key question raised is the nature of the incommensurability of temporalities involved, which, in their working out, are in fact quite antithetical to the aspirations of the long term if they are defined as the fulfilment of ambitions of national cohesion and unity.

FREEDOM AND THE FORCES OF MATERIALISM

In 1889, Eugen Zintgraff, the first European to penetrate the Grassfields region of Cameroon, established a post in the chiefdom of Bali-Nyonga near the present town of Bamenda. His appearance, accompanied by a hundred Vai carriers armed with guns and cutlasses, quickly destabilised the local regional balance of power between Bali-Nyonga and the other chiefdoms. It also formed the pretext for a revolt by the young against the authority of the notables. The first evidence of this is found with the appearance of young irregulars called 'kamenda', 'tapenta' or 'free boys' drawn from a number of chiefdoms in the Grassfields, who defined themselves as becoming independent or free by working for the German colonists or the Presbyterian missions (Warnier 1993: 206).

Neither the chiefs nor the Germans were able to prevent the spread of these bands of 'free boys' who were identified by their wearing red caps and by the large numbers of young men and women who flocked to join them. In 1914, Brother Spellenberg of the evangelical mission at Bandjoun described their depredations in the following manner:

> The appearance of the Tapenta promises nothing of any good. Corrupted by the magic of the Whites, they attack like ferocious animals, men, women and children. They steal everything that is not nailed down. When one of them is arrested, he will cry 'Lef me, mi be big boy, mi be Tapenta boy.'

> (van Slageren 1972: 84)

The escapist society of 'free boys' promised an alternative social vision of future liberation, not from that of colonial rule but rather that of the chiefs and the notables (Warnier 1993: 206). Freedom meant entering into the German colonial service as servants ('kamenda' is pidgin for kommandant, 'tapenta' probably for interpreter). It was these 'free boys' who went to the coast to work on the plantations to gain the European goods to pay bridewealth and be independent of the elders. Chiefs in turn struggled to reimpose their control by persuading the German colonial authorities to levy a head tax on the labour supply and to prevent young men being paid on the plantations in cash or trade goods.

During most of the German period, the chiefs and the Christian missions maintained contradictory and often opposed relations with each other in the struggle against the 'free boys'. The chiefs, seduced by the power of the whites, initially opened the chiefdoms to all sorts of innovations and the means to acquire them, such as allowing schools and churches to be built as adjuncts to their palaces. Between 1903 and 1916 the Basel Mission established stations in many of the Grassfields chiefdoms, providing schools and training in skills like carpentry and joinery and the first pupils were often sons of chiefs and notables. Van Slageren has shown in his history of the missions in Cameroon that the honeymoon between chiefs and churches lasted until 1913. Already by 1908, with the first baptisms, the chiefs began to have doubts about the Christian message. The demand by the missions for converts to renounce polygyny and any participation in 'secret societies', the stigmatising of the consumption of alcohol and what was seen by the missions as the exploitation of the young by the notables, led many of the chiefs to turn against the missions. At the same time the educated youth who were taught to read and write in German, either converted to 'tapenta' or entered the mission service. The interregnum between the end of German rule and the British/French mandate after 1916, saw brutal repression of the youth by the chiefs, the mission schools were closed and attempts made to have the students returned to the discipline of their fathers' compounds. But the Christian converts had experienced a sense of release that they sustained by establishing links with Cameroonian pastors on the coast who made frequent trips into the Highlands to encourage converts and invite them to their seminaries. The reaction of the chiefs, who had finally 'seen through' the implications of church and mission attendance on the young, focused particularly on banning the rite of baptism and the burning of mission books and objects, prohibiting attendance at the missions' weekly services and the mission schools, which were either banned or only allowed to be built on non-chiefdom land. The colonial authorities, which needed both to support the chiefs and to placate the missions, played a double game for a while but increasingly sided with the chiefs against the missions.

The annual Conference of evangelical missions to Cameroon in 1925 made clear how the chiefs viewed the missionaries:

> They are thieves and liars. They legitimise all the 'free boys' and that makes them believe they no longer have to obey us.
>
> (van Slageren 1972: 170)

Van Slageren, the missionary turned sociologist, musing on the implications of this statement, poses the question:

> When studying this phase in the Bamiléké revival, one has to ask oneself if the Christian movement had not been confused with an act of liberation.
>
> (van Slageren 1972: 172)

But equally it was the rapid penetration of the colonial economy that provided the economic alternatives for the christianised cadets to escape from the hierarchy of the notables. Whilst the French administration surrogately supported the order of the chiefs and closed its eyes to their abuses, the missions expressed increasing concern about the consequences of the freedom they had helped unleash. In the annual report for 1923, the missionaries worried that:

> The development of our churches in the quest of liberty is probably in great part responsible for the depopulation of the region. It's a terrible charge against us but we must have the courage to recognise it.
>
> (Quoted in van Slageren 1972: 252)

From 1923 till the 1950s there was a stagnant but growing tension in the Grassfields between the youth, the churches, the colonial powers and the chiefs and notables without any significant advantage being gained on any side. Whilst to some extent we have access to the Western view through the writings of church and state, the subjectivity of chiefs and the youth is pretty well unknown. But the demands for European consumer goods as signs of modernity are the most consistent evidence of the identifications being sought. From the first contact with Europeans, the realisation that access to the wealth and technical innovations associated with these newcomers would confirm or subvert hierarchy, both chiefs and the young threw themselves into the techniques of appropriation. Whilst the chiefs did so by initially inviting the missions to build schools and churches as adjuncts to the palace, the young took the market route and, by acquiring literacy or technical skills through mission education, made themselves indispensable to the trading houses, plantation owners and other commercial interests within the mandate. Incontestably the losers, were the lesser notables/lineage heads who, by not having any access to the colonial administration except through the chiefs, were totally unsympathetic to Christian conversion and were forced to compete with the missions for control of the young. Chiefs did and still do maintain control through the redistribution of gifts from the administration in both money and kind. Generators, water supplies, building materials, tarred roads and health facilities were and are the sort of resources that chiefs were and are expected to provide their subjects. New shoes, clothes, bikes, radios and guns were the wealth of the young. It would have been impossible to remain chief if the supply of gifts from the administration were to dry up or be checked by the actions of the young. On the other hand, the dependence of chiefs on the administration linked their interests in the reproduction and modernisation of local societies. It also sustained widespread abuses by the chiefs that came to figure in colonial annual reports as a problem in maintaining good order. The peremptory replacement of titled notables by appointees of the chief, the taking of daughters for wives without compensation, sale of people and the arbitrary banishment of the non-compliant became typical of the exercise of autocratic power by the 1940s (Warnier 1993: 210).

Whatever might have been envisaged by the young as an alternative society to the chiefs in the colonial period, the manner of the transition to independence was to ruin the slightest chance of such an alternative emerging. The outcome of an anti-colonial revolt was to set the conditions for a reinvention of traditional hierarchy in the post-colonial period but on very different principles. From May 1955, a wave of assassinations, burning of palaces and compounds and general banditry was carried out in the Grassfields by young revolutionaries and their leaders educated in France or French schools in Cameroon (Joseph 1976). The main campaign was directed against the traditional chiefs and notables who were accused of siding with the colonisers in the perpetuation of the 'colonial disorder'. The rebellion in the Grassfields quickly became identified as an undisciplined armed revolt against the chiefs without any sign of the coherent political programme that characterised anti-colonial revolt elsewhere in Cameroon. Instead the rebellion was very similar to the 'free boys' revolt at the turn of the century. The young in full emancipatory fervour consumed everything in their path. Some particularly bloody atrocities against chiefs and 'petit blancs' and the absence of political objectives beyond the demolition of the power of the chiefs and their French colonial supporters demonstrated both the power of the young to mobilise support and the absence in their minds of any significant political alternative to the principle of hierarchy (Joseph 1976).

What emerged in the 1970s and 1980s was the creation of a new class of notables based on wealth who reinvented the hierarchy previously destroyed to reimpose control over the labour of young men and women as the means of economic and political accumulation. Whilst this was more radically the case in the francophone than the anglophone part of the Grassfields where lineage heads were less affected by colonialism, the wholesale reinvention of the chiefdom in the post-colony, in some cases by the leaders of the revolt in the 1960s, re-established the conditions of expanded exploitation of the young by their elders. Succession to the office of chiefship has more often than not gone to one of those who possessed significant political contacts and formal education. Nowadays, succession to chiefly title most often will go to a member of the Cameroonian establishment: civil servants, lawyers, doctors or businessmen. As often as not they will use their salaries as chiefs to invest in business and accumulate on a fairly large scale. In those chiefdoms where the older title-holders had been swept away during the anti-colonial revolt, the positions have been reinvented and filled by educated men frequently absent abroad or away politicking in the capital (Miaffo and Warnier 1993: 65). The lack of development of 'civil society' after independence reinforced the belief that success in gaining a share of the national cake could not be a product of local party politics but a result of bringing ethnic and regional clout to bear on the administration. Individual career opportunities, both political and business, have increasingly had to depend upon the recreation of 'traditional communities', the tribalism so derided by the state rhetoric of nation building in Cameroon, as the realpolitik of getting a share of the national cake (Burnham 1993).

It is symptomatic that the vigour with which ethnicisation of state politics is pursued is more or less a mark of the nature of the present political crisis in Cameroon. At the moment this is signified by the degree of political unrest in the Grassfields centred on another 'free boy' revolt against the reinvented chiefs and the post-colonial elite. In the 1992 multiparty elections, it was gangs of 'boys' who burned the chiefly palaces in Bamenda, 'necklaced' a prominent supporter of the President and burned to death a District Officer who had ordered gendarmes to fire on looters. The leader of the principal opposition to one-party state politics in Cameroon at present is an anglophone who appeals particularly to the young and to women in the urban slums by speaking out, in pidgin English rather than French, against ethnic politics, against the francophone elites and the chiefs and for the 'urban poor'. Invited, along with Nelson Mandela, to Clinton's Presidential inauguration, Ni John Fru Ndi used a familiar language to attack the collusion of the chiefs with the administration and the regional deprivation produced by the ineffective role of anglophone ethnic politics in the national political scene. But behind the rhetoric is the transformed status of 'tapenta' boy into national politician, freedom through anti-hierarchy of whatever transformed kind, and espousal particularly of American consumption as the vision of a modern non-hierarchical, non-ethnicised future.

INDIVIDUALISING TRADITION

Patrick Ngango (pseudonym) is a businessman who lives in a large villa on the outskirts of Bamenda. He is one of the older generation of businessmen who began his career in the commodity boom years of the 1950s. Ngango started by selling newspapers in Nigeria and acquiring a licence to import magazines from Britain. From this he diversified into transport and now has the Shell petrol distribution licence for West Cameroon. Generally regarded as one of the top three to four businessmen in anglophone Cameroon, Ngango also owns a house in Douala, the economic capital of the country, and another in London, which he visits two or three times a year for business purposes. He also has two sons in university in Britain, a third in the US and a daughter following a hotel management course in France. A man who professes to feel best at home in the village, he lives in Bamenda, speaks only in pidgin to his two wives and children and runs his business on strict hierarchical principles of a junior/elder kind. This includes a collection of unmarried and unpaid youths sent to him by their fathers from his village to work for him in anticipation that, if pleased, he will eventually give them the means to set up on their own.

His villa is a large, palatial affair and deliberately modern in appearance. The use of marble, sliding aluminium and glass windows and doors, brass fittings, and the modern imported furniture communicate an image of wealth, cosmopolitanism and sophistication. The house is equipped with electricity, running hot and cold water, air conditioning, telephone and fax facilities, TV and video. Both his wives have their own suitably equipped apartments where they stay with their children, each with their own Mercedes car and driver. The house is set in a large Western-style garden landscaped with lawns, trees and flowers. The furnishing of the sitting room is a particularly significant representation of modern achievement. A room over 15 metres long and 6–7 metres wide, it contains four executive 'suites' each made up of a sofa and four armchairs. They are ranked according to quality and status. At the far end of the room are the less prestigious Cameroonian-made chairs in the area kept for local visitors and people from the village. At the other end, in an area made slightly private by a room divider, there is the prestigious imported leather-covered suite arranged around a mock antique coffee table and a drinks cupboard containing a wide range of imported whiskies and champagnes. Prominent in one corner of this part of the room is a carved wooden stool with a lifelike bust of the owner sculpted in clay and painted in the bright colours of traditional 'country dress'. Off from this part of the room is a dining room with imported glass and chrome-metal table and chairs and a side cupboard for storing glasses and crockery. Visitors are shown to one or other of these areas of the room depending on their status and attended by one of the 'boys' with something to drink until Ngango arrives. The time this takes again depends on your importance to him.

Ngango is a supporter of Fru Ndi and generally of anglophone politics in Cameroon, which means essentially recanting on what is widely seen as an imposed act of unification between the anglophone and francophone parts of the country and a return to federal or independent status. In his politics he sides therefore with the majority of the population although against some of the more powerful chiefs who are supporters of the Biya francophone regime. In this respect, as with many other Grassfields businessmen, he invests directly in the 'traditional' political organisation of the region and draws on it for the benefit of his affairs. He comes from one of the smaller chiefdoms where he maintains a house and also has extensive interests in land, including a food farm and an estate of 300 dwarf oil palms that he imported from America hoping they would be more productive and easier to harvest than the indigenous varieties. Access to land and to the labour of young males are good reasons for a man like Ngango to retain an interest in his chiefdom. He does so by regular visits, making contributions to the village rotating credit association which he belongs to, by 'paying' to join various palace associations and also acting as a close confidant of the chief or *fon* in running the chiefdom.

This reinvestment of new wealth into the chiefdom and into chiefly titles is a cause of significant conflicts with chiefs and the holders of authentic titles. Notables and lineage heads accuse the chiefs of selling titles for gain to those without ancestry. The link to the acquisition of land, a right that is distributed through customary law, means of course that significant resources are involved in sustaining tradition. Moreover, Grassfields societies were and still are highly inegalitarian and stratified so that access to titles results in significant control over the circulation of marriageable women and the labour of young men. Since at least the 1930s there have existed major diaspora of Bamiléké and Bamenda in the major cities and coastal plantations of Cameroon. In recent years this control over junior labour has extended more widely to diaspora in Central Africa, Europe and the USA where the labour producing tourist art in the sweat shops of Paris or running taxis in Washington is recruited as an extension of the village elder/junior relationship. Warnier (1993: 113) has carried out significant investigations into this aspect of ethnicised labour recruitment and hierarchy in urban contexts in Cameroon and I shall rely on his argument here. The invention of tradition in the diaspora takes the particular form of father–son rights and obligations and the kinship metaphor embodies working relations. The paternal role is meant to combine authority, wisdom and, eventually, material help in return for the son's or daughter's absolute loyalty and unswerving obedience. Questions about competence, virtue or efficiency are not at issue and rarely raised. Instead a language of trust and mutual assistance is deployed within a general ethos of maintaining the undivided patrimony of the extended family which an entrepreneur manages on behalf of the pseudo-family constituted by the enterprise. This need not entail that anyone working for the patron should necessarily be ethnically Bamiléké or Bamenda but rather that, whatever their origin, as far as his enterprise is concerned, they will be bound by an ethic derived from that tradition.

How does this affect someone like Patrick Ngango? He runs his various business interests from an office in Bamenda and another in Douala that he visits twice a month. His right-hand man is not from the village but a francophone who is also qualified in accountancy and deals with the books. Nevertheless he is bound to Ngango in unswerving loyalty, has never married, accumulates and anticipates a personal future autonomy when Ngango retires or dies. Ngango's older brother runs his import/export business in Douala and another one manages the petrol-licence agency in Limbe. In conversation he appears relaxed and non-committal about the way he manages his affairs and how decisions are made. 'Listen', he would say, 'I know everything about them, all the people who work for me. I helped them get married, I give them money for medical bills and I keep them in work.' Which of course reflects his paternalism and may be what he likes to think rather than what happens. Just as frequently he expresses fear of losing money due to the duplicity of a brother or a son or trusted worker. Hence an ideology of trust and mutual assistance is retained often regardless of the painful realities of business life.

Ngango's lifestyle, as with many others in his position, sits uneasily with a reliance on an uncertain state of cultural belief created when the archaic emerges in the margins of modernity. The 'double' in his case is associated with the uncanny process of a 'double-time' which engages anyone who so much as visits and sits down in his living room. Such an apprehension of a split time cannot be resolved in the fullness of history nor mediated as a flexible set of alternatives depending upon context, but leads us to a questioning of the ideal of an homogeneous and synchronic view identified with an imagined community. In part the archaic is subversive and emerges as a displacement of and a means of reinterpreting the strategies of the modern. As such it is a pedagogy that is based on a pre-given or constituted historical origin in a past. At the same time it is embedded in a process of signification that erases any prior or originary presence to demonstrate the living principle of contemporaneity. This suggests that positions of authority are themselves part of a process of ambivalent identification, what Gellner called the rags and patches of everyday life (Gellner 1983: 56). People like Ngango represent the nation-space in Cameroon as a double movement turned into a coherent identity when in fact it is in the movement of the signification that the ambivalence of being modern reveals itself and robs identity of the stability of centre and closure.

EMBODIMENT AS CONTAINMENT

How is it that modernity becomes conceived as an incomplete project that intervenes as historical event into the self-reproduction of archaic community? The sameness of time, turning everything modern and pluralistic into tradition, turns outside event into inward time. Whilst this moment of domesticating the event is represented as 'the work of ancestors', as unavoidable and from which there is no escape, what this means in Grassfields practice is a more literal bio-politics of the body. The eruption of the archaic, the repetitive theme of the same, centres around an insurance of somatic well-being and a conception of community as a timeless *blindage* counterpoised to the forces of temporal instability. In fact it is nothing of the sort and the somatisation of identity has itself internalised colonised categories derived from the missions, hospitals and health practices, but within a dialogue that clearly distinguishes it as separate and antecedent to them.

Grassfields chiefs and notables have been described as 'tirelire vitales' or living piggy banks by Warnier (1993: 126). The metaphor was proposed by two Catholic fathers, both of them Bamiléké (Fathers Tchouanga Tiegoum and Ngangoum 1975: 33).

> A notable [chef de famille] is a living piggy bank for the whole descent group: in him is contained the plenitude of blood received since the creation, through a chain of ancestors.
>
> (Warnier 1993: 126, my translation)

Blood stands as a metonym for transmissible life essence, breath, saliva, semen and blood which of course all males possess, but unless one is coopted as a 'father' into a descent group, these substances become impotent. They have life but cannot be transmitted. This is a very widespread cosmology in Africa but transmission of body substances, and transmission to whom, takes on a particular hierarchical form in the Grassfields. Succession to title is positional, which means that one of the sons of a father is selected by him to take his name, titles, wives (except his own mother) and all persons and things. Brothers now become 'sons' to the 'father' who was gone but has now returned. In other words the piggy bank is not broken and the contents have not been dissipated. Instead a man is selected and the installation ritual transforms his body into the piggy bank of the descent group, containing its blood and semen, which, together with camwood and oil, also his possessions, forms the corporate estate of the lineage. All family heads would transmit their substance by taking as many wives and producing as many children as possible. Hence, males who do not succeed to title, are prevented from taking wives and effectively are denied adult status. As a result there are two categories of men. Uninitiated cadets are perceived as and treated as children regardless of their age. Whilst symbolically impotent and incapable of transmitting lineage substance they are, however, perfectly capable of work. The other category comprises the married men who at some level are coopted into the line of descent of a notable. Such men would never be allowed to forget their role as a conduit of paternal substance. Normally a father must provide the first wife for each of his sons and the latter stay in his compound until they have found the means to marry a second wife which makes them economically independent. Only then can a son go to the father and ask for the ritual of separation which allows him to build his own compound. Until then the father considers the wives of his married sons as his own and also the children produced by him. Elders will be heard telling their daughters-in-law: 'Bring me my wine. Remember I am your real husband. He [speaking of his son] is only the stud [the he-goat in the vernacular]' (Warnier 1993: 132). His married sons have sex but not fatherhood whilst his unmarried sons should not even have sex.

What is transmissible life essence? In a recent survey based on Phyllis Kaberry's field notes, Chilver has described what the Nso call *sem*, best translated as life breath or seed, as a genderless principle located or rather contained in the stomach (Chilver 1993). It can project itself in a number of different forms, as an animal transformation, a rushing wind, as a witch or a witch-finder at night. More generally it is the principle of transformation of beings and material things into each other, and accordingly it is both a principle of matter and its reproduction which 'explains' fertility since it is also the principle which transforms blood and semen at conception into the hard and soft tissues of the human foetus. The father feeds the growing foetus with semen whilst in the womb and the mother feeds it with milk when it is born and for the first two years of its life. Both substances are made into bone or flesh by *sem* and a plump baby when born is seen as a sign of proper sexual feeding and a thin or wasted baby or a stillbirth is a sign of witchcraft. A woman who commits adultery and mixes the semen of husband and lover will suffer a breach birth and die in agony. Semen and milk are also irreconcilable since they come from the father's father and the mother's father respectively and should be kept separate because semen spoils milk. Hence feeding women should not have sexual intercourse. Since *sem* is genderless, both parents should possess it but it has to have different origins (the blood/semen opposition) to produce a viable human being. *Sem* also varies in potency and effect depending on how it has been 'fed' with magical substances by the members of the lineage since its origin. That of the *fon* or king is the most powerful and is associated with the leopard. Its strength is detected by wind; breath on the back of the hand is *sem*, so is a violent storm sent by the *sem* of a distant *fon*. It is strongly associated with speech and anger through the power to curse. It is the mother's father's speech that is most powerful and can harm and even kill the offspring of a daughter if the son-in-law has displeased him (Pradelles de Latour 1994). The life essence of a dead elder is transmitted to his chosen son at the succession ritual which aims to convert the body of the incumbent into an efficient container for lineage *sem*. Hence there is no formal male initiation rite which equally distributes lineage substance to all males at a prescribed age. Instead the marriage rite and the installation ritual to succession of title selectively transmit both lineage substance, the capacity to be a person, and position in hierarchy as a totalising act.

However, it would be inconceivable that a rich and successful man like Ngango would not be credited with a powerful *sem*. Presumably, up until colonial contact a powerful *sem* would have been a result of, and predicted by, hierarchy. However, access to the colonial economy meant that possession of *sem* outside hierarchy could be demonstrated through economic and political success. The fundamental motive of demonstrating wealth and success outside succession (sic) for many marginalised young men and, to a lesser extent, for women, has been revenge fuelling an ambition to return to the village as the possessor of a powerful *sem*, which would have to be acknowledged by the titled elders otherwise such a potentially destructive force could be turned against them. The expansion of hierarchy through the creation of new titles as well as conflicts over the possession of old ones is therefore a dispute over legitimacy embedded in a bio-politics of the body that wields considerable destructive potential. It is also antipathetic towards any claim that an individualised route to success can deny recompensing kin for the possession of a powerful *sem*. 'To behave like a white' is an accusation frequently made against the young who leave the village, achieve success and no longer fulfil kinship obligations. It is the envy of the old, poor but titled successors in the village that young, urbanised men and women fear most as the cause of premature illness and death. But their ambivalence in rejecting the ethic of the village betrays precisely their acceptance of such beliefs in the identification of the person. The wish to possess *sem* freed from hierarchy is therefore not to deny it or to imagine that one could do without it but to use it in a modern, national setting as a prerequisite for a more individualised success.

In part this is as much to do with understanding the conditions of failure and misfortune as it is to do with ensuring success. If the body of a notable is a container which must retain, accumulate and transmit, then the worst thing that can happen is for him to suffer waste or loss of substance. There is a Grassfields notion of such a person as *balok* (having bad luck) or possessing *ndon* (mystical danger) which describes anyone who, through no apparent fault of his own, suffers loss or misfortune (Dillon 1990: 67–75; Warnier 1993: 149). It is literally seen as a wasting disease manifested in illness, miscarriage, poor harvests, loss of money or poor business sense. With low-ranking people it doesn't matter much except that they should be avoided, since the presence or the participation of a *balok* jeopardises the result of any venture. But if it affects a notable or a *fon* it is more serious and should be prevented through protective medicines. Modern urban forms of witchcraft, called variously *msa*, *'famla'* and *kong*, which roughly describe loss of people through the contemporary occult slave trade (a close agnate dies and will work in another world to make the killer rich) follow much the same pattern that one person's accumulation is at the expense of another's disaccumulation. However, these are extreme forms of a more widely understood principle in the Bamiléké and Bamenda urban diaspora, the necessity to conserve and retain wealth and possessions of all kinds and the threat to a sense of self of any action that wastes resources.

For a man such as Ngango, the emphasis on retention and saving has tremendous advantages when extended to the conditions of savings and accumulation in business. It means he is able to refuse the demands of close kin for financial help and he can rely on the loyalty of the young who expect him to be retentive and mean. Bamenda and Bamiléké traders are renowned in Cameroon for their propensity to save through rotating credit associations and for their capacity to invest in business rather than wasting money on celebrations and meeting the demands of opportunist kin. Described popularly as 'slaves to money' or *'les ordinateurs'*, envy of them frequently means political riots will turn into the looting of Bamiléké shops and businesses. There is no doubt in the minds of most Cameroonians that containment is fundamental to the economic success of the Bamenda and Bamiléké and that it is an essentialist virtue that historically constitutes the virtue of their difference.

The envy that accompanies the success of a man such as Ngango is matched by a feeling that, as a non-successor to title, his material success is a mere substitute for a more authentic identity. Both Bamiléké and Bamenda titles (hence access to proper adult identity) are inherited through a decision made by the previous holder which he trusts close agnates to carry out after his death. Non-succession to title entails marginalisation and a stark choice for the other sons. In the past the options were limited to remaining as a dependent of the successor and working for the latter to acquire the means to marry and found a compound. The possibility of choice came with access to the colonial economy and the appearance of alternative sources of wealth. But, ultimately, realising personal success through alternative routes entails a return to roots and recognition by the successor of the power of a personal *sem*. Burial on compound land and the proper feeding and service to the body of the deceased by descendants in the form of 'cry-dies' means that his *sem* will not be lost and its achievements will be remembered. This must entail recognition through the bestowal of title and the right to transmit it to a successor through an appropriate installation ritual. There is no guarantee that such an ideal life cycle for the non-inheritor will be recognised by the elders of the village unless his anger poses a threat to their security. Containment as bounded closure is therefore a concept rooted in the realities of separation, exclusion and cleansing that must maintain a strict inside/outside dichotomy in personal politics. Although this suggests a 'double consciousness', the janus face of the modern and the traditional as separate worlds which follow the individual from the cradle to the grave, it is the absence of an explicit sense of alienation in the behaviour of men like Ngango that needs to be understood. Indeed it is the inter-penetration of apparently inconsistent temporalities, such that each erupts in the midst of the action of the other, not as conflict or contradiction, but as constraint and as part of the self-consciousness of identity that defines existence through the eyes of dominant others in the political culture of Cameroon.

COOPTING MODERNITY BY THE STATE

For the modernisers, the ostensible solution to the alienation of a 'double consciousness' of the archaic and the modern has been that of education and the faith laid in the powers of rationalism for the promotion of 'nation building'. It was the classic and still unresolved ideal of modernisation theory that the vast and potentially contradictory streams of thought encountered in development could be reconciled only through an educational practice that stressed the unity of informed knowledge. Ironically it was the promotion of the most highly educated – ministers, doctors, intellectuals and technocrats – that came to characterise the purest form of a modern identity and the greatest degree of self-estrangement.

Yet such ideals are still firmly in place in the authoritarian populism that characterises multiparty politics in contemporary Cameroon (Rowlands and Warnier 1988). The link between education, credentialism and the bureaucratic state has been mediated through consumption to disparage ethnic origins and promote an immediate and tangible modernity. Bayart has described national politics in Cameroon as a pattern of consumption he calls 'la politique du ventre' ('the politics of the stomach', Bayart 1993). He sees the absence of 'civil society' as characteristic of the state in much of post-colonial Africa and the development of a bureaucratic elite that takes as its prerogative a special relationship with the means of ensuring a future of development and progress. A well-known aspect of this modernist formula is a hostility towards 'traditionalism', 'tribalism' and ethnicity which are associated with an alterity of non-development, ethnic violence, disease and famine to which the state stands opposed as modernity incarnate. A rejection of tradition as past is a necessary aspect of subscribing to 'la politique du ventre', as long as it assures those with education, credentials and a budget that they and their careers have a future.

Both Bayart and Mbembe (1992) have given a depressing account of Cameroon as an example of a post-colony operating on the basis of bureaucratic rationalism, raw power and surveillance supported by acts of conferment of prestige and symbolic violence. The post-colony rules through the exercise of a modernising regime whereby the legitimacy of the state is perpetually and extravagantly authorised. In the rounds of administrative authority, ceremonies and banquets, official visits of dignitaries, the presentation of medals, and the holding of national holidays as occasions for unrestricted spending on food, wine, sex and ostentatious prestations, the grandeur of the regime is put on display. Contrary to what he condemns as simplistic dualistic theories of domination and resistance, Mbembe argues that authority depends on inscribing everyone within the same symbolic field. In the conviviality of the ruler and the ruled, an intimate tyranny links them in the desires that are shared across all its disparate groups. The *commandement* is a legitimising horizon, an episteme of consent, conviviality and adulation which seeks the status of a fetish in possessing magical powers. If there is a post-colonial subject, Mbembe writes, he or she is publicly visible only at the point where two activities overlap – where formality, concerned with ensuring future success, articulates with the ludic in the celebration of achievement and the escape from failure. A regime of consumption is played out which articulates the subject's capacity for play and a sense of fun (which create a *homo ludens* par excellence) with the common daily rituals (such as an obsessive concern with bureaucratic detail and exactitude or the formalities of hierarchy and the demands for respect and esteem) that ratify the process of institutionalisation. Everything is there to be enjoyed once a position, a salary or a budget in the state apparatus has been acquired. Through laughter, jokes, ribaldry and rumours a sort of de-authorisation of power is threatened and the regime responds by opening up a space for others to enter and be seduced (Toulabour 1994). Hence everyone has to be involved, cynics, poseurs, critics, academics, power-holders. It is by way of these mediations of signs and mundane practices that the dominated and the dominant come to share the same episteme, the same aspirations and sense of achievable futures. In watching football, shopping, going to church, drinking in a bar, the aspiration that links modernity as a future to state power is experienced and made palpable so that it can be possessed by the greatest number. This is not the grandeur of the *belle epoque* – the let them eat cake kind of obscenity – it's the sort of sign that marks the uncertainty and vulnerability of elites – that makes having the 747 waiting on the runway the only alternative form of political action.

What is so striking about Bayart's and, in particular, Mbembe's rendering of Cameroonian reality is the emphasis on bodies and objects as items for visual display: the bodies of the guilty awaiting jail or public execution and of the public audience invited as part of an 'economy of good manners' to applaud as the shots drown out the cries of the condemned; the newspaper pictures of captured thieves lined up like the national football team with their stolen consumer goods piled at their feet like trophies and the guards standing at each end like referees (in the article they are described as the national team of armed robbers); the bodies of male officialdom at the reward ceremonies dressed in three-piece suits or elaborate military uniforms waiting to receive the medals 'Cameroonians love slick gabardine suits, Christian Dior outfits, Yamamoto blouses, shoes of crocodile skin' (Mbembe 1992: 28). The parallels with other descriptions of francophone Africa are striking, in particular Gandoulou's discussion of the cult of elegance of 'le sapeur' in Brazzaville where the self-esteem of the urban youth is determined by the range of brands of clothing that they are able to wear (Gandoulou 1989). This intersection of formality and the ludic, Mbembe declares, means that 'the postcolony is a world of anxious virility, hostile to continence, frugality and sobriety' (Mbembe 1992: 9).

It must be said that most of this does not appeal to anglo-Bamiléké Cameroonians who regard these as the antics of the 'Frenchmen' and to be treated with considerable distaste. Cameroon TV, for example, will regularly show dance and music from the different regions of Cameroon as a way of demonstrating the rich cultural diversity in unity that characterises the Cameroon nation. Dances from the francophone southern Cameroon forest, which are well known for their explicit sexual content, are greeted with derision by anglophones who view them as symptomatic of the sex-crazed, depraved lifestyle of the francophone, a sign of their laziness and incapacity for hard work. In the face of the degeneracy of the francophone, an explicit post-colonial 'anglo-saxon' identity has grown around what are viewed as the reverse values of honesty, hard work and probity. The general view is that their francophone brothers know the 'anglos' to be superior in all things to do with economic development, democratic pluralist politics and administrative probity, which accounts for why they have spent the last thirty years doing everything possible to suppress them. Absurd antics and displays by francophones, administrative, academic or otherwise, are dismissed as another good reason why the act of union should be repealed and a return made to a federal structure. At a certain level, the debate concerns the difference between anglophone and francophone alternative roads to modernity. The anglophones, consistent with a history of exclusion in post-independence Cameroon, avoid the state and emphasise an entrepreneurial, free-market politics that reinvents hierarchy as a means of controlling labour and regulating capital accumulation and disaccumulation (Rowlands 1993). By contrast they see the southern Cameroon 'francophone' road to modernity as based on a corrupt monopoly of state power and resources, soft loans and development aid to fuel an ethnic politics rooted overtly in displays of the obscenity and arbitrariness of power.

It is no doubt part of the convenience of ethnic politics that such stereotypes can be turned to multiple uses. The theme of the 'cannibal state' devouring its own people is after all not peculiar to Cameroon and has been widely ascribed to other regimes in sub-Saharan Africa. There is

also a despair in the writing that links together a number of African intellectuals who are themselves products of modernist educational
programmes that encouraged them to pursue futures that they now despise
and live in exile from (cf. Mbembe's own autobiographical article 1993).
What is rejected as a desirable future is a modernity that owes nothing
to any past, whether conceived in terms of repetition or origin, and everything to 'naturalising' the arbitrariness of the sign of the nation-space.
Benedict Anderson has argued that this 'naturalising' process depends on
the replacement of one form of simultaneity by another in the shaping of
a national consciousness. He suggests, borrowing an idea from Walter
Benjamin, that in early modern Europe the fissuring of a medieval
cosmology of simultaneity by an idea of 'homogeneous, empty time'
enabled a new form of temporality to emerge. If previously simultaneity
marked the here and now as something which has always been so and
will be so in the future, in modern consciousness 'simultaneity permits, as
it were, transverse, cross-time marked not by prefiguring and fulfilment
but by temporal coincidence, and measured by clock and calendar'
(Anderson 1983: 30). The desire to reject the past and create an identity
that coordinates events and lifestyles in different nation-spaces is used by
bureaucratic elites in Cameroon who imagine that they live in a style
exactly equivalent to their peers living in Paris or New York. Indeed,
travel to such places for celebrations confirms the temporal coincidence
of those believed to hold equivalent positions and to share fraternal bonds
of mutual support and dedication. This provides the imagined world of
the nation-space in Cameroon with a sociological solidity; it links together,
in a synchronicity of times, diverse acts of actors who are otherwise
unaware of each other except as sharing a project that will realise itself
in the fullness of time (Bhabha 1994: 158). However, whilst modernity
struggles to establish itself as the dominant if arbitrary signifier, it does
so by claiming to exist in radical disjunction from those other temporalities that bear down on individual identities. The decentring of a prophetic
visibility embedded in messianic time is deemed a prerequisite for the
emergence of the homogeneous and horizontal community of modern
society. The violence of a certain kind of consumption and body politics
is part of this struggle to break up a received coherence and establish
the conditions for a new cultural signification and power relations. But
if this is so, then in the midst of this establishment of a new cultural
homogeneity, emerges the inconsistency of minority discourses and temporalities. The fact that this assumes a radical spatial disjunction, realised in
terms like village, bush and underdevelopment, recognises that this is not
remnant time but an alternative to the linear and progressive time of the
national will. But through turning this into a form of resistance, we risk
missing the ambivalence that Bhabha, for instance, recognises as lying
deep within the account of modernity; the need to sustain supplementary
spaces for the articulation of cultural knowledges that are adjacent and

adjunct rather than teleological and accumulative (Bhabha 1994: 163). In contemporary Cameroon it is not necessarily contradictory for Fru Ndi to call on the language of the 'tapenta boy', or for the modern bureaucrat to return to the village to consult a healer; they are simply taking advantage of the inconsistencies that exist.

CONCLUSION

The starting point of this paper was the same as other writings in a Gramscian tradition which have documented that the politics and cultures of subalternity are inherently oppositional or, to use Gramsci's phrase, structured by a 'series of negations' (a particular influence in this chapter has been the seminal work of the late Roger Keesing). The operation of hegemony in colonial situations explored by Keesing but going back to Fanon and other writers has shown that 'one of the dynamics in the colonial situation has been the deep internalisation by the colonised of the discourse of domination with regard to race, cultural inferiority and the ancestral past' (Keesing 1994: 54). In part this is a matter of appropriating the language of the dominant or, as Keesing describes it, 'as a strategic realisation that one must meet the enemy on his own turf' (ibid.). But subtlety in creating opposition through appropriating the codes of a dominant discourse also implies its affirmation.

One aspect of this is to rediscover the past as heritage, tradition or custom precisely at the moment when it is being finally eradicated as a living force. All of which may be regrettable but unproblematic within an historicist discourse that affirms the present as a process of becoming in the signification of a people as a nation developing a culture. In Cameroon, as in much of Africa, this has been shaped by a dominant language of nation building that has in turn reshaped the meaning of colonial time in the present. But the figure of the people that emerges is marked by an ambivalence of disjunctive times and meanings that has produced what Fanon called profound cultural undecidability (Fanon 1969). In such circumstances, national cohesion can no longer be signified as the achievement of a sociological solidity (using Anderson's term) where the social space is a public space securely occupied by symbols of modernity – schools hospitals, prisons, government and business offices. If this is so then oppositional currents, through their appropriation of dominant codes, share in historicist expectations of a future, although disagreeing as to who should possess it. Contemporary events in Africa no longer make even this stance believable. They pose not only essential questions of the representation of the nation-space as a temporal process but predict more disturbing nightmarish scenarios that are now becoming only too chillingly apparent. If each nation is not to have a modernity consistent with its sense of precedent then the jettisoning of well-established modes of thought, both dominant and oppositional, is an urgent necessity.

ACKNOWLEDGMENTS

Sections and the spirit of this chapter owe a great deal to collaborative research over the years with Jean-Pierre Warnier.

REFERENCES

Anderson, B. (1983) *Imagined Communities*. London: Verso.
Bayart, J.-F. (1993) *The State in Africa*. London: Longman.
Berman, M. (1983) *All That is Solid Melts into Air*. London: Verso.
Bhabha, H.K. (1994) *The Location of Culture*. London: Routledge.
Burnham, P. (1993) L'Ethnie, religion et l'état au Cameroun. *Cahiers d'Etudes Africaines* XXXIII: 313–57.
Campbell, C. (1987) *The Romantic Ethic and the Spirit of Modern Consumerism*. Oxford: Blackwell.
Dillon, R. (1990) *Ranking and Resistance*. Stanford: Stanford University Press.
Fanon, F. (1969) On national culture, in *The Wretched of the Earth*. London: Penguin.
Friedman, J. (1989) The consumption of modernity. *Culture and History* 4: 117–30.
Gandalou, J.-D. (1989) *Dandiès à Bacongo*. Paris: L'harmattan.
Gellner, E. (1963) *Nations and Nationalism*. Oxford: Blackwell.
Joseph, R. (1976) *Radical Nationalism in Cameroon*. Oxford: Clarendon.
Keesing, R. (1994) Colonial and counter-colonial discourse in Melanesia. *Critique of Anthropology* 14(1): 41–58.
Lerner, D. (1968) *The Passing of Traditional Society*. New York: Free Press.
Mbembe, A. (1992) Provisional notes on the postcolony. *Africa* 62(1): 3–37.
Miaffo, D. and Warnier, J.-P. (1993) Accumulation et ethos de la notabilité chez les bamiléké, in Geschiere, P. and Konings, P., eds, *Itinéraires d'accumulation au Cameroun*. Paris: Karthala.
Miller, D. (1994) *Modernity: An Ethnographic Account*. Oxford: Berg.
Pradelles de Latour, C.-H. (1994) A Lacanian analysis of Bangoua kinship. *Africa* 64(1): 21–33.
Rowlands, M.J. (1993) Accumulation and the cultural politics of identity in the Grassfields, in Geschiere, P. and Konings, P., eds, *Itinéraires d'accumulation au Cameroun*. Paris: Karthala.
Rowlands, M.J. and Warnier, J.-P. (1988) Sorcery, power and the modern state in Cameroon. *Man* (n.s.) 23(1): 118–32.
Sennett, R. (1986) *The Face of Public Man*. London: Faber & Faber.
Slageren, J. van (1972) *Les origines de l'église évangélique au Cameroun*. Yaounde: Clé.
Tchouanga Tiegoum, P. and Ngangoum, B.F. (1975) *La verité du culte des Ancêtres en Afrique chez les Bamiléké*. Ed Essor des jeunes (mimeo), Nkongsamba.
Toulabour, C.M. (1994) Political satire past and present in Togo. *Critique of Anthropology* 14(1): 59–75.
Warnier, J.-P. (1993) *L'esprit d'entreprise au Cameroun*. Paris: Karthala.

3 Creating a culture of disillusionment

Consumption in Moscow, a chronicle of changing times

Caroline Humphrey

The turn towards a market economy has brought a flow of goods from all over the world to Russia. They range from franchises for expensive cars and designer clothes, through cheaper manufactures from China and Turkey, to a mass of quickly run-up clothing, handicrafts and southern fruits sold by traders from the former Soviet republics. By late 1993 basic foodstuffs were also pouring in. All these things are seen as *ne nashi* ('not ours', i.e. foreign).

One might have expected Muscovites, after decades of imposed homogeneity, to delight unambiguously in the possibility of using consumption for self-expression by means of exotic and global signs. Undoubtedly there is pent-up demand in Russia. But nevertheless attitudes to consumption are complex, sometimes negative, and subject to rapid historical change. Soviet society had earlier created consumers, that is people conscious of living through objects and images not of their own making. However, this consciousness was significantly different from that of late-industrial market economies. In fact a large section of the population continued to produce for subsistence in their own households,[1] but more important than this was the Soviet ideology, which insisted on the citizen's conscious identification with the activity of the state. Virtually all industrial and manufactured goods, and most agricultural ones, were produced by state enterprises and distributed throughout the Union according to state plans. This meant that, although the vast majority of products and images were consumed by people who had not created them, it was ideologically enjoined that people feel them nevertheless to be 'ours' (*nashi*). At some level people did make this identification, while simultaneously realising this to be part of the gigantic deception (*obman*) of the Soviet regime. What we need to try to understand now is how people conceive of consumption when the category of state products is shrinking by the month and 'foreign' goods are flooding in, even foods, which people literally consume in their own bodies.

This paper supports the view that consumption is the key means of creating culture in the urbanised and industrialised societies of the modern world (Miller 1987). This view may be contrasted with the idea that some pre-existing culture moulds consumption, which thereby appears as an outcome of culture. The idea of a pre-existing culture suggests something timeless and homogeneous, but it is evident that neither of these qualities is appropriate for our times. In Russia today attitudes to consumption cross-cut the various ethnic 'cultures' of that vast country. One may find more in common between the consumption cultures of youthful urbanised Russians and Buryats, say, than between different classes within the Russian population. This is not to deny ethnic diversity, but it is to challenge the idea that it can be the sole or even main explanation of consumption patterns. It would be interesting to explore whether the revival/reinvention of ethnic traditions is not in fact leading to parallel phenomena in 'different' ethnic groups, somewhat like Wilk's 'structures of common difference' discussed in this volume. However, the focus of this paper is elsewhere. It will be suggested here that certain immediately preceeding economic practices and attitudes of the late Soviet period have been like the motor-drivers pushing current consumption in particular directions, and that the extreme compression of historical changes in the past few years has polarised the population; this has occurred most notably by generation, separating those people whose attitudes were formed by the Soviet regime from those who came to adulthood after the advent of Gorbachev in the mid-1980s.

Perhaps it seems extravagant to write as if there were much choice when so many people struggle only to survive. It is true that the vast majority of Russians have very low incomes and quite simply cannot afford to buy foreign goods. Over 30 per cent of the population of Russia has an income below the 'threshold of survival', i.e. they must use existing stocks, sales of property, or loans from kin and friends in order to stay alive (Valyuzhenich 1993). However, poverty alone cannot explain the present Russian attitudes to consumption, since even the most desperate are conscious of other times and of themselves as 'poor people' within the diversified world of the city.

If contemporary culture is being created by consumption we need to ask what are the dynamic mechanisms that influence attitudes and affect actual choices. Friedman (1990) has made an important step in suggesting that we think about consumption attitudes not as intrinsically ethnic, but as the specific product, in any given situation, of a series of historical global transformations. However, in the case of contemporary Russia a purely externalist analysis of economic and political developments risks diverging from Russian understandings and producing an over-coherent analysis remote from the actual chaotic situation. Therefore this paper explores three quite different representations of the historical transformation out of Sovietness as seen from inside. The first two of these were suggested to me by reading Bukovskii's *Letters of a Russian Traveller* (1981), his images of 'deception' (*obman*) and the 'crisis of values'. The third is the image of the *Novyye Russkiye* (the New Russians), the perception that business and entrepreneurship have produced a totally new kind of person. In this paper, rather than using standard categories like price and demand, I use these historically formed value-laden perceptions as ways of getting at the factors influencing people to consume in the ways they do.

'We know that they [the Soviet government] always want to deceive us, and because of this we seek deception in everything', wrote Bukovskii (1981: 43). He was writing about attitudes to the press, but it is clear that, just as the Soviet ideology was in fact an attempt at a totalising hegemony, the sense of deception among ordinary people also extended into virtually every sphere of life. It seems that from the mid-1960s onwards the fitful opening of Soviet society to the world outside, and glimpses of global technology and consumer goods, began to play a role in the internal relations of state and people.

> It is strange, but totalitarian regimes are very sensitive to social pressure, though they carefully hide this. These regimes are maintained by fear and the silent complicity of those who surround them. Each person should be absolutely powerless before the state, completely without rights and generally to blame. In this atmosphere the *word* (even spoken from abroad) comes to have a huge strength (it is not by chance that they executed poets among us). At the same time both the powers and the people understood perfectly the illegality of the regime, its *illegitimacy*. In this hidden civil war the external world (*zagranitsa*) becomes the highest arbiter. Just as a gangster, who has become wealthy through fighting, attempts to be accepted by high society, arrays himself in a dinner-jacket and imitates the habits of the profit-making businessman, the Soviet regime thirsts to be accepted as an equal in world society. The exclamations about being the most just, the most happy, the most progressive, and absolutely the most socialist state have long disappeared into the shadows. 'It's no worse among us,' or 'Do they have it any better?' – these are the subtexts of present Soviet propaganda.
>
> (Bukovskii 1981: 29)

If the illegitimate and deceiving regime itself came to mimic the West, this placed all emulation in an ambiguous light. What was 'real' when everything produced by the quasi-hegemonic regime at the same time copied and denounced the outside world? Russians, habituated to cynicism, continued to search for the fraud of the even more powerful West, and this rendered people perpetually aware of a certain conditionality, removing any possibility of simply and directly accepting capitalist consumption patterns at face value.

Bukovskii describes an instant from his own life to illustrate the 'crisis of values' as the Russian economy faced that of advanced capitalism. He had been freed from camp and reached the West:

It is just the same as when I stood in the airport in Zurich over my bag of prison odds and ends – completely amazed that all my valuables, penknives, razors, and books, accumulated over years by generations of convicts, were turning under my eyes into nothing. I myself had hidden them, I had sewn them into linings, and trembled over them at each frisking. And I even brought a condom to Zurich, what a blockhead. . . . You see Soviet people spend a great part of their lives in endless cares, how to get hold of, how to obtain, how to dig out the most elementary things. What trickery, what resourcefulness is needed to do things that over here take only five minutes. And now all this experience, all your property, collapses in a single instant.

(Ibid.: 83)

If such a crushing realisation brought bewilderment and dejection to each Soviet person, that time has passed now. Three or four years have gone by in which Muscovites have become accustomed to there being an array of glittering goods and to their vastly high prices in comparison with those of local manufactures. Nevertheless, the historical instant of the 'crisis of values' has made its mark, so that all attempts to come to terms with the new economic circumstances, to somehow make a life with all of these goods, take place in its shadow.

The Russians' exaggerated cynicism and despairing sense of loss of value emerged from within their own, radically different, economic experience. Furthermore, perhaps only a professional economist could separate out such an object as 'the Soviet economy'. For everyone inside, it was experienced as a *political economy*, that is, imbued at every point with policies and ideology. The habit of seeing all 'economic' activity as intrinsically also activity laden with political-ideological value is particularly marked and conscious among former Soviet people (though it must apply in other kinds of economy too). One aspect of this was the glorification of production/labour and the condemnation of commonplace trading for profit, called 'speculation' in Soviet parlance. The quasi-illegitimacy of the Soviet regime itself did not thereby make speculators a positive category. Nor have they become so today. Rather, the historical (and so far only partial) transformation of the economy has seemed to Russians to produce an original breed of business-people, the 'New Russians'. New Russians are seen as a continuation of the speculators, but with the shocking difference that their activities are now approved by the government. These political-moral attitudes set the New Russians apart, and they have reacted with a bold-faced rejection of all such views. In the following section I give a description of the consumption situation in Moscow, and this is followed by a discussion of the role of the three perceptions introduced here in influencing consumption decisions.

AN ETHNOGRAPHY OF CONSUMPTION IN MOSCOW, 1993

In the Soviet period the people of Moscow bought basic goods mostly in state shops and, if they were relatively well-off, in the few state-run markets, where vegetables and fruit were sold by collective farms and peasants at higher prices. Besides this there was an extensive system of allocation of difficult-to-obtain goods through the workplace, sometimes paid for 'by order' and sometimes distributed free as a bonus (Humphrey 1991). Meanwhile, of course, people sought every means, the black market, networks of acquaintances, barter and exchange magazines, patrons and back doors of all kinds (*blat*), to get hold of other things they needed.

In Moscow in spring 1993, there were not only the state stores and official markets of old, but also private and foreign shops, kiosks, street peddlers, informal markets and huge weekly fairs, such as the arts and crafts fair at Izmailovo Park. However, all this did not make shopping in Moscow like shopping in London, Paris or Rome. Somehow, the sovereignty of the Western shopper, enticed to wander and inspect, to titillate desire, to take pleasure in the whole process – that is, shopping promoted as a leisure activity – had not occurred and seemed indeed far from Russian reality.

In Soviet times there used to be an underlying sense that for the most part goods were not really bought by choice, but allocated. This intensified during the first years of economic collapse (1989–91) before the freeing of prices. During those years there was an increase in workplace orders and state distributions to various needy and honoured social groups, and rationing was introduced everywhere for basic goods such as meat, flour or butter. Thus, even though the Soviet consumer formally engaged in buying – went to a shop, decided what to purchase, and paid money for it – the ways people talked about this reveal that at some level they realised that they were at the receiving end of a state-planned system of distribution. People said that goods were there to buy because 'they' (the authorities) had given them out. 'What are they giving (*dayut*) in GUM today?' people would ask. In slang 'they' threw out (*vybrosili*) or chucked out (*vykidivali*) the goods to the people.[2] This was recognition that shops and markets were lower-priority parts of the same system as the specially distributed packages of luxuries to officials and the nameless, closely curtained buildings that contained foreign-currency stores. Voinovich (1985: 113) wrote ironically, 'With socialism, as everyone knows, there can be no *uravnilovka* [egalitarianism, a pejorative term in late Soviet times, C.H.]. From each according to ability, to each according to rank. Even Marx said that. Or Lenin. Or maybe I dreamed it up myself, I can't remember when.'

In working-class Moscow in spring 1993 the stark signs of the distributory era, 'Bread', 'Footwear', 'Meat', were still virtually the only labels a shop was likely to have. Most of them, private or not, did not bother with anything much in the way of window displays (though they were not as downright misleading as they used to be: in the old days, if you saw something in a shop window it was a guarantee that it could not be bought inside). Strangely, rather than private shops approximating to some Western model, and state shops being forced by competition to emulate them, almost the reverse was the case. State stores remained unchanged, and private shops, which were often only state ones taken over by the collective of workers, were usually indistinguishable from them in any outward way. Only locals could tell if a given rouble grocery was in private hands (though the prices were higher). It is true that private and foreign shops selling in dollars were somewhat different, since hardly anyone could afford to buy at them;[3] but here too minimal effort was made to make the goods attractive. Decorated Italian sweaters jostled with Swedish fridges, lace underwear with salami, whisky or videos. The idea was simple: these things are foreign, bring your dollars and pay up. Inside state shops for basic goods, on the other hand, there were crowds and the sales-people, as of yore, had precedence. The shoppers were subjected to the triple queuing system, as irritable shoulder-to-shoulder masses shuffled in three lines to order the goods, pay for them, and collect them.

In its way, the Soviet state shop was like a microcosm of what Bukovskii called the 'hidden civil war', and essentially this system continued into spring 1993. As befits the idea that the state managed this microcosm to its own olympian benefit, the manager remained invisible in a separate room and the cashier's desk was often elevated on a stand, so buyers had to pass money up to someone sitting at shoulder height. This made it feel as though one was petitioning to be allowed to pay. The cashier might refuse to accept anything but the exact sum, or alternatively might throw down (literally) some sweets as change. The shoppers cursed, or agitatedly counted through their packets of multifarious banknotes. In the ordering queue something of the distributive mentality remained, partly because pre-packaging of goods in units a shopper might want to buy was still a rarity. So when buying butter or cheese, for example, the purchaser named a weight and the shopworker cut a certain amount off a huge block with a spatula and weighed it, often with a bored and careless look, so the buyer had to glare or remonstrate that it was too little, and then a bit more would be added, all with the facial expression, 'This is as much as you deserve.' Frequently shoppers were turned away if they had not brought their own wrapping paper. In the case of meat, people could reach the top of the queue only to find that the shopworker refused to give a good piece unless some scrawny, dried-up bits were taken too. So mistrustful of one another were the two sides that payment by cheque (were such things to exist) was unthinkable. In 1993 a few large stores introduced their own 'credit cards' and some people were attracted by such a seemingly Western modernity. But not only did purchasers have to buy the cards by paying up to their 'credit limit' in advance, they soon found that the goods in these stores were regularly more highly priced than outside. Shoppers were not really surprised to be disillusioned, and queueing continued, though during the year it changed its goals.

The queue, heaving involuntarily forwards and looking with gimlet eyes at each transaction, could not be said to be supportive of the shopper at the head. An almost palpable vexation arose if someone 'bought too much', and it was almost as bad if they 'wasted time' by querying the weighing, or insisted on picking and choosing between good and rotten fruit, or made a mistake in their sums and arrived from the cashier's queue with a chitty that did not exactly correspond with the price/ weight of the items. Of course, queues varied: in neighbourhood shops people often kept places for friends or jumped the queue by prior arrange-ment with the shopworker (this was grimly borne by those behind). In the fashionable Western franchises in central Moscow, it was more a case of each for himself and physical elbowing into a more advantageous position.

The Russian queue (*ochered'*) was not simply a social presence but was also a social principle, one which regulated social entitlements in time. It enshrined the social and psychological idea of consumption through state distribution. As Voinovich (1985: 42) wrote, and it is still true, 'Queues [*ochered'*] are various. They can be for a few minutes, over-night, for several days. People stay in the queues for cars or apartments for years.' Russians fleeing from Tadjikstan report that the Dushanbe riots of 1991 were caused by the rumour that Armenian refugees had been allotted places at the head of the queue for apartments. The preservation of the queue for flats in the metropolis was the main reason given by the Russian Federal Migration Service for their support for the residence permit system, despite its 'non-democratic' nature and the fact that it serves to exclude their clients (refugees) from all major cities (Baiduzhi 1993).

How did this change through 1993? On the one hand, the system of consumption through the allocation of benefits if anything increased. On the other hand, the old Soviet-type queuing, where the availability of scarce goods rather than price was what mattered, has to a great extent been replaced by the desperate search for cheap goods.

One of the reasons why allocated benefits have increased relative to money wages is the newly introduced income tax (Hansen 1993: 92). Wage increases over government-regulated levels are subject to punitive taxes up to 60 per cent, as a measure to control inflation. But social welfare benefits are exempt from taxation. Many state organisations and com-panies therefore choose to give workers rises in the form of vouchers or coupons, calling them something like 'subsidy for food'. A recent study of living conditions in a northern province of Russia (Hansen 1993) showed the benefits to be: free/subsidised transport (27 per cent), vouchers for purchase of consumer durables (7 per cent), humanitarian aid from

Western countries (7 per cent), free meal at the workplace (6 per cent), food-orders for families with many children (2 per cent), food-orders for invalids and veterans (15 per cent), food-orders through the workplace (35 per cent). This essentially continues an old practice of the Soviet state, but it is now supplemented by the distribution of imported goods which companies can obtain by purchase or barter for their own locally gener- ated profits.

This system may take the edge off subsistence shopping for some employed people, but it leaves the unemployed and the dispossessed in a desperate situation. Furthermore, state wages do not keep pace with infla- tion and many loss-making factories, though they do not dismiss their workers, close down for months on end without pay. During 1993 large numbers of state and collective farms were unable to pay wages for as much as six months. Russians divide their 'money' into *nalichniye* (cash in hand) and *beznalichniye* (notional money owed to one). There is a terrible shortage of *nalichniye*.[4] Thus the glittering goods are mostly things people are unable to buy, and the Soviet search for scarce goods has been replaced by combing the city for cheap basic products.

However, this is exactly what the market is not providing. There are many reasons, perhaps the main one being that state shops (and even privatised state shops) still to a great extent rely on their old suppliers, and these are the doddering collective farms and ramshackle factories which themselves have problems with supplies. Here, however, I shall focus on the activities of entrepreneurs, which are another major factor. Entrepreneurs in Russia, not surprisingly, started out by trading the most profitable goods, in other words, those luxury items not found in the Soviet economy. This explains the historical appearance first of foreign liqueurs, 'designer' jeans, expensive flashy jackets, etc. on the Russian marketplace. People rushed to buy them in 1990–2, but now they are beyond the pockets of ordinary workers. Only a few Western goods have penetrated everyday consumption, notably Mars bars and Snickers ('Karl Mars and Frederik Snickers'). In 1993 entrepreneurs started to import American and European foods (Norwegian salami, American butter, etc.), which have appeared in state and private shops. But the prices are still too high, and today, if you see a crowd of people, you know the queue is for cheap Russian produce – the very opposite of the situation a few years ago.[5]

A friend of mine 'in business' said that if a certain item sells well her reaction is not to get in more of the goods but to raise the price. Muscovite shoppers describe how you may hear that something (soap, tights, cassettes) is cheaper in one quarter of the city than another, but it never makes sense to trek over there to get it, because by the time you get there the price will have gone up. It is clear how pricing tricks work locally: there is a row of kiosks all selling the same items. One has a lower price for something. Thinking they have got a bargain people eagerly buy it. The kiosk-holders are in league and divide up the profits. In fact, local Mafias ensure that prices are never truly lowered.

The purchaser thus encounters a different kind of anxiety from the queue: a threatening kind of lawlessness. The kiosks which cluster around railway stations and the entrances to the Metro sell a range of profitable goods: Western cigarettes, cans of drink, electronic equipment, Italian shoes, CDs, briefcases, tights and obscure (but always the same) liqueurs. Near the kiosks sit the peddlars, with their trays of local cigarettes, ice-cream, Mars bars, or apples. But round about, sometimes hidden, but often sitting openly alongside, are the minders. There is not a single old woman selling Marlboros and matches who does not have her allotted stretch of pavement and pay her protector for the right. One kiosk cannot lower prices or the owner would immediately be beaten up by the others or by the minders. If a customer spots a fraud and complains about it aloud, a number of leather-jacketed men are likely to appear instantaneously at his or her elbow. They do not hestitate to threaten or even beat ordinary women shoppers.

In the case of the kiosks with their threatening entourages people buy there in the teeth of what is to them certain knowledge that they are being 'cheated'. They know a good proportion of the price is going to the minders and the higher-level Mafia, not to speak of the 'good-for-nothing' young kiosk-holders themselves. The goods are suspected to be counterfeit and defective. A kiosk worker I knew, a Russian drop-out student, worked for Chinese merchants, and she realised she was hired to do the face-to-face selling because foreign traders are so resented. I heard people liken them to cockroaches. Where this differs from negative attitudes to ethnic groups as traders elsewhere in the world is the universal cynicism in every single relationship down the line. All sides cheated one another: the owners under-paid the sellers, the purchasers tried to steal, the buyers were given defective goods, and the sellers hid some of the takings from the owner. Massive takings nevertheless ended up with the main Chinese trader (early 1990s), but my friend was almost sorry for him because, since banks took high taxes, he had to sit day and night by his trunk of rapidly devaluing money.[6]

As for the street peddlers (*perekupshchiki*), Muscovites know exactly how they operate. Often they are old people who have fallen on hard times, and almost all are women. They get to know the managers of large shops located in inconvenient places. Having paid a bribe they are able to buy up quantities of the goods before other shoppers get access. They then take the goods (say, cans of beer or flowers) to strategic spots where people are in a hurry and are prepared to pay far more than the usual price.[7] Sometimes goods change hands through several traders before they reach the streets. A money-conscious Muscovite would not buy from these peddlers, but would prefer to do without, or to make the trek to the original shop and pay the lower price. Nevertheless, passers-by, being certain

Figure 3.1: 'St Petersburg: street sellers near Primorskaya metro station', 1993

Source: Susannah Rogers

they must have been driven to it, are horrified at the plight of the elderly street-sellers, who stand meekly in rows, with their prowling minders nearby.

As the structure of the Soviet Union collapsed, two things happened: there was a phenomenal growth in the number and type of economic transactions, and the old system of laws became obsolete. New laws hurriedly passed have failed to keep pace with the economic life of the streets, and the growth of some kind of 'protection' for transactions was inevitable. This has become so pervasive that the authorities, colluding with at least some parts of the Mafia, have so far only ventured to attack relatively powerless outsiders (traders from the erstwhile 'younger brother' peoples of the Caucasus and Central Asia).

The following newspaper report is noteworthy because it links such anti-foreign drives with new consumer reactions. In October 1993 the Mayor of Moscow, Yuri Luzhkov, justified the use of the state of emergency as a way of expelling from the city several thousand Armenian, Georgian and Azerbaijani traders without residence permits.

> Mr Luzhkov ... said that after the state of emergency ended, he would probably introduce an entry visa regime to prevent those expelled from returning to Moscow. As for the markets, they might offer fewer 'exotic fruits' in future, but 'honest traders from Tambov, Lipetsk, Bryansk and other [Russian] towns will arrive with good products and will sell traditional Russian food.'
>
> If Mr Luzhkov carries out his threat, Muscovites will face a diet of potatoes, beetroot, cabbage and pickled cabbage. But they don't care. Because some Caucasians are involved in crime, they blame them all and welcome the police action. 'It's just a pity this state of emergency can't be permanent,' said Vera Vladimirovna, a pensioner looking for something affordable on the few stalls left at the Chernomuzhkinskaya Market.
>
> (Womack 1993)

Sometimes at a market one can see heaps of unsold meat. It is not just that many people cannot afford it, a large number refrain from consuming altogether as far as possible. They prefer to save or invest, for reasons that will be explored below.

It is interesting to try to discover what people do actually buy. Some information is available from large-scale, all-Russian statistics, although it is not clear how these were gathered. In 1991–2 Russians spent between 30 and 40 per cent of their incomes on food, 40–50 per cent on non-food manufactures, around 12–15 per cent on services, and 8–10 per cent on alcohol. In 1992–3 the amount spent on food rose to 40–50 per cent, payments for manufactures and services declined, and alcohol remained the same (Struktura ... 1993). A probably more reliable survey in 1992 in the Kola Peninsula suggested that householders spent between 70 per cent and 82 per cent of their budget on food (Hansen 1993: 99).

I close this section with a description of the budget of a Moscow middle-class family with whom I stayed during March–April 1993. I wish to use this to make two points: first to show how consumption even in the middle class was largely devoted to basic necessities, and second to indicate the kind of *bouleversement* that people are living through, since only six months later such a consumption pattern became impossible. The family in spring 1993 regarded itself as not particularly well off, less so, for example, than that of an experienced factory-worker. Their income for the month 15 March to 15 April was 70,100 roubles.[8] In December 1992, a Russian economist from the Ministry of Labour estimated that the 'threshold of survival' of such a family (three adults and a child) would be around 16,100 roubles a month, while the 'poverty line' would stand at around 40,000 roubles a month (Valyuzhenich 1993).[9] Extrapolating this by the 70 per cent price rise between then and 16 March 1993 (Goryacheva 1993) we can estimate that the family's income of 70,100 roubles was around the official 'poverty line', though well above the survival rate. The family's food for the month cost 25,955 roubles; payment for services (including transport, and one-off payments for school repair and a foreign passport) were 14,319; non-food manufactures were 5,121; alcohol was 550. The total spent was 45,695 roubles. Potatoes, bread, cabbage, pickled cabbage and beetroot indeed figured prominently in the budget, though the family was also able to afford meat, fish, eggs and cheese. Fearful of total economic collapse, the household also kept stockpiles of food like flour, tea, noodles and sugar, and these were being gradually used up as such Russian goods became more and more difficult to obtain.[10]

We should note that the budget was provided by the wife, and assumed to cover the whole family. This is a characteristic Russian assumption regarding the household, according to which it is the wife who has to make do.[11] In fact the housewife's budget did not take into account certain expenditures of the husband and older daughter. I have estimated these to include around 8,600 roubles for cigarettes, 1,000 for vodka, some 1,000 for newspapers, and around 5,000 for dress-making. The family's total expenditure would therefore have been at least 61,295 for the month. Any savings were put towards purchase of a *dacha* (country cottage) outside town.

Although the family did not spend their entire income, they felt hard-pressed. Steep inflation was perceptible even during the month. The housewife, the main shopper, went to great efforts to find products that were good bargains. She was dependent on the fact that it was possible to buy good bread cheaply (bread is subsidised and people buy it even several times a day from numerous local bakers). Very little was spent on clothing, and nothing on books, cinemas, music, etc. What is most noticeable about this budget is that, with the exception of one piece of imported butter, *nothing* in it was foreign. 'American butter' was regretted and bought only because 'our fatherland (*otechestvennyi*) butter' was sold out.

The cigarettes were Russian and so were a door-lock and a pair of child's skis. It was as though the global influx of goods to Moscow had never taken place.

Before discussing the thinking behind this kind of consumption, I should explain that its Russianness is no longer an option. Even the state and collectively owned shops are now full of imported products, and to the amazement of Muscovites these are packaged in convenient units and in such a way that they can be preserved longer. But people told me they would rather go without, or restrict their food to a few repetitive items, than buy foreign produce. However, they do not have much choice. The Caucasian and Central Asian traders with their fruits and kebabs continue to be kept out of Moscow. Unless you can grow produce yourself or have relatives on a farm, it is a case of imports or nothing, and these tightly packaged foods many Russians find 'doubtful' and 'likely to cause illness'.

DECEIT

From the 1920s onwards the Communist Party's propaganda sections put forward Soviet styles for people to emulate. They were styles of clothing, house interiors, food, etiquettes of behaviour, etc. that were designed to express the classless, health-conscious, labour-oriented direction that society should take. In the Khrushchev era (1950s–1960s) an important change took place. Rather than representing goals for the future, the propaganda images were presented as if they really existed (see Figure 3.2). At first these images were deceitful because they were utterly un-attainable – the items represented either were absent from Soviet shops or so expensive as to be beyond ordinary people's most extravagant hopes. But later, as these very goods became available for the middle class (I have often sat in sitting-rooms *exactly* like the one in the photograph) it became apparent that the range of products was so limited as to enforce an involuntary homogeneity on all consumption.

Thus there was another aspect to the feeling of being involved in a gigantic deception. This derived from the growing sense during the 1970s–1980s of being removed, by being entombed in the Soviet Union, from another, more real, but curtained-off history, that is from the history of the world. Soviet citizens were told that they were at the forefront in every sphere, they led the world, and yet disorienting glimpses on TV, and above all foreigners themselves, seemed like evidence that this might not be so.

So propaganda images were widely seen as a deceit (*obman*), and yet they aroused consumer desire. Furthermore, as Verdery (1992) has percep-tively observed, this desire was constituted as a 'right', since material plenty was an essential measure of the advancement of the Soviet socialist system. Quoting a Romanian friend, Verdery wrote: '"What everyone strives to do is to figure out how not to have frustration be too costly:

Figure 3.2 'In the family circle', Dushanbe, 1967
Source: photograph supplied by Viktor Buchli

not to want something so much that being denied it will devastate you. The test of character becomes managing to accept yet another denial without being undone by it." ' Verdery continues,

> Socialism intensified this experience ... for the regimes themselves paradoxically abetted the emphasis on consumption. First, organised shortage made procuring something – anything – a major triumph. Second, even as the regimes prevented people from consuming by not making goods available, they insisted that under socialism the standard of living would constantly improve.... Socialism ... aroused desire without focalizing it, and kept it alive by deprivation. That is, in socialism desire floated free in endless search of goods people saw as their right.
>
> ... The arousal and frustration of consumer desire and East Europeans' consequent resistance to their regimes led them to build their social identities specifically *through consuming*. Acquiring consumption goods and objects conferred an identity that set one off from socialism. To acquire objects became a way of constituting your selfhood against a regime you despised.

(Verdery 1992: 25–6).

Russia under the Soviet regime was more pervasively subject to hegemonic propaganda than Eastern Europe, and this ensured that Western goods were not merely representative but constitutive of social identity (cf. Friedman 1990: 318). Ordinary people would hide things, such as tape-recorders, of obviously Western provenance, since they were associated with resistance to the regime. The *fanaty* (football fans), *khippi*, *punki*, *rokery* and other counter-culture groups in Moscow during the 1970s to 1980s used English for their graffiti, wore approximations of Western fashions and hairstyles, and conceptualised their way of life by 'English' terms: *flety* ('flats', or crash-pads), *grin* ('green', dollars), *askat'* ('to beg/ask'), and so forth (Bushnell 1990: 116–17). Just looking like a *khippi* was enough to provoke the authorities. Many were dispatched to short terms in the *kreiza* (loony-bin) just for their appearance (Bushnell 1990: 115).

There is a crucial difference between Eastern European countries, discussed by Verdery, and Russia. In the former, the Soviet system was easily seen as alien, whereas in Russia it had to be acknowledged as 'ours' (*nash*). Consequently the experience of deception was both interiorised and globalised, as though that was the way things were in the world in general. So 'the West' too was read as some kind of mirage or trick. Both Bukovskii and Voinovich describe this reaction of the Soviet visitor first faced with the unimaginable plenty of the West, the 'pointless' diversity, the objects 'of whose use we know nothing, even old people can't remember them' (Bukovskii 1981: 82). Voinovich recounts how an elderly Russian came to visit his daughter who had emigrated to Germany; she took him into a shop. He looked around and frowned, 'No', he said. 'Take me to a real shop, this must be a special one for foreigners. Show me one for ordinary people' (Voinovich 1985: 44). Bukovskii (1981: 82 describes the same feeling of the visitor to the West: all these things must be for show (*napokaz*) like in a Soviet shop-window, and of course no-one will buy them. That is why there are no queues and such huge quantities of goods lie around unsold. Real goods must be procured with difficulty (*dobyvat*), unearthed (*otkopit*), obtained on the side (*nalevo*), from under the counter, or from such crafty places as are known only to the dedicated.

A first reaction to 'the West' was to buy everything in sight. The second was depression and inertia, *slyshkom khorosho – tozhe nekhorosho* (too good is also no good), and the feeling that it was impossible to find anything unique in these jungles of wealth. 'I stood before a counter with twenty-four kinds of salad oil, and I couldn't choose one, I only got tired. What is oil, after all, one can live without it' (Bukovskii 1981: 83). It seems to me that these reactions are not irrelevant to the stages of the opening of Moscow to global goods in the early 1990s. Muscovites now are tired, having experienced the 'deception' they were expecting. 'Sophisticated Western equipment is not for us', people often say, suspecting it to contain some hidden drawback or delicate mechanism which will prevent it functioning in Russian conditions. My Russian friend, whose budget is given above, had rushed to buy a magnificent German washing-machine. It does not work. Nobody quite knows why, but not many efforts are devoted to finding out. 'We should have realised', sighs my friend. Now the machine stands there, taking a lot of space in the bathroom, and everything is washed in a 'reliable but rough' Soviet contraption or by hand. Likewise glossily packaged produce like salami is suspect. Why encase it in such brightness? People say 'At least with our Russian sausage we won't be eating all those chemicals.'

This feeling that Western goods are in some way a sham, contaminated, or somehow unassimilable and unsuited for Russian life, has transformed the politicisation of consumption noted by Verdery for the late Soviet period. Now, for many people at least, they are no longer a goal in themselves and they have lost much glamour. Above all, using Western consumer goods no longer confers a defiant social identity against the regime. Rather, they are associated with the new businessmen created by the Yeltsyn government's economic reforms. Their suspectness is compounded by their contiguity with shady dealings and what is guessed to be an insubstantial, dangerously risky kind of existence. Hundreds of thousands of Muscovites have been turning in another direction; they are forgoing Western consumer goods for the sake of more down-to-earth values: plots of land, *dacha*s (cottages), or, if they have country relatives to look after them, cows, chickens and pigs.

Prices for vegetable plots, small farms, etc. have grown enormously, and in the more desirable, unpolluted environs of Moscow they are now always quoted in dollars. It is possible to build a *dacha*, plant a few trees there, and sell the whole thing a year later for a large profit. Thus both entrepreneurs and ordinary workers invest in land, but they do so for different reasons. Even in 1991 over 30 per cent of Muscovites owned a *dacha* (Hansen 1993: 100) and since then the country cottage has become even more a part of city life. The produce of the plot is important to subsistence. But the *dacha* also has a symbolic value. It represents space, repose, 'Russianness'. The *dacha* may be no more than a hut, the journey to get there may involve several wearisome and expensive trains and buses with a walk at the other end, but people say it is worth the effort, since in the country they can re-create a familiar, age-old security lacking in Moscow. All this requires effort, saving, self-denial and forethought. Sudden huge drops and gains in income have torn apart relationships, but the situation has also welded together families in new strained dependencies. Saving is a survival strategy, and there is almost a frenzy to produce safety against the unpredictability of chaos. This pulls people back from 'the market' and turns them inward to networks of security. The *dacha* is one of these, and combining a city job and even a moderately productive plot is not something anyone can do on their own.

THE CRISIS OF VALUES

Bukovskii's image, his small bag of prisoner's treasures confronted with the opulent plenty of Zurich Airport, is in one sense a contradiction of values that exists in any complex economy: the incalculable value created by a person and the socially measured values of industrial production indicated by their prices. But there is a difference between Russia and the West. As Alexander has argued, in the West:

> Deep down inside, we all know that commodities and services have an appropriate price – a fair price – and should normally be traded at this price, although in special conditions prices may be lower. One reason for the robustness of this view, is the continuing stress in advertisements on value for money, another is the observation that prices seldom fluctuate . . . and that the gradual increases are always justified in terms of increasing costs. 'Firms not only behave that way, but also condition their customers to expect them to behave that way.'
>
> (1992: 91)

Admitedly Alexander goes on to suggest that the supposition on which this close relation between price and value rests – that firms will act relatively honestly by raising prices only when costs also rise – is 'the most unrealistic assumption of modern economic theory' (1992: 91), but my point is that the assumption of there being such a relation has never existed in Russia since the 1930s.

The state fixed the prices for all goods at 'arbitrary' rates, that is to say, with a whole variety of rationales (here for political reasons, there to make a profit, here to subsidise some necessary branch, there to buttress some ideological policy). The state also promoted essentialist-ideological values; in other words it designated items that were beyond price. The range of these was different from in the West, and much wider. Land was the most central, but other natural objects such as timber, coal, oil or building materials also became quasi-sacred 'people's wealth' (*narodnoye bogatstvo*). Ordinary people could in fact only gain access to them by fiat of the state. It was absolutely forbidden simply to cut down a tree in the forest. Other state-imposed values were negative, for example typewriters: however much a typewriter cost and however many were sitting in the shops, it was illegal to own one without permission (they were regarded, rightly, as powerful potential dangers to the regime). Since I wish to illustrate how the disjunction between price, ideological value and what I call 'value-in-life' was experienced by everyone, let us take the case of bread.

Bread had a symbolic value to Russian peasants before the Revolution; for example, it was offered, together with salt, to welcome visitors on behalf of the village community. In the Soviet period, bread was first and foremost simply the epitome of food. Bread was part of every meal. 'Almost all of us, growing up in the conditions of Soviet reality, earlier or later in our lives experienced war or hunger and we have got used to relating to bread as something almost sacred', wrote Voinovich (1985: 26). Now all through the Soviet period the state kept the price of bread extraordinarily low. For decades bakeries made the same sizes and shapes of loaves, and all of them kept the same prices, which were as axiomatic as the unchanging fare on the Moscow Metro. It was part of Soviet life that bread was ideologically beyond price:

> How many angry lines have I read in poems and prose about people who have forgotten about the war and the blockade of Leningrad and fling bread into the rubbish shute in loaves. I think I have read considerably more verses about this than there can have been cases of its happening.
>
> (Voinovich 1985: 26)

People were instructed to save every crust, to pick fallen pieces from the floor, to moisten dried-up bits with water, to remember that even mould contains beneficial penicillin.

However, Russians were past masters at dealing with sacrosanct values; some peasants used to feed bread to their pigs. In the end, bread had a value-in-life just like anything else. It was the disjunction between price and value promoted by the Soviet state itself that provided scope for divergent values-in-life. Some ordinary product like onions could have two quite different prices in neighbouring provinces. Of course the people knew about this and state agencies had to spend unknown resources in clamping down on the main lines of smuggling. In all this, prices, being unrelated to any kind of value, were just what they were, a mystery, and yet people got used to them. So when travellers came back and said that prices in the West were higher for some goods than in Russia people refused to believe it. In the Gorbachev era classes were introduced in schools to explain that price depends on the cost of production. 'But look around you,' people of that generation now say, 'it's obviously not true.'

These days almost the whole consumer sector is under the control of various Mafias, and this renders it unlike other economies where trust is difficult to establish. The age-old method of the bazaar, bargaining in public, is ruled out. We cannot be surprised at the bewilderment, anger and mistrust of consumers. Even though prices in Russia are still significantly lower than in Western Europe (from where many of the goods come), a fact which is published in the Russian newspapers, many people would rather not buy anything than put a rouble in the pockets of traders they consider must be cheating them. When a 'fair price' can only be guessed at, and you cannot bargain, then you look at who is selling.[12]

THE 'NEW RUSSIANS'

The attitude described above does not apply to the 'New Russians', the business-people, stock-brokers, commodity traders, Mafiosi, personal assistants, computer specialists, bankers, private hotel owners, masseurs or taxi-men of the metropolis. They know the rules of the bribe and the pay-off, and are firmly attached to Western styles and to the accumulation of elite and luxury goods. One of the first things they do, if successful, is to travel abroad and then try to reproduce the signs of capitalist practices in Russia. So they have personal bank accounts and credit cards at Western banks, use e-mail and faxes, and make arrangements to have their children taught in English. They have no interest in Russian nationalism, and little respect for the state.[13] Taking Russia as a whole they are a tiny proportion of the population, but many more yearn to join them, especially among young people.

It is not entirely clear why the New Russians are nevertheless so bitterly disliked. One can hardly hear a good word said about them among factory-workers, farm-hands, government and service employees, or elderly people. One of the explanations must be the extraordinary success of the Soviet propaganda against 'speculation'.

Speculators are people who make a profit by buying and re-selling goods without adding any value by means of their own labour. This became a crime in Soviet times, and especially in the provinces it remains a grey area today. For example, if you lived in Chelyabinsk, took a train to Moscow, queued up and bought twenty bottles of shampoo, brought them back to Chelyabinsk and sold them for more than the Moscow shop price, you could be punished with a prison sentence. Not only was this a crime, but people in general condemned it, and many would still do so today. This blanket, almost unthinking dislike is oblivious to the economic reality of 'speculation', the fact that people in Chelyabinsk needed shampoo or that the trader was put to trouble, danger and expense to get it.

Negative attitudes to trading are not an instrinsic part of Russian peasant culture, though some writers maintain such a view (Nikol'skii 1993). Historical evidence indicates that in the sixteenth to eighteenth centuries a greater proportion of Russians engaged in trade and manufacture for profit than in any other European country and furthermore they 'had a passion for it' (Pipes 1974: 192–3). After the Revolution, during the Civil War and into the 1920s, the peasantry in fact successfully revived both barter and market trade, even though the new Soviet government was ideologically opposed to it (Figes 1989: 26).

The reaction that developed during the Soviet period rests, of course, on the Marxist teaching that true value is created by labour. It was reinforced after the late 1920s by the Soviet social organisation which ensured that labour was all that Soviet people gave. There simply were no legitimate people in the Soviet Union whose activity was conceptualised

as creating wealth in any other way. Even workers for state trade organisations received only wages for labour, and except for the director they
would have no idea (or concern) whether they were trading at a profit or
not. An extensive vocabulary developed to obscure the very existence of
'profit', because this idea was incompatible with the unique institution
which in fact gathered it, the Soviet socialist state. All of this is another
way of saying that the great hidden 'speculator' was the state itself, which
would brook no competition.

It is interesting to consider this in relation to Parry's theory (1989: 84–5)
on the hostility to commerce in Europe and Latin America. Parry suggests
that ideological commitment to a traditional householding economy
oriented towards self-sufficiency was accompanied by mistrust of trade
and money, which were seen as a dangerous drain on subsistence needs.
In India, on the other hand, the caste order was founded on the fundamentally different premises of a division of labour between castes.
Not even the local community was seen as an ideally self-sufficient entity.
In India, without an ideology of autarky, trade and commerce were not
condemned. To explain Soviet Russia we need to add to this theory the
political element. The USSR actually involved an extremely complex
division of labour, but this was disguised by the fact that the positive
function of distribution was taken over by the 'fatherly' state. Thus independent trade became subversive of its monopoly. For their part, ordinary
people perceived traders as siphoning off the scarce goods that the state
should distribute to them as their due. This explains why extravagant
consumption by highly ranked officials and their families was seen as
their right, even if one that was grasped in the teeth of popular envy. The
reaction of the privileged was often defiant and crude: load on the jewels,
the furs and the perfumes, because *we are in power*.

It should not be forgotten, nevertheless, that in the 1950s, 1960s and
even early 1970s there was also still an austere Soviet style, a declaration
of respect for the old revolutionary ideals. There were professors who
dressed in workmen's clothes, officials who indignantly refused to use
foreign-currency stores, people who had their false teeth made of grey
proletarian metal. But such plainness withered away during the Brezhnev
years and people began to seek all possible methods of differentiating
themselves from the mass by small signs.

The black market existed surreptitiously in every town. It was called
tolchok or *tolkuchka* (from the word 'crowd', 'push' or 'bustle'), and this
expressed its mobile reality. In the old days it was fed largely from the
depots (*baza*) of imported goods, where employees regularly stole whatever they could for distribution to traders. Closed down in one alleyway,
the market would spring up in another. 'Where's your *tolchok*?' strangers
would ask, as they looked for the only institution in town that might make
their visit *vygodno* (profitable). In Soviet times almost all city people had
some consumer goods which clearly must have come from the black

market, a Hungarian sweater here, a packet of Western cigarettes there. Such goods sharply divided opinion. Some would react angrily to 'strange' (*chuzhiye*), non-Soviet things; others would remark, with envy, 'She dresses from the black market' (*ona odevaetsya s tolchka*). Now, criticism of buying black market goods has disappeared. But dislike of those selling them remains strong.

The early years of perestroika suddenly liberated street markets from their back-alley existence. The largest ones sprung up in the focal point of the city: in the Arbat in Moscow, in Revolutionary Square in Ulan-Ude, right outside the doors of Ikh Delguur in Ulaanbaatar (the only state department store in the city). In the last year or two, city authorities have tried to curb markets. Essentially, they are still thought of as 'black markets' and they are still known as *tolchok*. Thus, for example, the newspaper *Buryatiya* of 3 November 1992 gave out a schizoid message. On the front page was a long article: 'The Buryat Republic: the way to the market'; on the back page was another long article, about how to put into effect the mayor's decree closing all street markets.[14]

It is very difficult to discover what are the meanings of 'the market' to Russians. The market as a rational system sits uneasily with earlier values. In the following newspaper clipping the market seems to represent a mysterious process of natural justice, but certainly it has nothing to do with visible trading. The article is about a herdsman in the Tuldun state farm who had been refused a change of house by the farm bosses:

> As we see, the question of housing moves into the sphere of politics. True, they do not now put people in prison for politics, as was the case in times of yore, but now the market can enquire about political malpractice. For the market is created by the producers of material wealth, and not by trader-speculators and not by shady dealers. The Tuldun bosses, having cheated the producer, are sabotaging the triumph of the politics of the market.
>
> (Ubeyev 1992)

Much is unclear in these remarks (the impression is that the author is toeing some political line he doesn't quite understand); however this may be, 'the market' is clearly a good thing, and therefore allied with producers and their labour, while traders are a bad thing and their activities do not create 'the market'.

With these attitudes still prevalent, it is not surprising that to engage in trading professionally is to step over some invisible line of decency. This, in my view, is one reason why cheating, protection rackets and gang violence have accreted to markets and trade. Traders live metaphorically in a different layer, the layer of grease (the slang for profits is *navar*, the grease on top of soup). Society was unprepared for morality, let alone legality, in this sphere. Public markets have become like huge fairs of disingenuousness, spreading wider and wider as people set up booths here and there, or turn their flats into little shops. Petty traders are too insecure to turn their backs on trickery and quick profits: not only do they have to pay bribes and protection money, they are also the 'last in the line' – they stand to lose or gain personally from every transaction. Those who make serious profits from all these activities, the New Russians, glide past in their Mercedes, keeping well apart from the peddling on the streets.

Thus the New Russians are dividing into different groups. It might seem that New Russian consumption is continuous with the blatant opulence of the old Soviet high-ranking officials. However, we should be careful about making such an assumption. Top managers and ministry officials, it is true, were the first to to be able to take advantage of privatisation. But their selling-off of state assets for their private benefit has been surprisingly little resented, especially as they have normally carried on as local bosses and patrons of great power. It is the *New* Russians people dislike, the jumped-up youthful businessmen whose education is being used to no-one's advantage except their own, and whose conspicuous consumption is no longer a marker of rank or ability to pull strings in the system.[15] We can now perhaps discern four groups, the old managers, their young entourages of kin and clients, the high Mafiosi, and the aspirant traders and racketeers of the kiosks.

All of them love sheer wealth, but different styles are beginning to emerge. The old managers retain sober suits and put their money in opulent furniture and bushy fur coats for their wives, while their younger kin prefer sleek brand-marked Western clothing. The seriously wealthy Mafia buy private aircraft, whole plumbing systems for their houses, or new kitchen systems. The aspirant traders affect black leather, dark glasses and sports clothes. Behind this lie different rates in the appreciation of the importance of information technology. The old manager would get a gold-plated dinner service and then a fax machine. The new business people would first get English lessons or acquire a Mercury telephone line to the West, and only then branch into conspicuous consumption (which, I am assured, includes an obligatory mistress as well as a wife). In any field involving large amounts of money the different interest groups in fact meet and carve out their domains, so the high bureaucrats, old managers and new Mafia are not strangers, though they may be enemies. But the public at large knows little of this and reserves its dislike for those New Russians who seem to have become rich by invisible and foreign means. Theirs is regarded as unjust consumption, the outcome of some unfair magic, outside the huge struggle to move upwards in the power game of Russian society. It is this that makes saving and consuming *nash*, be it for choice or necessity, a political statement.

CONCLUSION

This paper has suggested some connections between the constitution of the consumer under the Soviet regime and present patterns of spending. The Soviet person was ideologically constituted as legitimately producing and consuming only within the state sphere. Thus, consumption was in theory non-alienated. The terms 'ours' (*nash*) and 'native' (*otechestven-niye*) referred to the products of state Soviet enterprises, not to their ethnic or cultural origin. It followed that non-state products, or goods whose social life had been transformed through the black market, were 'not ours'. This nicely coincided with the fact that the vast majority of black-market consumer goods were of non-Soviet origin. Even stolen state products were tinged with the otherness of 'speculation'. Consumption thus was an activity which took place in two different modes, that of struggling to get one's due (the state allocation mode) and that of battling to obtain something extraordinary (the black-market mode).

In the present period of bewildering change, consumption and the refusal to consume are creating a heterogeneity of culture. 'Ours' and 'other' are changing places, and the old coincidence between foreign goods and foreign traders has ended. In the early years of reform, it was easy for Central Asians, Caucasians, Chinese, Vietnamese, etc. to take on the role of alien 'speculator' set out for them. Now, the foreigners have been largely expelled and Russian traders are overseeing a flow of imported goods that is seeping even into the sphere of basic foods. The great redistributive mechanism of the state is faltering in its attempt to contain the social consequences of this rush of new transactions. In this suddenly open field millions of consumption decisions are producing a differentiated culture, now crystallising into new patterns. To understand what drives the actual practices of consumption I have suggested that we can look at certain value-laden perceptions held by Russians, all of them specific to recent historical time: the experience of deception, the instant of exposure to global values, and the projection forward of moral ideas concerning the political economy. The Russian economy is as deeply 'embedded' as it ever was, not only in the politics of the struggle for rank and power, but also in the ideas of what lies beyond. The global economy is seen by most as the domain of the great deception, the more so as it seems to be producing new (and dubious) kinds of Russian person.

ACKNOWLEDGEMENTS

I am grateful to Ira and Sergei Panarin, Tanya Medvedeva, Marina Mongush and Balzhan Zhimbiev for generously providing me with information. David Anderson and Danny Miller gave valuable comments on an earlier draft of this paper, for which many thanks.

NOTES

1. I refer here to production on the private plots (also herding, fishing and hunting) by virtually all workers in collective and state farms.

2. The expression gave rise to an inevitable anecdote: an American goes up to a queue and asks what is being sold. People tell him, 'They're selling (throwing out) boots!' He has a look and says, 'Yes, in America they throw out those too' (Voinovich 1985: 42).

3. Dollar sales were eliminated at the beginning of 1994. Shops continue to give prices in dollars, but purchasers must pay in the equivalent roubles at that day's exchange rate.

4. Cash is worth up to 20 per cent more than the equivalent sum in *beznalich-niye*.

5. During 1993 Moscow benefited from the disastrous situation in the Ukraine and Belorussia. The total collapse of these economies and currencies has made even the rouble an attractive proposition, and peasants from these countries came to sell their produce at railway stations and roadsides.

6. Banks and money-changing kiosks sprang up during 1993, but ordinary people still avoid using them. Not only are deposits taxed, but the state sometimes forbids withdrawals point blank.

7. In March 1993 a single rose at the Orangery nursery in north Moscow cost 125 roubles; in flower shops the price was around 300; street-traders charged 1,000 roubles.

8. This was made up of a man's salary of 33,000, a grown-up daughter's income of 12,000, the wife's pension of 15,000 and two smaller state benefits for a school-age daughter who was in bad health.

9. This was calculated using the minimum of buyable foods estimated necessary for survival for adult men, adult women, the elderly and children per day. The portions did not represent the actual diet of any studied group of people, but theoretical dietary requirements. Added to this were sums for heating, rent, etc. and the absolute minimum of products required for sanitation and health. The costs of clothing, furniture, footwear, television, etc. were not included, as 'unfortunately the situation today is such that it is necessary to make do on existing reserves of these things' (Valyuzhenich 1993: 3).

10. Hansen (1993: 95) notes that over 60 per cent of households in the Kola Peninsula kept stockpiles in 1992, and that these included not only food but also medicines, clothing, footwear and consumable durables. A majority of his respondents said they drew constantly from their stockpiles and expected them sooner or later to be exhausted.

11. As Bukovskii has written (1981: 99), 'It is not in the Russian character to economise. 'Eh, devil!' concludes the husband, 'We've never lived well and now is not the time to start. Somehow or other the woman will manage', and he drinks away the cash with his mates. At home there's a row, of course, but if you look, somehow or other it seems they do manage. Our families are maintained by women, and all their economy consists of buying cheap products.' This gender difference in consumption is an issue I have not been able to develop in this paper, though it is highly important. With the new emphasis on subsistence production (such as potatoes) even among urban families, the expectations of women are even more burdensome. This is a subject that requires further research.

12. There is more trust in the sphere of private services for known people. Many of those on low incomes are beginning to develop little sidelines to make ends meet: mending furniture, selling medicinal herbs sent from a relative in Siberia, massage, 'consultations', etc. The prices for these are subject

to bargaining and agreement.

13. A recent study of the 'new class' in Ulan-Ude showed that virtually none of them supported Zhirinovsky in the recent elections, although 60 per cent of the rest of the regional population backed him (Osinskii 1994).

14. The ambivalent status of markets (and probably many other financial institutions too) is exacerbated by their quasi-illegality. It is not forbidden to trade, yet it is forbidden to trade at given places (in Ulan-Ude it was banned everywhere in the city in 1992). In practice, this only adds another layer to the labyrinthine connections between financial and other institutions. Because the mayor banned markets in Ulan-Ude, the police were able to take fines from all the people who nevertheless went on selling, fines which went into the police fund; at the same time there appeared numerous 'inspectors', empowered to take a sizeable 'state tax' from the same traders.

15. A study of the 'new class' in Ulan-Ude in early 1994 showed that most of its members are aged between 25–30, are well educated (though not second-generation intellectuals), and most had left jobs like medicine, teaching, engineering or management. Only 9 per cent were from the working class (Osinskii 1994).

REFERENCES

Alexander, P. (1992) 'What's in a Price?', in Roy Dilley (ed.) *Contesting Markets: Analyses of Ideology, Discourse and Practice*, Edinburgh: Edinburgh University Press, 79–96.

Baidduzhi, A. (1993) ' "Tat'yana Regent:" Rossiya ne mozhet vypolnit' svoi obyazatel'stva v otnoshenii bezhentsev' [Tatyana Regent: Russia cannot fulfil her obligations with regard to refugees], *Nezavisimaya Gazeta*, 23 April 1993, p. 6.

Bukovskii, V. (1981) *Pis'ma russkago puteshestvennika* [Letters of a Russian Traveller], New York: Chalidze Publications.

Bushnell, J. (1990) *Moscow Graffiti: Language and Subculture*, Boston: Unwin Hyman.

Figes, O. (1989) *Peasant Russia: Civil War, the Volga Countryside in Revolution, 1917–21*, Oxford: Clarendon Press.

Friedman, J. (1990) 'Being in the World: Globalization and Localization', in M. Featherstone (ed.) *Global Culture: Nationalism, Globalization and Modernity*, London: Sage Publications, 311–28.

Goryacheva, I. (1993) 'Stoimost' produktov s nachala goda vyrosla na 70 protsentov' [The cost of products has risen by 70 per cent since the beginning of the year], *Izvestiya*, 24 March 1993.

Hansen, E. (1993) *Living Conditions on the Kola Peninsula*, FAFO-SOTECO report no. 155, Oslo: FAFO-SOTECO.

Humphrey, C. (1991) ' "Icebergs", Barter and the Mafia in Provincial Russia', *Anthropology Today*, vol. 7, no. 2, pp. 8–13.

Miller, D. (1987) *Material Culture and Mass Consumption*, Oxford: Blackwell.

Nikol'skii, S. (1993) 'Agrarnaya reforma i krest'yanskii fundamentalizm' [Agrarian reform and peasant fundamentalism], *Krest'yanskiye Vedomosti*, no. 11, 22–8 March 1993.

Osinskii, P. (1994) ' "Novyi klass" v zerkale sotsiologii' [The "new class" in the mirror of sociology], *Buryatiya*, 14 Jan. 1994.

Parry, J. (1989) 'On the Moral perils of Exchange', in J. Parry and M. Bloch (eds) *Money and the Morality of Exchange*, Cambridge: Cambridge University Press.

Pipes, R. (1974) *Russia Under the Old Regime*, London: Penguin Books.

'Struktura potrebitel'skikh raskhodov rabochikh i sluzhashchikh na chlena sem'i' [The structure of consumer spending of workers and employees per member of family], *Argumenty i Fakty*, no. 12 (649) (1993).

Ubeyev, S. (1992) 'Sem'ya – tema vechnaya' [The family – an eternal theme] *Burgatiya* 28 October, p. 2.

Valyuzhenich, G. (1993) 'Porog vyzhivaemosti' [The threshold of survival], *Argumenty i Fakty*, no. 4, 1993, p. 3.

Verdery, K. (1992) 'The Transition from Socialism: Anthropology and Eastern Europe', Lewis Henry Morgan Lectures, 1992, University of Rochester (in press, Cambridge University Press).

Voinovich, Vladimir (1985) *Antisovetskii sovetskii soyuz* [The Anti-soviet Soviet Union], Ann Arbor: Ardis.

Womack, H. (1993) 'Moscow expels traders', *The Times*, 13 October, p. 7.

4 Bureaucratic erasure
Identity, resistance and violence –
Aborigines and a discourse of autonomy
in a North Queensland town

Bruce Kapferer

In the last twenty years Australia has witnessed a major shift in the general public attitude and in Federal and State administrative policy towards minority populations. The Federal Government defines Australia as a multicultural society and is committed to the pursuit of policies of ethnic tolerance. Aboriginal Australians have become highly active in asserting their rights and have achieved some success. The assimilationist policies of the recent past which sought to create an homogenised mass, an Australian society defined negatively or positively in relation to Anglo-Saxon or British values, have been abandoned officially. These new developments are, of course, not completely disjunctive with what went before. They are extensions within discourses powerful in Australia of egalitarianism and individualism and achieve growing popular accept-ance accordingly. They gain force within, as they propel, a reinvigorated Australian nationalism which is eager to sever the remaining and largely symbolic ties of British colonial subordination.

Britain or England in the Australian nationalist imagination has always communicated the antithesis of egalitarianism and individual autonomy. The absurdity of English hierarchy and the unjustness of class rule is present, for Australians particularly, in the current theatre of the English Royal Family, much information for the script coming via the Australian mass media. But the changes towards multiculturalism and the redirec-tions in administrative policies are responses both to the effects of immigration of peoples for whom a British past is irrelevant and of global processes, postmodern in theme, which stress narratives, for example, other than those authorised in imperialism or devised by those in commanding power.

Identity is at the heart of the new narratives. The discourses over iden-tity in Australia as elsewhere challenge and subvert previous conceptions and, most importantly, are vital in the construction and constitution of identity itself. Discourses surrounding identity in Australia concretise what they construct. They create communities in fact whose social and political reality is forged through the imagination and style of the discourse itself. Encouraged in the administrative and policy shifts of the state, the ever-expanding field of discourse about identity is also integral in forcing the shifts which contribute to the energy of a discourse over identity and, indeed, the construction of discourse communities.

All this is apparent throughout Australia among most sections of the population. It is particularly so in the discourse concerning identity among Aboriginal groups. Here the discursive practice generates communities of identity and authenticates their presence. It is integral to their 'registration' within the bureaucratic order of the state. The discursive process highlights my general theme – identity as a process integral to contemporary bureaucratic orders, to the transformation of these orders, and to the problematic of the political power of modern states and their internal bureaucratic dynamic.

The events I discuss here occurred in 1990 in the town of Mossman located 70 kilometres north of Cairns in northern Queensland. Mossman is a small town of some 1,500 people situated on the coast at the edge of the Daintree Rainforest, an important site of ecological protest.

The core members of the Mossman Aboriginal population are of the Kuku Yalanji tribe, the largest section of which is located in a reserve area to the north along the Bloomfield River. The Aboriginal people at Mossman broadly fall into two groups: those who live at Mossman Gorge just outside the town; and, for want of a better term, the townies who live in Mossman itself. Those at the Gorge are viewed by Whites and Aboriginals in the town as 'traditional', oriented to tribal ways, whereas those in the town are considered by Whites especially as being 'detribalised' or oriented towards White society but 'unassimilated' and incapable of organising their lives within modern society. The townies are at the bottom of the social heap and display their marginality in the occupation of marginal and public space, streets and parks. This marginality, of course, is a consequence of racial exclusion and prejudice – these days illegitimate with changes in government and administrative policies. The marginality of town Aborigines and, indeed of Aborigines as a whole, and the public display of dissolution, evident in open drunkenness and violence, is the historical product of White racism. Linked factors such as chronic unemployment and lack of education are reproductive of Aboriginal marginality.

I stress that the contrast between Gorge and Town is integral to the imagination both of Aborigines and of Whites who are engaged in a discourse concerning Aborigines. Empirically the Aborigines of Town and Gorge broadly share in a common abjection. Drunkenness and violence is as much a routine dimension of everyday life in the Gorge as in the town, and people from the Gorge are as much routine *habitués* of open, marginal, public space in the Town. The two categories register equally high rates of unemployment. There is residential movement of Aborigines between Gorge and Town, although this is restricted to those who have close kinship with the people at the Gorge.

The higher valuation by many whites of the Gorge over the Town as legitimate Aboriginal space has to do with the presentation of the Gorge Aboriginals as being traditionally oriented. Tradition is valued whereas modernity – usually conceived through metaphors of disorganisation and chaos – is devalued. In various discourses among non-Aboriginal Australians, Aborigines are symbolic types of the errors of modernity – of what happens in urban/industrial societies if the bonds of community are broken and there is a shift away from the authority of the family.[1]

Fundamentalist Christianity is a feature of much small-town life in Australia and Mossman is no exception. The Lutheran, Seventh Day Adventist and Jehovah's Witness churches are strong in Mossman and their ethos of community and family value supports a general tendency of country-town Australians to imagine themselves as representing a bulwark against the disordering possibilities of change. The valuation of the Gorge Aborigines is part, therefore, of a much larger discourse among non-Aboriginals.

This discourse has less to do with Aborigines in themselves than with debates within non-Aboriginal worlds in Australia. These debates have at their heart issues concerning notions of personal morality, individual and community autonomy relevant to what I have elsewhere called 'egalitarian individualism' (Kapferer 1988). They gain particular force, I suggest, in small-town Australian society and especially among those fundamental-ising Christian communities who often take a particular interest in the plight of Aborigines. Aborigines refract dimensions of the problematic of small-town non-Aboriginal worlds caught in the mesh of encompassing global and 'outside' forces.

The Gorge Aborigines, as is common with many such groupings throughout Australia, have their own white interlocutor, a go-between who mediates their interests with the various government and non-govern-ment agencies who affect the lives of the Gorge community.[2] Paul, the go-between, an ex-Vietnam veteran and now a pastor of the Christian Brethren (Plymouth Brethren), has lived with his wife (a schoolteacher at the Mossman secondary school) for 11 years in a house at the edge of the Gorge community. The doors of the house are plastered with religious slogans. 'ALL MUST BOW BEFORE CHRIST' is written above the entrance. He stresses as his Christian message that individuals must live by their own interpretation of the Bible's meaning and that there is no 'higher authority than themselves' for the meaning they ascribe.

Paul describes himself as a practical person and suspicious of intellec-tuals (among whom he counts his wife). Paul is proud of the fact that he has learnt the Kuku Yalanji language without any outside academic assis-tance and written a short history of the Gorge community. He sees in the Kuku Yalanji a reflection of his own individualism and intense practicality. Thus Paul regards the Kuku Yalanji as being 'like us really', who manip-ulate others for their own interests. He sees himself as being manipulated by members of the Gorge community and that this is a necessary survival strategy as relevant to the Kuku Yalanji forest-dwelling past as to their present.

Paul's personal mission among the Gorge community is to work to restore their sense of traditional identity, unity and autonomy. This, in his view, is dependent on asserting their linguistic and cultural homogeneity and developing leadership and administrative capacity. These must be encouraged in preference to any expansion of 'welfarism' or tendency to depend on Federal Government grants which denies Kuku Yalanji individual initiative. Paul considers that the worth of his views is borne out by some of the limited success of the Gorge community. He points to their entry into the tourist industry – their organisation of a dance troupe and their efforts to communicate traditional rainforest knowledge to visitors. Paul compares the relative homogeneity and unity of the Gorge community with other Kuku Yalanji at Bloomfield River who are riven by factionalism and so dependent on government funding that they run inefficient and uneconomic businesses.

This kind of observation is a widespread non-Aboriginal criticism of Federal policies. This does not ignore the fact that it is also a feature of Aboriginal self-criticism. However, I stress the perspective as vital in the imaginary of Whites. This imaginary is an ideological shaping, a conscious reflecting within common-sense ground, a vision from out of doxic habit-uated space, whereby non-Aboriginals engage their own situated problematic through representations of the condition of Aborigines and its causes.[3]

Whites in Mossman, as I have already stated, those who are antagon-istic to Aborigines and those who are active or sympathetic to their cause, conceive of themselves as at the periphery of centralised state bureau-cratic apparatuses and often as being its victims. It is a powerful element of the cultural or ideological construction of the region of Cairns, an emotional aspect of the epithet of the region as being part of FNQ (Far North Queensland), as a place at the edge of the state, at the extremity of its controlling tendrils. The migration of persons, transient and more permanent, into the region is influenced by a 'romance' of shifting to a dream world of individual autonomy freed from the negating force of the State. Much non-Aboriginal discourse is directed to constituting a world of their imagination. Their constructions of Aborigines and, indeed, recon-struction of Aborigines are significant in the process.

Within the context of the non-Aboriginal imaginary the force of the State and its bureaucratic agencies erases or subdues the 'individuality' or 'individualness' of the person. This is the meaning behind non-Aboriginal conceptions of Aborigines as having lost their identity. Their identity is seen to derive from their participation in a larger 'ordered' whole, or community. No community, no identity or an identity which is devalued. Furthermore, the identity should embody community values, which most often is the value of 'tradition' defined in contrast to modernity. The autonomy of the part is maintained in the autonomy of community. State and bureaucracy threaten the unity of the individual and the autonomy whereby such unity is achieved.

Aborigines, through such non-Aboriginal mytho-logic, represent the 'truth' of this non-Aboriginal imaginary. Their manifest drunkenness and violence is often referred to as testimony. I underline Paul's assertions that it is the dependence of Aborigines on the bureaucratic institutions of the State that contributes towards their dissolution. The reconstitution of identity autonomous and independent of the State recovers both the order of the individual and of the community. Thus the Gorge Aborigines in Mossman are valued by Whites, regardless or not of their sympathy towards Aborigines, over Town Aborigines. Town Aborigines in their apparent disorder represent the negation of identity in State and bureaucratic control.

Town Aborigines embody the alienating and destructive potentiality of State and bureaucratic power vis-à-vis non-Aboriginals. Objectified as disordered, they are conceived of as being virtual manifestations or symbolic types of the destructive force of the state in the lives of non-Aboriginals.

The racism or prejudice shown by Whites towards Aborigines in regions such as that of Cairns is undoubtedly born of still-continuing notions of racial inferiority. But I point in addition to a prejudice or to a prejudice created in a white fear, a fear or terror generated in a non-Aboriginal discourse in which individuality and personal integrity (what I have elsewhere called egalitarian individualism (Kapferer 1988)) are perceived to be under threat from the control and institutions of the state.

Certain aspects of white fears and thus of their prejudice generated in towns such as Mossman were apparent in a town meeting called by the head of the Cairns region police. The regional Superintendent of Police had been touring outlying localities attempting to initiate a new regime of local community/police consultation. It was part of a propaganda drive to give a new humanitarian look to the police. The Queensland Police have a particularly bad reputation for brutality and corruption. Aborigines in particular are the victims and this is demonstrated in numerous commissions of enquiry in Queensland and elsewhere in Australia.

Large sections of the non-Aboriginal population in northern Queensland, often because of their own feelings of victimisation, have sympathy with Aborigines. The Queensland Police are the symbolic representation *par excellence* of the potential of State agencies to offend egalitarian ideals and to outrage individual autonomy and integrity. The Fitzgerald Commission of Enquiry, just published at the start of fieldwork, had revealed not only the appalling corruption of the Queensland Police but also the complicity of the National Party Government of the erstwhile Queensland Premier, Sir Joe Bjelke-Petersen, just ousted by the election to power of the Queensland Labor Party under Wayne Goss. Bjelke Petersen's free-wheeling *laissez-faire* policies in effect had been exposed as disguising the role of powerful inegalitarian economic and political interests at local and state levels. But Goss's new and explicitly reform government threatened forms of State and Federal Government intervention perhaps more threatening to white notions of autonomy and integrity, especially those in small towns such as Mossman.

At this time, the sense of uncertainty in the midst of considerable political changes in Queensland was given expression at the meeting of all interested local citizens in the Mossman Returned Serviceman's Hall in March 1990, summoned by the Regional Superintendent of Police and chaired by him.

THE MOSSMAN MEETING

The meeting as a whole condensed major dimensions of the broader context in which it was set. It expressed divisions within the town population – the separation between white and black, the internal oppositions among whites and among Aborigines, especially the opposition between the Gorge and Town Aborigines and, above all, the racial hierarchy of the town, the domination of whites over blacks. This last was represented in the spatial location of whites and Aborigines. The latter were seated or standing at the rear of the Hall expressing their historically produced marginalisation at the fringe or base of dominant orders. Non-Aboriginals were seated towards the front immediately before the table at which the Superintendent was seated. The Mossman police sergeant stood to one side behind the Superintendent.

The meeting opened with the Superintendent admitting the responsibility of the police in the corruptions exposed by the Fitzgerald Enquiry. He declared that it was his intention to reinstitute the appropriate relation of the police to local communities, in effect the police as guardians of order and the upholders of the will of the people. He saw the failure of the police as a 'communication problem' and that if a closer working relation had existed between the police and local citizenry then '50 million dollars would not have been wasted on the Enquiry'. He then invited suggestions from the gathering on the way the police could improve their service.

A large beer-bellied white male immediately stood up and complained about police breathalysing tactics. It was a thinly disguised personal gripe. Everyone in the hall knew that he had recently been caught drunk-driving and was presenting his own case. He rambled on for some 5 minutes communicating both a self-importance and a role as community spokesman. In fact, he had recently put himself forward in the local council elections but had failed in his attempt. The Superintendent appeared to grant him his role and responded almost apologetically insisting that the breathalysing tests were done at random and that there was no intention to target and trap particular persons – an implication of the rambling complaint.

This first spokesman – whom I shall call Barry – claimed a leadership of the town's citizens as a whole, including Aborigines. He was married to a Torres Strait Islander. Categorised by Whites and classified by the State with Aborigines, there is considerable tension in the Cairns area between Islanders and Aborigines. The former have gained greater acceptance by Whites and this has sharpened an Aboriginal sense of their exclusion from the white-dominated system and their marginality to it.

Barry's speech and the Superintendent's reasoned response continued the status quo; that is, the arrangement between State and citizen, the citizens with power being white with Aborigines being at the edge or virtually outside citizen status and being spoken for rather than themselves having a voice. The very civility of the meeting breathed the continuity of the past into the present – the address by the legitimate authority of the State, the negotiative, oppositional response, respectfully presented by the citizen, the reasoned rejoinder, etc.

I have noted the State/people opposition which expresses the problematic of autonomy in State structures whose democratic process is grounded in an ideology of egalitarian individualism.

Opposition is internal or ideologically systematic to the dynamic of order and reproductive of it. Until recently, this was not so for Aborigines. They were not citizens with the political rights of citizens determined within State or State-supported institutions. Aborigines who voiced opposition to the State that controlled them could be interpreted as antagonistic and subversive of the State. This was critically problematic for a population who were made dependent on the institutions of the State for their very survival. In such a circumstance silence could be expected as a routine strategy of survival. I stress the overall point by way of contrast. Whites, in their expressions of opposition to the State, confirm their thorough membership of it, and indeed their relative freedom within its process and their capacity to engage in defining the boundaries and other parameters of State order. Aboriginal opposition was in contradiction of their non-citizenship status (they had no rights of opposition) and could be seen as directly disconfirming of the very ideological terms whereby the State determined the life chances of Aborigines.

Collmann (1988) makes a similar observation for Aborigines in a detailed ethnography of fringe-dwellers in Alice Springs in the Northern Territory of Central Australia. Aborigines maintain their identity, or better, total individual integrity as Aborigines in their own eyes and in the eyes of Whites, in their separation and location in spaces marginal to the State. When they come to occupy similar organisational spaces to those inhabited by Whites in the State order they lose their individual integrity as Aborigines in relation to Whites and perhaps to themselves. I have emphasised the role of White discourse – even well-intentioned discourse – in producing this circumstance, for example, the relatively higher value placed on the Gorge over those Aborigines living in the town. While a white discourse about Aborigines frames many of the ideo-logical terms wherein non-Aboriginal orders are continually defined and internally resisted, such discourse is or was engaged in reproducing the political marginality of Aborigines and effectively disempowering them or else only empowering them insofar as they remain clients of non-Aboriginal-controlled organisations or provide a symbolic capital for non-Aboriginal-defined political interests.

Barry's holding the floor was in thorough bad faith as was the Superintendent's response. The Whites present colluded in this bad faith by their composed and restrained acquiescence before Barry's self-presen-tational display and by their implicit acceptance of the rules of civility that governed the meeting – rules integral to the preservation of non-Aboriginal hegemony and the continuity of the status quo. Perhaps this prompted their silence.

Aborigines by remaining silent risked an even greater compounding of bad faith. While the silence of other Whites in fact was the silence of the relatively powerful, the silence of Aboriginals confirmed a powerlessness and, indeed, an effacement of their identity by the bureaucratic order of the State, a practice which they were now witnessing and, theoretically, participating in.

They were absent in their presence. A violence, a symbolic violence, was being perpetrated which negated changes that were in progress. Aborigines now have the rights of ordinary citizens but were being deprived of their voice as citizens. It was their awareness of their demo-cratic rights which accounted for the number who came to the meeting, a fact which surprised many of the non-Aboriginals present. The marked attendance of Town and Gorge Aborigines was encouraged by the larger political changes, particularly Federal Government policies which aimed to give Aborigines greater autonomy and to reduce their client status. Federal Government changes were intended to shift the relation of Aborigines to the State, granting them the right to define and pursue their interests as Aborigines within the State apparatuses. In other words, the aim was for them to participate in the practice of State politics as insiders rather than as marginalised outsiders.

At the time of these observations the situation of Aborigines was in radical transition. The old Department of Aboriginal Affairs had just given way (5 March 1990) to the Aboriginal and Torres Strait Islander Commission (ASTIC).[4] Ideally, Aborigines were to have control over their own affairs through representatives whom they elected on a nationwide regional basis. In principal, the new idea is a kind of Aboriginal State within a State, Aborigines having a dual citizenship, one in the Federal and State structures and one in a polity subject to their sole control. At the time of the meeting the new organisation was far from established and most Aboriginals were unsure what was involved in the changes. Many had not been informed.

There was considerable suspicion among all sections of the Aboriginal population in the Cairns region, some fearing a loss of the autonomy they had achieved. This was especially so among reserve Aborigines and those relatively independent communities like those at the Gorge who had their own local councils. The general message was that they were being given greater power but there was widespread suspicion that this was yet another white ruse entailing more stringent controls on, for example their financial affairs and the organisation of government grants than there had been hitherto.

However, all being said, the silence of Aborigines at the meeting meant that their new political terrain remained untested and that the subordinating violence of old regimes remained. To continue in silence might also be interpreted as collusion, all the more so in the changing political climate.

Barry's domination of the stage was even more outrageous in his particular role or appropriation of the position of symbolic victim of State persecution. His was the victimhood of a rational State order gone wrong in which he had voice. Moreover, Barry's victim role could be seen as even more reducing of the power of Aborigines.

Increasingly, especially over the last twenty or so years, Aborigines have discovered a vast reservoir of symbolic power, perhaps convertible into actual power, in the exterminations, land alienations, divisions of families, abductions, rapes, incarcerations, etc. Aborigines have been writing increasingly of their own experience of such shattering events, attesting further to the historical record. They are archetypal victims whose experiences challenge the very principles of those white-controlled orders which threatened to annihilate them. Unlike Barry's victimhood, that of Aborigines challenges the very techo-rationality which legitimises the institutions of dominant power. Non-Aborigines are these days acutely conscious of the depredations and destructions of Aborigines and it is to some extent a recognition of white guilt which yields power to Aborigines as victims.

Marge, a middle-aged Aboriginal woman seated against the right/back wall of the hall, used this power. Marge lives at the Gorge, is a well-known 'character' around town, usually drunk. She is an embodiment of the Aborigine as victim. Marge is crippled and walks on crutches. After a particularly heavy recent bout of drinking she had fallen down and been severely bruised and cut. On this day one of her legs and an arm were swathed in bandages.

Engaging her power as victim, Marge explosively interrupted Barry's peroration. 'Bloody shut up, you talking too long, saying nothing.' Barry, visibly embarrassed, was stunned into silence. Marge continued to shout out but unintelligibly. The Whites in the gathering remained silent, eyes fixed to the front. Their silence might now be interpreted as a paralysed silence, not the silence of moments before which was conditioned by and thus active in a discourse organised in the very terms of white dominance. Marge rendered that power impotent, subverting that discourse of white power which had hitherto framed the meeting. Marge confronted the assembled Whites with the full force of their guilt and made them speechless in it. Paradoxically, the destructive fact of their power, its irrational and humanly fragmenting possibility, was displayed as a mirror to itself, rendering it impotent in the explicit revelation of its very potentiality.

Marge kept up her noisy disruption and so held the stage. The Police Superintendent and the Mossman sergeant made no move. They were trapped by their own project to present the new humanitarian, non-autocratic, free and open face of the police. The egalitarian air which filled the hall and was critical to the life of the meeting placed limits on who could command the will of others. Given public declarations in Mossman and other towns in the area that the racism of the past had gone, the subjection of Marge to any white present would have risked falsifying the image. Despite many indications to the contrary (a case of the exclusion of Aborigines from a hotel in the nearby town of Mareeba on the Atherton Tablelands was receiving considerable press coverage), non-Aborigines were committed to mirroring to themselves their racial tolerance. A reporter for the local Mossman newspaper was present. He was known for his pro-Aboriginal views. His photographer was busy taking shots. Marge, in effect, was putting to severe test an image which public officials and locally dominant groups wished to present. Their legitimacy and the power which flows from legitimacy depended on such successful presentation. Aborigines are generally aware of this, their political energies being directed towards revealing the contortions of this public face.

The non-response to Marge's intervention sustained the image. Indeed, the longer Marge continued her disruption without non-Aboriginals stopping her, the more she upheld the tolerant frame of the meeting. Moreover, her action sustained and validated a common knowledge openly held by many non-Aborigines in the room that Aborigines had lost all sense of inner communal control and order and that 'traditional' Aborigines were out of place in the institutional contexts of the democratic practices of State and town.

Many of the other Aborigines in the hall now took action. They called to her to quieten down. Some spoke in Kuku Yalanji. Marge had created space in which Aborigines could express their voice *as Aborigines* and, moreover, disconfirm the validity of those non-Aboriginal values that lay beneath the surface civility of the meeting, which until Marge's disruption were a force in maintaining Aboriginal silence.

Clara moved from where she was seated in the rear body of the room to Marge and put her arms around her. Clara is an albino Aborigine, she had moved from the Gorge and was now living with her sons in town. Her sons have had frequent brushes with the local police and are described as 'troublemakers' by the town Whites. Clara is known for her active and angry defence of her sons against the police. Clara's joining of Marge communicated a unity between Gorge and Town Aborigines that white constructions tended to deny.

I note Clara's embodiment of contradictions that have significance in the white hegemonic imaginary. Clara is a 'white' Aborigine, she literally expresses in the reality of her body, in her albino-ness, a non-Aboriginal view that Aborigines who are separated or distanced from tradition or their 'true' reality (as dreamed by non-Aboriginals) are neither of the dominant white world nor of 'authentic' (however destroyed) Aboriginal realities. In this conception Town Aborigines, for example, are not so much marginal in the 'betwixt and between' (people-of-two-realities-but-members-of-neither sense of the liminal term), but are negativised, annulled, erased identities in the more radical usage of the liminal concept by Victor Turner (1969).[5]

Thus, Aborigines separated from their tribal source (in the numerous ways this may be understood) and located in white worlds have the valued (by Whites) aspects of their Aboriginality erased by these realities. Moreover, their Aboriginality prevents them from completely assuming identities presumed to be relevant to white worlds. The Aboriginality of Town Aborigines becomes a fundamental negativising principle which becomes active in excluding them from all situations. Their Aboriginality, conceived by Whites and Aborigines to be a vital embodied part of their being, becomes more than a representation in an imaginary of dominant worlds such as a sign of tradition lost, of personal and social disorder. It becomes in itself a disordering, disintegrating power, which inhabits the body and with which one must daily live. Aboriginality as a function of white construction and its institutionalisation in the political orders of the dominant world is made continually destructive of the person as a coherent, integrated unity.

The dynamic intensity of a politics of identity among Aborigines, of course, has everything to do with transforming a negative force into a positive one. This revaluation of identity involves contradicting the devaluing prejudices, even of those who are sympathetic, of non-Aboriginals. Thus the importance of asserting that those outside traditional contexts maintain a vital relation to tradition. Here is the significance in Clara's expression of unity with Marge and also the attempt to 'control' Marge through the use of Kuku Yalanji.

Marge's disruption opened critical space for a new definition of the situation to be proclaimed, which to a large extent confused the constructions whereby non-Aboriginals attributed significance to different sections of the Aboriginal population. This redefinition publicly communicated the fact that Town Aborigines exerted traditional knowledge and power and, moreover, the fact that the identity of all Aborigines, regardless of location, is relevant in the space and practice of dominant institutions.

Marge's play did not end with Aboriginal attempts to subdue her, nor with Clara's expression of unity. She stopped her disruptive talking and shouting. The Superintendent resumed addressing the gathering. But Marge now got up and advanced towards the Superintendent seated behind the table at the front of the hall. He made a valiant effort to ignore her, to treat her as a non-person, to use Goffman's highly relevant term. Marge now draped her arm around the Superintendent and began to stroke his hair. She kept doing this for quite some time and despite the Superintendent's trapped irritation. No-one moved to remove her and all in the hall – except the Superintendent and the Mossman sergeant – visibly enjoyed the scene before them.

Marge simultaneously exposed the joke in the structure and insisted that the Superintendent live the rhetoric of his presentation and the discursive frame of the meeting. The joke is the idea of the humanitarian, listening, mutually respectful idea of the police. Marge underlined the absurdity of the idea, given Aboriginal experience of police abuse and that they are the most frequent victims of police excess. A government-sponsored investigation of Aboriginal deaths in custody was in train at the time and a team led by Aborigines was interviewing in Mossman. Marge, virtually embracing the body of white power, made it symbolically evident that she and, by extension, all Aborigines, as the once-externalised victims of State authorities, were manifestly citizens as well and were to be treated in accordance with professed democratic and egalitarian principles.

Marge's intervention cleared the way for Aborigines to realise in this context the possibilities of wider political changes affecting their position. She also enabled Aborigines at the meeting to demonstrate a unity of interest with non-Aboriginals at the meeting vis-à-vis bureaucratic and state authority and to expose common concerns. In some ways her disruption swept aside some of the cant that surrounded the meeting and facilitated a less constrained and formalised airing of grievances from Whites as well as from Aborigines.

The meeting closed as a virtual apotheosis of the moral virtues of egalitarian individualism, persons from all sections chorusing the values of individual autonomy and familial authority. Blacks and Whites asserted the importance of traditional family values, although Town Aborigines stressed Aboriginal cultural distinction and the crucial significance of extended kin ties.

The theme of police violence, a major concern of most in the gathering but so far largely submerged, broke into open discussion. Whites and Aborigines gave instances of police excesses and presented a unified front as victims. Simultaneously, however, some of those who declared themselves as victims also openly accepted the need for control which might involve the use of physical violence. Such acceptance can be perfectly consistent with the terms of the discourse of individualism and egalitarianism which framed the meeting.

Thus violence defensive of the body of the person is legitimate and is valued as a sign of individual autonomy and integrity. The exercise of power, both as a physical expression of the individual body, as emergent from the resources enclosed by the body and not dependent on extra-bodily sources, is valued within Australian egalitarianism. This is certainly so when constrained in the interests of the morality of egalitarian individualism directed to the maintenance of an order based in the autonomy and integrity of individuals.

With the open discussion of physical violence, the Mossman police sergeant assumed that he was the target of attack. He defended his own actions in egalitarian terms with reference to the art of the body and the operation of a practical rationality, both vital in Australian individualism. The sergeant described himself as a 'pretty fit man' and if he is 'smacked' he will smack back. The idea, he said, is to 'hurt' the assailant in order to protect himself, for he patrolled alone, and to bring the situation under control quickly. This was regrettable but technically practical. He supported police patrolling in twos because it reduced the necessity of hurting assailants, in other words violating the other's body. Those gathered not only backed the sergeant but vindicated their own violence. One who declared his support was a white male whose tattoos marked the violent autonomy of his body. A large cross with the letters R.I.P. marked his right thigh and his upper left arm showed one man whipping another. He announced that he had had his fair share of run-ins with the police but he recognised the importance of authority. An Aborigine who identified himself as a 'full blood' said that Aborigines should help the police in maintaining order. The sergeant won further support from the gathering in stating that he had been the object of some '200 investigations into his conduct' by police authorities controlling the region but had been vindicated. It might have appeared that the sergeant had assumed the role of victim and, too, as a community member threatened by outside forces.

The convergence of attitudes that emerged in the course of the meeting should not be seen as a move towards the establishment or expression of community harmony or of unity in opposition, popular in a functionalist anthropology. The conflicts and tensions which surfaced in the course of the meeting were deep and continuing aspects of the structures of practices of everyday life. The appearance of consensus was born of the fact that all present were internal to the discourse, although differently positioned within it. The meeting, of course, was a practice of the bureaucratic state but its dynamics were integral to a more encompassing and deep-seated 'bureaucratic life-world'.

CONCLUSIONS AND EXTENSIONS: RESISTANCES, PREJUDICE, AND THE FORMATION OF BUREAUCRATIC LIFE-WORLDS

The general terms of the discourse were those of what I have called egalitarian individualism, the ideological ground, with variations, of many contemporary nation-states. A thesis at the heart of my argument is that notions of the individual and related terms such as those of 'citizen' and 'identity' are value constructions that are integral to the formation of contemporary states and develop and shift in their meaningful use in the ongoing historical formation of such states. Moreover, the experience by persons of their individuality is a function of the way they are so constituted in the instituted practices of the state and of its agents. People at the Mossman meeting expressed pleasure in the occasion, a satisfaction that their voices had been heard. It was the pleasure of participation in a world which they resisted (and there was excitement in this), but which nonetheless conditioned its routine existence and, perhaps its mode of sociological description.

A discourse of individuality is a legitimating practice of contemporary democratic states and this is particularly so in Australia. Moreover, it centres upon the Hobbesian dilemma or potential contradiction that the instituted order and practice of the State may defeat that upon which its very existence is premised, the autonomy and rights of the individual. This is especially so in contexts like Australia where a cult of the individual achieves an intensity in a powerful egalitarian individualist ethos.

Ideas of the individual at terrible risk of defeat are a feature of philosophies born or developed in the conditions of modern state formation. Marxian notions of alienation and Sartrean/existentialist theses of negation are among the best known. They are no less a dimension of popular romanticism. Australia abounds with a symbolism of State/anti-State discourse engaging a symbolism of defeat and negation. Convicts, Ned Kelly, ANZACs and Aborigines are outstanding examples made all the more potent because of their historical facticity.

The value of the individual is virtually fetishised in modern democratic states, especially of the Australian kind. No doubt capitalism, the emergence to dominance of free-market principles and ideologies and the growth of commodity-based cultures are key factors of global proportion. They embrace individualist ideologies and produce them. I take all this for granted but focus on the broad nature of bureaucratic institutions and practices which are vital in all modern states; they condition though not necessarily determine the populations enclosed by contemporary orders of the nation-state.

An increased pressure towards individualist assertion is integral to the bureaucratic order of contemporary states. This is so because the individual autonomy of vital value in egalitarian orders may be denied or subordinated. These are a likely consequence of the appropriation or concentration of power away from individuals into state-controlled bureaucratic agencies. This is part of ordinary consciousness, a common-sense axiom of everyday life conditioned in the circumstances of the State. It is largely in the State institutional suppression of autonomy and also a failure to effect ideals of equality often conceived as being at their root – a furious impetus in egalitarian concerns with corruption – which are high on the list for anti-bureaucratic attack.

Assertions of autonomy and of individual autonomy are treasured expressions of those enclosed in contemporary state orders. The pressure towards such expression may well be universal in human nature as many Western philosophers and sociologists maintain. But, of course, in demo-cratic systems especially, the voicing of autonomy is integral to a discourse of State legitimacy. The Mossman meeting is an obvious example of state-instituted practice for the expression of autonomy, the sheer occasioning of it being an important means for the agents of the state to ensure their acceptance. This was all the more significant in the context of a reasser-tion of the rational principles of bureaucratic order in the wake of vast allegations of State Government corruption. But in extending the point, I stress the idea of individual autonomy, the particular shape in which it is dreamed, imagined and practised, as being closely related to the recent historical formation of modern political systems.

Thus in Australia, individual autonomy, often as a valued mode of resist-ance to the State, is envisaged as a fleeing from the bureaucratic control of the State, an escape to the wild margins, where communities and societies may be formed anew, or where individuals can rediscover them-selves – hence the counter-culture or alternative movements so much a feature of recent Western history, Australia included. These popular processes are no more internal to the system than are scholarly abstrac-tions which tend to obscure such facts. Victor Turner gives notions of liminality and marginality a universal analytic value. In Australia, however, they are terms deeply resonant in the doxa of everyday life and gener-ated in imagination and practice from within the circumstance of the contemporary state.

Idealisations of individual and community as being autonomous, integrated and whole are constructions cast in the process of popular and scholarly debate about the nature of the bureaucratic State. The reality of the bureaucratic state, its role in conditioning the routine of life is vital to the way State bureaucracy is fantasised as, too, are the ways the 'indi-vidual' and the 'community' as social constructions are imagined. Each is dialectically a process of the construction of the other. Thus, a vision of the state as a consuming monster is as much a product of the idealisations of individual and community as unitary wholes as vice versa. But these imaginaries and their diverse styles of naturalisation, essen-tialism and reduction – all part of legitimating concerns to assert the truth value, or better, the immutability or incontestability of their claims – are, nonetheless, formed in worlds where the bureaucratic practice of the State is vital in lived experience regardless of how the significance of this experience is constructed.

In bureaucratic practices the individual is an abstraction. They specify particular human beings (dead or alive or who may never have existed), but the totality or profile of the individual is one which has its significant elements defined in the bureaucratic system. It is disembodied, as it were. Moreover, and as a process of this disembodiment, the individual is broken down into classifiable parts relevant to various bureaucratic functions, and hierarchialised. Through such a practice individuals are internally differentiated, these differentiations of the individual being significant for categorisation with or separation from other individuals. Indeed, depending on the bureaucratic task, the individual as bureaucratically identified may be very different and separated things. To put it another way, a classified part of the individual will operate as the totality, in relation to which other classified elements of the individual will be organised.

I stress the bureaucratic process as a disembodiment and fragmentation (and reduction) of human beings who otherwise live their worlds as larger and more fluid embodied totalities, that is, all experience of the world is grasped and interconnected or lived as a unity through the fact of experience as being always an experience of the body. The rationalism of Western bureaucratic practice which Weber explored in his comparisons gives objective primacy to the category superordinate to embodied experience. Foucault (1974) has very similar things to say in his discussion of the development of taxonomic organisation in the Classical Age of the seventeenth and eighteenth centuries, exemplified in Linnaeus' natural history, and its transmutations into the modern sciences. As Handelman (1981) argues, Foucault's account of the development and forms of scientific knowledge is applicable to modern bureaucratic practice, expanding Weber's understanding. I note Foucault's stress on the stasis of the taxonomic schemes, their attention to surface features or what can be ascertained visually from which the basic characteristics of structure are determined, the virtual draining of content from the categories, and the disappearance of life, sometimes the object of their concern, from their analytical orders. Foucault develops his point in relation to a discussion of the classifying procedures of ordinary language to which the taxonomic categories of Linnaeus relate, but as a transformation which rules out the play and ambiguities of ordinary speech or what Foucault calls 'badly constructed language' (Foucault 1974: 158–60).

Developing further, but a fairly explicit dimension of the works of Weber and Foucault as a whole, the orientations of bureaucratic practice, and partly as a function of the dominance of the political form of the bureaucratic State, is the cultural order of daily life in Western systems. It is integral to the way people construct themselves in relation to others as much as the agents of bureaucratic power are given to define them and is tantamount to a cosmology. I assert this in order to avoid simple oppositions of the kind that separate the thinking and practice of bureaucrats from those of the people to whom they attend, even though such separation is very much part of 'folk' belief, especially in places like Australia. Weber's iron cage may be stronger than even he feared.

Categorical thinking and practice, and especially the subordination of the person or the individual to the rules of the category, the distancing or alienation of human beings from the continuous and fluid totality of their lived existence through the operation of categorical imperatives, may not just be the way things are – an assumption of much ethnography – but intensified and changed in the cultural orders established in the growth of bureaucratic systems. Racism and prejudice are functions of the categorical practice that pins subjects within the stereotypy of certain abstractions and which defines the whole in terms of the part. What I am suggesting is that such practice may be impelled in the rationalism of bureaucratic worlds which are part of the habitus, the space of everyday life, of those who live them.

It is worth noting that the term 'identity' appears to come into English usage, largely as a technical term in algebra and logic, round about the sixteenth century (Gleason 1983). Notions relevant to identity are, of course, powerful in the development of the logical discriminative structures of natural history, particularly with Linnaeus. The use of identity in the sense of 'personal identity' first seems to occur in Locke's 'Essay 'Concerning Human Understanding' (1690) and in Hume's 'Treatise on Human Nature' (1739). Therefore, the usage of the term coincides with the emergence of the bureaucratic nation-state in its contemporary form and with the development of that technical, scientific and philosophical rationalism which is at the centre of the legitimation of modern states. The concept explodes into common usage with the development of the human sciences (psychology, psychoanalysis, sociology) in the late nineteenth and in this century. This is especially so in the advanced technical/rational bureaucratic orders of North America where the technical/rational management of immigrant (and native indigenous) populations is at a premium and, too, matters of the reconstruction of 'self' and 'person'. The observation can be extended to Australia and to other colonial contexts where the bureaucratic technical and scientific management of observed difference is considered critical to the order of the State. Those sections of the social sciences explicitly concerned with identity tend to be in a close practical relation with the agents of state control or else in resistance to their policies. Either way the term 'identity' reveals its close discursive connection, indeed ideological internality, to the matters and process of the bureaucratic State.

In my view, models and theories developed in anthropology concerned with identity, especially ethnic identity, share much with the principles underlying bureaucratic state practice (e.g. see Gluckman 1957, Mitchell 1956, Barth 1985). This is so whether they stress primordialist or interactional constructivist positions: the former essentialises and dehistoricises what the latter treats as vitally labile and reorganisable. Both place great emphasis on the analysis of parts as representing or signing the character of the whole and concentrate and overdetermine the role of particular elements (labels!) of persons, e.g. ethnic identity, in the exploration of processes where they are relevant. Identity is examined as a technically manipulable aspect of persons engaged by them and others to structure their position or relationships in the world. Often in analysis identity terms are drained of content or their content is equated with structure and the complexity of the life-world, in which the parts achieve considerable emotional force, recedes from understanding.

I am not questioning the validity of a vast array of studies but drawing attention to the fact that they inscribe dimensions of bureaucratic rationalist realities, which may not only be instrumental in the way questions of identity are approached, but are productive of issues of identity and the problematics that surround it.

Interestingly, as Langbaum observes, Locke and Hume in their usage of identity 'cast doubt on the unity of the self' (Langbaum 1977: 25). Early on then, discourse in the world of the formation of the bureaucratic State implicitly recognised the disembodying and fragmenting processes of what I have previously discussed. Langbaum (1977) also notes the later reactive development expressed in the works of writers like Wordsworth and D.H. Lawrence who stressed the 'integrity of "the self" '.

Aborigines in particular are prisoners of the categories of white discourse and of what can be called the bureaucratic categorical imperative. This is not merely a function of their forced submission to administrative orders which an ever-expanding literature documents as destroying their worlds, radically dehumanising them, and also engaging in their 'reconstitution' at the periphery or within dominant orders (see Rowley 1973, Beckett 1988, Collman 1988, Morris 1989, Lattas 1992). The reconstitution was and is frequently radical, their being formed, by various authorities and by themselves, in accordance with the representations of the colonial mirror. Thus, at the Mossman meeting one Aborigine describes himself as a 'full blood', a bureaucratic term indicating the 'purity' of category, its non-hybridisation.

The taxonomies of bureaucratic operations were and are significant in the distribution and redistribution of Aborigines across space (in the settlements, missions, reserves of habitation and, in Queensland, of frequent relocation) and in the formation of their social relationships. Relatively static differentiations within the encompassing term 'Aborigine' limit the extent to which Aborigines can 'situationally select' or move between different identities, or even aspects of Aboriginality, according to the 'logic of the situation' (an analytical approach to ethnicity which assumes a notion of the autonomous individual as the underlying base and not inconsistent with axioms of bureaucratic practice in egalitarian individualist worlds). Their lived experience constituted through the category is constantly divided and set against itself.

Much of the Aboriginal action at the Mossman meeting was directed against the internal divisions of the categories that separate Aborigines from others and from within themselves. Marge and Clara demonstrate not just the fracture of taxonomic differentiation but the distortions wrought on the body as the living embodied totality of such fracture.

A paradox of the present context for Aborigines is that they enter inside the State, and now achieve power within it as citizens, by virtue of their Aboriginality. The reforms in the administration of Aborigines – the formation of ASTIC from the Department of Aboriginal Affairs – reflects this paradox. Ideally, within ASTIC they constitute the various dimensions or identities of Aboriginality. Outside ASTIC, as citizens of the nation-state as a whole they have an individuality as any other citizen capable of taking on a variety of identities independent of their Aboriginal status. But within the new administrative structure they remain caught within the relatively static categories of the past still active in the present bureaucratic practices and in the wider culture of bureaucracy of dominant social and political worlds. Moreover, in the world at large, outside their own organisations of control, Aborigines are impeded in the expression of an individuality independent of their Aboriginality.

The revaluation of Aboriginality in non-Aboriginal understanding (as well as for Aborigines) means that the destructive relation of the category to their embodied experience of the world is reduced. But unlike non-Aboriginals, whose individuality is constructed ideally as beneath or in some ways independent or autonomous of lived realities, the individuality, the unit being of Aborigines and the coherence of their individuality as this is constructed, is never apart from their Aboriginality. Aboriginality once exclusionary, or masked or denied, by the force of social processes integral within a bureaucratic life-world and integral to their non-recognition as persons, now is vital to their individuality and to their status and power as citizens. This carries its dilemmas and can be active in the creation of prejudiced antagonism even where there may have been none. Their actions as individuals are always maintained as relevant to the value of the category.

Aborigines, for example, are rarely just drunks; they are usually understood as *drunk Aborigines* whose drunkenness is, in the dominant imagination of many non-Aboriginals inseparably a function of their Aboriginality, a function of the totalisation of the person in the category. This is true too when they are sober – their sobriety too being a function of Aboriginality.

That Aborigines have their individuality as members of a category is sustained in what I have called a culture of bureaucracy and the dynamics of its internal resistances. Aborigines increasingly in recent years have been further constructed as representations of the virtues and vices of non-Aboriginal dominating realities. Revalued, Aborigines are the symbolic types who must not only carry the burden of their own recent history in the white settlement of Australia, but must be the mirror to the nature of the realities which non-Aboriginals construct and live. Specifically they become the mirror of bureaucratic reality, the measure of its discordancies as non-Aborigines may experience the motion of the State. This is an aspect of the attitude of the Kuku Yalanji go-between whose views I presented at the start of this paper.

In the early years of the establishment of white bureaucratic power in Australia Aborigines were the objects of a natural history, examples in the evolution of life who were often rendered lifeless in the process of their dehumanising examination. It would be a gross distortion to equate current practice with this past and it would deny the many benefits of recent reforms. But still a trace of the past persists. Aborigines are maintained as a category against which to measure the progress of dominant realities, to express resistance and criticism of them, and to demonstrate theories in practice. They are still the categorical objects of 'experimentation', the site for testing those theories of the world emergent in the process of dominating realities. At the time of fieldwork, a moment when considerable changes were being mooted for Aborigines in North Queensland, Aborigines were being conceived by Whites still in control as sites for bureaucratic experimentation – much of it probably needed. Others were concerned to give back that traditional identity that history had destroyed, such restoration of tradition – as this was imagined – to be essential to the reformation of the damaged self. This is an idea, I have suggested, central in the motion of bureaucratic realities and resistance to their disembodying abstraction. It reimprisons Aborigines in the tyranny of the category and makes them the focus of contradictions which they may be powerless to overcome.

Numerous Aborigines are escaping this observation of the category, indeed, they are playing with non-Aboriginal visions of them and trapping non-Aborigines in their own conceptions. But this should not minimise the importance of what I have referred to as dominating cultures of bureaucracy which condition forms of experience and resistance and are germane to the production of modes of categorising knowledge and constituting the person which dehumanise and destroy.

NOTES

I wish to acknowledge grant support from the H.F. Guggenheim Foundation and a Wenner-Gren Foundation Small Grant for a research project in northern Queensland between 1989 and 1991 which provided some of the material upon which this paper is based.

The fieldwork for this paper pre-dates the Mabo decision of the Australian High Court in 1992. This decision recognised that the alienation of Aboriginal land at the time of 'discovery' was in contravention of British law at the time. The Mabo decision has altered the political context of Aboriginal rights in Australia, especially in relation to land. The decision has given added clout to Aboriginal claims and has in many ways heightened the tensions and uncertainties in Australian country towns of the kind I write about in this paper.

1. Jeff Collmann (1988, but published as his Ph.D. in 1980), has in my view given the most thorough analysis of the traditional/urban dichotomy in everyday discourse and in scholarly work. Collmann is the first anthropologist to have developed a strong critique of Australian ethnography and to have insisted that Aborigines be explored in terms of the complexities of their relations to the State. His work (and that of Barry Morris 1989) is vital as a background to the arguments presented here.
2. See Collmann (1988, Chapter 1) for an in-depth analysis of the role of white brokers among Aboriginal fringe dwellers in Alice Springs.
3. Postmodern analyses (e.g. the essays in Attwood and Arnold 1992) have established the importance, following E. Said and others, of representations of the other in constructing the unity of self-identity. This point, of course, is not the discovery of postmodernists but is well established in European psychoanalytic and existentialist traditions. The position I adopt here accepts such argument but examines processes internal to the structure of dominant discourse which produces its own internal distancing and the necessity for certain kinds of construction of the other. Lattas (1992) shows how Aborigines fill a lack which white Australians find in themselves. He sees this as a general process in 'Western culture'. I try and locate it in a more limited way in the 'culture of bureaucracy'.
4. At the time of the meeting the transition was still in progress.
5. Turner initially developed his concept of liminality through an analysis of Ndembu circumcision ritual. The aim in these rites is to abolish entirely the identity of the boys who are central to the rites, preparatory to their re-identification as men. This point was extended by Turner to other social processes such as those of pilgrimage during which the participants suspend their ordinary and everyday identities and statuses (identifications which differentiate and separate). During the process of pilgrimage, Turner argues, the pilgrims ideally recognise no distinctions born of ordinary social and political life and enter into relations of equality (which Turner describes as 'existential communities').

REFERENCES

Attwood, Brian and Arnold, John (eds) (1992) *Power, Knowledge and Aborigines* (special edn of *Journal of Australian Studies*), Melbourne: La Trobe University Press.
Beckett, J. (1988) *Past and Present: The Construction of Aboriginality*, Canberra: Aboriginal Studies Press.
Barth, F. (1985) *Ethnic Groups and Boundaries*, Norwegian University Press.
Collman, J. (1988) *Fringe Dwellers and Welfare*, St Lucia: Queensland University Press.
Foucault, M. (1974) *The Order of Things*, London: Routledge & Kegan Paul.
Gleason, P. (1983) 'Identifying identity: a semantic history', *Journal of American History*, vol. 69, 4.

Gluckman, M. (1958) *The Analysis of a Social Situation in Modern Zululand*, Manchester: Manchester University Press.

Handelman, Don (1981) 'Introduction: the idea of bureaucratic organisation', *Social Analysis* 9

Kapferer, B. (1988) *Legends of People, Myths of State*, Washington DC: Smithsonian Institution Press.

Langbaum, R. (1977) *The Mysteries of Identity*, New York NY: Free Press.

Lattas, A. (1992) 'Primitivism, nationalism and individualism in Australian popular culture' in B. Attwood and J. Arnold (eds) *Power, Knowledge and Aborigines* (special edn of *Journal of Australian Studies*), Melbourne: La Trobe University Press.

Mitchell, J.C. (1956) *The Kalela Dance*, Manchester: Manchester University Press.

Morris, B. (1989) *Domesticating Resistance*, Oxford: Berg Press.

Reynolds, Henry (1987) *Frontier*, Sydney: Allen & Unwin.

Rowley, C.D. (1973) *Outcasts in White Australia*, London: Penguin.

—— (1974) *The Destruction of Aboriginal Society*, London: Penguin.

Turner, V.W. (1969) *The Ritual Process: Structure and Anti-Structure*, Chicago IL: Aldine.

5 Around a plantation: the ethnography of business in Cameroon

Jean-Pierre Warnier

This paper is based on a case study of a plantation located in Cameroon. It produces a tropical fruit, glossed here as 'pinana', for export towards European markets. The plantation is owned and managed by a Bamiléké businessman whose pseudonym is Tadji It is roughly 140 ha. in size with 100 ha under actual cultivation. Tadji has some 200 employees. It is located in an area with a history of nearly a century of plantation economy and migrant Bamiléké labour. Tadji belongs to a generation of Cameroonian businessmen with a low level of formal education and a strong investment in the life of his chiefdom of origin. He behaves like a traditional notable, has two wives, and employs low-ranking labour with junior status.

For several years, the Tadji plantation remained marginal to the interests of its owner because the pinana was commercialised by the Pinana Marketing Board (PMB), an overstaffed and poorly managed parastatal which succeeded in bringing the national production from some 100,000 tons in 1985 down to a mere 40,000 tons in 1988. As a result, in 1990, the Tadji plantation was in rather poor condition, had a low productivity and put on the market inferior quality fruits. Fortunately for Tadji, the PMB was dismantled in 1988 and its estates sold to the private sector. The Tadji plantation happens to be next to a large expatriate concern called the Nong Valley Pinana Plantation (pseudonym, henceforth NVPP) with 1,200 ha. The NVPP has invested heavily in the plantation since its foundation in 1991. The capital is mostly French and private, with some Cameroonian private capital and an involvement by France Développement (pseudonym. henceforth FD), a French public funding agency. The Tadji plantation represents a double hazard for the NVPP – phytosanitary and commercial – insofar as its proximity and its poor state of maintenance can cause the spread of pests and fungus to the NVPP plantation, and that the reputation of the 'Cameroonian pinana' abroad can be jeopardised by the inferior Tadji product. Consequently, the NVPP proposed a contract to help Tadji, with technical assistance and the commercialisation of its fruits. For political reasons, this contract met the interests of the Cameroonian government and of FD because it not only promotes expatriate business but also Cameroonian private plantation economy and a category of local notables.

Since 1986, Cameroon has been experiencing a deepening politico-economic crisis. The withdrawal of expatriate capital, the growing pressure from the IMF and the World Bank, a vast programme of privatisation, reduction of state intervention, and structural adjustment, all have a strong flavour of triumphant capitalism.

In Cameroon, there is hardly any African big business worth the name. Rather, there are business networks connected to the world market and to Western big business. Such networks can be explored starting from any local nodal point such as the Tadji plantation. Selecting the plantation as the point of entry provides access to the traditional Bamiléké chiefdom, its hierarchy, its notables, to the NVPP as part of expatriate big business, to the interests of FD, and to the Cameroonian government.

I do not think that any of those partners, however 'big and near', can be considered as 'global'. To begin with, fieldwork on the case has demon-strated that the knowledge each of them has of its partners – and this is true of high-ranking FD consultants – is strikingly local. The 'global' does not exist except as a network, and 'global knowledge' can only be an anthropological construct. This is perhaps the ultimate conclusion that I would draw from the case because it shows what no-one can achieve in such a context except the anthropologist, that is, produce a global knowl-edge that otherwise would not exist. No agent belonging to the network has any interest in trespassing the boundaries of his local group, main-taining connections and identifying with other groups.

In this paper I shall give a sketchy ethnography and analysis of Tadji's life history against the Grassfields historical background, then come back to Tadji's action as a 'neo-notable' in the reinvented Bamiléké chiefdom. This will provide access to Tadji's partners: to the NVPP with which he negotiated a contract, to FD as the funding agency for the modernisation project of the plantation, and to the global politico-economic context. Finally, I shall focus on the knowledge the different partners have of each other, to conclude on the construction and use of global knowledge.

Before I start, let me add a last point: with the modernisation scheme of Tadji's plantation, we have a neat case of what I would call a 'working misunderstanding', that is, each nodal point in the system has a partial knowledge of the network and pursues its own interests. Yet by chance they all fit together in such a way that they favour the enforcement of the technical and commercial contract between NVPP and Tadji. In that respect it is a rather unusual and interesting case.

TADJI'S LIFE HISTORY AND BUSINESS AGAINST THE GRASSFIELDS HISTORICAL BACKGROUND

Tadji was born in 1935 in a Bamiléké-polygynous family. He was lucky enough to be sent to primary school by his father. He then learned typing in a private school. In 1953 he was recruited as a typist on contract in the colonial administration. The salary was low. He resigned and found employment with a French private company. He earned 7,500 F CFA a month (three times as much as before) and was able to save a substantial part of his earnings. He resigned again after three years and started trading in foodstuffs with his savings as initial capital. He bought a new minibus for 425,000 F CFA in 1959, hired an experienced driver, and started trading in coffee and cocoa at a time when prices were high and the trade profitable. In 1963, he built a coffee factory, purchased a car, and started touring the small plantations to buy coffee. He processed it, and sold it to Hollando, a Duch trading company well established in West Africa. He purchased a plot in Douala in 1970 and started building houses for rent. In 1973 the pinana plantation was for sale. It belonged to the widow of its former French owner and manager. Tadji bought it. In the meantime, he had married two wives. He now has nine daughters and seven sons.

His trajectory is quite typical of Bamiléké businessmen. In Cameroon, they are notorious for their success. Although the Bamiléké represent 17.5 per cent of the national population, they control between 35 and 95 per cent of Cameroonian capital investment and business, depending on the branch of activity. Such a success is puzzling. It is rooted in the history of the Cameroon western Highlands over the last three centuries, to which I have devoted two books (Warnier 1985 and 1993). This is where Tadji's case gives access to the local ethnography of his chiefdom and region of origin. In the Highlands or Grassfields, the typical political organisation is the chiefdom with its hierarchy of polygynous notables dependent on low-ranking categories of women and unmarried men. There are about 150 such chiefdoms of very unequal importance.

Towards the end of the nineteenth century, tension was running high between the notables and the cadets. With the onset of colonisation, the latter had an opportunity to rebel or escape. Both options are documented as early as the 1890s. Escapism in the form of conversion to Christianity, involvement in market economy and urban migration emptied the Grassfields of part of its younger male population, followed later on by the women. As a result, about a third of the total Grassfields population lives in urban and rural diasporas in Cameroon and neighbouring countries. One of the earliest areas of colonisation was the Douala hinterland, where the Tadji plantation is located.

Some of the migrant cadets succeeded in accumulating. They succeeded at the expense of those who failed. The latter survived by subordinating themselves to the wealthy. The hierarchy was reinvented by such 'neo-notables' who took to marrying several wives, purchasing titles of nobility and land in their chiefdom of origin, and behaving like 'traditional' notables.

It is no wonder that Tadji does not seem to have any problem with his 200 Bamiléké employees. Strikes are unknown in his plantation, and the hierarchical order is never challenged. In the neighbouring NVPP, the political unrest of 1991 was accompanied by strikes, riots and a severe clash between the workers and the gendarmes. During the 'ghost town operation' the workers blocked access to NVPP with heavy stones laid across the road. The Bamiléké Head of Personnel, who had notoriously conflictual relationships with the workers, asked a boy who happened to pass by with his two-wheeled cart to help remove them. The boy refused and in anger the man shot him dead with his automatic hand pistol. The infuriated workers started burning down lorries and equipment and made for the pumping station that feeds the NVPP irrigation network. They meant to destroy it. The gendarmes arrived within minutes from the neighbouring town, and 'calmed down' the mob of some 1,000 plantation workers of the NVPP. 'Otherwise', says Tadji's wife who told us the story, 'there would have been nothing left.' Meanwhile, the Tadji plantation remained undisturbed. Throughout this period, lorries loaded with fruits from the two plantations had to travel to the coastal harbour of Douala under military escort. The Bamiléké Head of Personnel had to be removed to France where he was given employment in one of the companies with a share in NVPP.

Tadji, like many Bamiléké chiefs and some businessmen, is a supporter of President Paul Biya, who was re-elected in October 1992, whereas the Bamiléké population stands firmly with the opposition. The official portrait of the Head of State is displayed in Tadji's living room, just across the entrance. The explanation of this apparent paradox rests in the historical background and the conflict that developed around the presidential campaign between Paul Biya and his most vocal opponent, John Fru Ndi, an anglophone Grassfielder. Fru Ndi is a small trader who used to run a bookshop in the provincial capital of Bamenda. He is the candidate of the cadets, the women, the low-ranking migrants of the Bamiléké diaspora and of the urban slums regardless of 'ethnic' affiliation. During the campaign, he addressed them in Pidgin English which was a means of reaching the people beyond the limits of his own anglophone constituency, since Pidgin is a standard means of communication among low-ranking Cameroonians even in francophone Cameroon. It was also a political statement: his party – the Social Democratic Front – was the party of the women and cadets against the state nomenclature and the hierarchy of chiefs and neo-notables who make it a point to speak either French or English or both. As a result, many chiefs and entrepreneurs, such as Tadji, with labour-intensive businesses supported law and order and the status quo offered by President Paul Biya. In October 1992, the latter was re-elected, although claims of fraudulence were made, against John Fru Ndi.

It should be clear by now that the 'traditional' political organisation of the Grassfields chiefdoms, and its social cleavages are an important part of the background to Tadji's business and action. I shall only mention it briefly, just to suggest that the ethnography of business is rooted in the kind of local ethnography that anthropologists have been trained, and used to do, and of which we have many examples in the work of Brain (1972), Kaberry (1952), Chilver and Kaberry (1967 and 1968), Ghomsi (1972), Pradelles de Latour (1991), Tardits (1980). Hurault (1962), Geary (1976), Dillon (1990), Nkwi (1976), Warnier (1985) and others. There are lots of local variations, but basically a chiefdom is made of aggregated unrelated descent groups or residential wards. Those groups are held together in a single polity by a number of associations of hereditary notables presided over by a chief or *fon*. The higher-ranking notables, usually numbering seven or nine, are said to be the successors in line of the companions who surrendered their ritual powers to a *primus inter pares* who became the *fon*. Men and women of the various descent groups or wards congregate in hundreds of associations – each with its specific dance, musical repertoire, orchestra and paraphernalia.

There is much evidence for high population densities from at least the second half of the eighteenth century. The sheer size of population provides a broad base upon which hierarchies of notables could develop, accumulating wealth from regional and long-distance trades, maintaining large polygynous households and controlling matrimonial alliance networks. A large number of male cadets remained bachelors for life in the household of their 'father'. Grassfields societies were, and still are, stratified and extremely inegalitarian. This must be kept in mind when reading the life history of a man like Tadji: a migrant cadet who is taking his revenge and reversing the roles. He does not feel uneasy regarding his own status as a notable and the subordination in which he keeps his labour force. The contract he arranged with the NVPP is just one more means to achieve these ends.

THE NVPP AND THE CONTRACT WITH TADJI

We now turn to the other key agent in this business network, that is, the NVPP. Perhaps the single most important factor in its activity is the constraint imposed by the annual climatic cycle on the organisation of work and production. From October to April, the Nong Valley enters a drier period in the yearly climatic cycle. Pinana production drops accordingly. The fruits are smaller, with a higher sugar content. Part of the labour and equipment remains idle. The cashflow is reduced. The adverse impact of seasonality on business does not need to be stressed. Irrigation is the technical answer to this. The NVPP has invested in a vast scheme of nearly 900 ha. of irrigated land (out of 1,200), with a permanent network of pipes buried deep into the ground, fed by powerful pumping stations along the Nong River.

The Nong Valley is located in a volcanic area. The soil is a mix of rocks of various sizes and very fertile volcanic ashes. Because of the rocks it cannot be ploughed. The only suitable machine to till the soil is the bulldozer. Besides bulldozers, the NVPP is equipped with a helicopter for the phytosanitary treatment of the plantation, a vast shed in which the fruits are sorted out, prepared and conditioned in 20 kg. cartons, tractors and platforms to transport the fruits from the fields to the shed, and a fleet of lorries to transport labour within the plantation and fruit to the harbour of Douala. The NVPP has its own mechanical workshop for the maintenance of the equipment. It employs some 1,000 persons, including a dozen expatriates, Cameroonian agricultural and mechanical engineers, a few laboratory technicians, mechanics, and a large number of plantation labourers.

The production cycle is spread over nine months, after which the fruit is harvested and an offshoot of the plant allowed to grow. After five cycles, the plants are uprooted, the soil turned over and allowed to fallow for about one year. The rotation from one field to the next is planned so as to even up the production from month to month and from year to year, and to stabilise it at around 40,000 to 45,000 tons per year. Work on the plantation includes weeding, cutting surplus offshoots, pruning the plant, spreading fertilisers, spraying fungicides and pesticides, and harvesting.

The Company has made a net profit of several hundred million F CFA since its foundation in March 1991 until June 1992. Expectations for the years to come are optimistic provided new regulations of the European Unified Market are such as to maintain the price of the African pinana high enough against competition from the Caribbean, Latin America and South-East Asia.

Thus, the NVPP is actually an agro-*industrial* plantation. The cost of equipment is high. The bill for the irrigation scheme for the Tadji plantation amounted to nearly 1.3 million FF for 80 ha. It is ten times higher for the NVPP. To this must be added the cost of the vehicles, the helicopter, etc. New investments from March 1991 to September 1992 ran up to 17 million FF. It cannot be seen purely as a labour-intensive enterprise.

The capital is shared between a number of partners: four French private companies with interest in the agrobusiness in France and abroad, several Cameroonian private share-holders (politicians and businessmen belonging to the entourage of President Paul Biya), two funding agencies operating in and for the benefit of developing countries (one French: France Développement; and one European) though financing private expatriate business, and a couple of smaller share-holders. This state of affairs is the result of the privatisation of Cameroonian parastatals in accordance with the structural adjustment policy of the World Bank and the IMF.

The project of making a contract with Tadji originated within the NVPP itself. The rationale behind this proposal, as already mentioned, was purely technical. The French Director of the NVPP approached Tadji and suggested that his plantation could be modernised with the financial support of FD. If this could be achieved, the NVPP would provide its own technical expertise and services and commercialise Tadji fruit under a common label.

Available evidence does not reveal any other hidden motivation on the part of the NVPP. We shall see that Cameroonian politics is very much part of the picture. In an area heavily dominated by political opposition to President Biya, the NVPP is concerned with playing down its all too obvious connections with Cameroonian political leaders. But the offer made to Tadji will not make relationships between the NVPP and its labour force any better or worse. They are poor anyway, the workers being Bamiléké, low-ranking and followers of John Fru Ndi, whereas the capital of the NVPP is mostly expatriate, involving the participation of Cameroonians who are the supporters of Paul Biya. Besides, as an expatriate and successful concern, the NVPP knows that it is rather unwelcome regardless of the present political context. However, the tension between the agro-industrial plantation and its workers is somewhat lessened by the fact that salaries are fully and regularly paid, which was far from being the case with the parastatal from which the NVPP took over. We find here the usual ambivalence vis-à-vis the white employer. Both parties seem to put up with it, and for the NVPP the motivation behind the contract is mostly technical and commercial rather than political. Tadji agreed with the offer, and lodged an application for a loan of 200 million F CFA with FD, strongly supported by NVPP. I shall now turn to FD as a key agent in the case at hand.

FRANCE DÉVELOPPEMENT AND THE GLOBAL CONTEXT

FD is a public funding agency, investing French State money in the agricultural and industrial sectors – both private and public – in developing countries. I shall now focus on the motives behind its aid to Tadji, leaving the ethnography of FD for the last part of this paper. Usually the aid takes the form of a share in the capital, with low interest rates, to be reimbursed within five to ten years. The feasibility and profitability of any project are the major conditions of its acceptability. But political motives loom large in the activities of FD. For example loans should be spread as evenly as possible among 'ethnic' groups and regions of a given country. The project should have at least the tacit approval of the political authorities. In the case of the Tadji plantation, the political motive was clearly stated by the Head of the FD local branch: supporting small Cameroonian plantations is a basic condition for the local integration of the large ex-patriate agro-industrial ones. It can lessen the resentment caused by their creation around 1990, which has increased ever since because of their spectacular success. Cameroonian State authorities, and French policy defined at ministerial level, both agree that small local plantations should be helped in order to alleviate tensions between Cameroonians and expatriates and to promote a strong agro-industrial branch. The Tadji project is seen by FD experts as the first step in a series of contracts to be negotiated in the coming years. The final success of such long-term plans depends partly on the more global politico-economic context that I shall now discuss.

The pinana market is a highly competitive world-wide market. Not that it is a free market. Far from it. It is a political market on which quotas are negotiated between producing countries in Africa, Latin America, South-East Asia and the Caribbean on the one hand, and industrial coun-tries on the other hand. France for example has to arbitrate between the interests of its former African colonies and its Caribbean territories (Guyana, Guadeloupe, Martinique). It also tries to obtain the support of the European Economic Community. Thus, in mid-February 1993, France obtained from the EC a large quota for the pinana imported from the French Caribbean and from francophone Africa. This new regulation became effective on 1 July 1993. It explains much of the confidence displayed by the producers and the government in Cameroon as regards the profitability of such plantations as Tadji's and the NVPP's.

The EC agreement is especially welcome at a time when Cameroon is experiencing a deepening politico-economic crisis. From 1955 to 1986, the country provided one of the rare success stories in Africa. The annual growth of the PNB averaged 7 per cent per year throughout the period, and the development of a market economy, mass consumption, the health, educational and communication systems was spectacular. Crude oil production started in the late 1970s and financed large state projects such as the building of a new Presidential Palace. In 1982, President Amadou Ahidjo resigned from the presidency if not from power in favour of Paul Biya who was then the Prime Minister. It turned out that A. Ahidjo had meant to keep control both of Paul Biya and the state through the One Party presidency. The conflict between the two men ended up in two coup attempts and a deep split within the political elite. At the same time, profits from exports dropped with the declining price of raw products on the world market and the increasing burden of the internal and external debt. In retrospect, it is clear that already in the late 1970s, private and public establishments, banks, the state had given out massive loans to promote investment and mass consumption without appropriate guaran-tees. Since 1986, when the tide turned, the economy started crumbling to pieces and Cameroon came under an IMF-imposed structural adjustment policy.

To these factors of decline must be added the development of predatory practices widely shared by many Cameroonians, which had been more or less domesticated under the presidency of A. Ahidjo. This is what Bayart (1989) calls *la politique du ventre*. Its extent is obviously hard to assess, but it is believed by many well-informed observers in various quarters (including FD and the World Bank) that it has taken an unheard of extension in Cameroon since the onset of the politico-economic crisis. Bayart (1991) goes so far as to speak of a mafia within the state and the criminalisation of politics.

Since 1986, many expatriate companies have left Cameroon, and the unemployment rate among qualified people is running high. In such circumstances, any foreign investment is welcome by the state and, with very ambivalent feelings, by the population. So is the NVPP and the help it provides to Tadji.

To sum up: in December 1992, at the time of the enquiry, the contract had been signed between the NVPP and Tadji, a loan of 200 million F CFA had been awarded to the latter by FD, a new shed had been built, and the irrigation scheme of ca. 80 ha. was nearly completed. The parties seem to have a good knowledge and understanding of each other and to be in agreement. Yet we shall now see that this is not quite the case, and that each local set of knowledge is more or less marginal to the others.

THE LOCAL BODIES OF KNOWLEDGE

Let us begin with the body of knowledge associated with the Bamiléké chiefdom: what is it all about, and who shares in it? It is the kind of knowledge that used to be the staple of classical anthropology: local polities built out of unrelated kindred or descent groups; local hierarchies of notables and their chiefs: regional hierarchies of chiefs; marriage alliance systems by bridewealth between men of equal rank and by deferred exchange between notables and lower-ranking men; rituals functioning to reproduce the chiefdom as a bounded unit of descent groups and households. This body of practical knowledge is associated with a rich set of representations regarding the dead elders, gender relationships, seniority, substances and qualities such as blood, semen, camwood, high and low, dry and wet, hot and cool.

This set of knowledge, well studied by anthropologists, is in the process of being reinvented by businessmen and neo-notables. In the new tradition as well as in the old, who is who is an important bit of useful knowledge: hereditary titles and who holds them, who has succeeded to whom, who is likely to succeed, who has money whether he hides it or not, who has married whom, who is doing business with whom, who are the people who belong to such and such rotating credit association?

A man like Tadji is socialised into that sort of knowledge. To him, this is a question of survival. His position is in fact insecure. In national politics, whether rightly or wrongly, the Bamiléké feel ostracised. They are actually disliked by a majority of the population because of the control they are believed to exercise on the economy, on trade, transports, plantations. As a Bamiléké, Tadji knows that in the long run, his security lies more with his chiefdom and with the Bamiléké as a group than with the Cameroonian nation as such, although he certainly shares the nationalist pride of all Cameroonians in their country. Let us say rather that if the worst came to the worst and an anti-Bamiléké pogrom were to take place in the country, he would have to fall back on the Grassfields community. Already during the presidential campaign, and especially afterwards, when John Fru Ndi with his Grassfields supporters was identified as the main opposition by Cameroonians at large, a number of Bamiléké traders saw their shops sacked in the southern towns, despite the amount of local support they enjoyed.

Yet when he turns for support to the Bamiléké community, Tadji has to face the hostility of the low-ranking cadets, plantation labour, urban migrants, unemployed, and many women, who support John Fru Ndi and his Social Democratic Front against the small minority of dominant Bamiléké chiefs and neo-notables. This social cleavage in Bamiléké society is as old as its hierarchy. It was very much part of the rebellion of the cadets against the 'colonial disorder' and the abuses of the chiefs between 1955 and 1970.

Most Bamiléké leaders have to play a double game. They want to support the Biya regime to keep the cadets in check. Also if they have reached any visibility on the national scene, they must support it while redistributing its favours. At the time of the presidential elections, there were stories of Bamiléké chiefs receiving money to campaign for Paul Biya, and sharing it back in the village with his opponents. Tadji does that sort of thing, at the same time enforcing his dominance over his employees, voicing threats and meting out punishment, and offering rewards, protection and some amount of security. Tadji's wife told us: 'the workers are "strong heads". We tell them *c'est la crise*. You are lucky to be paid at all. There are thousands of unemployed knocking at the door. If you don't have the pinana, what will you have?' His employees are his clients. This emerges clearly from their number. Whereas the NVPP employs less than one person per hectare (1,000 employees for 1,200 ha.). Tadji employs two (200 employees for 100 ha. under cultivation). Yet he does not have to do the maintenance of the irrigation and phytosanitary equipment, the commercialisation of the fruits, etc. His plantation is grossly overstaffed, and it is probably difficult for him to avoid this.

It is hard to tell what knowledge the cadets and the labour force have of the chiefdom and of Tadji's partners at the NVPP, FD and the state administration. This is certainly the most glaring gap in our knowledge. In the Grassfields and in the Bamiléké diaspora, most if not all enquiries were made from the point of view of the hierarchy. Women have received some amount of attention because they are the primary agricultural producers, and Kaberry (1952), Goheen (1984), Van den Berg (1993) among others, have established a scholarly tradition in that domain. But male cadets have been ignored altogether, although their rebellion in the early years of colonisation and again from 1955 to 1970, their massive conversion to Christianity, their migration in diaspora, demonstrate that they have never been the passive victims of their condition. The difficulty with them is that they escape or rebel but seldom speak up. They constitute a muted category, even more than the women, and when they start speaking, it is because they have succeeded and they tell only the success story. In fact the discourse they produce is mostly that of the hierarchy. As long as they are on the wrong side, they remain silent and it is difficult to know what is on their minds. Besides, hardly any scholar has ever ventured to ask the question.

What little information we have concerning the Bamiléké diaspora shows that from the second generation onwards, people have a rather scanty knowledge of the chiefdom or chiefdoms of origin of their parents and their traditions. Yet they have internalised the hierarchic principle because the village has been reconstructed in town or in diaspora, with its notables and its men's and women's associations. As a result, the ambition of any cadet is not to destroy the hierarchic principle as such but to rebel, overthrow the notables and take their place if they can, or to graduate peacefully to the status of a notable. Accordingly they all have some amount of knowledge of the rules of the game and of who is who around them.

Tadji himself is between two or perhaps three worlds. To bring out this point, it is perhaps best to discuss the local knowledge shared by the staff of France Développement and see what access, if any, Tadji is able to have to it.

FD SENIOR STAFF

FD is a large establishment, based in Paris, with local residencies in the major African towns, mostly but not exclusively in francophone Africa. Whereas the Ministry of Foreign Affairs and the Ministère de la Coopération provide development agents and not development money, the latter is the *raison d'être* of FD. It is a funding agency. It enjoys some amount of autonomy within the French Civil Service, under the control of the Ministère de la Coopération, the Ministry of Finances, the Ministry of Foreign Affairs and, above all, the presidency. Its senior staff of experts is recruited among graduates of the highest ranking schools of management and engineering (Polytechnique, Centrale, H.E.C., Institut d'Etudes Politiques de Paris). The staff works at the headquarters in Paris and in the various residencies abroad. Decisions regarding loans such as the one awarded to Tadji are taken at the headquarters, after enquiry and a recommendation by the local resident and his colleagues. An important proportion of the senior staff make frequent travels between the head-quarters and the residencies. Such travels are short, usually from two to ten days at a time. A given expert may thus visit ten to fifteen different African towns within a year. They are often dispatched to assist local governments in such matters as monetary policy, renegotiating the public debt, privatisation of the public sector, providing the local government with an audit of a private bank or a parastatal.

They are accountable only to FD. As members of the Civil Service, their careers depend on the internal criteria of FD. They enjoy much freedom and the high prestige awarded by the handling of large state funds. Their ethos is that of the public service, not business. They share high moral standards, although they have to put up with the *politique du ventre*. Most of them would see their calling as one of promoting good business and good governance without actually doing business or partic-ipating in government. Their status is such that their opposite numbers in African countries are seldom below the rank of Director. In fact, both their African counterparts and their own establishment would find it some-what inappropriate, perhaps even distasteful if they dealt with people below that rank, except as informants when they conducted an enquiry. It would show some amount of distrust of their African counterparts and an attempt to undercut their knowledge and authority.

Such an establishment does not promote an intimate grassroots level knowledge of Africa amongst its staff. The three key people who studied the application lodged by Tadji have probably never read a single page of serious ethnography on the Bamiléké. Why should they anyway? They know that Bamiléké businessmen are their best bet in Cameroon although they would not disregard other ethnic groups for local political reasons. They know next to nothing of the expectations and the life histories of the businessmen. They have a poor understanding of their lifestyle. They find it at best exotic, at worse irrational and wasteful. Their knowledge of Africa is sometimes crude. The FD resident in Douala told me that the force behind John Fru Ndi was United States interests, because if he became the President of Cameroon, being an anglophone and hostile to French interests, he would open the oil fields to American companies, and even perhaps replace Elf-Serepcam (the Franco–Cameroonian petroleum company) with an American company. He viewed the support given by the United States to Fru Ndi as a clear indication of the interest that the White House and the State Department have in gaining access to the Cameroonian oil fields. This is an extreme case of ignorance by a man who was new to Africa and new to his job. He had been trained as a banker. He denied Africa any claim to civilisation anyway. He missed entirely the local political dynamics. This case, however extreme, shows that one can be recruited at a high level by FD without knowing anything about Africa.

Is such a knowledge believed to be irrelevant at FD? Certainly not. Rather, the question is: how far should it extend? All the experts think that they can become usefully acquainted with Africa on the spot. The knowledge acquired in that way includes economic statistics, who is who in politics, administration and business, current and potential resources of the country and the like. Should it include an anthropological expertise regarding local dynamics, ethnic groups, social cleavages, representations such as occult powers as an idiom in contemporary politics? Most of them would think it is beyond their reach and probably irrelevant to the current issues of structural adjustment and privatisations. This means that they actually have some knowledge of it but that it is mostly a matter of stereotypes about Africa and the Africans.

Such stereotypes are often glossed by the experts as 'cultural obstacles to development' and best left to the scrutiny of the anthropologist until the process of modernisation discards both the obstacles and the anthropologist. For the expert, the relevant body of knowledge currently revolves around the question of structural adjustment, privatisation and good governance. Henry (1993) demonstrates the ambiguity of such a word as 'privatisation'. It raises many questions left without any proper answer, such as the lack of reliable technical and financial data concerning the firms to be sold to the private sector, the absence of economic, fiscal, legal, social and administrative state policies that should be carried along with the privatisation. The concept itself varies from one expert to another depending on their ideological background, the organisation they belong to, and their nationality. It is far more important for the career or mere survival of a senior FD member to acquire a good knowledge of the current issues about privatisations and structural adjustment policies, what doctrines are in or out of fashion at ministerial level, including the complexities of technical and financial data, than to cope with the subtleties of Bamiléké political dynamics or the balance of occult powers within the Cameroonian state apparatus as analysed for example by Rowlands and Warnier (1988).

Yet Henry (1993) convincingly argues that without an intimate knowledge of Cameroonian or African society, the discourse of FD (or other) Western experts is no more magical than the discourse of Cameroonians on the balance of occult powers. To their African counterparts, 'privatisation' is the latest to date of all the 'White man's sorceries'. I would add that it is no less comprehensible to the outsider than the discourse of occult powers is to the FD expert, except that the Cameroonian establishment knows that it is a good opportunity for private accumulation (and accumulation is what occult powers are all about). A. Henry points out the fact that structural adjustment policies leave one important question unanswered: what are the *locally* acceptable methods of efficient organisation in African business and administration? Such methods do exist, witnessed by the success of some purely African firms, both private and public. They may vary from one branch of activity to the next, and privatisation as such leaves that question open. The enquiry into locally acceptable methods of management would require some amount of ethnographic research into the local sets of knowledge, or into what Bayart calls the local trajectories of politics. There is however a small minority of FD experts who agree on that line of argument. They are found mostly among the local residents, or those with a good background in Africa, rather than those at headquarters. Understandably, they are marginalised by the mainstream official wisdom of the organisation. I expect we are now in a better position to ask how Tadji copes with the arcane customs of the FD tribe.

TADJI'S KEY POSITION

Tadji stands in a key position: his plantation leads him to deal with his employees, the NVPP, FD and the Cameroonian administration. He has to form some knowledge of their motives and rules of behaviour. His background is that of his chiefdom of origin. He has a low level of formal education. In principle, he is poorly equipped to understand his partners, except his employees. He does not have much difficulty in empathising with the NVPP expatriate staff. They are in Cameroon to make money, and the motives behind the contract they offer to Tadji are profoundly selfish; they want to solve *their* phytosanitary and commercial problems caused by the proximity of Tadji's plantation. Unfortunately, fieldwork conditions did not allow us to probe into the ways in which Tadji perceives FD and the Cameroonian administration beyond his obvious puzzlement about their real motivations. The rationale behind FD's action cannot be business or making money. So, what can it be? Tadji does not seem to know for sure. The research team was not actually working for FD, but enjoyed some of its facilities, and Tadji did not seem to know what to do about this. As regards the Cameroonian Ministry of Agriculture, Tadji's permanent complaint is that it is meant to promote agriculture and the agrobusiness – it claims to anyway – and yet it seems to put every conceivable obstacle in the way of the producers. This complaint is voiced in a petition addressed to the Ministry by Tadji and a dozen other *planteurs* regarding the reimbursement of some money given to them several years before, the status of which was unclear: loan or grant-in-aid? Tadji's wife gave us another example of what to her looked like an insult from the Minister in person. At the time of the presidential campaign, the Minister visited the area and compensated the small farmers for the lack of income due to a glut of cocoa and coffee. He distributed cheques for 700 to 5,000 F CFA payable to the bearer in the political town of Yaoundé, about 300 km away. The largest cheque did not even cover the cost of the return journey by bus or train.

The account I have given of Tadji's case is far from being complete. It is in fact no more than a sketch. It leaves out the ethnography of NVPP, of the Cameroonian administration and of plantation labour. However, a number of conclusions can be drawn from it regarding the production and use of global knowledge.

ANTHROPOLOGY AND GLOBAL KNOWLEDGE

First, although Tadji's plantation does not belong to a vast business organisation that could qualify for 'globality', it belongs to a global rather tightly knit network of socioeconomic relationships that includes the workers, NVPP and its share-holders, the Cameroonian political establishment, the state bureaucracy and France Développement.

Second, there are local bodies of operational knowledge corresponding to the various nodes in the network. One should not think that each of them is closed in upon itself and that they are disconnected. Far from it. Although Tadji expresses his puzzlement regarding the motives behind the action of the Ministry of Agriculture, it would not require much talking with him to produce a number of statements on the logic of the *politique du ventre*, presumably associated with some amount of ethnic prejudice against the administration which is, quite wrongly, supposed to be recruited among non-Bamiléké. He would also recognise that the action of the Ministry is not always predatory. Except in extreme cases exemplified in Zaire and Uganda, intelligent predation does not go without some amount of catering for the population on which the predator can feed itself. And that is what a 'good' *politique du ventre* is all about.

Those bodies of knowledge are not entirely disconnected, yet they are opaque to each other. The most extreme case in that respect is the nearly total lack of communication and understanding between the FD experts – especially the headquarters senior staff – on the one hand, and Tadji's world – especially his personal motives as a neo-notable – on the other.

Yet – and this is my third remark – contrary to common-sense wisdom, the lack of communication and understanding is not necessarily a cause of failure. Far from it. Let us consider the case of one FD expert who eventually resigned after many years spent in Africa. He could not bear any longer the cognitive dissonance he was experiencing. In an interview with a member of the research team, he pointed out that in most cases you cannot expect that the motivations of all partners in a business venture will coincide. Yet the condition for its success is that they should be stated. Fair enough. The trouble is that, in nearly every case, not all but at least some of them are not only impossible to put into words but are opaque to the actors themselves. Their statement requires some amount of analysis and conceptualisation. In fact, the synthesis is provided by the action itself: in the case of Tadji's loan, it happens that all parties agree on the action itself for all sorts of different reasons that are not necessarily understood or even stated. In fact, most FD reports are confidential and released with much reluctance to the researcher, let alone to Tadji, NVPP or the Cameroonian administration.

If such is the case – and that is my fourth remark – who can produce any kind of global knowledge unless it be the anthropologist, who has been trained to watch and to listen – except that he has been used to applying these skills to the small and exotic rather than the big and near? If he agrees to take on the global view, his construct can only begin with the ethnography of what is small and local: the chiefdom, the plantation, and (why not?) the ethnography of FD or the Cameroonian administration. But then how can such a knowledge be put to use?

One should stress (and indeed it causes stress) that such global knowledge is disturbing for most partners in such a venture as Tadji's. An FD expert likes to think of himself as an impassioned missionary of efficient management and good governance. There is indeed a fair amount of truth in this view, as P. d'Iribarne (1989) has demonstrated regarding what he calls the *Logique de l'honneur*. But it should also be said that, more or less consciously, an FD expert is actually acting to pursue his career when he conforms to the constraints and expectations of the organisation, to such an extent that he can even miss important components of any action towards economic development. Now to point this out to him is like practising wild psychoanalysis. It will not be heard, or it will hurt. It will be worse than useless because it will contribute to built-up resistance. I can put this in print precisely because the present paper is unlikely ever to be read by mainstream FD experts.

This is perhaps the main critique that I would address to the way anthropology as critique (Marxist or other) was advocated and practised by some anthropologists until the 1970s when growing unemployment among graduates led them to knock at the door of big corporations which, at the same time, began to invest more and more in cross-cultural management and in human resources. Anthropology as a critique reached a readership of radical intellectuals. It could not be read or heard by those it was meant to criticise (except the anthropologist himself) just as with wild psychoanalysis: precisely because it is true and misplaced. At times, it had a strong flavour of narcissism ('Look, I am more radical than you are.').

At this point, I do not wish to enter the debate over applied anthropology and the various uses of the knowledge produced by the growing number of anthropologists working for such institutions as Xerox Corp., General Motors, the World Bank or the US Federal Government – some 3,000 of them in the USA according to Corcoran (1993). I would rather raise the following question: in line with the present case study, what are the conditions under which the discourse of the anthropologist as a producer of global knowledge could be heard by the various parties? This is the question of anthropology as critique revisited in the 1990s.

The question arose from the fieldwork setting itself. A team of three, including a Cameroonian University lecturer in management, an FD expert and an anthropologist, was studying medium-size Cameroonian business. The FD expert was not there as such, but as a member of a permanant research team on cross-cultural management. The research developed from the idea that medium-size business depends on a network of customers, bankers, consultants, etc., and that the enquiry should focus as much on the network as on the internal organisation of the firm. Given the fact that partners in the network were worried, sometimes to a considerable extent, about the information and the fantasies each of them had regarding the others, the researchers were very soon cornered into producing some global discourse or denying any competence to speak on behalf of, or about any third party. In actual fact, we navigated as best we could between those two positions.

Several months after the enquiry was conducted, it is clear that the global knowledge which is emerging from it could be of value to the partners, by providing each of them with a chart indicating where he stands, how he acts and how he is perceived. This is especially true of FD senior staff, who are far from being all of a piece, and among whom development is a permanent concern. The question we are now faced with is this: what are the rules and procedures to be observed if we want to put our knowledge to good use with FD (or any other partner)? This is not a question raised out of context. In fact a meeting is planned between two members of the research team and several FD experts, but the rules have not yet been discussed.

The kind of knowledge we have acquired is likely not to be considered as legitimate among experts. Its lack of legitimacy deserves analysis. In my opinion, it comes from the conditions of its production, that is, where it is produced, and by whom. Some of it is produced at grassroots level, that is, with people who do not share in the expertise that is found higher up in the social and professional hierarchy. Another way to express it is to say that it is concerned with what Latour (1991) calls a hybrid object, that is technique *cum* social relationships, whereas legitimate knowledge is concerned with pure technicalities. Further, an anthropologist is the wrong person to produce it because he is not qualified in such matters as engineering, management, finance and public administration. Part of the answer to this lies in the setting up of a research team: the anthropologist is expected to procure his own legitimacy vis-à-vis other anthropologists who have some reasons to deny it to the economist. The FD expert on the team does the same thing the other way round. The Cameroonian's contribution is an important asset as regards his fellow countrymen. However, this is only a small part of the answer because legitimacy means technical *purity*, and what we propose is a *hybrid* team, and its product which is *hybrid global* knowledge. Is there any hope of overcoming this difficulty and how?

ACKNOWLEDGEMENTS

This paper is based on research carried out in Cameroon in November and December 1992 by A. Henry, E. Kamdem and myself on Cameroonian-owned and managed medium-size business. The data were shared between the three researchers. I acknowledge with thanks the contributions of my two colleagues and comments by M. Rowlands and D. Miller. The analysis however is mine. The research was supported by the French Ministère de la Recherche et de l'Environnement and by the CNRS laboratory Gestion et Société, I also wish to express my gratitude to all the Cameroonian and French experts who agreed to help us in our enquiry.

REFERENCES

Bayart, J.-F. (1989) *L'Etat en Afrique. La politique du ventre*. Paris. Fayard.
—— (1991) 'Mafia et répression au Cameroun'. *La Croix*, 29 August 1991.
Brain, R. (1972) *Bangwa Kinship and Marriage*. Cambridge: Cambridge University Press.
Chilver, E.M. and Kaberry, P.M. (1967) 'The Kingdom of Kom. West Cameroons'. In D. Forde and P.M. Kaberry (eds), *West African Kingdoms in the Nineteenth Century*. London: Oxford University Press. pp. 123–51.
—— (1968) *Traditional Bamenda. The Pre-Colonial History and Ethnography of the Bamenda Grassfields*. Buea: Ministry of Primary Education and Social Welfare, and West Cameroon Antiquities Commission.
Corcoran, E. (1993) 'Anthropology Inc.'. *The Washington Post*, 21 February, H1 & H6.
Dillon, R.G. (1990) *Ranking and Resistance. A Precolonial Cameroonian Polity in Regional Perspective*. Stanford: Stanford University Press.
Geary, C. (1976) *We – Die Genese eines Häuptlingtums im Grasland von Kamerun*. Wiesbaden: Franz Steiner Verlag.
Ghomsi, E. (1972) *Les Bamiléké du Cameroun: Essai d'étude historique des origines à 1920*. Thèse de doctorat de troisième cycle, Paris.
Goheen, M. (1984) *Ideology and Political Symbols in a West African Chiefdom: Commoditisation of Land, Labour and Symbolic Capital in Nso, Cameroon*. Unpublished Ph.D. dissertation Harvard. UMI n° 84–19290.
Henry, A. (1993) 'Les privatisations, nouvelle sorcellerie des Blancs?' *Afrique Contemporaine*, La Documentation Française, juin 1993.
Hurault, J. (1962) *La structure sociale des Bamiléké*. Paris: Mouton.
Iribarne, Ph.d' (1989) *La logique de l'honneur*. Paris: Seuil.
Kaberry. P.M. (1952) *Women of the Grassfields*. London: HMSO.
Latour, B. (1991) *Nous n'avons jamais été modernes. Essai d'anthropologie symétrique*. Paris: La Découverte.
Nkwi, P.N. (1976) *Traditional Government and Social Change: A Study of the Political Institutions among the Kom of the Cameroon Grassfields*. Fribourg, Switzerland: The University Press.
Pradelles de Latour, C.H. (1991) *Ethnopsychanalyse en pays bamiléké*. Paris: E.P.E.L.
Rowlands, M.J. and Warnier, J.-P. (1988) 'Sorcery, Power and the Modern State in Cameroon'. *Man* (ns) 23: 118–32.
Tardits, C. (1980) *Le Royaume bamoum*. Paris: A. Colin.

Van den Berg, A. (1993) *Women in Bamenda. Survival Strategies and Access to Land*. African Studies Center, Leiden, the Netherlands.

Warnier, J.-P. (1985) *Echanges, développement et hiérarchies dans le Bamenda précolonial*. Stuttgart: Franz Steiner Verlag Wiesebaden.

—— (1993) *L'esprit d'entreprise au Cameroun*. Paris: Karthala.

6 Learning to be local in Belize: global systems of common difference

Richard Wilk

What makes us all the same is that we're all different.
(Television advertisement for AT&T communications, 1993)

Interviewer: What's your advice to the next Miss Belize with regards to her participation in the Miss Universe pageant?
Miss Belize: I would advise her to go to the pageant feeling *first* that she is the chosen representative of her country and is just as special as every other contestant there. Secondly, she should be herself, never trying to imitate anyone else.

(*Amandala*, 1 August 1986)

When I went to Belize in 1989, the furthest thing from my mind was the topic of beauty pageants. I intended a study of imported consumer goods, and the structure of taste and value among the middle class. But when I began to look into clothing and jewellery and the sites where they were put on public display, I could no longer ignore the pageants and contests. They were simply the most common and popular form of public spectacle, held in almost every community and school. When I later mentioned this to colleagues working in other parts of the world, they reported a similar profusion of beauty pageants in places as diverse as Thailand, Liberia and Moscow.

Here is an institution, invented in its present form by the American circus impresario P.T. Barnum in 1848 (Banner 1983), which has now expanded to a global, if not universal scale. The beauty pageant presents the basic paradox of globalisation in an especially clear form; in each place the pageant is made into a local institution, embedded in specific social relationships, invested with meaning by unique groups in a particular historical context. But at the same time, in some ways, the pageant also creates larger relations of uniformity, casting local differences in ways that, on a global scale, are predictable and surprisingly uniform. This paper is an attempt to think through this contradiction, to show how the replication of diversity can produce homogeneity, and to think about whose interests are being served by this process.

This paper could be read as another account of commodification, of the production of national culture, and the progressive penetration of global commodities into every crevice of daily life, turning even the beauty of the human body into an image to be bought and sold. But this is far from my intention; in fact my ultimate goal is to subvert this now-traditional narrative and challenge some of the basic oppositions that it depends upon: indigenous and imported, authentic and false, local and global.

The intent is to suggest some ways to move beyond the polarities of global hegemony and local appropriation. I argue that in the process of absorbing the beauty pageants into a local context, Belizeans have also been absorbed into global *contest*. By asserting their distinctiveness and difference through this medium, they have entered what I call a 'structure of common difference', creating one of Appadurai's 'global localities' (1990). The parallels with arguments made in other papers in this book are obvious; we are all dealing in some way with the complex interplay *between* local context and global content, rather than arguing for the primacy of one over the other.

As I define it, the global stage does not consist of common content, a lexicon of goods or knowledge. Instead it is a common set of formats and structures that mediate between cultures; something more than a flow of things, or of the meanings attached to things, or even the channels along which those things and meanings flow. As in Friedman's concept of 'hard globalization', the connections between localities are created by widespread and common forms of contest for the exercise of power over *what* to produce, consume, watch, read and write. These contests follow channels that put diversity in a common frame, and scale it along a limited number of dimensions, celebrating some kinds of difference and submerging others.

THE LOCAL IN THE GLOBAL IN BELIZE

Belize, independent from Britain since 1981, has a tiny but diverse population – less than 200,000 people who speak more than six languages. Today the country is increasingly cosmopolitan. The economy is open to foreign capital, the stores full of imports. Belizeans themselves are transnational – their families scattered across the United States and the Caribbean, with most of the young expecting to spend parts of their lives abroad. Those at home are bombarded by foreign media – there are nine stations broadcasting a steady diet of American and Mexican satellite TV, and one can hook up to full-service cable systems in every town with more than a thousand people. When Belizeans turn off the TV they can look out the window at a parade of foreign tourists, resident expatriates, and students in search of authentic local experience, traditional medicine, untouched rainforests and ancient ruins.

The paradox is that amidst all this transnational influence, Belize's national and ethnic cultures have never been so strong or so distinct. In fact, until foreign cultural influence became so pervasive, most people denied that such a thing as 'Belizean culture' existed at all. When I began to work in Belize in the early 1970s, people carefully explained to me that the numerically dominant African-European group, the descendants of slaves and their masters collectively labelled 'Creoles,' had no culture of their own. They were 'really' British or Caribbean. The predominantly Spanish-speaking rural communities were 'just Mestizos', the same people as neighbouring Guatemalans or Mexicans. The only people in the country who were generally acknowledged to have culture were marginalised minority immigrants – Mayans, Hindus, Lebanese, Chinese, Garifuna and Mennonites.

When I asked about 'Belizean food', I was met with blank stares or nervous laughter, or a patient explanation that there was no such thing. 'Creole food' was a term of embarrassment; like the local English-Creole dialect, it was considered a 'broken' and imperfect version of the metropolitan English standard. By definition, cooking was the preparation of European and American dishes with imported ingredients, a skill that required sophistication and training. As an honoured guest from the north, I was usually treated to something from a can (Wilk 1992).

In those days when I looked for Belizean gifts for my friends in the US, there were simply no distinctive or emblematic objects one could take home to prove that one had been to a place called 'Belize'. Only stamps, coins and bottles of 'local' Belikin beer (brewed next to the Belize City airport by an American, in a Canadian brewery using Dutch malt concentrate and English bottles). Belize was an ethnographic blank. While *I* found something there quite special and distinctive, there were no public symbols, no public discussions about that distinction.

About the only other people who seemed to believe in something called 'Belizean culture' were politicians, especially in the nationalist Peoples United Party, which had engaged in some fitful cultural decolonisation projects after achieving internal self-government in 1964. Black woollen coats and ties were banned as official garb, and a plain Guayabera dubbed a 'Belize Jack', or a neutral safari suit were briefly in vogue. The party leader and first Prime Minister George Price gave speeches about the need to develop a Belizean culture that would bring together the country's diverse ethnic groups, sometimes hinting at American-style syncretism, but more recently favouring the pluralist metaphor of the stewpot over the blender (Judd 1989).

But the content of this national culture was never specified, beyond that it was to be a unique blend of the best of the Caribbean and Latin American.[1] Starting in 1975, local intellectuals and public servants tried to fill the void by staging an annual cultural festival, modelled explicitly on the Jamaican 'Carifesta'. But through the 1970s and early 1980s,

'Belizean culture' was still the project of a small minority – in the countryside it was still an oxymoron.

Today all of this has dramatically changed. Belize is awash with emblematic local goods – woodcrafts, hot pepper sauces, dolls and dresses. There is a literally booming local music industry, boasting its own 'Punta Rock', now internationally marketed. A Belizean cuisine has appeared, first in expatriate Belizean restaurants in New York and Los Angeles, then in the form of a 'Belizean Dish of the Day' at tourist hotels. Belizean cookbooks were produced by the Peace Corps, and today almost every eatery which isn't Chinese is advertising 'authentic Belizean food'. There is a touring national dance troupe, a national theatre movement, a new historical society that is designating landmarks and choosing national heros. Art galleries feature oils of village life by Belizean artists, Belizean poetry flourishes.

This furious rate of cultural production is not just a preoccupation of an educated or economic elite. When I conducted a large-scale survey in 1990, reproducing the format of Bourdieu's *Distinction*, I found that a majority in all ethnic, occupational and income groups believe there is a national culture, and are proud of it. In ranking their favourite music, food, home decorations and entertainment, they consistently placed local products above foreign imports. Even as actual consumption of imports of all kinds has increased dramatically, as frozen and packaged foods from the United States have entered every home, pride in emblematic local products has risen too (Wilk 1990, 1991).

This is not to say that Belizeans in any way agree about the content or meaning of their national culture. Controversy and political contest over the cultural content and effects of local and foreign television, sports, music, arts, dance, food, money, drugs and migration are intense. But 'culture' has emerged as a legitimate topic, as an objectified matter of debate and dispute in everything from political campaigns to the wildly popular radio call-in programmes.[2] There is now a daily programme of 'cultural music' on Radio Belize, 'cultural dance' graces most public events, and shops feature cabinets of 'cultural goods'.

The emergence of a public national culture in Belize provides an interesting contrast with the similar process documented on the Caribbean island of Nevis by Olwig (1993). In both Belize and Nevis national identity has emerged through an interaction between local cultural politics and the cultural processes of diaspora. In Nevis the island economic base is weak, and the rate of emigration is enormous. Nevisian national identity is now largely a performance for the benefit of returning expatriates, for whom the island provides a 'cultural homeland'. In Belize the expatriate community has a much smaller role, and contestation of identity is played mostly by local actors for a local audience. As the size of the Belizean expatriate community increases, this may well change in the direction that Nevis has taken.

The emergence of an objectified national culture in Belize is a clear example of what Friedman calls 'the production of local difference on a global scale' (Chapter 7, this volume) and his description raises important questions about the status of the local within the global. First is the issue of whether or not this production of local culture is something new, radical and transforming; the symptom, sign or substance of a new cultural world order, creolised, commodified and transnational. A second and related question asks how these objectified and politicised phenomena relate to everyday social practice in a place like Belize – do they merely overlay other, more immediate forms of lived identity that preserve the local in the form of habitus? Do the public and objectified forms parasitise practice, sucking away its power and substance to leave only a shell? Or is it the everyday world of lived practice that absorbs, organises and coopts the public rhetoric of group identity, domesticating the national into a stable and continuous regime of localised meaning and small-scale social groups?

I suggest that there is indeed something new about the emergence of a national culture in Belize, but that trying to understand this novelty in terms of '*the local and the global*' is futile and unproductive. The local and the global (or at least the foreign) have a long-term relationship in Belize; there has never been a vestige or illusion of an authentic and autonomous local regime of value. This situation is hardly unique to the Caribbean, as demonstrated by recent studies of cultural importation in France (Kuisel 1993) and Japan (Tobin 1992). Such examples show that there is nothing contradictory in the maintenance of distinctive local cultural practices and identities while awash in imported goods, language and ritual.[3]

While anthropology has long surpassed an equation of objects or customs with culture, this conception is still at the core of the popular imagination in most modern states. The emerging 'folk model' of national culture in Belize identifies foreign words, ideas and goods as evidence of cultural intrusion, threatening a parallel loss of authentic local culture. People in every social category accept and lament the Belizean taste for imported goods (even as they raise their voice over the sound of country and western music on their stereos), and only disagree over the degree to which resistance is possible or desirable. They interpret consumption in a context of foreign domination and local resistance, as external modernising forces standing against long-standing local practice, the major cause of recent cultural changes. Like the French (on both left and right) who resisted the importation of Coca-Cola in the 1950s, Belizeans thereby implicitly accept a concept of culture as a limited taxonomic corpus which can change through substitution (Coke replaces wine), not through expansion (adding new categories of beverages alongside wine) (Kuisel 1993). The most benign possibility is dilution of the national essence.[4]

Anthropologists also often implicitly accept this model of culture, when we try to make the opposite point; that global media or goods are effectively localised and incorporated into local cultural lexicons. (The literature on the different ways that the TV program *Dallas* has been locally interpreted is a good example of this tendency (Liebes and Katz 1990).) If we follow this logic far enough, we can lull ourselves into thinking that the global spread of goods and culture is nothing new, that each culture will just absorb global culture and recontextualise it. And there have been a number of excellent recent anthropological studies of how foreign and international ideas and objects are effectively localised – incorporated into local systems of meaning and value, in the contexts of long-standing local structures of power. This is what James Carrier has called the 'It's All Right, They've Appropriated It' school of thought (personal communication, 1993).

In this way a focus on commodities and goods, on the specific content of consumption, can lead us right back to the time-worn theme of domination and resistance, of hegemony and the localised struggle for autonomy.[5] Historical evidence shows on the contrary that the content of Caribbean culture has been thoroughly globalised for hundreds of years, that the foreign and the local have long been deployed in a stable regime of competition (for thorough discussion see Olwig 1993). They are part of a semiotic landscape in which people have pursued a variety of strategies, without challenging the underlying order. Below I will sketch something of this order, and then go on to suggest some of the ways in which it is changing, as the local drama is increasingly played out on a truly global stage, constituted through *structures of common difference*.

THE LOCAL STAGE AND FOREIGN CULTURAL CAPITAL

Many scholars have remarked on the dualism of English-speaking Caribbean culture. One system of values, often labelled 'respectability', revolves around the home, stable marriage-based family relations, participation in churches and social advancement through education, community service and support of a mostly European 'high culture'. In most of the area, as Miller (1993) points out, this set of values is celebrated and re-affirmed in home-centred Christmas ritual. A second set of values forms a complex of 'reputation' that centres on the streets and rum-shops, and elevates promiscuity and fertility, verbal performance and play, popular music and dance, and opposition to a social order based on wealth and position (see Wilson 1973 for an original formulation; Manning 1990, Pyde 1990, Abrahams 1983 and Austin 1983 for critical commentary). Reputation reaches its ritual climax in the bacchanal of carnival.

Most analysts trace this dualism back to the regimes of slavery and emancipation, linking respectability to the ideology of colonial domination and reputation to resistance by those excluded from wealth and power.

As Austin (1983) points out, the 'plural societies' debate about the Caribbean was partly an argument over whether these value systems should be seen as constituents of a single cultural order, or as separate cultures, or as modern and traditional sectors (M.G. Smith 1965, R.T. Smith 1967). Most anthropologists now see them as a single system, pointing out that most individuals 'code shift' between them situationally and during their life courses (Abrahams 1983).

Other authors have tried to link this dualism to gender, with women as the keepers of respectability and men the followers of reputation; the values have also been linked to colour and class divisions and to divergent class-based economic strategies of communalism and individualism. The common assumption in all these interpretations is that respectability somehow expresses an imposed, foreign (British) value system, a slavish mimicry of the old colonial elites. Conversely, reputation is cast as an indigenous response, an authentic form of local cultural production.

But explaining Caribbean cultural dualism as a global/local regime of domination and resistance simply doesn't work. If anything, Miller's work on Trinidad suggests an inversion, as the transient ritual of carnival looks outwards to the global stage of world music and mass migration, while respectability looks increasingly dowdy, stagnant and local (1990, 1994). While it may seem like this sets the stage for a dramatic change in the cultural balance, it is probably no more than a stage in a continuing cycle – for historically both reputation and respectability have always drawn on foreign sources for key symbols and goods that bolster their legitimacy.

My surveys in Belize followed Bourdieu in tracing the relationships between economic power, inherited cultural capital and that acquired through education.[6] But the stable cycles of accumulation of cultural capital in a coherent class hierarchy, which Bourdieu finds in France, do not exist in Belize. Tastes and preferences are very weakly related to educational levels, wealth or class background. Travel abroad, short-term migration and having family members abroad were much more highly correlated with tastes and preferences. This is similar to the situation Appiah describes in post-colonial Africa, where the European hierarchy of high and low culture is replaced by a ranking of the degree of access to Western cultural capital (1992: 148).

At one time, when foreign travel was much more restricted, it may have been that only the cultural elite in Belize had *direct* access to foreign goods. The elite effectively controlled the diffusion of high culture through their grip on the media, churches and schools (Wilk 1994). Today, however, foreign goods and tastes enter from many directions at all levels of the economic pyramid. They do not just enter at the top through the elite, to percolate downwards. Uzi machine guns and LA gang colours appear in Belize city these days, just as Harlem fashions, Garveyism and Jazz appeared 60 years ago.[7]

Reputation can be gained through sexuality and fertility, by mastery of local gossip and verbal performance, but also with the latest New York hip hop, untied pump basketball shoes and a 'dread' belt. Acquiring respectability can entail visible public service or a church marriage into a light-skinned family, but may also involve an American college diploma, an imported pure-bred Alsatian or a passion for wildlife conservation and birdwatching.

What integrates the constant flow of imports and permits something Belizean to continue to emerge? Surely it is not the meanings or valences of the objects themselves; I have seen dreadlocks change from a generally recognised symptom of the lowest outcast street-life, to an emblem of the educated and politically conscious pan-Caribbean, and then into a sign of middle-class teenage rebellion, all in less than five years. The coherence lies in the circuits, in the connections forged not by common agreement, but by a common system for communicating difference, a shared political and moral contest, in which all Belizeans take part (elsewhere I have likened this to a common *drama* (Wilk 1991)). A central problem of interpreting the role of imported and local goods in this drama is confusing contest (agreement on the terms of conflict, on what is at stake) with consensus (agreement on substance, on what goods mean). Belizeans themselves rarely make this mistake – they are quite aware that goods and styles are deployed strategically, and that public display is a persuasive assertion, not a fact (and there are pertinent local proverbs that make this point).

I now want to move on to suggest some ways in which the arena of cultural contest in Belize is undergoing structural change. Until the last decade Belize could be seen as a relatively stable arena; while goods, language, fashion and capital flowed in and out quite freely, they were effectively naturalised and localised in the context of structures of common difference, of which the drama of respectability and reputation is only one. The props, sets and costumes changed, but the players and the dramatic themes did not. What is happening now, however, is that the boundaries that previously defined the local Belizean stage are breaking down. The Belizean arena is losing its autonomy, as it is incorporated into *global* structures of common difference.

GLOBAL STRUCTURES OF COMMON DIFFERENCE

In several important papers, Jonathan Friedman has discussed a variety of ways that local cultural systems have interacted with hegemonic Western modernism in a 'global arena of potential identity formation' (1992: 837). He equates hegemony and homogeneity, and sees the recent increase in the number and vitality of local cultural phenomena as a product of the breakdown of that pervasively powerful modernism. The master narrative is passing, and so are the subaltern dialogues with which it was engaged.

I would argue, instead, that the nature of cultural hegemony may be changing, but it is hardly disappearing, and the consequence is not de-homogenisation or global fragmentation. The new global cultural system *promotes difference* instead of suppressing it, but difference of a particular kind. Its hegemony is not of content, but of form. Global structures organise diversity, rather than replicating uniformity (to paraphrase Hannerz 1990 and Appadurai 1990). Another way to say this is that while different cultures continue to be quite distinct and varied, they are becoming different in very uniform ways. The *dimensions* across which they vary are becoming more limited, and therefore more mutually intelligible. In this way the societies competing for global economic and cultural dominance build their hegemony not through direct imposition, but by presenting universal categories and standards by which all cultural differences can be defined.[8]

In other words, we are not all becoming the same, but we are portraying, dramatising and communicating our differences to each other in ways that are more widely intelligible. The globalising hegemony is to be found in *structures of common difference*, which celebrate particular kinds of diversity while submerging, deflating or suppressing others. The global system is a common code, but its purpose is not common identification; it is the expression of distinctions, boundaries and disjunctures. The 'local', 'ethnic' and the 'national' cannot therefore be seen as opposed to or resisting global culture, but instead, insofar as they can be domesticated and categorised, they are essential constitutive *parts* of global culture. As Fusco (1990) points out, recent intellectual discourse about 'the other' functions inside this system, rather than constituting an external critique.

I want to emphasise that my argument for the expression of locality through a system of common difference is not an attack on the *authenticity* of those differences. The typical postmodern critique of commoditisation of culture on the global stage argues that all local cultures are becoming equally inauthentic, distanced and incoherent, as images become disconnected from experience (see Featherstone 1991: 122–8). In sharp contrast, I see a world where very real and 'authentic' differences in experience and culture continue to exist, but are being expressed and communicated in a limited and narrow range of images, channels and contests. Furthermore, people have very good reasons to want to express themselves in this way.

Structures of common difference are built through processes of commoditisation and objectification that do produce an appearance of artificiality and homogeneity. They are especially powerful because they often act directly on the human body, promoting particular kinds of uniformity and regimentation. But people still infuse commodities, goods and their own refashioned bodies with meaning grounded in local practice, to their own ends, and the result cannot be pushed to extremes of global hegemony and/or arbitrary artificiality. Let me provide two examples, one from the United States and the other from Belize.

Just before last Christmas, while visiting relatives in New Mexico, my wife and I stayed up late watching cable television, which we do not have at home, but remember fondly from our last stay in Belize. Long after midnight we strayed onto ESPN, the sports channel, and to our surprise encountered the final events of the American Double-Dutch League Jump-Rope Championships, for fourth grade through high school.

What we had thought to be a simple recreation, as the unregulated fun of kids at play, was presented with all the features of a professionalised contest – the moves were named and standardised, along with a precision scoring system based on 'how well you execute your tricks and how difficult they are'. The performances were divided into required compulsory patterns, and 'free style' expressive and artistic performances, graded separately. There were corporate sponsors, a panel of judges, computerised scores flashed on the screen following slow-motion replays, and truly dazzling, well-practised performances by teams of young people in matching costumes and expensive brand-name sportswear.

The jump-rope contests organise both time and space – there is a hierarchy of regional competitions from local through state, regional and nationals, an annual season starting in the spring, and a sense of continuity as 'old championship teams come back year after year', and players become coaches. The events classify performers by age grades – all team members had to be in a narrow range, and they could only compete within that category. At the same time, other kinds of distinctions were deliberately muted; boys and girls could be on the same team together though most competitors were girls. There was no explicit mention of race or ethnicity, though all the teams but one were all-black or all-white, and there was a powerful sub-text of rich white suburbs pitted against the inner city. The teams were surrounded by adult coaches, clearly family members and friends, tied together in local networks in which they invest tremendous energy and large sums of money for little material reward.

We heard interviews with the winners and coaches after each competition; they spoke of the way the sport uplifted and disciplined performers, 'developing self-respect' and giving the kids a chance for travel and experience. But besides becoming cosmopolitans, they developed a sense of local pride: 'Seein' ourselves last year on TV was real important, especially comin' from a small town like we do.'

I have to say, I am not much of a sports fan, but I found this program riveting. Before a tiny late-night insomniac audience, I found the cutting edge of global commodity culture, and a model for what I have been seeing and experiencing over my twenty years of visiting Belize. The National Double-Dutch League of Washington DC, with the willing complicity of competitors, is professionalising jump rope as a public performance, taking a lived, contextualised tradition of play and turning it into a commodity. The contest formalises a particular set of distinctions and places them in the foreground, while moving others into the background. It reifies and emphasises particular kinds of hierarchy based on time and geopolitical space, and it groups people according to some kinds of physical biological characteristics, but not others. The competition is exactly what Bourdieu speaks of in *Distinction* as a system that 'classifies and classifies the classifier'.

Since watching the rope-jumpers, I've noted other similar events, from professional ballroom dancing on American public television at prime time, to the national mixed doubles free-style canoe championships, covered in *Paddler* magazine. In the United States almost every town, county and state fair and festival features local folk practices like baking, hollering, lying and calling animals that have been transformed and elevated into competitive aesthetic performance.[9] But the pattern also extends to the competitions I have been studying in Belize, where beauty pageants have recently become the most popular public events.

BEAUTY PAGEANTS IN BELIZE

In the 1930s and 1940s the 'variety show' was a popular entertainment in Belize, with singing, dancing, monologues, skits and comedy from local amateurs and visiting professionals. This was a middle- and working-class entertainment, distinct from the sacred and classical concerts, poetry recitals and Shakespearean dramas staged by the elite to 'enlighten' the populace. Beauty pageants took on the format of the variety show, but also blended elements of the street display of the annual September festivities, which are the local equivalent of the *carnival* celebrated elsewhere in the Caribbean. The pageant also amalgamated some elements of the poetry, essay and cooking contests promoted by schools and churches throughout the 1920s and 1930s. Pageants therefore blended elements of rituals of respectability and reputation, of high and street cultures, though there was no question that respectability remained dominant. A sexual gaze is focused on the bodies of young women in a way that speaks directly to the values of reputation, but the stage performance stresses talents, education, patriotism and other respectable values.[10]

The emergence of beauty pageants as a popular entertainment has deep roots in local politics, particularly the local responses to the economic stagnation of the British Empire in the late 1930s and 1940s. When nationalist, labour-union, populist and anti-British movements began to grow, members of the urban middle class, who dominated the civil service, reacted by forming the 'Loyal and Patriotic Order of the Baymen' (LPOB) in 1945. Organised by neighbourhoods into 'lodges' modelled on existing fraternal and Masonic organizations, the LPOB's main public activity revolved around the annual celebration of the battle of St George's Cay on 10 September. While the nationalists and trade unionists argued that the British were dominating and exploiting the country, the LPOB stressed their pride in being British subjects. The battle of St George's Cay dramatised the unity of British Hondurans with the British, for this heavily mythologised eighteenth-century event was supposedly a time when Baymen (as the local white inhabitants were then known), slaves and British troops stood 'shoulder to shoulder' to drive back a Spanish fleet. The Baymen were eulogised for their 'Deeds that won an Empire' (*Clarion*, 7 September 1945). Reams of patriotic songs and poems were composed and performed, and schoolchildren competed in a 'Bayman Quiz' and in writing patriotic essays.

The Queen of the Bay was added to the celebration in 1946 at the instigation of several older women in the LPOB. They conceived of the contest as something which would bring the lodges together, and add respectability and a reminder of royal leadership to the celebrations. One of the organisers told me the goal was to 'bring up' (give status to) the celebration; she kept careful track of the girls' family backgrounds and personal characters and made sure they had no babies: 'We were looking for a real queen.' A contemporary contestant looking back said: 'The black colonials acted like she was the real Queen Elizabeth, they wanted someone who would be like royalty as part of their celebrations.' So there was an explicit goal of emulation in the origin of the pageant, but there was also a specific and local context in which the mimicry was embedded.

Each lodge selected a candidate at a meeting of its membership. A week before the celebrations, the pageant was held as part of a dance to an orchestra. The girls would march on stage to patriotic music. One organiser told me that the contest was judged 'not much for beauty, light skin or curly hair, it was just for dignity'. Three judges would ask them questions about colonial history and the battle, and they would recite patriotic verse. 'It was to try to enlighten them. The queen must be dignified! The answer would have to be intelligent. Not like today with bath suit!' Nevertheless, the first queen of the Bay *was* white skinned with straight hair.

The winner of the pageant then became the centrepiece of the parade on 10 September, riding on a float, surrounded by her ladies-in-waiting. Each lodge, and many social clubs (including the 'Queen Elizabeth Club') decorated a float on an historic or patriotic 'empire' theme, and the floats were judged. The queen was expected to give a patriotic speech at Memorial Park, but after the pageant she took her modest prize and went back to private life (with considerably enhanced prestige). After the festivities there was revelry and public drinking, though the event remains a pale reflection of the bacchanalian carnival celebrated elsewhere in the British Caribbean (Miller 1990).

The LPOB strategy was to fight the *political* issue of independence and self-government, within the *cultural* arena of respectability, education and 'taste'. Their strategy equated the foreign with the upper-class British and thereby with respectability; the local could not be a source of culture in these terms. For some participants there was an underlying and unspoken goal of continuing the privileged position of a small, educated middle class in a stagnant and marginal local economy. But for many the issue was one of 'uplifting' the masses with a respectable spectacle.

The need for public affirmation of respectability grew from the increasing popularity of the populist and anti-British 'People's Committee', which held unruly mass street demonstrations in favour of independence and against West Indian union and the devaluation of the Belize dollar (Shoman 1987). Many members of the LPOB whom I spoke to about that era said that they agreed with some of the political goals of the People's Committee radicals – but they saw the group as a source of *cultural* disorder. As one respondent said 'Some of what they said about the need for democracy was sensible. But I could not forgive the way they treated the flag [Union Jack].' The supporters of the LPOB were the pillars of respectability, they owed their position to their role as cultural brokers, retailers of British metropolitan values.

The People's Committee, prevented from direct economic or political action through harsh libel and labour laws, was forced to attack the colonial order in its symbolic heart. In 1950 their supporters attended the tenth celebration, but wore the Committee's colours of blue and white instead of the Union Jack. They refused to participate in the celebration of the Battle of St George's Cay, and publicly questioned whether the battle had ever really occurred. They popularised the use of the term 'Belizean' (instead of British Honduran) and objected to the symbolic merging of the local to the British in such practices as marching under the Union Jack and singing 'God Save the King'. Early meetings of the People's Committee were held under the flag of the United States (meant to signal independence from the British) and were accompanied by singing 'God Bless America'. The political party that emerged from this movement quickly created its own flag and song, and never gave up its opposition to the celebration of the battle (Judd 1989).

The spread of beauty pageants went along with the extension of political parties into the countryside. The very first local beauty pageants in many towns and villages in 1950 sparked heated controversies, for the selection of a single local queen in public made it clear what faction was locally dominant. The newspapers were full of letters complaining that queens were selected 'undemocratically', in a secretive way, favouring candidates for their political connections rather than beauty or elegance (e.g. *Billboard*, 17 September 1950).

Therein lies one of the central themes of the public drama of the beauty pageant in Belize, one which is as strong today as it was in 1950. The

pageant encompasses the two dramas of power in the Belizean democratic system. On the one hand there is a respectable public contest of
open democracy, where there is open expression of opinions, and expert
representatives (judges) vote on contestants according to their objective
merit (judges are supposed to stand above the contest). On the other
hand there is a hidden, covert process of the exercise of power and
privilege based on wealth and personal ability, where factions scheme
and manoeuvre for advantage and influence in ways the public can only
imagine or gossip about (they often attack the putative objectivity of the
judges). Both systems of power exist in a stable relationship, and while
in rhetoric they are seen as opposed, they are in many ways dependent
on each other.

The consequence is that selecting a beauty queen always brings to the
fore existing divisions within the community; even if factions do not fight
for 'their' candidates, the public believes they do. The crowd at a pageant
always identifies candidates with factions – ethnic, local, political and
family – and acts as if the pageant is a struggle for power. An unpopular
winner faces a hostile crowd, ready to complain that the contest was
rigged, that the process was not really open or democratic. The same
people who blame the system for its corruption will turn around and in
the next breath advocate covert and corrupt tactics on behalf of their
favoured contestant! So the pageant foregrounds both the divisions
between factions in the community *and* the differences between the
respectable politics of public democracy and those of repute, private power
and influence.

Division and replication of pageants

Under the loyalist LPOB, the extension of Queen of the Bay pageants
into the countryside began to play a role in nation building. In 1946 all
of the contestants came from Belize City, but in 1949 some contestants
came from LPOB chapters in the districts, and the winner was from the
mostly Hispanic Cayo district. In 1949 most district capitals, and some
small villages elected their own queens, who served in local festivities, but
in 1950 a hierarchical structure was built. The district queens went to
Belize City for a final competition called 'The National Beauty Pageant'.
The complexities of ethnicity, class and politics were now partly submerged
under a theme of competition between districts.

The pageants were an important method of fund-raising and publicity
for the loyalists, who contested their first city council elections as the
National Party in 1950. In the same year the People's Committee became
the Peoples United Party (PUP), and the colonial governor responded to
their demonstrations by declaring a state of emergency, and eventually
jailed most of its leaders for sedition. Amidst this turmoil, as the British
rewrote the colonial constitution, with its leaders in jail, the Peoples

United Party plotted not a revolution, but a beauty pageant – 'Miss British Honduras'. The PUP committees in each district selected contestants, who were presented in local meetings that were notable more for their lack of British trappings than for the presence of anything local (American styles and popular songs were prominent). Significantly, the winner's prize was a trip to Guatemala, a strong statement of the PUP's policy of seeking closer ties with its Hispanic neighbours.[11] The National Party's Queen of the Bay went to Miami (no winner ever took the more expensive trip to England, where few Belizeans live).

This dual structure of Belizean pageantry is still very much alive. The two major political parties each conduct their own annual pageant, organised as a contest between representatives of the six districts and Belize City. The final contest is held in the city, and the winner becomes a focus of each party's separate September festivities. The content of the pageants symbolically mirrors the political programmes of the two parties. The rightist United Democratic Party (the descendant of the National Party) stresses high culture, deportment, marching, grace and 'refined beauty', accompanied by more respectable forms of European band music. The populist and now mutedly leftist PUP pageant emphasises talent, sexually nuanced speech and dancing, and ethnic culture, to the tunes of the latest popular American and Caribbean music.

Changes in national politics have affected the pageants. In 1964 the PUP changed their winner's title to 'Miss Independence'. The National Party then took control of the Queen of the Bay pageant out of the hands of the LPOB lodges and made it more overtly political. Both pageants began to accept contestants nominated by interest groups within the political parties (unions, youth groups, women's associations). And when the PUP began its long electoral dominance in the 1954 elections (they were not defeated until 1984), their party pageant became the official 'national' event, while the Queen of the Bay was often ignored by the government's publications and radio.

When an Africanist 'black power' movement, inspired by US models, began in the late 1960s, their group held a 'Miss Afro Honduras' pageant. The front page of the *Belize Times* in 1969 had pictures of Miss Independence in a miniskirt, the Queen of the Bay in a formal gown, and Miss Afro Honduras in African-style cloth. There was also an ethnic proliferation of pageantry. The Garifuna, historically discriminated against in the colony, have a long history of forming associations based on ethnicity which celebrate 'Settlement Day' each 19 November in Belize. As early as 1946 they held a coronation of the 'Queen of the Settlement', and by the 1970s had a national 'Miss Garifuna' contest with contestants from each Garifuna town and village. The Hispanic northern districts have 'Miss Panamericana' crowned on Columbus Day, who travels to Yucatan on the Mexican pageant circuit.

Pageants of an explicitly nonpolitical and non-ethnic nature have also proliferated in splendid abundance. Secondary schools, church associations and youth groups around the country hold 'popularity contests' to raise money, and their winners often enter other pageants. Industrial associations sponsor the 'Sugar Queen', 'Citrus Queen' and 'Miss Agriculture' competitions at district and national agricultural shows and fairs. The annual Easter bicycle races are graced by 'Miss Cycling'. Larger merchants and corporations sponsor contestants in most of these pageants, blending political and commercial patronage.

The most recent trend is to broaden the appeal of pageants through age segmentation. In 1985 the Minister of Youth and Culture promoted a Miss Youth pageant, which drew contestants from five other countries in the Caribbean. During 1989 there were local and national Miss Teen and Miss Preteen Belize competitions, and a variety of Ms Elegant, Ms Middle Age and Ms Maturity pageants for older women. All were staged by private promoters as money-making ventures. One organiser told me she planned a 'Miss Big and Beautiful' pageant for 'larger' women.

On one level this proliferation of pageants may appear divisive; each interest group selects its own symbol to represent separate aspirations. But while the winners differ in complexion, ethnicity, party affiliation, class, employment and region, the common format of the pageant is an underlying unifying structure. The pageants try to domesticate (in the sense of tame and control) and encapsulate the many differences between citizens within a single dramatic theme.

The international connection

The international development of pageantry in the years after World War II was a global phenomenon, which quickly took a hierarchical form (see Deford 1971). The first moves were for regional pageants; in 1947 a representative of the 'Miss Caribbean' pageant was soliciting a 'Miss British Honduras' entry (*Billboard*, 15 September 1946). The local groups did not have the money to send a contestant, however. As a poor and isolated colony, Belize was not equipped to enter the 'pageant of nations' in the immediate postwar years.

Instead the international connections that emerged were a product of the rapid upswing in migration from Belize to the United States in the early 1950s. Belizean migrants, a tiny minority within the polyglot of Caribbean immigrants in New York, Los Angeles and Chicago, began to organise national associations with an interest in politics and education back at home, tending to favour the loyalist National Party. One way they maintained their distinctiveness in the United States, *and* maintained cultural ties with the home country, was to hold concerts, dances, parades and festivities which were modelled on those of Belize. They also held beauty pageants, and the winner's prize was usually a trip back to Belize to appear in the September festivities (ironically, in Belize the winners usually got tickets to the United States!). As early as 1957 the Queen of the Bay pageant in Belize City was attended by the 'Queen of the Belize Honduran Association of New York'.

It was not until the early 1970s (when British Honduras was renamed Belize by the PUP) that Belize had the resources to send entries to the major international pageants. Both political parties, at times, have put resources into local franchises for Miss World or Miss Universe, and some of the wealthiest foreign companies involved in the Belize economy have been patrons. By 1988 Miss Belize or another local contestant were going to both pageants, as well as to regional events (La Reina del Costa, Miss Caribbean USA) and smaller global competitions like Miss All Nations and Miss Wonderland.

The professionalisation of the international pageants now requires coaches, consultants and accoutrements which are so costly that Belizean contestants find it hard to compete. Many Belizeans still remember the name of the only Miss Belize to survive into the final group of twelve in the Miss Universe pageant, in 1979. Despite these handicaps, attending the international competition is both an incentive for the local contestants and an assertion of sovereignty at the same level as other countries. The local organiser of the Miss Universe pageant said it concisely: 'To show we *can* compete with the rest of the world.' But that competition also highlights the subordinate position of Belize in a global hierarchy.

The organiser of the Miss Belize pageant in 1990 told me that when people come to her office they always look at the picture of the 110 contestants in the Miss Universe pageant, and they want to pick out Miss Belize. But they are always surprised that Miss Belize looks as good as most of the other women. They expect her to 'stand out and be ugly'.

This expectation reflects the understanding that most Belizeans have about the pageants – that they are a part of a world stage. Well over 70 per cent of Belizeans now have direct access to foreign television through cable or rebroadcast (Wilk 1992). They watch the Miss America, World, and Universe pageants, and are intimately aware of every failing of the local events in comparison. Everyone I spoke to about the pageants, even the sponsors, began the conversation by excusing the poor quality of the local shows and contestants. Everyone praised the pageants where foreign entertainers appeared, and disparaged the local talent. Global media create a withering contrast, and in their new sophistication, most Belizeans know that their pageant ranks low in the international league. The important thing, however, is that Miss Belize is there at all.

In many interviews with organisers and contestants, I heard the same explanation of why Belizean contestants cannot win an international competition. They say that Belizeans have different standards of beauty from those of the global pageants. As one organiser said,

The [international] judges like tall, thin and beautiful girls. In Belize they like girls who are shorter – here 5 feet 6 inches is tall – and stockier. To qualify for Belizean men, you must have some shape, you must have bust and hips. It's something completely different. If you choose a girl for the international competition the Belizean men will say 'E too maaga' [she's too thin]. Bones alone, not enough *flesh*. But them [foreign] judges will look at the Belizean girl and say 'E too fat'.

Part of the drama of the contest, then, is the collision between local standards of beauty, deeply embedded in cultural constructs of gender and sexuality, and international standards which are widely believed to be those of the dominant white nations of the north.

The widespread awareness of this difference is the crucial link between the local scene and the global drama. While Belizean pageants are full of local, contextualised meaning, they are performed and observed with an intimate awareness of the global gaze. Foreigners do not even have to be present to watch the local competition (though they are often included on the panel of judges), because the global standard has become an ever-present (and perhaps internalised) 'significant other' by which the local is defined and judged.

The local pageant of difference

The organisers and sponsors of the pageants see them as events that unite the nation in diversity – following the official pluralist line of the state that each ethnic group contributes something to a unique mix. As Miss Teen Belmopan 1990 put it: 'Even though we all a different race, Belize da one place.' The pageants attempt to organise and domesticate differences between Belizeans, by an appeal to objective standards of beauty and talent, and they provide a common code for the expression of differences.

Contestants often dress in fancied regional or ethnic costumes, perform 'ethnic' dances or sing 'ethnic' songs, and may themselves be considered official representatives of particular groups (though this is by no means universal). But as each pageant progresses towards the semi-finals, the ethnic themes are dropped and national unification takes over. Speeches, songs and discussion focus on Belizean culture and nationalism. In the semi-final interviews, contestants are usually asked questions about the country, and how they will represent the whole nation.

In 1990 the aspiring Miss Belize candidates were asked 'What would you as a Belizean, selling your country to tourists, tell them about Belize?' The responses mentioned the democratic government, the harmony among diverse people, and the natural environment's touristic attractions. 'Belize is rich in natural beauty and we should be proud of it.' 'Belize is peaceful and democratic.' 'Belize is truly a paradise.' 'Belize is a curious colourful mixture of cultures such as the Maya, the Mestizo, Garifuna, Creole, Lebanese and East Indians. I am proud to be part of this mixture.' These questions, and the answers they elicit, are meant to place Belize publicly in the foreigner's gaze; they project Belize outwards as a unique place, in the common descriptive terms of all the unique places that make up a global pageant.

This presentation of ethnic diversity in the context of the pageant cordons off a potentially dangerous and divisive issue by placing it in the 'safe zone' of expressive culture – music, art, dance and 'customs' (see Wilk and Chapin 1990, Wilk 1986). Ethnicity is officially sanctioned and is even supported by a government 'Director of Culture,' as long as it remains focused on self-consciously artistic performance. Safe ethnic culture is ornamental, attractive to tourists, part of an international genre of 'our nation's wonderful diversity'; it is mostly disengaged from the concerns with land, labour and rights which predominate in ethnic discourse at the community level. It almost goes without saying that such performances are recent products of cultural professionals, and have only a mimetic (or parasitic) relationship to the everyday practice of music and dance.

Recent history shows the Belizean government is unsupportive or hostile towards ethnic expressions of a political, economic or territorial nature. Ethnic organisations which assert legal rights, or which try to organise labour or economic cooperation are gently or violently repressed, or are coopted with offers of support for 'safe' projects. When the Maya in the southern districts formed an organisation to press for land rights in 1984, the government response was to offer them money and equipment for videotaping their ritual dances (Wilk and Chapin 1990). Keeping ethnic diversity a safe and nonviolent issue is certainly a laudable goal; but in the long run it does not address the underlying disparities and discrimination that feed ethnic politics. This is not to say that the safe zone of ethnic culture is superfluous or cosmetic, merely that it is a limited arena that organises political discourse into fairly narrow and common terms.

CONCLUSIONS

Beauty pageants organise and objectify many kinds of differences between Belizeans. Like the jump-rope contests they channel space and time, space into a hierarchy and time into annual cycles of competition, linked by the careers of the participants. They provide regular institutions that link small communities of competitors and supporters together into larger and larger structures reaching upwards to a global level. Like jump-rope, pageants make an appeal to objectivity in the competitive distinctions they make, through the use of judges, a scoring system, and organised displays of both innate talent and acquired skill. Like other competitions, they classify the participants by essentialised biological characteristics, especially gender and age. And also like the rope jumpers, they publicly justify pageantry as educational and uplifting for the contestants, a chance for them to become cosmopolitan, gain poise and begin careers.

There are other common characteristics to the cultural forms of these competitions, both in Belize and elsewhere. While their ostensible purpose is to bring people together as equals, they inevitably dramatise particular kinds of difference, often in ways that the organisers do not intend. This is because they derive some of their power from the tension between foreground and background, from the audience's knowledge that the public performance is only a part of the story, and that there is a world 'behind the scenes' where the competition is anything but objective and fair (cf. Cohen 1991). Like other global competitions, beauty pageantry is hierarchical; it moves upwards towards standards that are defined at the centre, not the periphery. On the global stage the fact remains that most winners of national pageants who will go on to international competition are indeed light skinned and tall – they appear to conform more to the New York standard of beauty than that of Belize City. Can we see this as another form of colonialism, as the percolation downwards of a more powerful and superordinate set of standards and ideals, the cutting edge of cultural hegemony? Will this pressure, in the long term, lead Belizeans to change their own ideas and values and accept the subordination of their local standards to the global and foreign?[12]

But Belizeans have been under exactly the same kind of pressure for hundreds of years; their whole conception of the local has emerged, first under slavery, then in stark class stratification, in the context of a superordinate global empire. For 350 years the people of Belize have been confronted with standards of beauty and value that purport to be superior. These standards *have* percolated downwards and all Belizeans are aware of them – they believe that light skin and straight hair are prettier, and they often disparage each other as 'black pots' and 'bushy'. But this does not mean that other conceptions of beauty do not flourish as well, that a person cannot be both ugly by one standard and beautiful by another at the same time, to the same person. Many Belizean men and women say that a woman with a full head of brightly coloured hair curlers is sexy and attractive – an aesthetic that certainly does not come from American television. Many other examples abound, and these are not vestiges of some isolated past system, the remnants of an earlier autonomous aesthetic. They have grown and developed in concert with, in close relationship to the externalised, powerful and global white images in newspaper advertisements, bibles, television shows and children's dolls (cf. Lundgren 1988).

A key point here is not that the pageants and competitions eliminate differences between the local and the global. They are not hegemonic tools that create homogeneity. All they do is provide a common channel and a point of focus for the debate and expression of differences. They take the full universe of possible contrasts between nations, groups, locales, factions, families, political parties and economic classes, and they systematically narrow our gaze to *particular kinds* of difference. They organise and focus debate, and in the process of foregrounding particular kinds of difference, they submerge and obscure others by pushing them into the background. They standardise a vocabulary for describing difference, and provide a syntax for its expression, to produce a common frame of organised distinction, in the process making wildly disparate groups of people intelligible to each other. They essentialise some kinds of differences as ethnic, physical and immutable, and portray them as measurable and scalable characteristics, washing them with the legitimacy of objectivity. And they use these distinctions to draw systemic connections between disparate parts of the world system.

I would argue that in accomplishing these tasks, competitions serve political and polemic purposes for many different and contending interests. They are not hegemonic in the sense that they allow one group to simply extend and exercise its power over others. They never manage to purvey true 'false consciousness' and conceal underlying differences in power and resources. (Belizeans remain quite aware that their country is tiny, poor and dominated.) The competitions are hegemonic only in the way they involve disparate groups in a common contest, and thereby limit their ranges of possible action.

And a place like Belize has *never* had very much range for autonomous action; not under British colonialism and not under Cold War discipline. But the growth of a global order of communication and of systems of common difference forces us to think about autonomy and dependency in very different ways. The same processes that destroy autonomy are now creating new sorts of communities, new kinds of locality and identity. The kinds of hierarchical, linked structures that I describe in this paper create communities of fans and contestants that are very real, and are no more imaginary than the lineages and tribes that anthropologists have traditionally studied.

ACKNOWLEDGEMENTS

An earlier draft of this paper was read at the meetings of the International Studies Association in Acapulco, Mexico, 23–7 March, 1993. I appreciate comments by Janet Abu-Lughod, Joel Kahn and Jonathan Friedman on that draft; I am also indebted to James Carrier, Anne Pyburn and Danny Miller for thorough critiques which have helped me in the present revision. This is a slightly amended version of the paper circulated in advance of the ASA decennial meetings.

NOTES

1. The question of how much would be Latin has continued to be controversial and politically charged, especially in recent years as immigration and emigration have made the once-dominant Creoles into a numerical minority.
2. Following Friedman's recent discussion of Ainu and Hawaiian identities (1990), we have to be careful not to portray this new Belizean culture as a kind of inauthentic pretence. It demonstrates instead that identity requires a significant 'other' (Friedman 1990: 321), in this case provided mostly by the United States, and that it emerges in particular historical forms and circumstances.
3. See Munn (1986) for a discussion of the ways foreign goods were essential in the production and maintenance of local distinctions in smaller-scale 'traditional' societies.
4. After writing this I found a parallel passage in an unpublished manuscript by Jonathan Friedman (n.d.). He notes that the nationalisation of culture proceeds through objectifying culture as concrete things, and advocates a re-emphasis of the anthropological concept of culture as practice as an antidote.
5. Austin (1983) points out, in a perceptive review of Caribbean ethnography, a number of reasons why foreign domination and local resistance are inadequate terms for the historical analysis of cultural complexity in this region.
6. The survey, conducted in 1990, included 389 interviews in Belize City, a smaller city and a large rural settlement.
7. There *has* always been a tendency for respectable culture in Belize to be drawn from British sources, while reputation has used American expressions. Here the local cultural dualism has a further global aspect.
8. These are not just categories for defining cultures and groups through censuses, maps, etc. They include economic categories of unemployment, GNP, standards of living and the like, which define and shape policy in a wide variety of political arenas.
9. I am indebted to James Carrier for pointing out the example of fairs and festivals.
10. The crowds who attend Belizean pageants (both men and women in about equal proportions) judge the contestants on a variety of counts. They tend to appreciate women who 'have spirit' – who are outgoing, well spoken and engage the crowd in some direct way. Women focus on the contestants' costume, grooming and manners, on how current their fashion and where it was obtained, while men's comments revolve around the women's reputations and performances as well as their physiques. As at many of the Caribbean public performances described by Abrahams (1983), when the stage projects respectability, the audience subverts and challenges their message. The crowd delights in gossip about contestants already being pregnant, having highly-placed lovers or sponsors who expect more than a good stage performance.
11. The PUP sought an alliance of working-class Creoles with Hispanics, but were constantly accused by the Nationalist Party of 'trying to turn Belize into a Hispanic republic'. One frequent charge against the PUP leader, George Price, repeated to this day, was that he sought to 'sell out' the country with a secret plan to become part of Guatemala.
12. It is clear that one of the things that makes beauty pageants so attractive to Belizean audiences is the way they allow a familiar play of reputation and respectability, of the overt and covert, of political power and faction. Does this mean that the foreign form has simply been localised and appropriated into long-standing patterns? I think not; it may have started as a relatively simple tool of local political conflict, but in the long run it has played a role in transforming the local scene (I do not mean to imply that it is the only, or even the major source of such transformations (see Wilk 1993)).

REFERENCES

Appadurai, A. (1990) 'Disjuncture and Difference in the Global Cultural Economy', *Theory, Culture and Society* 7: 295–310.

Abrahams, R. (1983) *The Man-of-Words in the West Indies*, Baltimore: Johns Hopkins University Press.

Appiah, Kwame (1992) *In My Father's House*, New York: Oxford University Press.

Austin, D. (1983) 'Culture and Ideology in the English-Speaking Caribbean: A View from Jamaica', *American Ethnologist* 10(2): 223–40.

Banner, L. (1983) *American Beauty*, Chicago, IL: University of Chicago Press.

Bourdieu, P. (1984) *Distinction: A Social Critique of the Judgment of Taste*, Cambridge, MA: Harvard University Press.

Cohen, C. (1991) 'Queen Contestants in a Contested Domain: Staging National Identity in the Post-Colonial Caribbean', Paper presented at the 90th annual meeting of the American Anthropological Association, Chicago.

Deford, F. (1971) *There She Is: The Life and Times of Miss America*, New York: Viking.

Douglas, M. and Isherwood, B. (1981) *The World of Goods*, New York: Basic Books.

Featherstone, M. (1991) *Consumer Culture and Postmodernism*, London: Sage Publications.

Friedman, J. (1990) 'Being in the World: Globalization and Localization', *Theory, Culture and Society* 7: 311–28.

—— (1992) 'The Past in the Future: History and the Politics of Identity', *American Anthropologist* 94(4): 837–59.

—— (n.d.) 'Global System, Globalization and the Parameters of Modernity', unpublished MS in possession of the author.

Fusco, C. (1990) 'Managing the Other (A Gestao do Outro)', *Lusitania* 1 (3): 77–83.

Hannerz, U. (1990) 'Cosmopolitans and Locals in World Culture', *Theory, Culture and Society* 7: 237–51.

Kuisel, R. (1993) *Seducing the French: The Dilemma of Americanization*, Berkeley, CA: University of California Press.

Judd, K. (1989) 'Who Will Define Us? Creole History and Identity in Belize', Paper presented at the Annual Meeting of the American Anthropological Association, Washington, DC.

Liebes, T. and Katz, E. (1990) *The Export of Meaning: Cross-cultural Readings of Dallas*, New York: Oxford University Press.

Lundgren, N. (1988) 'When I Grow Up I Want a TransAm: Children in Belize Talk about Themselves and the Impact of the World Capitalist System', *Dialectical Anthropology* 13: 269–76.

Manning, F. (1990) 'Celebrating Cricket: The Symbolic Construction of Caribbean Politics', in F. Manning and J. Philibert (eds) *Customs in Conflict*, Peterborough, Ontario: Broadview.

Miller, D. (1990) 'Fashion and Ontology in Trinidad', *Culture and History* 7: 49–78.

—— (1993) 'Christmas against Materialism in Trinidad', in D. Miller (ed.) *Unwrapping Christmas*, Oxford: Oxford University Press.

—— (1994) *Modernity: An Ethnographic Approach*, Oxford: Berg Publishers.

Munn, N. (1986) *The Fame of Gawa: A Symbolic Study of Value Transformation in a Massim (Papua New Guinea) Society*, Durham: Duke University Press.

Olwig, K.F. (1993) *Global Culture, Island Identity*, Chur, Switzerland: Harwood.

Pyde, P. (1990) 'Gender and Crab Antics in Tobago: Using Wilson's Reputation and Respectability', Paper presented at the annual meeting of the American Anthropological Association, New Orleans.

Shoman, A. (1987) *Party Politics in Belize, 1950–1986*, Benque Viejo, Belize: Cubola Press.

Smith, M.G. (1965) *The Plural Society in the British West Indies*, Berkeley: University of California Press.

Smith, R.T. (1967) 'Social Stratification, Cultural Pluralism and Integration in West Indian Societies', in S. Lewis and T.G. Mathews (eds) *Caribbean Integration: Papers on Social, Political and Economic Integration*, Rio Piedras: Institute of Caribbean Studies.

Tobin, J. (ed.) (1992) *Re-made in Japan: Everyday Life and Consumer Taste in a Changing Society*, New Haven: Yale University Press.

Wilk, R. (1986) 'Mayan Ethnicity in Belize', *Cultural Survival Quarterly* 10(2): 73–8.

—— (1990) 'Consumer Goods as Dialogue about Development: Research in Progress in Belize', *Culture and History* 7: 79–100.

—— (1991) 'Consumer Goods, Cultural Imperialism and Underdevelopment in Belize', in Third Annual Studies On Belize Conference, *Spear Report* No. 6, Belize City.

—— (1992) 'I Would be Proud to be a Belizean – If I Could Figure out what a Belizean Is', Paper presented at conference 'Defining the National', Lund, April 1992.

—— (1993) '"It's Destroying a Whole Generation": Television and Moral Discourse in Belize', *Visual Anthropology* 5: 229–44.

—— (1994) 'Colonial Time and TV Time', *Visual Anthropology Review* 10(1): 94–102.

Wilk, R. and Chapin, M. (1990) *Ethnic Minorities in Belize: Mopan, Kekchi and Garifuna*, Monograph No. 1, Society for the Promotion of Education and Research, Belize City.

Wilson, P. (1973) *Crab Antics*, New Haven: Yale University Press.

7 Global complexity and the simplicity of everyday life

Kajsa Ekholm-Friedman and Jonathan Friedman

INTRODUCTION

In the literature on modern society, on world systems, on contemporary culture, the term complexity often appears. We confess that we think this term lacking in significant content, especially for the understanding of the contemporary world, as it is founded on a superficial and quite ideological dichotomisation between the assumed face-to-face simplicity of traditional society versus the extensive division of labour, the market and social differentiation of modern societies. We have no intention of entering into a discussion of a word that is best left to common usage. Instead we shall relate it to the context which we find relevant for this analysis. In cultural terms, global systems are obviously complex. In such systems the local is produced in an articulation with broader processes. The local is encompasscd and consituted within the global, which is not to say that it is a mere product of external forces. On the contrary, we have insisted on the articulation between the local and global as central to the generation of specific social realites.

The question of complexity, on the other hand, is more closely related to perspective itself. A position based on social distance, the bird's-eye view of the cosmopolitan, especially the cosmopolitan self-identified as culture expert. This complexity is part of the experience of the traveller encountering a myriad of cultural differences jumbled together with ketchup, McDonalds and MTV displays. The natives in this very naive view are not what they used to be, and there is a tendency to think of them as Baudrillardian simulacra, hybrids, moderns toying with the ideas of their identities. But this is indeed the self-identity of the cosmopolitan culture critic, and not of those whom he observes. We shall be arguing that while all social systems are complex, everyday life tends to reduce this complexity to schemes of meaning and action that are significantly simplified. The complexity to which we shall be referring is not a cultural complexity except for the external observer. The global perspective embraced here is simply an awareness of that larger set of reproductive processes within which local social fields are encompassed and maintained. Global systems are, in their very nature, historical, in the minimal sense that they are processes of social reproduction, i.e. temporally defined. The analysis of such systems consists of the study of the degree to which and the way in which local structures are constituted in and by global relations.

Global processes encompass much more than what is referred to as cultural process. They are directly involved in the production of the social frames within which culture is constituted. Thus, the appearance of the nation-state, individualist ideology and experience, the novel, evolutionary thought, are all linked to the processes that transformed Western Europe into a hegemonic centre in an emergent world system. Such processes do not preclude the existence of local strategies but merely define the framework, the context, in which they develop.

Until quite recently, African cloth was made primarily in Holland and Germany. The production was targeted to specific regions and 'tribes', i.e. based on specific patterns, and the cloth was not for sale in Europe. The production of local difference on a global scale is proof of a global relation in production and consumption. Now, for the cosmopolitan culture expert, this may become a matter of some amusement – the innocent tourist who buys genuine African cloth in the local market and returns home to find 'made in Holland' printed into the edge – and one might go on to surmise that the local African culture had become hybrid or Europeanised, on this basis. This is not, of course, the globalisation of culture, but global control over local consumption via product differentiation. However, the appropriation of the cloth and its uses is not deducible from this fact. In other words the global circulation of products is not equivalent to the globalisation of meaning, except, perhaps, for the global observer who ascribes meaning in global terms.

In several previous publications we have discussed a phenomenon called *la sape*, whereby young men from the Congo and Zaïre, usually from more impoverished urban areas, systematically accumulate designer clothing, moving up the ranks of finery until moving to Paris, *l'aventure*, in order to engage in becoming *un grand*. The emergence of a kind of cult group surrounding this process is well documented, with clearly defined age classes and competitive cat-walking, organised by returning to Brazzaville, centre in the periphery, sewing the accumulated labels into a single jacket and performing *la danse des griffes* at the local *sape* club. Now in one sense this process is about globalisation, the globalisation of people, or garments, a veritable traffic in people and goods, sometimes including drugs and often resulting in the re-import of low-end jeans and t-shirts to be sold in the African markets. What is not occurring, however, is a mixture of culture, not unless the notion is confined to the museological definition of ethnographic objects. A lumpenproletarian Congolese who flaunts his Versace suit and Westin crocodile shoes is not, in my view, a Westernised African, nor is he something 'betwixt and between'. This is because he is engaged in a specific practice of accumulation of 'life-force' that assimilates the Western good to an expression of a process that is entirely African. The Western is encompassed by the practice of *la sape*. The clothes are contained within a different project, and the properties of the clothes do not alter those of the project. The content does not shape the container. On the other hand, his entire project, as a social practice, is in its turn encompassed by the larger global processes upon which it is, in its global specificity, entirely dependent.

Thus, instead of falling back on a model of complex cultural flows or other similar metaphors, we think it better to conceive of such global cultural processes in terms of positioned practices such as assimilation, encompassment and integration in the context of social interaction. This is a relation between container and contained in the sense of the variable forms of incorporation of the products of a global field of interaction into the practice of local strategies, and the relation of these processes to the practice of identification, i.e. of meaning attribution. The global processes of commercial world systems contain three very broad levels of integration:

1 The assimilation of the global to local systems of practice (social reproduction)
2 The integration of the local into the reproductive cycles of the global
3 The interaction of identification processes
   (a) global identifications of the local as part of the self-identity of the centre
   (b) local self-identity
      (i) via the mirror of power, i.e. the assimilation of the gaze of the other, the localisation of global categories
      (ii) via the elaboration of local and historicised representations
   (c) the practice of authority, i.e. the institutionalisation of identity.

In the Congolese case the strategy of appropriation of the world is strongly other-directed and consists in the identification of the foreign as life-force to be appropriated, as the definition of well-being, power, wealth and health. This is a practice of dependency that defines social selfhood as part of a larger whole whose source of power is external to the local society. The Hawaiians discussed below practice precisely the opposite form of selfhood, one that builds a blockade to the outside world and that transforms all those people and things that enter into the local. In both cases, we have an assimilation of the global to local systems of practice, but the forms of identification are respectively exo-social and endo-social. In either case, what may appear as complex from the outside is integrated into a life-strategy that is considerably simpler.

In the following discussion, we shall attempt to concretise the way in which the Hawaiian village of Miloli'i is at once engaged or, perhaps, entangled in the larger world system in terms of material transactions which are, of course, social, while at the same time it is driven by a strategy of self-preservation, self-isolation, what we refer to below as endo-sociality.

As this is a rather descriptive discussion we might detail the course of the argument in advance. The first section describes the historical processes involved in the formation of the modern village. It concerns the way in which the village has become increasingly isolated as an economic unit from a former regional economy and reintegrated into the larger economy of the islands, and the simultaneously increasing force of attraction of the village as a refuge for Hawaiians. This is followed by three aspects of contemporary village life: first, a concentric presentation of social relations from the village itself to the relation to tourism; second the representation of the village in the media and the Hawaiian movement, detailing the symbolic significance of the village, and the way the former affects village self-identity; finally, the physical context of the village as a central place on the sparsely populated coastal plain. This is followed by a discussion of the relation between the complexity of the place when seen from the outside and the simplicity of everyday life seen from the inside.

The case studies exemplify the argument that the relations between the village and external forces are changing due to changing global relations and their expressions in a declining modernism and an expansive cultural identity among Hawaiians. Miloli'i has gained from this change but it may be changing from this gain.

A SMALL VILLAGE IN A BIG SYSTEM

Miloli'i is a small village of less than 200 inhabitants in the South Kona district of the island of Hawaii. It is one of perhaps two well-known villages in the state, known for their continuity with the Hawaiian past, a continuity of settlement that is rare in the islands, where the Hawaiian population was more or less ousted from its lands from the middle of the nineteenth century until the struggles of the 1970s.

The Kona coast of Hawaii is well known for its beauty and its perfect weather. Even the Hawaiian nobility gathered there for sport and leisure in the late pre-European period. Miloli'i is located today in an area that is far to the south of the more lucrative tourist areas. Travelling down the coast from Kailua, once the capital of the islands, now a wealthy tourist centre, one passes a string of small towns overlooking the Pacific until coming to Captain Cook, and then Honaunau, after which it is said one enters Hawaiian territory. Until recently, there was a sudden decline in housing density after this point, as well as a decline in basic infrastructure, electricity and then water. The 1980s expansion led to the beginnings of real-estate speculation in this area as well, but the 1990s have put a stop to that.

From Honaunau to the southern tip of the island, the percentage of Hawaiians increases significantly, mostly because the percentage of other peoples declines. Here is the famous Kona coffee district on the slopes,

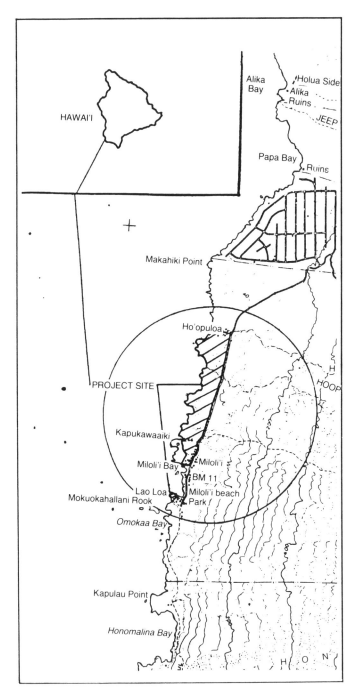

Figure 7.1 Milol'i on the southwest coast of the island of Hawaii, showing the subdivision to the north adjacent to Papa Bay

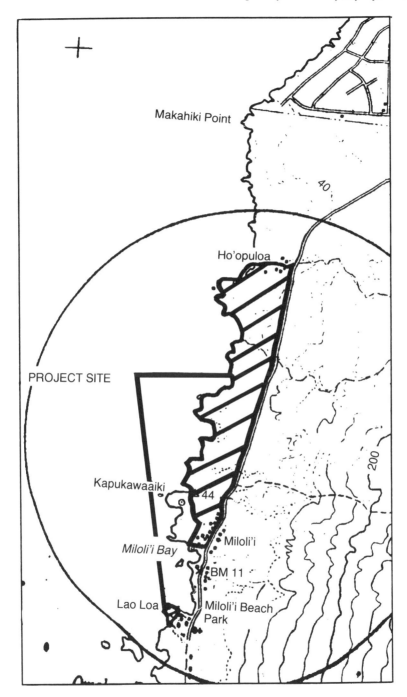

Figure 7.2 Closer view of Milol'i, showing the previous squatter area for 1926 refugees from the lava innundated village of Ho'opuloa

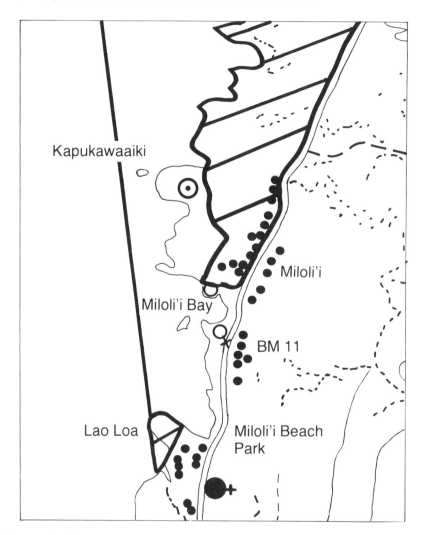

Figure 7.3 Close up of Miloli'i village, showing distribution of dwellings and two old churches (Catholic and Protestant), one in old Ho'opuloa refugee area and one in the original village of Miloli'i

fruit trees and, as one moves south, the great macadamia-nut plantations and some of the most advanced marijuana growing in the world. The further one goes up the slopes the more booby traps, pit bulls and automatic weapons one is likely to run into (literally). The marijuana industry is unofficially the largest industry in the state, producing an income of upwards of $10 billion compared to the $9 billion in the tourist industry. Large syndicates are involved, but the original growing base consists of hardened middle-aged hippies who were often on their way to India in the 1960s and settled down in Hawaii where almost everything was free. Here, over the border from Kona in the southern district of Ka'u, is the community of Ocean View, a vast lava slope where lots can be bought relatively cheaply, where infrastructure is minimal by white Hawaiian standards, and where a large part of the population consists of ordinary pensioners who can't afford the more lucrative localities in paradise.

Driving along the highway one can peer out over the Pacific. Along the coast there were once a great many fishing villages. Today only Miloli'i remains, although there is a tendency for certain villages to become repopulated. Miloli'i is located 5 miles and 1,300 feet down from the highway. From a distance it appears as an oasis settled at the end of a desert of lava flows. Until very recently it possessed neither electricity nor running water. Next to the village is a famous development scam from the 1970s, a number of lots totally without infrastructure set out on a lava plain where rain is practically unknown. Some wealthy restaurateurs, builders and mainlanders have built large houses on these sites, but there are others who camp out on their own lava lawns. The total lack of vegetation here is quite awesome, compared to the relatively luxuriant fishing village next door.

FRAGMENTS OF AN ARTICULATION

Miloli'i, as other fishing villages, was part of a larger political unit called an *ahupua'a* stretching from the upper slopes to the sea. As an economic unit the *ahupua'a* was essentially self-sufficient in terms of subsistence. The entire island was divided vertically into smaller or larger pie-shaped slices which were organised into political units of the chiefdom structure. Throughout the second half of the nineteenth century, after the introduction of private property, the vertical structures tended to become divided into horizontal strips. An ecology based on self-sufficient access to the products of a wide range of zones, from mountain to sea, was transformed into a privately owned horizontal specialist economy of ranches and plantations. This all occurred in a period of severe depopulation, and a massive importation of foreign plantation labour. Miloli'i as a fishing village was known at the end of the last century as a producer of *olona*, a strong water-resistant twine used for making fish nets and rope. Later on in the twentieth century it became famous for its dried sea mackerel, *opelu*. Once a month a sampan or even larger boat would come to Miloli'i and exchange rice, flour, salt and other necessities for dried *opelu*. There was a pier in Miloli'i Bay where the ship landed and which is still used today. Contact with the outside world in this period was via shipping and, to a lesser extent, overland. There was trade between the fishermen and dry- and even wetland taro growers from the upper slopes and from the north, as far as the illustriously fertile Waipio valley. Many of the inhabitants of the village however, had other residences in the uplands and moved between the upland and seaside zones on a seasonal basis, thus practising the essentials of the former *ahupua'a* economy. The neighbouring *ahupua'a* of Ho'opuloa was intact until 1926. In that year the fishing village with that name – neighbour, that is, to Miloli'i – was destroyed by a lava flow. Most of the families from there became squatters on land just above Miloli'i itself, part of the Ho'opuloa *ahupua'a* but without its own port and physically an extenstion of Miloli'i. The territorial government 'set aside' this land as refugee land, but never gave the residents legal access. They were, in legal terms, squatters until 1982. Much of the upland above the former village was taken over by the major land companies and ranches, either by trickery, or by adverse possession.[1] Until World War II there were still quite a few coastal fishing villages between Miloli'i and Kealakekua Bay,[2] some of them quite large. In the war this was all changed radically. Many of the villages were totally depopulated as a result of military evacuation and induction into the armed forces. After the war the villages were simply not repopulated by returning veterans. The latter had been introduced into new ways of life, new jobs, new education, often within the military. Many of them left Hawaii altogether in the 1950s as the plantation economy drew to a close and began to be replaced by tourism, the 'new kind of sugar'. The economy of the Kona coast was essentially coffee, and, in spite of its luxury quality, it was not lucrative. The introduction of Hawaiians into the larger American economy as wage workers was for many an escape from poverty and stigmatised status. Many Hawaiians in the interviews conducted in the village told of how they identified out, a possibility since they were all part something or other (e.g. Chinese, Filipino, Japanese). Miloli'i was not new to foreign contact, of course. During the war, a large number of Filipinos moved down to the village in order to fish commercially. They worked for a couple of Hawaiians, a Filipino and a 'part-Chinese' who ran commercial fishing businesses based in the village. Quite a few of them married into village families. Other Hawaiians also gravitated toward Miloli'i. Small settlements south of the village were emptied by the war and moved to the larger agglomeration and still others from villages to the north, such as Ho'okena moved south. Often this was a question of marriage since, formerly, there were alliance relations along the entire coast. There is continuity in social relations here, but increasingly geographically compressed.

In the 1950s, Miloli'i had a reputation for being an isolated village that held to the old traditions, while the rest of the coast was being rapidly modernised. Whereas most Hawaiians had lost their land, Miloli'i still maintained control over its land and sea base. While the refugees lived on state land, land confiscated by the territory after the lava flow of 1926, Miloli'i proper was the property of the villagers themselves. In the 1950s people still spoke Hawaiian, and there was a school in the village that

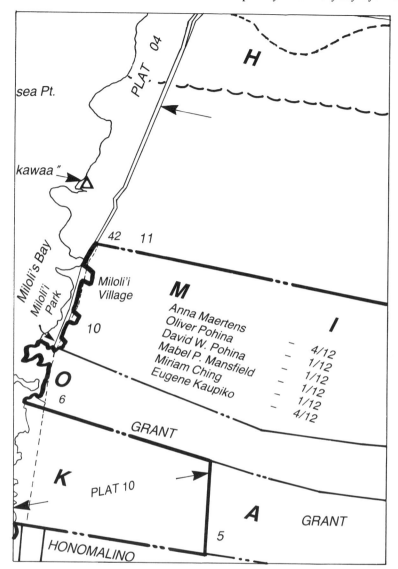

Figure 7.4 Miloli'i and adjacent Ahapua'a Omoka'a, showing family land titles

assured in part that Hawaiian was not totally repressed, i.e. while Hawaiian was officially forbidden in school, the location of the school in the village, and close friendship between teacher and villagers, made it possible to maintain the language. Secondary education and the goals of modernisation led to the exodus of a large percentage of the following generation to Kona and to Honolulu. During the 1950s Hawaiians in general had a tendency to leave the islands entirely, often via the military, and they often identified as part Chinese, part Filipino, part Portuguese, rather than part Hawaiian. Miloli'i experienced various waves of exodus as Hawaii became increasingly integrated into the United States. Many worked in Honolulu Harbor, in shipping, in the merchant marines, and in a number of trades related to the development of the tourist sector, construction, painting, hotel services, etc. But Miloli'i-born usually returned home after several years, or sometimes decades in the outside 'fast' world.

Miloli'i had until very recently become a kind of city of refuge, a place of security and freedom, where one can always go down and get food from the sea. It is far enough from the mainstream life of island and the islands to be able to maintain its own separate existence. It has become in some ways a closed corporate community, although this is more a question of identity to be presented to the outside world than a material reality. The distinction 'inside/outside' has been used to refer to the nature of closed corporateness in world systemic terms (Ekholm and Friedman 1980, Linnekin 1991). Applied to the village of Keanae on Maui it has been used as a kind of model, a representation of the relation between Hawaiian villagers in a non-monetary world and the larger capitalist society (Linnekin 1991). For Miloli'i residents being inside is not so much a way of interpreting experience but the experience itself, one that many non-Hawaiians may have also felt in descending the South Kona slopes to the tiny fishing village. Being inside, as we shall argue later, is practised and practical. The village is a place of refuge where Hawaiians can survive doing things that are by and large unacceptable in the larger society. In this sense, the metaphor is constructed on much less than a general understanding of the larger world, and more immediately on the experience of literally being inside a community that is a shelter from the outside world.

PRACTISING THE LOCAL IN THE GLOBAL

Self-isolation has the effect of packing experience into a small geographical space. Demographically, Miloli'i is quite complete, unlike many Third World villages which often contain only the very old and the very young. Miloli'i maintains a rather high rate of endogamy. Almost all of the twenty or so households are closely related to one another, forming half a dozen extended families that are and continue to be intermarried. This is a thick core. 'We are all family down here!'

There are many children,[3] many first-year birthdays, many marriages, many occasions for *luaus*. The villagers practise a kind of generalised reciprocity, a group fusion, rather than exchange. That is, they continually practise the non-existence of households as political units. Relatives, near and far, even friends, often move in for periods of several months or even longer without arousing the least opposition or surprise. Such phenomena are unmarked for the Hawaiian household. In this respect the latter is entirely open to the larger network of relatives and close friends. Expectations of generosity are high. One is to give oneself to the group and not exchange things with others. Conflicts and broken relations arise on the basis of the difficulty of maintaining this kind of giving/taking. At the same time the household is a fortress of privacy – 'kuleana rule', no butting into family business. The generosity is an expected behaviour, an overlay, upon the separateness of the household, that fuses the larger community into a family despite clear internal boundaries. Nobody demands, nobody asks. One can go to a *luau* and take home all that one can carry without offence – and one is expected to give what one has, in the sense of making one's wares available for others. It is not so much giving as balanced taking – i.e. 'to each according to his need', in this case from others in the community. Balance in transactions is only visible in the negative, i.e. in the visibility of non-generosity. This may be a correlate of closed corporateness. It clearly marks off the village from the outside world. Non-generosity is a heavily marked feature of village discourse. It defines the essence of evil and causes immense psychic pain among those affected. It causes fear of interaction and self-isolation. This experience of personal relations clearly resonates with the notion of *aloha* as it is used, politically, to distinguish the Hawaiian lifestyle. Village relations combine what might seem paradoxical; proximity and distance, openness and closedness, or perhaps, more accurately, distance in proximity and closedness in openness. It is the fragile and unstable encompassment of the centrifugal by the centripetal. This is fundamental to the social structure of the village, characterised by hierarchical households in which women are dominant and where separate projects are formulated and executed, and an egalitarian de-politicised (historically) public arena where men meet to practise equality, consensus and generosity.

The internal relations of the village are not accessible from the outside and are not part of the explicit model of village life. Various views of 'what goes on down there' are entertained by various categories of people. Resident whites, lower-middle and middle-class working people, would never dream of going down; for them Miloli'i is a frightening, mean, place.

> 'Don't go down there . . . it's a mean place . . . people, *haoles*, have got killed down there.'

One person, a Canadian, was in fact murdered along the coast after having spent some time in the village. And his accused murderer, an in-married Hawaiian, was sent to prison for his offence following a long series of false accusations, insinuations and painful investigations. The village is also associated with various criminal and dangerous activities by those who have never been there. For such people the fact that the village is on the tourist map and that there is a camping ground located in its centre, is a total mystery.

In contrast to this view, Miloli'i is a kind and generous place for the campers looking for a non-tourist Hawaii, 'the other Hawaii'. There is a state park in the middle of the village, parking space for ten cars or more – quite an institution in a village of 200. In the mid-1980s, the state park department built running-water bathrooms for the use of visitors, while most of the villagers had only outhouses and no running water of any kind. The system was based on brackish water that was pumped into the toilets and sinks while the sewage went down into the coral formation that at high tide could conceivaby wash out in the front of the village. This has never been tested but there have been rumours, and rumours, are central to the life of the village. Quite a few cars descend to the village and into the park area, which used to be the Miloli'i elementary school until it was destroyed by high surf. A Miloli'i summer programme used the building skills of the inhabitants, most of them teenagers, to build several *halaus* and an extended lava-stone sea wall. Many visitors get out of their cars for only a minute or two, to take photographs and then disappear, apparently rather afraid of the place, especially if there are no other visitors present at the time. Others come to camp, some families, some pairs, some singles. They wander around the village or at least around the park area. Some hike down the coastline, after asking villagers or the visiting anthropologist how to get to a well-known black-sand beach, Honomalino, which is inaccessible except by foot. A more interesting category is those who return year after year to the camping place. Some of these are older people who have established tourist-friendships with the local people, often via the Protestant church which is located just above the parking place. For many of these people, Miloli'i is truly a 'haven in a heartless world', a congenial place where folks are generous and the pace is human. There are also quite a few Alaskans, often from the salmon-fishing industry, who come to Hawaii in the off-season and often have boats that they launch from the village.[4] Many Alaskans have also bought second houses in the development known as Ocean View, 1,500 feet above the village and several miles south (see below). Relatives of the Hawaiian families may come, on occasion, from Honolulu or the mainland to visit the village of their childhood. In recent years this has sometimes been a step toward resettlement in the village. Finally, there are local residents who descend either to swim, fish or just camp out. They are known to the villagers and are part of the village support network. There are in this category quite a large number of Hawaiians, who have a tradition of coming to Miloli'i from Hilo, on the other side of the island, or from Ka'u in the south. Many are related to Miloli'i residents. The range of visitors spans the most superficial visual relation of cautious distance to the well-integrated Hawaiian from across the island or across the state.

Every year Miloli'i puts on two game-fish tournaments in which sportsmen from the entire coast, Honolulu, and even the mainland can participate. Miloli'i fishermen and women almost always win as they are so familiar with the waters, and there is plenty of money to be made both by the fishermen and by those who bet on the winners. It is true that the sportsmen and women are by and large people who return from year to year, and thus fall into the category of the perennial tourists or campers. The event combines a tournament with the usual all-night party and the visitors, if they stay, are easily assimilated into the occasion without in any way affecting its character.

Just as Miloli'i takes on innumerable visitors of different types, the villagers themselves are very often on the move themselves. To go *holoholo* as they say, to go travelling to visit others, is a generally known phenomenon that has sometimes been reduced to cultural instinct, as in 'Hawaiians have a penchant for travel' (Linnekin 1985:35). But Hawaiians travel in groups, in their own pickups, and stay in the homes of relatives in other localities, or at least in specially designated hotels, often Hawaiian owned. They manage, brilliantly, to avoid all contact with the larger society, i.e. travelling with their backs to the world they traverse, as if in conduits of their own making. Home is thus extended to the larger region via a complex of insulated networks. On the road they practise the obverse of that which is practised at home. But the larger strategy is identical.

Miloli'i entertains, literally, a great many different categories of people. On the surface there is no closure to the outside world. This is, in one powerful respect, the result of the politics and economics of the State of Hawaii. The existence of a public park and camping site in the middle of the village, the public access to its boat ramp, the neighbouring communities, all impinge upon the day-to-day existence of the village in physical terms. At the same time, as we shall argue at the end of this paper, villagers assimilate outsiders into their lives in ways that they choose, from complete obliviousness to incorporation into the activities of village life, festivities, fishing, coffee production etc. Those who are so integrated have to make sacrifices, to submit themselves to the needs of the villagers. This is the demonstration of their *aloha*, their eligibility for membership.

THE REPRESENTATIONAL CONTEXT

Miloli'i is thoroughly represented in the larger world, by films, from Hollywood to educational and Public Broadcasting, and in the news media, where their struggles for their land and against developers have usually been accorded a great deal of sympathy. Miloli'i is also represented in the Hawaiian image of its own lifestyle, as an ideal type. This context is part of a century or more old representational scheme for Hawaiians, who have represented the remote and romantic paradise of many an American dream, made ambivalent by the ambiguous relations entertained by white women and their men folk to the potentially dangerous sexuality of the colonised brown people.[5] The major shift in Western identity concomitant upon the decline of hegemony has been a globally orchestrated shift to respect for the native past and a longing for a past of one's own. The ambivalent primitive has become the symbol of that which we others have lost. This is the predominant neo-traditionalism of the period. Modernists, certain anthropologists for example, struggle against the Hawaiian self-image as a romantic falsification of its real past to which only anthropologists have unobstructed access due to their ideological neutrality. All of these public representations partake of the larger struggle for control over Hawaiian identification. This identity contest is clearly global.

Two very different kinds of film have been made in part or in whole in the village. In the early 1960s Paramount Studios made the Elvis film, *Girls, girls girls* partly in Miloli'i. They paved the 5-mile road down to the village which previously took a day to travel and which now takes less than 30 minutes. The film team was there for several months and a small shack overlooking the bay, belonging to one of the villagers, is called 'Elvis's House'. It is where he lived during the shooting.

In the 1980s Chevron Oil made a film of Miloli'i that was part of its educational series on Native American lifestyles. Here Hawaiian lifeways are celebrated as part of the American heritage. Villagers don't remember so much about this particular film except for the fact that they had to get hold of some real Hawaiian canoes, i.e. *koa* wood canoes, in order to fish in the traditional style.

A number of TV films have also been made about the village. Public Television has made a film, also celebrating the traditional lifestyle of the village, in the 1980s, very much inspired by the explosive increase of interest in Hawaiians, itself a partial result of the Hawaiian movement. Another film was made by the movement's own film team, *Maka'ainana* films, as a celebration of Hawaiian life on the land.

Miloli'i is a very important place for the Hawaiian movement. It represents something that has been lost to most Hawaiians. For ordinary Hawaiians it is not so much a question of tradition, but a place to live as Hawaiians. In Waianae, the largest Hawaiian non-urban settlement along the coast outside of Honolulu, there are a number of homestead lands as well as shopping centre based communities where a large portion of the population works in the city and commutes or is quite simply unemployed. In interviews conducted here, Miloli'i was often referred to as a kind of paradise – not so much in cultural terms, but as a true place of sanctuary from the fast life that had destroyed many Hawaiians, relegated them to poverty and a marginalised existence in the State. Miloli'i was known to both young and old: 'Oh they got that *ono opelu* [delicious mackerel] . . . can live off the ocean . . . no more worries.' All this in opposition to the Waianae coast, riddled with social problems, broken families, feuding, murder, drugs and organised crime, from local politicians down, and of course in a position of practised marginalisation from the state, racist schools, Japanese golf course invaders (there are upwards of forty golf courses on Oahu today – most of them Japanese, built in the 1980s – some on agricultural land and all taking huge amounts of the scarce island water for their greens).

The Hawaiian movement began its take-off in the mid- to late 1970s. This was not an entirely new phenomenon. Hawaiians have in varying degrees resisted both the takeover of their islands, the establishment of an American republic, territory and then state. But this was all resistance in a period of vast economic expansion in the Pacific, the development of a large-scale plantation economy, followed by the tourist industry, the era of USA global hegemony in which it was difficult to resist not only force but economic and political success. Hawaiians were not only oppressed, they were also in significant ways, shamed out of existence, very much by the parallel sequences of their own decline and the rise of a dominant white society. Poverty and stigma led to identification with other ethnic groups in a part-X society that enabled a number of choices of ethnic identity. The great change occurred in the mid-1970s, a change that cannot, as far as we can determine, be understood as the cumulative result of a long Hawaiian struggle, but as part of the breakdown of USA hegemony and the quite sudden dissolution of modernist identity. Hawaiian identity re-emerged in the scramble for roots in a more general way, a scramble that was legitimised by the hegemonic groups themselves. The Hawaiian movement was not an urban-elite-led nationalist type of movement as some have described it (Linnekin 1983). Elites have, of course, played a role, especially in later developments, but its roots lie in the rural areas where Hawaiian resistance is quite old and where it is difficult to speak of a single organised movement. Rather, there was a series of local groups, often calling themselves *ohana*, that became increasingly interconnected over time. There is, of course, a strong link to the renaissance of Hawaiian tradition, seen in terms of extended family, *ohana*, and a specific love for the land, *aloha 'aina*, set off against the creative destruction of modernity, more specifically modern capitalist civilisation, but this was not an invention of academic elites. The Hawaiian movement very early on became anti-civilisational in its content, a Fourth World movement, as much against socialism as against capitalism, i.e. against modernist notions of development. Hawaiian life had to be salvaged, not so much ancient Hawaiian society and culture as those values still thought to exist among the population. For the members of this movement, Miloli'i was and is an idyllic ideal type of what life could be about. For the leadership it is, surely, a question of culture, not so much of symbolic systems and ritual, but of values and lifestyle, the latter still part of Hawaiian existence. But, for many, the Hawaiian today still bears and can develop his culture. In fact the temples, *heiaus*, are now being restored and used on an increasing scale. Hawaiian language schools have emerged. The *ahupua'a* economy is being reinstated, or at least serious attempts exist. The Hawaiian movement has demanded the return of a land base equivalent to half of the lands of the islands, and there is a move in the direction of the establishment of Hawaiian self-sufficiency.

It should be noted here that the Hawaiian movement has had a powerful effect on the self-identity of the islands in general, including the other ethnic groups. In the election of 1986, a Hawaiian became governor for the first time in the history of the state, which had been dominated for more than two decades by Japanese-Americans and *haoles*. His vice-governor was and is a Filipino. The inauguration was an event very unlike the usual gubernatorial happening. Heads of state from the entire Pacific were invited guests. The inauguration, held on the grounds of the Hawaiian royalty's palace, was attended by a large number of Hawaiians, also unusual for such an occasion. And thousands of people held hands and sang the Hawaiian national anthem. The Hickam, Honolulu-based airforce, flew its jets over the palace grounds, creating a din that might have been the order of the day in another state, but was here understood as just a military noise staged to annoy and perhaps scare the new state government. There was a general atmosphere of jubilation and premonitions of change. Hawaii was, perhaps, to become more Hawaiian. While the ensuing years showed that this democratic government was very similar to the preceding Japanese-American dominated regimes, the context of identification was radically changed. Hawaiians now existed and the general goal of Hawaiian independence was introduced into the realm of real possibilities. The Office of Hawaiian Affairs, OHA, a state organ in charge of Hawaiian issues (challenged at one point as unconstitutional since it was based on special group interests) began to jostle for power. The current result is that there are two models of Hawaiian sovereignty, one non-government based, best represented by Kalahui Hawaii, the 'Nation of Hawaii', and OHA, the official road to a top-steered Hawaiian entity within the state. The difference between the two models of sovereignty is less significant here than the structure of the power relations. Miloli'i has been able to use the Hawaiian movement, OHA and the state itself in order to make significant improvements in its conditions of existence. This was not possible in the period from the 1950s to the 1970s. When the renowned double canoe, the *Hokulea*, returned to Hawaii from a voyage to the South Pacific, it stopped in Miloli'i for a number of days. This was, of course, a media event. But even as it placed Miloli'i on the cultural map of the islands, it was a veritable carnival of cultural identity for the villagers, whose status was greatly enhanced by the occasion.

For culture experts, for anthropologists interested in 'things Hawaiian', for Hawaiian modernists, Hawaiian is about a no-longer-existing reality, destroyed by the modern capitalist system or perhaps succumbing to a superior civilisation. One modernist view of Hawaiians is that they ought to join the lower classes in a more general struggle against the evils of capitalist domination. For others Hawaiians can indeed attempt to recall their heritage and even to be proud of it (although one anthropologist expressed his disbelief that such a 'mixed' population could maintain a Hawaiian identity at all), but the idea of reliving or practising this heritage is absurd. This is very much because Hawaiians no longer have any cultural project that they can really call their own. That project is the property of the anthropologists. They have been reduced to a mere ethnic group among others and must leave their nostalgia for traditions behind. For others, including many ethnic Hawaiians, the American ethnic strategy is the most adaptive. The latter is one in which ethnicity is carried in the body and in a certain number of practices that are clearly external to social life processes, economic survival, etc. Hawaiians should strive for success in American society while keeping their separate identity in the form of values and knowledge of history, i.e. the basis for ethnic pride.

The representational context described above is part of the institutionalised field of representation and discourse available for all those engaged in the highly politicised process of identification, either of self or of others. The positioned voices detailed here are not produced in the same way as the representations of those who are positioned in the immediate vicinity of Miloli'i, and we have kept them separate. Of course, local retirees who think of villagers as dangerous and engaged in illegitimate activities, may make use of the more general representations, as may ecological activists who support the village on the grounds that they are closer to nature. The distinctions are not categorical, but there are clearly two spheres of discourse and cultural production, the one establishing the framework for the other.

THE PHYSICAL CONTEXT

The representational context of Miloli'i encompasses the island, the state and the nation. The physical context concerns the immediate environment of the village, but that environment is itself deeply enmeshed in global economic and political processes. And to the extent that the region is a marketable commodity, its image; the romantic, the tropical, the sea, but not the lava, are instrumental representations in the organisation of that region.

Just to the north of the village in the *ahupua'a* of Ho'opuloa covered by lava from the 1926 flow, was a developer's paradise. Here, more than 1,000 feet below the main road, began, in the 1960s one of the land scams that are so well known in Hawaii. A developer bought a lava field from a ranch, 423 acres, and subdivided it into 1,000 house lots, advertised as Miloli'i beach lots, right on the Pacific. General Robert Lee Scott, of *God is My Co-Pilot* fame, became head of a community association for the potential military retirees expected to buy the lots. The owners paid $137,000 for the area and sold the unimproved properties for a sum of $3.5 million. If houses had been put up on all the lots it would conceivably have destroyed the integrity of Miloli'i, but as there is no beach and there was no infrastructure, no water and no electricity, the lots did not begin to be developed until very recently, and then only a few of them. Instead the lots have become a kind of suburb of Miloli'i, or what we call downtown Miloli'i. The owners of the houses there number some restaurant owners, builders and mainlanders who have retired to the island. Some relatives and even residents of Miloli'i have lots in this area and others rent houses there.

Miloli'i is surrounded by ranches, a macadamia-nut plantation and, further to the south, a number of housing developments, all in the uplands, i.e. more than 1,000 feet above the village. The scam subdivision to the north is the only settlement in close proximity. To the south there is nothing, but there have been several attempts to 'develop' some of the *ahupua'a* that are owned by large corporate interests. The enclave nature of the village is partly geographical and very much social. But the (en)closure of the village in the midst of a constant flow of transients, the movement of local goods and people back and forth between the village and the larger society, is a crucial property of the way in which the village reproduces itself, a foundational strategy of local existence in the global arena.

COMPLEXITY: AN EXTERNAL PERSPECTIVE

What is complex about the village of Miloli'i? From the anthropologist's perspective, arriving with the view of a world dichotomised into the modern and the traditional, Hawaiian villages, *both of them*, are very much within the modern sector. One anthropologist was very much taken with the fact that the other village of Keanae in Maui 'the taro place' was not a subsistence settlement but produced taro for the *poi* market in Hawaii, that it was very much locked into the larger economy and could not really be understood as a local organic whole (Linnekin 1985: 34–6). Even the population was seen as hopelessly mixed-up, an ethnic hodgepodge. Several families are left out of her study on the grounds that they are not Hawaiians but hippies. One has, perhaps, to draw the line somewhere, in the search for the *real thing*. The search for real things has been a hallmark of classical anthropology's attempt to simplify the complexity of the world. Nowadays, complexity itself, in all its cultural confusion, has become a new *real thing*. However, it might be suggested that the transition from the ethnographically pure-and-simple to the messy-but-real is about the transgression of preconceived categories which define both sides of the supposed transition.

Miloli'i is involved in several economies. There is a strong subsistence component, based on the use that can be made of the resources of the sea and the uplands, affording fish, vegetables and fruits, and game. There is a cash economy on top of this based on the sale of fish and of coffee and fruit. Today, coffee is milled and dried in the village on a significant scale and then sold after being sent for roasting. Villagers also work part time in the macadamia-nut plantation and in hotels along the coast. Welfare payments are a very large part of the local cash flow. The village might, in one sense, be a place of residence like any other poor modern rural settlement, but at the same time it has a very special local organisation, identity and symbolic activities. The practice of the economic reproduction of the village penetrates into the island's modern sector, but the social practice of villagehood sets a clear boundary between the village unit and the outside world. Miloli'i is a political unit, a practised and reproduced place defined against the rest of the world. This is so in spite of the apparent paradox that there is a constant flow of various categories of outsiders in and out of the village and a plethora of contacts, political, economic and otherwise with county and state agencies, upland communities, coffee companies and fish markets.

This identification is practised both ways and in several overlapping situations. The village is ascribed certain characteristics by the outside world, dangerous, primitive, pristine, traditional. It is native Hawaii as against *haole* Hawaii.

The village was formed by a regional depopulation and geographical implosion from the north and the south that transformed the coastline replete with fishing villages at the shore lines of their respective *ahupua'a* into a single village surrounded by a horizontalised organisation of ecological exploitation in which fishing became an increasingly specialised activity, ending with commercial tuna fishing. After the war the village became relatively poor in relation to its surroundings and Hawaiians lost increasingly in the status hierarchy with the emergence of the tourist economy, the decline of island food production, and increasing dependence on tourist income and imported products. Hawaiians identified out and moved out. Today it is estimated that over 100,000 Hawaiians live on the mainland, i.e. almost a third of all Hawaiians. In the period 1960–70 it even appears as if the Hawaiian population decreased. Self-identified Hawaiians declined by 16 per cent in the national census. Miloli'i children, sent to high school, especially the Hawaiian Kamehameha School in Honolulu, did not return home, not at first. Many found jobs in the city, or in the military. Many ended up in Germany or in Vietnam. Many, that is, entered the lower echelons of the national society, and many were confronted with a kind of racism that they had not encountered in Hawaii. Miloli'i contracted during this period which lasted until the mid- to late 1970s. In the latter period, of declining American hegemony and rising ethnic movements, the Hawaiian movement also began its long trajectory, from being part of a larger radical student-based movement to an increasingly national or at least cultural-based movement. By the 1980s it was good to be Hawaiian. The chief state demographer, in an interview, suggested that Hawaiians were beginning to re-identify, often changing their names. Both this decline and the subsequent renaissance of cultural identity are vaster phenomena than can be understood from the village alone.

Miloli'i had been known throughout the century as a community that resisted the encroachment of the landowners. The former 'mayor' of the village struggled for years against attempts to buy out his land above the village. Large landowners were and are known to have taken advantage of the complex ownership patterns of former *ahupua'a* lands, where often titles are divided among large numbers of heirs without clear boundaries having been established. Often one of the owners who found him- or herself in debt would sell off property that belonged to a dozen other cousins and siblings, by simply having access to the deed papers. Conflict, often ending in court, over the division of land title is still one of the great Hawaiian pastimes, one that goes well back into the last century, at least as far as the establishment of freehold title. Miloli'i is interesting insofar as the three main landowning families and their heirs have maintained large tracts of land intact throughout this century, although most of it is below the precipitation line.

The complexity of Miloli'i might appear bewildering from an external point of view, replete with ambiguities, a myriad of relations with out-siders, from intermarriage to beer parties, from land struggles to Hollywood films. Miloli'i is extensively entangled with the larger world, up to its neck in the modern sector. But, from the inside things are simpler. The following three cases illustrate the nature and complexity of the entan-glement itself, and the way it is quite consistently integrated into the village life-projects.

HAWAIIAN RIVIERA: CHILDREN OF THE LAND VERSUS THE STRANGER KING

The southwest coast of Hawaii, as we have indicated, lacks modern infra-structure, running water and, in parts, electricity. It is a dry area in which lava flows have left their indelible mark on the landscape. Here, as we also pointed out, a number of lava-flow housing developments have been spawned by speculators. Most of them have not succeeded. The south-ernmost district of Hawaii, Ka'u, famous for its historical opposition to chiefly power, became the target for a development project at the start of the 1990s. The land – some 2,000 acres on the lower slopes of a lava plain rift zone – had been bought in a very complex set of transfers by an international partnership.[6] The construction project included two large hotels and condominium complexes, at a cost upwards of $1 billion, the

A MEDITERRANEAN RIVIERA SEASIDE RESORT DESIGNED AROUND AN HISTORICAL HAWAIIAN THEME

Figure 7.5 Advertisement for Hawaiian Riviera resort

largest in the state's history. In order to start such a project, the site first needed to be rezoned by the Land Use Commission after public hearings. By rezoning what had been conservation land as urban land the value of the property could be significantly increased – and in this way it would be possible to acquire loans to finance the project.

The Riviera was intended to be truly global – with a Royal Hawaiian flavour (see Figure 7.5). The developers paid a public relations specialist to present the project to the local people, and an Environmental Impact Statement was prepared by Hawaiian consultants. The aim was to demonstrate that the local area would benefit greatly from the development. A debate grew up in the neighbouring village of Miloli'i (about 15 miles to the north of the proposed resort) between those who felt that the Riviera would offer employment and economic recovery, and those who felt that the development would undermine their Hawaiian identity and lifestyle. This was also a conflict between accepting the patronage of international corporate developers and maintaining village solidarity.

The Land Use Commission arranged a series of hearings. Representing the village against the project was a man who had had a career in Hilo politics and had been involved in helping villagers gain rights to their lands and funds to rebuild their houses. He had also successfully opposed developers in the past. The other representative, in opposition to the project, was a young *haole* of 'green' persuasion, who – taking the lifestyle/ecology line – argued for the rights of Miloli'i to continue their traditional way of life. The village summoned its old-timers who described the sacred sites, the love of the land and nature, the lifestyle and the subsistence base that was so essential for village survival – the survival, after all, of the last fishing village. Those in favour of the project argued for jobs and economic security.

The Commission itself was in principal sceptical towards the project, and the representative of the governor was entirely against it. The media soon became involved – Miloli'i became a real power to be reckoned with at the state level – on radio and television, in the Honolulu newspapers, the major financial magazine in the state and the region. It was the tiny traditional village that fought the giant corporate foreign developer, the children of the land versus the 'stranger king'.

An Ocean View resident said:

'We need the Riviera down here! They'll widen the highway, put in some restaurants and entertainment. That's what we need. It's so boring now!'

'But why don't you move to Kailua or Honolulu?'

'I would if I could afford it. And the development'll raise the property values down here so much that I can probably afford to get out!'

As anthropologists we were directly involved in this conflict, writing letters, making phone calls, negotiating and writing newspaper articles. The anthropologists offered moral support as well, which placed them in a difficult position when the village was split, but the question of the politics of fieldwork is not at issue at this conjuncture, since it applies to a more general problem in relation to fieldwork in a politicised situation, and the village has been politicised in the same way throughout the six years of our association. The situation was more complex for the anthropologists than the villagers.

The female leader came home from two days of hearings.

'Wow, that was too much! You think we got a chance? ... Common sisters[7] let's play cards.' It was 15:30 and the game of Hawaiian Rummy kicked off. The money changed hands faster than normal eye movement could track, all in the calmness of an afternoon ocean breeze. The beers came out of the freezer. They had done well, it was party now ... all night. Next day go pick coffee, after 3 hours of sleep. Then, finally, home at noon and sleep.

(field notes)

Miloli'i became a village of heroes throughout the state, at least for Hawaiians, for the media and for much of the population. The village became a strong single unit during the latter phases of the hearings. The number and size of parties increased and the village became more carnival-esque than usual. The Land Use Commission, did eventually grant permission to get the project underway, but only after meeting a number of stringent conditions, including up-front money. But by that time the venture was in financial trouble; Miloli'i's demands and objections had at least ensured that the development was financially hampered before work could begin. The village became a bastion of the Hawaiian struggle, a tiny village, but a force to be reckoned with, or as a Hawaiian from the 'other' intact village of Keanae has said,

We are few in number
But our love of the land is great.
      (Harry Kuhini Mitchell n.d.)

OPERATION BAD ASS

Miloli'i, as we have suggested, practises closure against the outside world. The view from the village enables anyone to know who is coming down and there is plenty of time to set things in order before the police arrive. The Kona uplands host some of the most lucrative marijuana plantations in the world. The product, Kona Gold (also the name of a coffee), sells today for upwards of $600 an ounce in the islands, making it more than comparable to heavier drugs such as cocaine. The police are always on the prowl, but also deeply involved themselves. One story relates how some Hawaiians were taken to the local police station to be charged for possession and saw out of the unfortunately open back door that there was a considerable plantation on precinct premises. The myth is a sign, clearly substantiated, of the general banana republic lifestyle of official Hawaii. The upland plantations, run by ex-hippies, heavily booby-trapped and defended with automatic weapons and pit-bull terriers have driven the police to the more or less innocent. Helicopters often circle the village, often at night with spot-lights. Miloli'i was also a centre for cock-fights, sometimes with high rollers, politicians, union bosses and the like making their appearance, because in the village it was safe. The world does impinge on village life.

Miloli'i people like to gamble, to play craps and cards. This is an old custom. Some anthropologists might say that they had 'a propensity' to gamble. Others might cite Queen Ka'ahumanu's (the wife of King Kamehameha) inveterate card playing and her insistence that she would only set foot in church if she could take her game with her. If this is mythopractice, so be it. If there is no myth, there is certainly a precedent, whatever that might imply for culture theory.

Sometime during the Riviera troubles an incident occurred. One morning at about 5 o'clock three police vans came down the Miloli'i road. They were the riot police, in their broncos and one ordinary police car. They were six or seven. They drove down to one particular house. The village was still asleep. They got out quietly with their loaded and cocked riot guns (sawed-off shot guns) and hand guns. Three surrounded the house and three others charged up the stairs, breaking down a door. They stuck their guns in the brutally woken victims' faces, one, a machine operator for the macadamia plantation and a fisherman, his wife, and a grand-daughter sleeping in the same bed. Downstairs the two sons were taken outside and held at gunpoint as well as a more distant relative visitor with a bad heart.

'Hey, you Harry Ho!' they screamed . . . Don't move! Don't move!
'Harry doesn't live here . . . I no see him!'

The police saw, across the roadway, the neighbours' son on his way to the outhouse. Guns up and cocked – 'Hey you! Don't move!'

'That not Harry!'
'Shaddup you!'

Harry Ho was accused of stealing a watch and a shirt by a Japanese store-owner in Ho'okena, 20 miles up the coast. Harry Ho was, in fact, sitting on his surfboard in the water out in front of the village! The police spotted someone and ran out to the shoreline and pointed their weapons. Harry, armed with only his board and bathing suit, tried to paddle away, but the police scared him into shore a little south of the village. They handcuffed him and drove him off in a truck. By that time the whole village was awake and out, mulling about and gravitating toward the house where the incident occurred. The police were still walking around looking in the various cars that were parked by the house, interrogating with their guns out and sometimes cocked. The police had come to the wrong house, broken in without a warrant, caused heart trouble, held a gun at a 2-year-old's head, and generally caused fear and trouble. The chief of operations was a Japanese[8] captain with a poor reputation among local Hawaiians.

The incident was reported. It appeared in both local and Honolulu newspapers. Hawaiian legal help was enlisted. The police department attempted to cover its tracks, first denying that anything was out of order, then running an internal investigation. The Office of Hawaiian Affairs representative came down and put a great deal of pressure on the local government. There was never a trial, but the policemen involved were all demoted to highway patrol or less. The police had swept down upon the village on numerous occasions, but this time the tide was against them. And the tide was constituted of the connection between the village and state organisations who had gained power as the result of the decline of the formerly hegemonic identity in the islands, a truly global shift.

CHANGING PLACES

The situation of Miloli'i has changed radically since the start of the Hawaiian movement. The upper village, once officially a squatter settlement, now has standard village status on 'state land' reserved only for Hawaiians. A Miloli'i village plan has begun to be realised, including low-interest loans for the reconstruction of local houses on a self-help basis, the opening of two new sets of lots, sixty in all, to accommodate the rapid expansion of the village, the installation of a solar-powered desalination plant for the village, fed by brackish water pumped up from beneath the shoreline lava, solar panels for all the new and even the old houses. Today there are well over twenty new houses, designed by a 'green' architect, all to get running water and solar power. Some of the youth of the village have got jobs including training in the construction industry. Some have no time to fish anymore, except on weekends. The interiors of these houses are unlike the ramshackle structures of the past.

One such house has wall-to-wall high-pile carpeting, an enormous stereo, a giant-screen TV, a super-modern kitchen with most finesses, including microwave and other appliances. It looks very like a high-end condominium, the latter having served as the model. A neighbouring house has a 60-inch TV screen and advanced video equipment. New plush sofas and enormous verandas characterise many of the houses. One individual was forced to take down his house frame, after building beyond the limit of breadth stipulated in the settlement plan. He had boasted that his house would be the biggest. He had planned a veranda almost as large as the rest of the house. When it was discovered that he had apparently stored extra lumber under his house the gossip exploded that he had a connection in the Housing Department. Another man was accused of building a house that was far too large, and the state agency was called in to measure his house site, which turned out to be well within the limits. Most villagers are quite simply satisfied with the gains they have made. The new conditions have, at least during the time of my stay, changed patterns of sociality in the village. The new housing areas had no public areas to compare with the village store. There were a couple of houses where people met regularly but no real centre. The area is, thus, more fragmented than the old village, especially during the daytime and especially for women with children who have become increasingly isolated. This is a change that is just beginning and it is, for the time being at least, counteracted by the continuing pattern of sociality delineated earlier in this discussion. In a more important sense it is encompassed by the more general strategy of villagers, their endo-sociality.

In the neighbouring subdivision, the upper middle-class owners of lots have been rather upset at the fact that the impoverished village of Miloli'i looks more like a real subdivision than their own subdivided infra-structurless lava. But they cannot summon the strength to fight for their rights. Hawaiians after all, are the aboriginals who were oppressed for so many generations. When one house-owner found a brackish water well by a cliff in neighbouring Papa Bay and put in a pump and piping, he managed clumsily to damage part of a well-known Hawaiian trail and an old graveyard. Another house-owner, seeing the damage, went to straighten things and was punched out. The police were summoned as well as the historical authorities. The said house-owner vanished from the island.

There are two new sections of land that have been opened for Miloli'i people and their close relatives to build upon. The second is located on top of the lava flow directly above the old fishing village of Ho'opuloa. Quite a few villagers complained that it was not right to build on top of the dead and at least one event became indelibly impressed on the village. The desalination plant is located just below the lava flow and the two tanks that fill with water are on top of the flow itself. One early morning when a couple of the Miloli'i men hired to help with the construction came to the well site, they saw two elderly women dressed in old-fashioned clothes. They were walking on top of the flow. The men ran home, thoroughly frightened. There had been problems with the well for some time. Each time they struck water it sank down, as if into a crevice, and disappeared. Several times they had even struck fresh water, but the same thing had happened. They knew that something was wrong, and when they saw the two old women they understood that this was no place to build anything. They were disturbing the dead of Ho'opuloa.[9] There was something about this hole that was unholy. They moved the drill back somewhat and within a single day there was running water.

We have indicated that Miloli'i's expansion is an effect of a more general change in the conditions of Hawaiian identity itself a reflex of a very broad global process. The villagers have fought sporadically for 30 years to gain control over their lands, just as rural Hawaiians fought for similar goals in other parts of the islands. But the process of expulsion and loss of land continued and Hawaiians were increasingly marginalised. The current change in Hawaiian status is part of a decline in Western hegemonic identity that has made Hawaiianness more viable, not only for Hawaiians but for other inhabitants of the islands as well. Miloli'i villagers have been able to exploit the new situation in order to regain control of their lands and gain numerous material advantages that were entirely beyond their grasp previously.

ENDO-SOCIALITY, THE REDUCTION OF COMPLEXITY AND SOCIAL SURVIVAL

These cases are examples chosen from a very large sample of similar scenarios. From a certain perspective village activities are hopelessly entangled with upland, coastal, state, national and international relationships. From the perspective of the villagers themselves, life is really quite simple. It is simple as long as the village is home and is practised as home. We indicated that impingement on the way the life course is organised, the way situations are immediately defined, is not tolerated. Miloli'i practises a strong form of assimilation of external circumstances. Villagers maintain their genealogies cognatically. If outsiders marry-in, their properties may be included, but the main lines of genealogy related to the village lands themselves are maintained with a vengeance. This includes court cases concerning inheritance, land boundaries, etc. which are a major local activity. Foreigners must adapt to the village in order to survive there. One wealthy resident of the neighbouring subdivision, who really loves Hawaiians because they are so different from his own life experiences, has bought an old coffee mill and gone 'into business' with a local coffee landowner. He works hard for his association with the village. Another resident has fallen in love with a Miloli'i man who is married in Honolulu and is getting a socialisation that cannot be discussed here. In-marrying men, as we said, get a clearly violent initiation into their village identity. Miloli'i is dangerous for those who would turn it into part of their own projects. Miloli'i has maintained integrity in some very difficult times. It is today expanding, building new houses for its growing local population and influx of other, more distant, relatives. All houses are now solar-powered, and there is a desalination plant that produces running water for the village, while the wealthy neighbouring subdivision is beginning to complain that Hawaiians get special treatment while they have to truck down water and pay for their own generators or solar panels. If we were to summarise the nature of village practices delineated here it might appear as follows:

1. The village economy is integrated in important ways into the larger region. Incomes are gained by both wage work and by the sale of fish. This implies movement of Hawaiians in and out of the village on a daily basis.

2. The social relations of the village span the island, other islands and Honolulu. When villagers go *holoholo*, travelling, they do so in clearly established conduits within which they meet only their own kind, either family or perhaps other local Hawaiians. They travel often in groups, in their pickups. They live in other people's houses or in one of several Hawaiian hotels. There is a concerted practice of endo-sociality in all of this which makes travelling with Hawaiians quite special. It is possible to move through the dense tourist areas of the islands without meeting any visitors or other non-Hawaiians.

3. Villagers may often move to other islands or to other places in the world during part of their lifetimes. This is often the result of working in the military, or in various construction trades. Many villagers return to the village in their later years. This is often the case among the young today who find it increasingly difficult to survive in a declining tourist economy. In this sense, the village acts as a kind of centripetal force against the centrifugal forces of the larger regional and global contexts.

4. This endo-sociality provides a high level of satisfaction for the villagers, even as it leads to high levels of conflict, due not least to the

contradiction between external resources and forces and the structure of everyday existence in the village itself.

5. The above is clearly evidenced in cases of in-marriage. The latter is of two types. The first and most common consists of downwardly mobile whites who marry or live with local girls. If they are white they usually go through a period of aggressive socialisation including beating, where they learn how to get along with the local boys. This is followed by partial acceptance. The next generation fares better. In-marrying Hawaiian men are accepted but do not in general play a significant role in the village. In-marrying women are usually Hawaiians. They too are very much marginalised and need to wait for the next generation which can then establish itself. The village, thus, does not practice exclusion but an aggressive form of assimilation that works through the second generation.

6. Endo-sociality entails a high level of intensity in social life. At any one time there are a number of activities concentrated in several different central places and in several different networks. The cores of these networks are kinship-based, often part of an extended family and a network of less closely related relatives and friends. Such activities include disputes over inheritance, marriage infidelity, conflicts over external intrusions, *luaus* for children or for numerous special occasions, night-time drinking at the store or on someone's porch. The level of commerce with the outside world is very high, and the assimilation of the outside into the practice of village life creates an activity level that is closer to an urban rather than a rural situation.

The relative success of Miloli'i, which harbours its own problems, is a product of the play of global forces as they have materialised in Hawaii. But the practice of villagehood still remains a constant through all of this, creating Miloli'i people as opposed to just islanders. 'Work hard, play hard ... go fish, get your welfare check, pick coffee, go to court, come home and play cards and then party or even *luau*.' Conflicts abound – but Miloli'i encompasses them. The woman-outsider-modernist referred to in our discussion of the Riviera, suffered great misfortune subsequent to the Riviera case. In the last Miloli'i fishing tournament she was asked to register the weighing-in of the fish. No conflicts were resolved by this act, but a potential exclusion was reversed. All of this occurred without reference to the heated past.

ENDO-SOCIALITY VERSUS EXO-SOCIALITY

The contrast between the situation in Miloli'i and among Hawaiians in general and the Congolese case is revealing. Hawaiians practice the forceful assimilation of the world to their own categories of existence. On the surface, the Congolese do something quite similar, if not by force.

Yet there is a clear difference between the Hawaiian steeped in his/her own world of practice and the Congolese attraction to the outside world. If the Hawaiian world closes itself off from its surroundings, the Conglolese world feeds explicitly on its surroundings. For it is here that the source of life-force is to be found.

Hawaiians assimilate the world by eradicating its original qualities or changing its signs. White status is negated in the Hawaiian enclave. The visiting anthropologist may indeed be useful in relation to state authorities and is readily used to achieve desired ends. But it is in the capacity of agent that this is carried out, not as a representative of a higher power. The *haole* is useful as a tool, but is not a source of well-being as such. And to be accepted in the community the *haole* must demonstrate his or her usefulness. In the Congolese situation, the white visitor is a resource in essence, in his or her very being. The transmission of power is achieved by way of clientship. There is no reversal of hierarchical roles, but their reinforcement. The definition of the situation is quite the opposite of the Hawaiian model. The latter invert the external relation of power, while the former make it into a religious truth. In both cases there is assimilation of external elements to the local situation, but the assimilation process is founded on opposing strategies.

The principal strategy that we have investigated in the Congolese situation consists in the appropriation of Western goods. This is an active and quite conscious strategy that is exemplified in a number of different social fields.

1. The President and the upper class are identical to the state, i.e. as a state-class. Their relation to the resources of the country, i.e. oil and aid funds is one of direct appropriation. This wealth defines their status and their strength (the same thing), the immediate expression of the possession of life-force. But this is not merely an upper-class activity. It is a common strategy. It includes not only the appropriation of foreign luxuries into local identities, but the bleaching of the skin, *se jaunir*, to become yellow, which also means to become wealthy and/or powerful.

2. The practice of medicine. Western medicines are especially powerful and included in the general practice of curing, connected to traditional methods of protecting the individual and ridding the subject of magical and witchcraft-based evil, an evil that eats the soul and diminishes its life-force.

3. The *sapeur* phenomenon refered to above, whereby links to Paris are part of a construction of the transfer of life-force that enables the subject to reproduce himself in a particular status or perhaps to raise that status. The practice of *la sape* is an active accumulation of such force, one that is highly socially organised and results in the production of 'great men' (*le grand*) and a rank system of age classes.

In all of these cases, the external world is part of the self-identification of the Congolese. Bakongo speakers of the southern Congo were the most transformed and/or modernised in the colonial period. Relative to the north of the country, these people identify more with aspects of white culture, with Paris and with all that is deemed 'civilised' and developed. The orientation is entirely dependent upon the appropriation of the superior other, a kind of self-induced clientalisation, which transfers life-force (*makindongolo*) and therefore status to the client. The elaboration of self in relation to external force is expressed in bars, churches and other public spaces where prestige is marked for others.

The formation of diasporas in Europe is part of the strategy of Congolese identity. Emigration to Paris, to *Paname*, as it is called is not migration in the ordinary sense but a pilgrimage to the centre where sacred force can be accumulated for utilisation at home. Migration is thus temporary, a stage in the achievement of greatness. One need only compare this to the relation to the external world that is evident in Hawaii from the early years of this century, when all foreign food and other goods were considered dangerous and even life-threatening, thus encouraging self-sufficiency in the extreme. Hawaiians throughout the period from the latter part of the nineteenth century established enclaves and built walls around themselves, especially in rural areas. The Congolese were, instead, increasingly attracted to the capital (more than half of the population lives in the two major cities) and ultimately to Paris, which became the source of identity for the entire country.[10] The one was centripetal the other centrifugal in principle. This contrast is, further-more, a question of historical variation, since the earlier material from Hawaii reveals an aristocracy that is quite absorbed in the accumula-tion of foreign goods as a means of self-identification and social com-petition (Friedman 1988, Kuykendall 1967: 89), where goods circulated downwards in the same strategy of prestige accumulation (Morgan 1948: 68). The prestige economy has been systematically discussed in Sahlins' major historical work on the period (1992: 57–81). The transition to the situation at the end of the century might be described as a shift from exo-sociality to endo-sociality. Without attempting a more elab-orate explantation of this process, we would limit ourselves to the differ-ence between the Hawaiian situation in which the indigenous popula-tion became a low-ranked minority in its own land and the Congolese situation in which the colonial elite was a small minority in the larger African society. And of course the general transformation of Hawaii from the early years of the century to the latter half is precisely the formation of a minority enclave in an increasingly foreign and increasingly domi-nant population.

CONCLUDING NOTE

The notion or non-notion of cultural complexity is a way of identifying the meeting, combination or fusion of practices and objects whose sources can be identified as disparate. But the way in which differences are combined in the life projects of a population can only be understood in terms of the practice of the relevant actors. We have argued here that the people of Miloli'i, in practising endo-sociality, reduce complexity in a radical way, by assimilation, often violent, of outsiders and by the active elimination or avoidance of ambiguity and complexity that might appear as extremely intricate to the observer. Cultural anthropological definitions of 'complex' situations often consist in a concerted effort to establish genealogies of 'cultural' elements, in order to correctly 'identify' the observed reality. This practice of historical continuity is just as specific, culturally, as the practices of those we observe. But the practice of cultural observation is not the practice of ordinary existence. The apprehension of complexity depends very much on perspective, on the position of the observer. It might appear strange to some dichotomisers that a so-called 'global anthropologist' can make a plea for 'the native's point of view', but this is, of course, the only way to resolve an apparently incommensurable opposition between observed complexity and practised simplicity. The fact that Miloli'i has been involved in the world system, both as an historical product of the formation of modern Hawaii and in its everyday relations with hotels, plantations, the police, welfare agencies, film productions, and the Hawaiian movement, implies, of course, that all kinds of objects, images and expressions from the larger world circulate in the village. But this circulation is not what the village is all about, although Hawaiian life is replete with America. Hawaiians, after all, are American citizens, and they are perfectly aware of this. Hawaiians, the great majority of them, do practise a specific kind of existence that is distinctive with respect and in opposition to the larger society in which they participate, whether or not they drink Coca Cola and ride American-style surfboards (the latter, apparently a creolised product), go to Hawaiian-language schools and engage in rituals on Hawaiian *heiaus*. The genealogies of the elements that participate in the structures that they generate are only of secondary museological importance. Otherwise the English are a motley blend of Celtic, Saxon, Scandinavian and Norman 'cultures', each of which in its turn is a motley blend of . . .

We have not denied that the village of Miloli'i is intricately involved in the larger world, via images and practices. On the contrary, the global perspective insists upon precisely such an involvement. Miloli'i is economically dependent and politically integrated into a state, national political sphere and, as such, into the global system. But that integration is not determinant of local strategies of social survival even if it sets the limits of their viability. Secondly, the integration is not merely a question of economic dependency, since conditions of identity and the politics of identity are directly involved in establishing the village's conditions of existence. The decline of Western hegemony, the result of a decentralisation of world accumulation, has led to conditions in which a hegemonic modernist identity (in its American variant) has declined. This in its turn has led to a broad change in identification including the renaissance of indigenous culture. In this off-shore state it has empowered Hawaiians and enabled them to make gains on a number of fronts that would have been unthinkable a decade ago. Miloli'i has had a tradition of self-isolation in the midst of outside contacts and this has combined with the recent upsurge of Hawaiian power in the islands to afford them advantages that were previously inaccessible. Endo-sociality is a general strategy in Miloli'i and it would appear to be rather widespread among the Hawaiians. It is not to be understood as what some anthropologists mean by 'culture'. A colleague of mine has commented,

> What are the people in the village maintaining in the face of their inte-
> gration with a global system? It appears to me that you are saying that
> villagers are maintaining only a separation from the larger world of
> which they are part. That is, they are preserving a distinctiveness, rather
> than any particular set of cultural or social elements. Hawaiianness,
> then is a chimera.

(Carrier, J. personal communication)

We include this comment because of what it reveals about the nature of perspective in the identification of phenomena. The question of cultural distinctiveness, i.e. of culture pure and simple, is not, in my view, a relevant issue here. The 'maintaining a separation' is a structure that is quite elaborated upon in Hawaiian society. It is central to maintaining Hawaiian existence in the larger social field. It is productive of metaphors and entire discourses of distinction, and of a very significant silence about encounters with the 'others'. That Hawaiians in Miloli'i practice numerous activities and discourses concerning Hawaiian lifestyles, morals and cosmologies that are continuous with, if transformed versions of, the past apparently indicates that they are somehow preserving a culture as well as keeping themselves apart. Village endogamy, or at least a high rate of endogamy within the *ahupua'a* is certainly evident from the earliest documents. Notions of *ohana, aloha 'aina, malama 'aina*, while politicised today, for good Gramscian reasons, are clearly not mere inventions in spite of some anthropologists' assertions (Linnekin 1983). But there are also the fishing shrines, the *luaus* and their special foods, even Hawaiian Christianity, and beliefs in *aumakua, mana*, magic, that permeate the life of Hawaiians, whether they live in Miloli'i or the outskirts of Honolulu. These specific ways of going about things and of interpreting the world, even, I would insist, of experiencing the world, are present even where Hawaiians do not have their own lands to maintain in the face of outside forces. The Hawaiian struggle is not a struggle to preserve a culture, not even for the official Hawaiian movement. The struggle to preserve culture can only make sense for anthropologists, perhaps because it is the preservation of their own identities, at least as masters of culture, masters of otherness, masters-in-fantasy, of the others. The struggle of the Hawaiian village is about life space, *lebensraum*, if I may; about the capacity to maintain a particular social existence no matter how we might classify the diversity of the elements it might contain.

NOTES

1. Adverse possession is a legal means of obtaining clear title to another person's land by using or occupying it openly for a certain time period, usually several years. Ranchers were able to snatch Hawaiian land by systematically grazing their cattle on it and then making claim.
2. Kealakekua Bay is the landing place of Captain Cook. It is approximately 125 miles north of Miloli'i.
3. The number of children per nuclear family ranges from four to ten and sometimes more.
4. Miloli'i's boat ramp is the only one for miles around, the closest being at South Point, i.e. the southern tip of the island more than 20 miles away.
5. This is best expressed in the famous Massie rape trial and its bloody aftermath, all recaptured in a well-known Hollywood film.
6. The central figure here was a Lebanese investor, whose history of less than clearly legal financial debts has been questioned.
7. They were primarily her 'sisters' even if by different fathers. There were four of them there. A brother, an old card shark, also played, as well as a daughter and a niece.
8. The term Japanese was used for Japanese Americans. Ethnic terms are common even where there is clearly a more generalised 'local' lifestyle, dialect, food habits, etc. Japanese Americans are more marked due to a rather strong tendency toward endogamy and stress on higher social status.
9. Now of course only one person died in the lava flow of 1926, so that the interpretation was of a more general nature – it was not good to build on top of formerly living villages, especially not above former graveyards, as soon became apparent in the interpretation of the event.
10. The centralism of this phenomenon is exaggerated by the French colonial mould and its post-colonial forms of canalisation of dependency to Paris: via language (with respect to anglophone areas), the educational system, including the university hierarchy which trains the academic core of most ex-colonies, and the financial control exercised via (until very recently) the franc zone and direct financial support for ruling elites.

REFERENCES

Ekholm, K. and Friedman, J. (1980) 'Towards a global anthropology', in *History and Underdevelopment* ed. L. Blussé, H. Wesseling and C. D. Winius. Leiden and Paris: Center for the History of European Expansion.

Friedman, J. (1988) 'Cultural logics of the global system', *Theory Culture and Society* 3(2–3): 447–60.

Kuykendall, R. S. (1967) *The Hawaiian Kingdom 1874–1893*, Honolulu: University of Hawaii Press.

Linnekin, J. (1983) 'Defining tradition: Variations on the the Hawaiian identity', *American Ethnologist* 10: 241–52.

— 1985 *Children of the Land*, Brunswick: Rutgers University Press.

— 1991 'Cultural invention and the dilemma of authenticity', *American Anthropolgist* 93: 446–8.

Morgan, T. (1948) *Hawaii: A Century of Economic Change 1778–1876,* Cambridge, MA: Harvard University Press.

Sahlins, M. and Kirch, P. (1992) *Anahulu: The Anthropology of History in the Kingdom of Hawaii*, Volume I, *Historical Ethnography* (Sahlins), Chicago, IL: University of Chicago Press.

8   On soap opera: what kind of anthropological object is it?

Veena Das

Soap opera came to India through *Hum Log*, which was modelled on the educational soap operas telecast on the television networks in Mexico in the middle of the 1970s. Consciously fashioned as an educational programme for the propagation of the message of family planning to the Indian masses, it was one of the best examples of how the global bureaucratic culture conceptualises popular consciousness in countries like India and seeks to transform this through the use of mass media. Yet for all the simplicity of this conception, it is not at all easy to decipher what kind of cultural object is soap opera in India. For no bureaucracy, however powerful, can shape the world totally as if it were a reflection of its own desires.

Most cultural theorists would agree that as a genre, soap opera finds its most suitable medium in television (Taylor 1989, Geraghty 1990, Cassata and Skill, 1983). As it was initially conceptualised and sponsored by the soap company, Procter and Gamble, it was targeted at female audiences. This is why most radio operas and later tele operas were scheduled for the afternoon hours when the housewife was alone in the house and relatively free from urgent domestic chores. The typical soap operas were dominated by the themes of intricate complications in familial relationships. By bringing to the surface the unofficial truths of familial relationships, many soap operas transformed the television screen into a space in which such forbidden themes as incest, adultery and illegitimacy could be projected. Hence while it is true that several cultural theorists have seen the popularity of the genre as evidence of the degeneration of mass culture (predictably represented as feminisation of culture),[1] others have looked at it as a subversive genre which manages to contest the patriarchal ideologies of male power by showing how women escape the male controls, operating in the official ideology of the family.[2] Yet it seems to me that this is the moment for hesitation. Before we can make a judgment about the nature of mass culture that is being produced through the medium of television, we should ask what kind of domestic object is television? Is the representation of familial relations on tele operas to be seen in continuity with radio soap operas and even with the romantic novels of which women are said to be such avid consumers? Or should one try to see it in relation to representation of familial relations in the context of programmes such as *Hello Zindagi* or *Shakti* in which the tele-screen was used to project problems experienced in the family by persons narrating their life-experiences or problematising these through letters or questions addressed to the producers of these programmes? In both cases we must ask whether a new relation between image, object and subject position emerges when that image is consumed on the small screen in the intimacy of domestic life. I do not have the answers to these questions. I shall only ask whether the relation between such television genres as soap operas and tele-documentaries on the one hand, and domestic life, on the other can be seen under a new aspect if we bring the anthropological eye to focus on these.

Many scholars have felt that the images we see on television do not belong, even as fictions, to life's reality. The most powerful proponent of this theory is Baudrillard (1982, 1991) who evokes television as an example of the dominance of the order of simulation in contemporary life. Oscillating between banality and fatality, television produces excessive visibility, information overload and an obscene plenitude of images (banality)[3] which can only be countered by a nostalgic return of the simulated past into the realm of the present (fatality). Recently Axel Honneth (1992) has argued that the destruction of metanarratives and the consequent pluralism of life-cycles considered typical of the postmodern condition can be traced in some part to the electronically produced images of culture that are globally produced and are not organically related to the social life-worlds of the people among whom they are consumed. Therefore the pluralism of lifestyles, he feels, is artificially produced and reflects a dissociation from the life-world of organic communities.

These formulations in culture theory, then, represent three aspects under which the production and consumption of these images on the television screen may be viewed. First, as a medium television creates images that do not arise from the life-world of any socially defined community – the community collapses into the mass of consumers. Second, as a domestic equipment its images are consumed by solitary individuals or families in the isolation of their domestic space. In this, television, unlike films, does not produce a community of viewers. Third, the intimacy between image and object belongs to the order of simulation in which it can be characterised as neither true nor false.[4]

Social anthropologists committed by their own disciplinary fantasies to a somewhat nostalgic view of the integrity of local worlds have contested these formulations. They have argued that local cultures do not simply kneel down in abject supplication before the onslaughts of global cultures. Not only are there important variations in theme and character in soap operas produced in different countries in accordance with local cultures but also the same soap opera may be very differently received in different parts of the world.[5] The viewer cannot, therefore, be seen as a passive recipient of images. Further, the life of these electronic images does not come to an end after they have been viewed within the confines of the domestic space. These become conversational objects and acquire a social life of their own. But the matter does not end with the consumption of images. Several social anthropologists have shown that programmes produced with specific local contexts in mind can acquire global popularity.[6] Thus, at the level of both production and consumption of meaning, the anthropological approach is to reinstate the importance of the integrity of local moral worlds.

Then what is the source of disquiet? I suspect that this arises from the fact that formulated in very general terms one can see the recycling of the same tired themes of resistance, pleasure, and political practices which leave the assumptions about the relation between culture and life-worlds unquestioned by uncritically valorising the 'local'. As Meaghan Morris (1990: 21) has expressed it:

> Recent cultural studies offer something completely different. It speaks not of restoring discrimination but of increasing cultural democracy. It respects difference and sees mass culture not as a vast banality machine but as raw material made available for a variety of popular practices ... but sometimes when distractedly reading magazines ... I get the feeling that somewhere in some English publisher's vault there is a master disk from which thousands of versions of the same article about pleasure, resistance, and the politics of consumption are being run off under different names with minor variations.

The only way to correct this tendency, it seems to me, is to move from the general to the particular and see how the relation between events on the tele-screen and domestic life play themselves out in the context of specific societies. While the nature of the 'mass culture' produced on television has been problematised by cultural theorists taking their lead from the writings of Adorno (1954), among others, it is possible that the emergence of the public culture might lead to a problematisation of the nature of the family, including the articulation between domesticity and sexuality – issues that the anthropologists have taken for granted in their description of family in India. Further, in the case of popular cinema, Ravi Vasudevan (1993) has already shown, with great finesse, that the possibility of mass culture producing from within itself a radical practice cannot be ruled out of court. His analysis of certain selected sequences in the case of two popular films of the 1950s shows what radical experimentations were possible with the psychic space of the mother in redefining the family. The point is that *Hum Log* or *Hello Zindagi* may turn out to be moments whose critical potential could not be realised, but they should not be abandoned with some kind of formulaic closure on the relation between mass culture and commodification or mass culture and resistance.

SOAP OPERA AND DOMESTIC LIFE

Let us first look at the kind of relation between soap opera and domestic life through *Hum Log*. The title, which means 'We People', itself signified the everydayness of the episodes of *Hum Log*. The everydayness of the middle-class family was, however, seen as raw material on which the state could bring about an effective transformation through the mediation of television in order to aid the tasks of social and economic development. Arvind Singhal and E.M. Rogers have traced the elements of this story with care in their numerous publications on the subject (see Singhal et al. 1992, Singhal and Rogers 1989a and 1989b)

The story of the production of *Hum Log* unfolds itself as follows. *Hum Log* was modelled on the pro-development soap operas or telenovellas which had enjoyed enormous popularity on the Mexican television networks between 1975 and 1981. The Mexican experiment was itself based upon the success of a Peruvian soap opera – *Simplement Maria* – which told of a rags to riches story of a girl called Maria and apparently had a great impact on young women in Peru. The idea behind the pro-development soap operas is to present socially desirable goals, which range from specific goals, for example, encouraging women to adopt contraceptive methods, to general ones, for example, promoting harmony in the family.

The technique of communicating the educational content of the soap opera through creating characters as role models was worked out by the producer, Sabido, in a precise manner. As Singhal, Rogers and Brown (1992) explain, each of Sabido's entertainment-educational soap operas begins with three sets of characters – those who support the values being posited and who are to act as positive role models; those who reject the values and act as negative role models; and those who are in a state of doubt and who are to be rewarded or punished according to which side they veer towards. The audience is not to be trusted to decipher the correct message without the aid of a celebrity who is to appear in a brief 30- to 40-second epilogue.

> The epilogue is in essence a thirty to forty second 'Advertising Spot' for the educational content of the soap opera, usually delivered by a respected national figure who relates the context of that episode with the everyday life of audience members. Each time a positive role model or a 'doubter' performs a socially desirable behaviour, he/she is rewarded immediately. Each time a negative role model or a 'doubter' performs a social act negative to the value that is being promoted, he/she is immediately punished.
>
> (Singhal and Rogers 1989b)

It was claimed that the Mexican soap operas or telenovellas modelled through this technique were successful beyond expectations in propagating the social values of literacy, family planning and promotion of social harmony. For example, it has been claimed that while *Acompaname*, the soap opera promoting the values of family planning was being telecast in 1977–8 in Mexico, the number of people visiting government family planning clinics registered a 33 per cent increase over the previous year. It is difficult to know how to assess such claims, for while the soap operas were seen as models of success by international bureaucrats and policy makers, sociologists have been more cautious in their judgment for they suspect that the commercial machinery of mass culture may be used by totalitarian regimes to impose cultural and social models of harmony that are most suited to the needs of these regimes (see, for example, Litewski 1982).

To take the story of the production of *Hum Log* forward, the claims of pro-development soap operas captured the imagination of international bureaucrats and social planners. Singhal and Rogers tell a fascinating tale of how Sabido's methodology was diffused to India through a network of international bureaucrats starting from David Poindexter, President of Population Communications International, linking scientist/adminstrators such as Dr Norman Borlaugh and Dr M.S. Swaminathan, influential politicians and ministers such as Mr Inder Gujral and other bureaucrats in the Information and Broadcasting Ministry such as Mr Jyoti Shankar Singh, Mr S.B. Lal and finally Mr S.S. Gill who was instrumental in trans-forming the idea into the actual television programmes.

Doordarshan, a government-owned TV channel, began telecasting *Hum Log* on 7 July 1984 and it was broadcast for 17 months with a total of 156 half-hour episodes. At the conclusion of each episode, the educational context was summarised by a well-known film actor – Ashok Kumar – in about 60 to 90 seconds. *Hum Log* was initially a disappointment in terms of popularity ratings, but after the didactic tone was diluted at the end of the first thirteen episodes it became one of the most popular television programmes, scoring 90% audience rating in some regions. It received 400,000 letters from viewers, some of which were instrumental in giving a change of direction to certain actors and events.

Hum Log approximated the form of soap-opera genre in several respects, the most important of which are:

1 The serial form is considered to be the genre most suited to telecasting. The continuity of the story for more than a year allowed a continuous interaction between viewers and the projected images.
2 The setting was clearly domestic with all the episodes revealing them-selves in interior spaces.
3 The episodes moved through conversation rather than action.
4 The action was located in the present.
5 The soap opera, as a genre, is dependent not on individual actors but on the entire community of actors and actresses, both for aesthetic

effect and popular appeal. *Hum Log* demonstrated the typical features of soap opera in that character, actor and interaction had the stiff, unchanging quality of a cast-iron cartoon.

6 In the conclusion of each episode, the educational content was conveyed by the foregrounding of a celebrity as celebrity.

Ashok Kumar, who made the guest appearance, is a famous character actor of Hindi films. Hence he derived his celebrity status not from his participation in *Hum Log* but rather as an inter-textual figure through which the characters from the film world were made available to the viewers in a new role. This inter-textuality is typical of soap opera as a genre.

In some other respects, the differences between the typical soap operas and the kind of telenovella based on the Mexican experiment are notable. They pertain to:

1. The limited duration of the telecast of *Hum Log*, as compared to the long life of the soap operas on Western television. For instance, the soap opera, *Love of Life*, died on 1 February 1980, when it was 28 years, 4 months and 8 days old with a remarkable eulogy delivered by the famed newsman Walter Cronkite on CBS nightly news. In contrast, *Hum Log* was telecast for a little more than a year and, although several viewers protested at its early demise, several critics welcomed the end of a programme that was viewed in the national newspapers as pandering to the lowest denominator in television viewing.

2. The typical soap opera was telecast in the afternoons. A major shift took place in the United States and UK when soap operas such as *Dynasty* or *All in the Family* were slotted for prime-time viewing. *Hum Log* made it to prime-time precisely because it was seen as an important instrument for propagating important social messages. It was the control exercised by the bureaucrats of the Information and Broadcasting Ministry and not the powerful commercial sponsors it could attract that secured a prime-time slot for *Hum Log*. One of the unanticipated consequences however, was the market success enjoyed by Maggi Noodles, the commercial sponsors of *Hum Log*, due to the tremendous popularity of the programme.

3. Unlike night-time soaps which depend upon melodrama and florid exaggeration, evident in say *Dynasty* or *Dallas*, *Hum Log* was quotidian in its conception. In this it was closer to soap operas on English television. In order to appreciate the quotidian conception of *Hum Log*, let me compare a dramatic episode of *Dynasty* with one of *Hum Log*. In one session of *Dynasty*, patriarch Blake Carrington struggles to control, variously, the rivalry between his wife and his former wife, his son Stephen whose sexuality oscillates between homosexuality and heterosexuality as the plot requires, his son Adam who turns out not to be his son at all, his niece Leslie who discovers that her lover is her brother, and his sister

Dominique who, in a wildly implausible but grand burst of TV affirmative action, is black.[7]

Contrast this with a dramatic episode of *Hum Log* in which the opening frame takes us to the humble kitchen of a middle-class family in which the mother is fanning the father while he eats. The image captures a traditional motif that appears in mythology, folklore and Hindi films. The eldest daughter, Badki, is called out of her room. She has been crying. Yet another prospective groom is coming to 'see' her. Badki complains sadly that when she thinks of how much humiliation her parents have to bear for her sake, she feels thoroughly ashamed of herself. The father interprets this as an accusation that he has been unable to fulfil his duty as a father by providing her with a good husband. A four-cornered quarrel ensues in which the father reacts in defensive anger, the mother tries to placate the daughter by assuring her that it is not a burden for parents to try and arrange for their daughter's marriage – indeed it is their sacred duty; the grandmother reacts with anger at Badki's mother (i.e her son's wife) for not inculcating respect for the father in the children. Cornered on all sides, the mother slaps Badki for daring to argue with her elders. Badki looks in hurt amazement and says 'Ma, you hit *me*?'. The hurt anger is itself a sign of the intimacy between mother and daughter and suddenly the mother hugs the daughter. This micro-event in the episode also draws on the complex emotional construction of anger from domestic life, for such forms of anger (which arise from a combination of love and helplessness) are characteristic of the mother's orientation to the daughter. Unlike American soap opera, *Hum Log* does not declare itself as florid exaggeration – leaving that field for popular films. Hence it weaves many quotidian images from everyday domesticity into itself. I should state here that this tradition has not continued on Indian television. The new soap operas of the 1990s such as *Junoon* (Madness), *Imtihan* (Test) play much more with the forbidden themes of adultery, murder, and are set in extraordinary places and circumstances.

4. The characters in *Hum Log* do not appear as social types. For example, many Hindi films of the 1950s and the 1960s were populated by actors representing social types which announced themselves through marked physical and verbal quirks. The Bengali would be marked by the tendency to mix grammatical genders in his speech; the Tamil by his propensity to use expressions like 'Aiy-aiy-o'; the Christian woman by her dress; and the generic filmic 'tribal' woman by her flared skirts that revealed plenty of leg. Although the setting and forms of speech used in *Hum Log* place it as a lower middle-class urban family from North India, the characters do not represent social types but rather conflict between values – tradition versus modernity, materialism versus spiritualism, etc. This is partly due to the fact that the educational content of the soap opera was sought to be conveyed through the typification of each character as representative of a social value which was in conflict with another

social value. Thus the specialisation of characters was to convey values perceived as 'correct' in accordance with the needs of the state. However, some typification did occur in the process of writing the script and giving it material shape. For example, names like Badki (the eldest), Majhli (the middle), Chutki (the little one) appear in folk tales to represent character types defined through positioning of a person in the family. Thus an intertextuality with folk tales is established, despite the fact that in *Hum Log* Badki represented tradition, Majhli, the evils of modernity and Chutki the possibilities of enlightened transformation that the state was trying to inculcate.

5. One of the most important differences in prime-time soaps in the United States and *Hum Log* was that the television culture in the 1970s in North America reflected the anxiety about the decline of family when social problems were being seen in the public mind as family problems. This was true not only in the official discourses of public agencies and of the social sciences but also in the imagery of popular culture. Television culture probably responded to this yearning for close familial ties. Yet, as I mentioned earlier, it ended up by evolving a sub-text in which new rules and new forms for familial living came to be articulated.

In contrast, *Hum Log* did not represent any anxiety about decline of family. I am sure that this is because family is seen in Indian public culture as an extremely stable and strong institution (Beteille 1991: 3). Although the attack on certain kinds of practices in the family such as child abuse, dowry, lack of freedom for women, have come in for criticism from time to time from social reformers and social activists, there has been no interrogation of the family as a fundamental institution of society. Thus there is no comparable anxiety about the decline of family which was a marked feature of the television culture of North America in the 1970s. What was interesting in the representation of family in *Hum Log* was the assumption that family values could be moulded in such a way that family could enter into an effective alliance with the state so as to act as an arm of the state. Thus women were to be freed from the tyranny of tradition enough to be able to make decisions to marry according to their choices provided the match was with a suitable boy according to middle-class norms. They were to be further encouraged to acquire enough autonomy to take decisions about limiting their families, but any desires that took them outside the accepted normativity of the family as an institution were to be severely punished. For example, Majhli, the middle daughter who dreams of a career as a glamorous singer (the heart throb of millions of young men, as a hoarding announcing her programme promises) is brought near the brink of disaster. There was no question, therefore, of permitting a sub-text to emerge which would encourage women to be radicalised. In the bureaucratic imagination, the family was to become a compliant surface on which to write the programmes of the state.

In the previous section I described the context in which *Hum Log* was created and compared its form to that of soap operas in the West, including night soaps. The characters and episodes of *Hum Log* were created to reflect the values that would be consistent with the direction that the agencies of the state were trying to give to the family through the manipulation of television culture in India. A prime-time family had been created. What kind of life did it lead in the social life world of the society in which it was created?

Just as it is given in the life of a commodity that it separates itself from the context of its production and comes to secure different social lives, so the characters of this prime-time family also acquired lives different from those that were embedded in their production. While *Hum Log* was being telecast in 1984–5 it provided a constant source of discussion among viewers. Unfortunately there has been no fieldwork to document the nature of this discussion. The letters received in response to the various episodes provide us with some clue of some possible relations forged between image, object and the viewer.

First of all one may distinguish between those letters which recognised the performative nature of the episodes and the simulated nature of the characters and those which somehow blurred the performance with life itself. The most prominent viewers in the first category were those who saw *Hum Log* as a form of theatre and for whom the question was – what kind of theatre was it? Thus one viewer wrote and asked Ashok Kumar whether he could join the theatrical company that was producing *Hum Log*. Another group of persons sent a script they had written for a film, asking Ashok Kumar to have it produced. Still others complimented the script writer for the lifelike script of *Hum Log* or complimented the cast for their realistic performances. One young girl wrote to Ashok Kumar telling him that she had always wanted to be a film actress but her parents were so tradition bound that they would not allow her to entertain such dreams. There was some irony in this for this letter recalled Majhli's dream of becoming a famous performer and the heavy price she had to pay for it, while this young girl was soliciting the support of Ashok Kumar for the fulfilment of these very dreams. Another boy wrote saying that he had always wanted to pursue poetry and music but his father pressurised him to study hard so that he could gain admission in medical or engineering college.

Singhal and Rogers inferred (1989a) that most letters came from members of lower-middle-class families. From the addresses, styles of writing, and the linguistic usages my own sense is that they have been correct in identifying the social background of the writers. The viewing of *Hum Log*, it seems, became an occasion for the release of certain kinds of desires among young persons of lower middle class for participation in the glamour of the world of film and television. These were desires that would have been thwarted within the family but the nearness with Ashok Kumar experienced through the television screen seems to have made the film world somewhat nearer and more accessible allowing one kind of expression for these desires. It is interesting to observe that these viewers never responded to any of the specific questions posed by Ashok Kumar (e.g., why is the world becoming more materialistic?) taking it to be part of the performance itself. In some ways they are the ones who called the lie to the bureaucratic fantasy that the programme would lead to different values being adopted in society and that Ashok Kumar's presence at the end would reinforce the educational content of the episode. Completely oblivious of all this, these viewers *re-placed* the actor back into the glamorous film world from which he had temporarily stepped onto the television screen.

The second kind of letters were those in which the performative aspect of soap opera slides under the notion that the characters have a life in which the audience can legitimately participate. For example when the eldest daughter, Badki, was torn between the traditional view of marriage as appropriately arranged by elders and her own desire to marry the doctor Ashwin, several viewers wrote encouraging her to go ahead and marry the doctor. It was reported that after the episode showing Badki's marriage with the doctor was telecast, markets in some towns remained shut to celebrate the marriage and sweets were distributed in some other places. There were other letters advising an actor or actress to be more tolerant or more assertive, or to lay off alcohol. After one episode, at the conclusion of which Ashok Kumar had commented adversely on the character of Badki's father, some viewers wrote to him urging him to show more understanding of the travails of a middle-class man. Such letters had their counter-life in the conversations among people on whether Badki acted rightly in her choice of partner, whether Majhli would be accepted back in society after her fall and so on.

A third aspect under which the relation between character and viewer emerged was a feeling on the part of some viewers that their own lives were, in some inexplicable way, linked with the lives of the characters. For example, when the grandmother was shown to have cancer several viewers wrote to Ashok Kumar urging him to see that she did not die. Although they were not successful in ensuring her immortality on television they were able to have her death postponed until several episodes later. In one of the letters a viewer said that he was very saddened by the discovery that grandmother had cancer because his own grandmother also had cancer and had died around that time. 'If you show granny's death in *Hum Log*, it will make us all very sad', he added.

Finally, there were viewers who responded at the cognitive level, using the occasion of the presentation of an episode and the summary presented by Ashok Kumar to discuss the many ills of modernity, the decline of family values and the harshness of society against women. For instance a letter[8] in which the author identified himself as 'a young citizen of the beloved country India and an admirer of *Hum Log*' stated:

And now your question: Why are there quarrels among us '*Hum Log*'. The answer is: there are three roots of all quarrels –
1. Money.
2. Livelihood. The Hindi word *roti* is used in the original which in its most restricted sense refers to bread and may be generalised successively to food and to livelihood.
3. Woman.

Due to these three reasons there are quarrels which are apparent in *Hum Log* – both yours and ours. One should find mutually acceptable solutions otherwise this life becomes poisonous. And in all this the opinions of elders must be into account otherwise this life becomes poisonous. And in conclusion, a couplet:

Empty handed we have come
Empty handed we shall go
Only memories of few moments
To our own we shall bestow.

Incidentally the writer of the letter identifies himself also as a secular person by drawing symbols of *svasti*, the star in juxtaposition with the moon, a cross and the symbol of *Om* in Gurumukhi script on the letterhead, showing his equal respect for Hindus, Muslims, Christians and Sikhs alike.

In a similar vein, another person, an employee of the State Bank of India, Indore, listed twenty-six reasons for unhappiness in married life which include falling prey to modernisation (literally expressed as coming under the sway of the new light), impotence or sterility, adultery, decline of electricity in the body, the wife becoming the dominant partner, etc. Although some people shared the troubles they were having with their own lives, such letters tended to use the tele-screen as a space in relation to which the threats faced by the family in India could be articulated.

If one summarises the subject positions from which viewers saw *Hum Log* one can make a separation between those positions from which *Hum Log* appears as a performance separate from everyday life and *Hum Log* as a cultural experience which links life on the tele-screen with the domestic life of the viewer. As performance it seems to have provided opportunities of two sorts. The first was the opportunity to lay claims to a theatrical experience made somehow more accessible by the presence of a film actor on the television talking to viewers right in their own domestic space. The episodes of *Hum Log* were not like those of *Dallas* or *Dynasty* that would bring the glamorous lifestyles of the rich and the powerful every day or every week within one's domestic abode. As mentioned earlier, *Hum Log* was quotidian in its conception – excepting only the presence of Ashok Kumar hinting at the glamorous world of film.

However, the inter-textuality of soap opera meant that Ashok Kumar's other life as a film star was constantly evoked and he became the addressee of several requests for a career on *Hum Log* or in Bombay films. Here the pluralism in conceptions of lifestyles introduced through the electronic media that so worried Honneth (1992) was not through imitation but by imaginatively bridging the gap between film and television.

The presence of Ashok Kumar on the small screen and the specific questions he posed about family and society also created a space for certain kinds of pop psychology and pop sociology to be enunciated. Not only did the actor freely pronounce upon the causes for the decline of moral standards, or the need for women to be encouraged to take on independent careers, but the viewers also responded with stock replies. For example, at the conclusion of one episode which showed the kinds of demands for dowry that the parents of a young girl have to face, Ashok Kumar gave a social message denouncing the evils of dowry. He contrasted the glorious position of women in ancient India when they chose a husband among the galaxy of famous men gathered through the ritual of *swayamavara* with the decline in modern India in which parents are compelled to 'exhibit' their daughters. At the conclusion of another episode depicting a woman doctor who had dedicated her life to the service of humanity, he asked: 'why are people becoming so materialist these days – why do they care only for money?'.

These observations, questions, as well as the answers received in response to them may suggest that *Hum Log* created a space from which the norms of family and society could be interrogated. Since the programme, however, was conceptualised as an *educational* soap opera, the questions were part of the didactic exercise meant to get the social message across. The interrogation did not arise from the experiential content of life but from certain rhetorical postures that inform the bureaucratic and political discourse in India. For example, the proposition on the materialist orientation to life is a standard, almost formulaic, posture for the criticism of modernity and of the West. Both Ashok Kumar's question and the responses it evoked were part of that rhetorical posturing that marks speech on public occasions. This does not mean that such rhetorical postures cannot ever be converted into experiential truths. But conversational gestures between an image on television, interrogating family norms through questions framed for didactic purposes evoked responses in which even that which may have been fatal at the level of experience (impotence of the husband, adultery committed by wife) became banal by being converted into an item on the list of twenty-six causes enumerated to explain the reasons for domestic unhappiness.

In both these cases soap opera provided performative space which, in order to be deciphered, relied upon the inter-textuality of the genre – its connection with the world of Hindi films on the one hand and its participation in other kinds of didactic, edifying discourses, on the other.

Interestingly, despite the intimacy of ordinary domesticity which was sought to be created on the small screen, both the subject positions converted television into a kind of public space related to theatre, politics, and public speaking.

The relation between image, object and viewer in the other two cases is more problematic. Why did viewers feel inclined to give advice to the characters on the screen about how to conduct their lives on television? What led them to participate in the events that occurred on television by, for instance, celebrating Badki's marriage by distributing sweets or mourning the death of grandmother? Is this to be accounted for by the particular characteristic of soap opera – *viz.* that it does not work within a structure of beginning and ending, of commencement and closure – or should we look for other forms of performance in which the audience takes precisely such subject positions? One must recall here that there are several kinds of performances in India in which audiences participate actively in shaping the events of the performance. Anuradha Kapur (1986) has described how the Ramlila of Rampur differs from the conventions of naturalist theatre precisely in the way in which the audience partici-pates in the events of the narrative so that they become synchronous with the events of one's life here and now. It is not only the collective suspen-sion of disbelief but an active creation of belief that allows a small stream in Banaras to be experienced as the terrible raging sea that has to be tamed by the might of Rama. Similarly, Rustom Bharucha (1983) has given a lively account of folk theatre in which a particularly good piece of acting may have to be repeated again and again (including stirring dying speeches) until the audience is satisfied with the performance. Roma Chatterji (1986) has suggested that certain narratives have a built-in formulaic closure (e.g. *kahani khatam paisa hajam*, i.e the story has concluded and the penny is digested) which insulate the narratives from events of one's life. She contrasts these with sacred tales (*katha*) in which the recitation of the story is part of the ritual activity and hence events occurring in the story are also happening in the lives of the people who are listening to it. So when shopkeepers distributed sweets to celebrate the marriage of Badki, or when a viewer complained that the marriage feast was no fun at all since the *hijdas* (eunuchs) who form part of the celebrations were not shown, as if he had gone for the celebrations and missed the risqué songs and the lewd gestures of the *hijdas*, how are we to interpret this? Is this the same kind of event as people celebrating the wedding of Rama and Sita by distributing special sweets? Despite apparent similarities. I believe that the complex of emotions that accom-panied these events was quite different and I shall try to formulate the nature of this difference. To my mind the crucial difference between the two kinds of events rests upon the nature of repetition.

The stories belonging to the *katha* genre can belong to both the order of narration and the order of life because they stand outside time. Events occurring in myths, even when the narrative time is the past, collapse the categories of past, present and future. In fact most of the framing episodes of Indian myths play with our categories of time. This is why sacred stories may be both eternal and historical. Hence when people distribute sweets to celebrate the wedding of Rama and Sita, which occurred in the *treta yuga* (one of the four cycles of time), they are recognising that this marriage was an event that occurs with regularity in every age in accordance with a ritual calendar. The devotee is magically transformed into a participant in the divine event by his or her devotion to the celestial couple. In this sense the time of the gods and time of men is made synchronous.

In the case of folk theatre a different kind of synchronicity is at play. It is the immediacy of the relation between actor and audience which allows the events in the performance to be moulded by the desire of the audience. It is because actors and audiences share the same life world that theatrical allusions can move out from the performance and gather meaning from the events in the life of the community of viewers. Consider the laughter that is produced when Laksman who is supposed to chop off the nose of Shrupanakha who is trying to seduce him, actually tries to inflict grievous harm on the poor actor who is portraying the unfortunate Shrupanakha because they are enemies in real life and this is as good an opportunity as any to take revenge! Life here intrudes into theatre and theatre intrudes into life because performers and audiences are part of the same social life-world. In a crucial way they are present to each other. As fictions, myth and folk theatre belong to life's reality.

In contrast, the viewer and actor are present to each other in the soap opera only through gaps in time. At one moment Ashok Kumar is speaking directly to the audience, including it in *Hum Log*, not only through the directness of address but also by the framing images of togetherness, in which different kinds of collectivities of Indians are shown. The signature tune *Hum Ek* – 'We are one' – emphasises the merging of the individual into a collective entity, the imagined community of the nation reinforced through the production of *Hum Log*. These images are received in the isolation of the domestic space, or at best a domestic space that has expanded to include neighbours. These images and messages now become conversational entities, woven into the different concerns of the face-to-face communities or the images sent to viewers are sent back to the sender in the form of letters. In one sense then, at any moment of time, the performers and the viewers are absent to each other, requiring the mediation of time for any exchange to occur. I want to emphasise that this is not essential to all electronic images, and certainly not to images in cinema. In the latter case the viewer is encapsulated in the scene of fantasy; although he may respond to this by writing letters to famous actors or actresses, the genre in itself does not require the day-to-day participation of the viewer in the events of the narrative.

The episodic nature of soap opera and the inter-textuality of the genre bring the past and the present into conjunction, but neither in a way that would suggest a play with the category of time as in myth, or the viewing of a frozen past in the reverential mode as in photographic images. Action in soap opera does not happen out of time and hence, unlike all the examples given earlier, the relation between the order of narrative and the order of life is neither in the mode of sacred myth nor in the mode of folk theatre.

Sacred myths and folk theatre are repeated in accordance with ritual calendars or other kinds of social calendars. The past in which their action is framed is brought into the present through repetition. In contrast, soap opera cannot be repeated, for its time flows parallel to the flow of time in life. It cannot provide the occasion for the creation of a collectivity in the Durkheimian sense by evoking sacred time through repetition nor can it be seen as a marked event of the past which has been brought into the present in the nostalgic mood. This is so even when bureaucratic decisions to repeat the soap opera for its educational value may be taken. For instance *Hum Log* has being telecast on Doordarshan since December 1992 in a strict linear sequence, but it has not evoked any response either in the press or in the viewers. The popularity *Hum Log* enjoyed when it was first telecast had simply vanished.

AND TELE-DOCUMENTARIES?

While the popularity of the kind of soap operas that were quotidian and didactic in nature vanished, giving way to a new genre of soap operas that is closer to the florid exaggerations of Hindi films, it is interesting to see that the everyday reality of the family finds new expressions in tele-documentaries and talk-shows. In 1991, Nalini Singh, who had already produced some very courageous documentaries on electoral corruption, police excesses and dowry deaths, decided to explore the life of the middle classes in India. Based on a mix of interviews taken in the normal habitat of the interviewees and expert comments from a panel recorded in the studios, she telecast the programme – *Hello Zindagi* – (Hello life), for one year on prime-time television. Like *Hum Log*, this programme also evoked an enormous response from the viewers. The letters received in response ran into *lakhs* (hundreds of thousands). Although the programme was not exclusively on the family, many episodes were constructed around the tribulations and experimentations in the relations between the family. Singh seemed particularly interested in exploring the nature of intra-familial communication, the creation of new kinds of desires, and the transgression of norms once held to be sacred. In the process she found that an enormous amount of suffering was encoded in the family.

Take some examples. In one of the episodes of *Hello Zindagi*, men and women talked about the nature of their relationships. The camera focuses on the face of a woman who is presented at a 180 degree plane to the camera verging on stasis, and who speaks of her longing that her husband might talk to her. 'But he says, what can one talk to a woman?' Another man with his back to the camera speaks in a broken voice of an episode in which his wife had hit him in anger. 'Could you not have hit her in turn?' asks the interviewer. 'Yes, I could have. Physically, I am much stronger than her. But when she lifted her hand against me, something in me just died.' In many other cases there were women and men who spoke of the enriching relations they had with other men or women outside marriage. Some faced the camera frontally while others preferred to have their faces blanked out. One woman spoke of an enduring relation which she had with a man for twenty years and how much tenderness and love she received from him. Yet she went on to claim that she did not consider this to be a betrayal of her husband, for she had fulfilled her role as a wife meticulously and that is all he seemed to need from her.

In one of the episodes on the middle-class woman's quest for beauty, Singh was able to show how desires created by advertisements are translated in the everyday life of the family. Some women stated that although they could not afford going to expensive beauty salons, they availed themselves of a whole range of services offered by neighbourhood salons which have mushroomed in metropolitan cities. Most women interviewed felt that their new looks were deeply appreciated by their respective husbands who compared them to various film or television actresses. Clearly images from cinema and television pervaded their lives. While Honneth (1992) would see this as evidence of plurality of lifestyles being artificially produced by the electronic media, one must ask whether the new possibilities that women were eager to explore in relation to their own bodies were not simultaneously commentaries on the articulation between sexuality and domesticity in the contemporary Indian family on which anthropologists have had little to contribute.

The tele-documentaries and talk-shows have also allowed a public culture to emerge in which new kinds of speech can be generated, breaking certain codes of silence. In one episode Singh talked to families in which women had sought amniocentesis in order to abort female foetuses. One learnt from these interviews that a mother who had borne three or four daughters and was under tremendous pressure from the family and by her own internalisation of the demands of the family to bear a son, could use this technology to avoid repeated childbearing. Some women spoke of the freedom that this technology had given them for they did not have to bear the taunts of their husband's mother that they were only mothers of daughters. The women and the men to whom Singh spoke were not afraid of facing the camera nor did they show any resistance to the interviewer. In contrast, in another episode in which families which had been compelled to abandon their daughters due to financial difficulties either to orphanages or to other childless families were traced and interviewed. Some of these parents, who were elderly couples now, found speech impossible when confronted with their own actions of long ago. One mother sat in an almost foetal position as if she would shrink into herself and cried in remembrance. In one poignant case, Singh found a mother who had just come to an orphanage to give up her illegitimate daughter for adoption. The camera faced the mother frontally feeding the baby for one last time and the sound track matched the image by the interviewer asking 'Is this the last time you are going to feed your baby?' with a numb reply 'Yes, the last time'.

Such tele-documentaries have broken the silence over the family in India – the variety of sexual and marital arrangements, the sexual abuse in the family, the commodification of relationships, is now available for thought not only in the form of didactic and rhetorical speeches of public persons but as voices of common persons. It is interesting to ask whether the response of the viewers differs when the families being watched on the tele-screen are not fictional families but what is represented a fragments of the life of real families. One clue to this is provided by the kinds of letters received in response. Although a systematic survey of the letters has not been possible since the audience-response cell of Doordarshan does not maintain these, I have had occasion to examine about sixty letters received in July 1992 which were available in the files of Singh. Some of these letters were narratives of the difficulties that a man or a woman was facing in the family, running into eight or nine pages. Others were reflections on the issues of a general nature without reference to the writer's own life. A few commented on the 'constructed' nature of the episodes with the suggestion that hired actors or actresses were used to suggest decline in family – hence the programmes were a conspiracy on the integrity of the familial values of Indian society. Let me give just one example of the kind of personal narratives that were unfolded in many letters.

This letter, written in Hindi, was penned by a woman in the midst of enormous difficulties with her conjugal and natal kin. It read:

Dear Nalini Ji,
We like the programme 'Hello Zindagi' very much. We feel good to see the truths of life reflected there. And when we see you we feel that women are not weak. They can also accomplish something. I get some courage that I may also be able to do something. I Hope you will understand my problems and try to help me to solve these or you will show me a good path.

    I am 24 years old and a mother of a 2-year-old daughter. My marriage was arranged by deceit. My husband is a very lowly kind of person. I am myself from a tradition-bound, well-off family. Before my marriage my husband gave us false information that he had a prosperous business. Afterwards we found he had nothing. ... His family also behaved badly towards me. To the extent that they started beating me. Initially I tried to be patient with my husband. When I told my parents [lit. mummy, papa], they tried to exhort me that I should bear this burden patiently. Everything would be alright. Those people would not allow me to leave the house. They would not allow me to come to my parents. But my mummy [*sic*] said, it will be alright, do as they say ...

The fights increased. One day I was badly beaten up. Even the neighbours came but my husband's mother said that I was just putting up a performance to embarrass them. Things reached a limit and my father came. But he said, it does not matter what they do – you should keep quiet. This is now your house. You have to stay here. One day I consumed a lot of sleeping pills but death also did not come to me. They did not call a doctor but they called my parents. My uncle who is a doctor took me to his house and revived me. But all my relatives scolded me and said my actions would reduce their honour to dust. But I did not want to return there. I have insisted in coming to my mummy's house. For the last six months I am enrolled for a course on stitching. My parents want to send me back to that hell. If I could become economically independent. Please Nalini Ji, help me. Will you have two minutes to meet me? Please reply to my letter ... etc.

This particular story of domestic conflict – a woman having to face violence by her conjugal kin; a husband who joins his parents in the aggression against his wife and who is dependent on them for economic survival; parents who push the girl back into the conjugal family despite the knowledge of the atrocities that she has to bear – this is almost the stable narrative of violence against young women. Such narrative organisation of the experience of violence can be found in the case files of women's organisations; in criminal and civil cases that come up in courts of law; in stories related in the process of psychiatric treatment or psychological counselling. When the script of *Hum Log* was being evolved, a well-known social anthropologist (S.C. Dube) was asked to write a background paper on traditional values of the Indian family so that the episodes could be realistic. In retrospect, the emphasis on family harmony as a basic value of Indian society and the peaceful transformation of values that the episodes of *Hum Log* portrayed, appear to be fictions created by social anthropologists.

The very process of portraying the family realistically on serials like *Hello Zindagi*, however, has raised important questions. In response to this documentary many viewers have used the analogy of a mirror and they want to see their own stories reflected in this mirror. Yet, given the nature of television, one wonders whether the appropriation of private lives into the public domain has not rendered life also more defenceless.

One can find episodes in which the camera clings too closely to the body; the cuts come at points so that the speech of the interviewee is made more crisp but at the cost of a loss of context; the severe imposition of time limits presents stories as floating fragments. Then there are the well-known devices by which the camera establishes its power over the narrative through the framing of presence, the juxtaposition of sound and image, the compositional devices by which the background disappears from view; as well as the voice of the commentary that establishes a transcendent privileged meaning.

While it is true that much of the social commentary in *Hum Log* was in the nature of clichés – not only the external clichés of sound and image but also the internal psychic clichés through which emotion was presented, its frankly fictional character and the inter-textuality it established with film, allowed issues on family to be framed in a manner that escaped the ethical issues on representation that the new genre of tele-documentaries has raised for our consideration.

As the nature of soap operas alters and new kinds of television experiences enter the home in India, especially through the operation of global commercial interests, it would interest us to see whether the confessional mode becomes a dominant mode through which our private experience begins to find public expression and whether that leads to a thinning of the richness of local experience as it is cast in globally perfected forms. My own sense is that the prognosis of epistemic and cultural domination through the medium of television may have been made rather too early. As the case of *Hum Log* showed, the capacity of Indian audiences to alter formulaic prescriptions whether for development or for entertainment cannot be underestimated even by its worst critics.

ACKNOWLEDGEMENTS

I am grateful to Pratiksha Baxi, Lester Cuitinho, Arvind Singhal, and Nalini Singh for their generosity in helping me to get access to the material on which this paper is based. The time I have spent with Raymond Bellour and Kumar Shahani, though fleeting, has given me an entry into the questions I may not have been able to ask otherwise. To Sanmay who typed large parts of this paper despite his gruelling summer schedule, I offer my grateful thanks. I am indebted to Daniel Miller for his patience in helping me to revise the paper for publication.

NOTES

1. The use of gender categories to represent high and low culture has been succinctly analysed by Huyssen (1986).
2. This point has been made forcefully by Geraghty (1991). There are others, however, who disagree, arguing that television texts identified as feminist

redirect independent, assertive female characters into safely traditional female categories. See, for instance, Rabinovitz (1988).

3. This point is made in a different way by Youssef Ishaghpour (1991) who feels that television tears aside all that is veiled and thus marks the advent of the world as obscenity.

4. See also Magny (1991) who says that the power of the image on television derives from the fact that it has reference and hence must be true. 'Yet, in practice, and in our individual experience of television especially as regards "truth" there is the experience of the lie' (p. 85).

5. See Ian Ang (1985).

6. Compare Miller (1992) for cultural innovations in the genre of soap opera in the Caribbean. See also Michelle and Armand Mattelart (1990) who have argued for the specificity of the telenovella that is to be seen as a Latin American art form distinct from Western soap opera.

7. This description is taken from Taylor (1989).

8. The names of all letter writers are being withheld to protect their privacy.

REFERENCES

Adorno, T. (1954) Television and the pattern of mass culture. *The Quarterly Of Film Radio and Television* 8 (3).

Ang, I. (1985) *Watching Dallas: Soap Opera and the Melodramatic Imagination.* London: Methuen.

Baudrillard, J. (1982) *A l'Ombre des Majorités Silencieuses.* Paris: Editions Denoel/Gunthier.

Baudrillard, J. (1991) *The Ecstasy of Communication.* Columbia: Semiotext(e).

Beteille, A. (1991) The family and the reproduction of inequality. *Contributions to Indian Sociology* (n.s.) 25 (1): 3–28

Bharucha, R. (1983) *Rehearsals for Revolution, Political Theatre in Bengal.* Calcutta.

Cantor, M. and S. Pingree (1985) *The Soap Opera.* California: Sage.

Casatta, M. and T. Skill (eds) (1983) *Life on Daytime Television: Tuning-in American Serial Drama.* Norwood, NJ: Ablex.

Chatterji, R. (1986) The voyage of the hero. In V. Das, ed., *The Word and the World: Fantasy, Symbol and Record.* Delhi: Sage Publications.

Contractor, N.S., A. Singhal and E.M. Rogers (1988) Metatheoretical perspectives in satellite television and development in India. *Journal of Broadcasting and Electronic Media* 38 (2): 129–48.

Derry, C. (1983) Television soap opera: Incest, bigamy and fatal disease. *Journal of University Film and Video Association* 35 (1).

Feuer, J. (1981) Melodrama and serial form in television today. *Screen* 25 (1): 4–16.

Geraghty, C. (1991) *Women and Soap Opera: A Study of Prime Time Soaps.* Oxford: Polity.

Honneth, A. (1992) Pluralization and recognition: On the self-misunderstanding of post-modern theorists. *Thesis Eleven* 31: 24–33.

Huyssen, A. (1986) Mass culture as woman: Modernization's other. In *After the Great Divide: Modernism, Mass Culture, Post Modernism.* Bloomington: Indiana University Press.

Ishaghpour, Y. (1991) The representable: The advent of the world as obscenity. In J. Kermaban and S. Kumar, eds, *Cinema and Television.* Delhi: Orient Longman.

Kapur, A. (1986) *The Ramlila of Rampur.* Delhi: Sage.

Litewski, C. (1982) *Brazilian Television in Context.* London.

Magny J. (1991) What is television? In J. Kermaban and S. Kumar, eds, *Cinema and Television*. Delhi: Orient Longman.

Mattelart, M. and A. Mattelart (1990) *The Carnival of Images: Brazilian Television Fiction*. London: Bergin & Garvey.

Miller, D. (1992) The young and the restless in Trinidad: A case of the local and the global in mass consumption. In R. Silverstone and E. Hirsch, eds, *Consuming Technology*. London: Routledge.

Morris, M. (1990) Banality in cultural studies. In P. Mellencamp, ed., *Logics of Television*. Bloomington: University of Indiana Press.

Motta, L. (1985) Debate on cultural colonization. *Tribuna ele Bahia*.

Rabinovitz, L. (1988) Sitcoms and single moms: Representations of feminism on American TV. *Cinema Obscura*.

Singhal, A. and E. Rogers (1989a) *India's Information Revolution*. Delhi: Sage.

—— (1989b) Pro-social television for development in India. In *Public Communication Campaigns*. California 331–50.

Singhal, A., E. Rogers and W. Brown (1992) *Entertainment telenovelas for development. Lessons learnt about creation and implementation*. São Paulo, Brazil: International Association for Mass Communication Research.

Taylor, E. (1989) *Prime-time Families: Television Culture in Post-war America*. Berkeley: University of California Press.

Vasudevan, R. (1993) Shifting codes, dissolving identities. The Hindi social film of the 1950s as popular culture. *Journal of Arts and Ideas* vol. 23–4.

9 The objects of soap opera: Egyptian television and the cultural politics of modernity

Lila Abu-Lughod

Circulating in Cairo in the 1980s was a joke typical for its urban contempt for the peasant from Upper Egypt:

> A Sa'idi [Upper Egyptian] came to Cairo and wanted to buy a TV set. He went to the appliance store and, pointing, asked, 'How much is that TV in the window?' The owner yelled, 'Get out of here you stupid Sa'idi!' He went away and dressed in a long white robe and headdress to disguise himself as a Saudi Arabian. He came back to the store and again asked, 'How much is that TV in the window?' The owner yelled, 'Get out of here you stupid Sa'idi!' He went away and changed into trousers and a shirt and tie, coming back disguised as a European. Again he asked 'How much is that TV in the window?' The owner yelled, 'Get out of here you stupid Sa'idi!' Puzzled, the poor man asked, 'How could you tell it was me?' The shop owner answered, 'That's not a TV, it's a washing machine.'[1]

In this joke, lack of familiarity with television was made symptomatic of rural backwardness. Television represents modernity, requiring for its production advanced technology and for reception an expensive instrument. Although introduced into Egypt in 1960, it took the slow spread of electrification and labour migrants' wages in the 1970s to bring television sets to the majority of households, especially outside the major cities.

In the 1950s, this new communication technology was celebrated in US discourses on the modernisation of the Third World. This was exemplified in Middle East studies by Daniel Lerner (1958) whose classic text, *The Passing of Traditional Society*, argued that mass media opened closed traditional minds by revealing the vast world of difference, facilitating the 'empathy' that was a prerequisite of the mobile, politically participating, opinion-holding personality essential to modernity.

Although Lerner's confident views of mass media have been countered by a more recent critical literature on cultural imperialism, followed by counter-critiques by anthropologists attuned to the creative and self-productive local appropriations of imported television (e.g. Miller 1992; Wilk 1993), in countries like Egypt, India and China with major television production capabilities of their own, the more pressing question may be how the internal cultural politics of government-controlled media articulate with contested visions of modernity. An anthropologist interested in Egypt would want to ask what sorts of differences Egyptian television actually reveals to its audiences and what difference this makes to those exposed to it. What, in fact, is the relationship between television and modernity?

More than any other form of mass media, especially in a place where many remain non-literate, television brings a variety of vivid experiences of the non-local into the most local of situations, the home. So when someone like Nobel laureate Naguib Mahfouz laments the decline of the Cairo coffee house, explaining 'People used to go to the coffee shops and listen to story tellers who played a musical instrument and told of folk heroes. These events filled the role played by television serials today', he forgets that this older form of entertainment, with the imaginary non-local worlds it conjured up, was only available to men (quoted in Hedges 1992). Television gives women, the young, and the rural as much access as urban men to stories of other worlds.

In Egypt, I will argue, a concerned group of culture-industry professionals has constructed of these women, youths and rural people a subaltern object in need of enlightenment. Appropriating and inflecting Western discourses on development they construct themselves as guides to modernity and assume the responsibility of producing, through their television programmes, the virtuous modern citizen. Especially in the dramatic serials which are Egypt's most popular television fare, they seek to 'educate' their public. Their faith in the impact of television is spurred by the debates their serials provoke among critics and other parts of the urban intelligentsia.

Yet a look at the place of television in these subalterns' lives suggests that this public subverts and eludes them, not because they are traditional and ignorant of the modern, as the joke about the country bumpkin would have it, but because the ways they are positioned within modernity is at odds with the visions these urban middle-class professionals promote. The nationalist message is broadcast into a complex social space where the very local and the transnational both exert powerful pulls. On the one hand, people live in the local worlds of their daily experience, of which television is only a small part. On the other hand, as multinational companies bombard the Egyptian market with their products, as Islamic political groups with broader than national identifications vie for loyalty, and as elites look to the West, television's nationalists have much to compete with.

TELEVISION IN A DISCOURSE OF THE MODERN NATION

In the discourse of some key culture-industry professionals in Egypt, television figures in a nationalist and elitist vision of modernity. When film

star and director Nur al-Sharif described the beginnings of Egyptian television, he noted that in a general atmosphere of national advancement
the government had a plan for using media and art to change people's
views on political participation and life.[2] Films and serials of the 1960s
were based on literary works in order 'to educate people, enlighten them,
and draw them into the policy of the new revolution in transforming
Egyptian society from a feudal, capitalist society into a socialist one'.
In the same breath, he added that many serials were based on novels by
Egypt's great writers 'to help the uneducated Egyptian youth in rural
areas, the provinces, and in cities other than Cairo and Alexandria, who
had no concern with culture, to become acquainted with those great
writers'.

This professed interest in educating and 'culturing' the poor and those
outside the urban capitals was echoed by Muhammad Fadil, one of Egypt's
foremost television directors, who argued that television in a developing
country plagued not just by illiteracy but by cultural illiteracy should not
simply entertain; it has to work to eliminate this cultural illiteracy. Linking
culture and social responsibility, he defined culture, in terms reminiscent
of Lerner's portrait of 'modern man', as 'familiarity with the news, appreciation of art, a taste for art, music, theatre. . . . Culture is the concern of
the individual with the problems of others, which comes from knowledge.'[3]
Fadil concluded that since drama was the most loved form, it had to be
exploited to teach people without them sensing it.

Essential to this construction of television entertainment as serious art
that is socially or politically uplifting is the contrast with commercial entertainment. Fadil distinguished between serials people enjoyed watching and
those whose effects carried on long after they had been broadcast. He
criticised colleagues for making pumpkin-seed serials – serials that were
fun to watch, like munching on seeds, but gave no real nourishment.[4] Nur
al-Sharif defended government policy regarding television in the 1960s
claiming that it enabled television 'to produce a common national dream,
not only inside Egypt but in the whole Arab world. It made people enthu-
siastic and optimistic.' He contrasted this to what had happened since the
mid-1970s when private companies began producing programmes, their
only interest being to entertain people and their hands being tied by the
necessity of selling their programmes in the conservative Gulf states where
political and moral censorship are highly restrictive.[5]

This contest between the idealistic vision of television drama as the
producer of a modern cultured citizen with a national consciousness and
the competing tendency of Egyptian television to present 'cheap' entertainment was dramatically played out during 1993 in the controversy, not
over an Egyptian serial, but over the American soap opera, *The Bold and
the Beautiful*. Beginning in late 1992, Channel 2, the channel that broad-
casts most of the foreign programmes in Egypt, began airing nightly
episodes of this successful American daytime soap that has been running

in the USA since March 1987 and has been exported to twenty-two countries.[6] In Egypt, cartoons in a weekly magazine caricatured its popularity; one showed a government minister on the telephone noting that the best time to raise prices on goods without anyone protesting was between 9.30 and 10.30 p.m., the time the soap was being aired.

The Bold and the Beautiful is set in the fashion world of Los Angeles and centres on two key families involved in fashion design and publishing. Nearly all the actresses are blonde and most of the actors are handsome, something that is not incidental to the success of the soap. Cartoons in a weekly magazine *Sabah al-Khayr* suggested that both men and women viewers had become smitten with the characters. One showed a woman viewer watching the female announcer introduce the show as follows: 'Dear Family Members, now is the time for our date with the adorable handsome boy who drives you crazy, damn him – Ridge.' Beside it was a cartoon showing a man strumming on a lute and singing as he watched television: 'O Night, linger over this pretty friend.'

Newspapers participated in and satirised viewers' immersion in the characters and their relationships, commenting on the way characters had become taken for real. A cartoon showed an older veiled woman talking to a friend on the telephone about the surgery of one of the female characters. 'Hey, people are all the same', she says. 'Come on, let's take two kilos of oranges and rush to visit our Aunt Logan, Brook's mother, in the hospital.' In a major magazine a serious article on USAID in Egypt introduced the argument that Egypt was actually subsidising the USA economy by saying, 'Would you believe that Egypt supports America? And gives it economic aid? . . . You don't believe that you subsidise that charming American woman, Brook Logan?'[7]

The contrast between *The Bold and the Beautiful* and the highlight of Egyptian television viewing over the past five years could not be more stark. Since 1988 during successive Ramadans, the Muslim month of fasting and the television season's high point, people had been emotionally riveted by a brilliant Egyptian television serial written by Usama Anwar 'Ukasha. This was the quintessential non-pumpkin-seed serial. Called *Hilmiyya Nights*, it followed the fortunes and relationships of a group of characters from the traditional Cairo neighbourhood of Hilmiyya, taking them from the late 1940s, when Egypt was under the rule of King Farouk and the British, up to the present, even incorporating into the final episodes the Egyptian reaction to the Gulf War.

Although many Egyptian television serials have captured large audiences and generated discussion and affection, and the local productions are generally more popular than foreign imports, the broadcast of this unusually long and high quality serial was a national cultural event.[8] Its popularity was not confined to the millions who regularly followed the evening serials but extended to the intelligentsia who were provoked by its political messages. The merits of the serial were debated in newspapers and magazines and a leading intellectual, Sayed Yassin, even used it as a metaphor for 'Egypt's real abilities'. In a brief essay in a major weekly magazine, *Al-Iqtisadi*, he contrasted the successful serial, with its excellent text, capable director, talented and devoted actors, and involved audience with the failures of current political activity in Egypt, suggesting that what Egypt needed was a better political text to guide its director (the President), more respect for its citizens, and the introduction of new political actors.[9]

With little daytime television and a state-controlled television industry until recently only minimally supported through advertising, there never developed in Egypt an equivalent of the US daytime soap opera.[10] Instead, since the late 1960s, the form of the evening dramatic serial (*musalsal*) consisting of anywhere from fifteen to thirty episodes broadcast on consecutive days, has dominated Egyptian television entertainment. Although as television critics have noted, the strict definition of television genres is becoming increasingly problematic, serials are distinguishable from daytime or prime-time soap operas in being finite and self-contained, offering viewers some sort of dramatic resolution by the final episode (Geraghty 1991). Like soap operas, however, most Egyptian serials are set in the domestic space, using limited and familiar sets; more importantly, their plots revolve around unfolding personal relationships often presented melodramatically. Much like the USA and British prime-time soaps of the 1980s (e.g. *Dallas*, *Dynasty* and *EastEnders*) that have deliberately sought wider audiences, Egyptian serials are believed to have women as their primary audiences while reaching out successfully to whole families, men included.

Hilmiyya Nights, more than most Egyptian serials, seems to be a hybrid product. Although its talented writer denied in print that he had given audiences an Egyptian *Falcon Crest* (an American prime-time soap that had aired several years earlier), there are numerous aspects of *Hilmiyya Nights* in which the influence of such American programmes can be detected. If the prime-time soap opera can be defined by its peculiar mixing of the aesthetics of melodrama, realism and light entertainment, then *Hilmiyya Nights* fits the description (Geraghty 1991: 25). Strong on emotional drama, the serial focuses on the faces and feelings of its characters and intensifies its effects through dramatic music.[11] As in other Egyptian serials tears are plentiful, if balanced by laughter and anger. Like the British soap operas (and unlike the American) that take realism more seriously, the serial is set in particular neighbourhoods and attempts to depict class differences and regional identities authentically and nostalgically.

What makes *Hilmiyya Nights* seem most like American prime-time soaps is that it partakes of the element of spectacle. The costumes are lavish, the sets sumptuous, and at least some of the women characters extravagantly glamorous and fashionable (Geraghty 1991: 27–8). The aristocratic central characters move elegantly among their villas and luxurious apartments, the key woman character elaborately made up and coiffured and dressed in a different outfit for each of well over a hundred episodes, trading sequined gowns for chiffon and furs, except when going in to the office when she wears stylish suits in striking colours.

In addition, the serial resembles the American prime-time soap operas in certain aspects of plot. As in *Dallas* the central action revolves around the rivalry between two wealthy men and their families, in this case an urban aristocrat and a rural mayor, both of whom become millionaire businessmen in the 1970s and 1980s. The financial wheelings and dealings of these two and the woman who at different times was married to each of them carry much of the narrative along. The adventures and love interests of their children become the focus as the serial moves into the present.

Though by definition serials differ from soap operas in having resolutions, this serial was unusual in deferring its resolution for so long. Drawn out over five years and far more episodes than any previous Egyptian serial, *Hilmiyya Nights* allowed for the development of the kind of attachment to characters that soap-opera audiences relish. Following the tribulations and successes of some of the characters from childhood to adulthood and others through marriages, divorces, losses, imprisonments and careers well into old age, audiences were treated to the pleasurable experience common to American soap-opera viewers: of finding meaning in scenes from their knowledge of the characters' histories (Geraghty 1991: 15). An intimacy was created by the deep familiarity viewers came to have over time with characters' personal histories and tangled relationships, especially since old episodes of the serial were re-run each year before the new instalment was aired and the whole serial, now complete, was being shown on successive Sunday evenings in 1993.[12]

Analysts have noted that among the distinguishing features of the soap-opera genre is the centrality of strong women characters. This too applied to *Hilmiyya Nights* with its important women figures in each generation. Not only do we have at the centre of the drama a *femme fatale* who is also a crafty and financially ruthless aristocrat turned businesswoman but also the long-suffering and moral wives and mothers of key male figures, the educated daughters of rich and poor pursuing professional careers while trying to manage love lives, and the odd belly-dancer. Although strong women characters are not uncommon in Egyptian dramatic serials, in *Hilmiyya Nights* the richness of the variety of women, their competence in the work sphere, and their dramatic centrality were striking.[13]

Despite these resemblances, however, 'Ukasha was right to deny that *Hilmiyya Nights* was the Egyptian *Falcon Crest*. This is not, as he charged, because *Falcon Crest* was made to dupe Third World people, full of beautiful women and sex, but because the series differed radically from any American soap opera in being historically contextualised. American soap operas have been characterised as a women's genre because they privilege the personal, depicting even the non-domestic work scenes in terms of personal relationships. This Egyptian serial similarly portrayed the personal lives of individuals but instead of having its narrative pushed along simply by events in the personal relationships among the characters, *Hilmiyya Nights* had the moral themes of loyalty, betrayal, corruption, thwarted desires and tragic errors embedded in an historical narrative that tied individual lives to Egyptian national political events. It did what no American soap would ever do: it provided an explicit social and political commentary on contemporary Egyptian life.[14]

Above all, *Hilmiyya Nights* promoted the theme of national unity. With the exception of a very few truly evil characters, selfish and corrupt individuals out for themselves, the characters of different classes and political persuasions were shown to be basically good and patriotic. Our hearts went out to them as many were led astray, reacting to romantic and political blows. But in the end, they saw the errors of their ways, prevented by their love of Egypt from pursuing the materialistic, immoral or corrupt paths they had taken. Even the young religious extremist (the first to be depicted in an Egyptian television serial) was sympathetically portrayed as part of a generation that had been led astray by the lack of national spirit.[15]

PROTECTING THE PUBLIC

Hilmiyya Nights sought to teach and enlighten. In response, intellectuals, critics, politicians and censors sought to protect the public from its messages. Both the writer and his critics, the urban educated elite who felt it incumbent on them to protect others, assumed the power of television serials and the vulnerability of subaltern viewers.

Hilmiyya Nights attempted to inform millions of ordinary Egyptians about their country's modern history. Its characters participated in such activities as anti-colonial raids against the British, the nationalisation of factories during Nasser's era, the wars with Israel, political crackdowns in a police state, the rise of Islamic fundamentalism and the scams of the new Islamic investment companies. Characters' lives were deeply affected by the economic liberalisation of Sadat's 'open door' policies, the increase in heroin addiction and drug trafficking, and the policies of state feminism.

The debates in the press focused on the political perspective presented. As the headline of an article in the centre-right newspaper *Al-Wafd* bluntly asked, 'Does the Author of *Hilmiyya Nights* Have the Right to Write History from the Nasserist Viewpoint?'[16] The serial then provided the occasion for setting the public straight. In the same newspaper, Dr Abd el-Azim Ramadan, the leading establishment historian of the Sadat period, defended himself for not criticising the serial, noting that *Hilmiyya Nights* was excellent drama, important for raising cultural standards in the Arab world, and that although the writer had glorified Nasser, he had presented the period as those living through it had perceived it. Ramadan explained why the people had worshipped Nasser; they thought he had achieved so many of their dreams: a republic, land reform, socialism, a strong army and Arab unity. They had not realised, he continued, that what Nasser had created was a military dictatorship. And because of media disinformation, they knew little about how many Egyptian thinkers of the left and right he had imprisoned. Ramadan concluded his articles with the two lessons to be learned from the Nasser period: that dictator-ship and justice do not go together and that people should distrust the mass media.[17]

The serial was criticised from other political perspectives as well. In the leftist newspaper *Al-Ahaly* 'Ukasha was asked why he made the capitalist pasha such a sympathetic character and ignored the everyday problems of ordinary people. In *Al-Sha'b*, another opposition newspaper that now presents the viewpoint of the Muslim Brotherhood, the paper's editor Adel Hussein defended the serial and 'Ukasha's right to free expression. He praised the new instalment for depicting everyday religiosity, noting that he had earlier criticised the serial, like all television drama, for never showing Islamic religious practices as part of daily life.

Those sympathetic to 'Ukasha's politics wrote articles complimenting the serial for its brilliance, invoking a discourse of art over politics. 'Asim Hanafy criticised those who treated the serial as a political tract rather than a superb artistic achievement that had made people realise the fraud-ulence and poverty of the past 30 years of television drama. Yet, in enumerating their political criticisms, he made his own position clear. Most pointed was his mockery of one writer who had accused *Hilmiyya Nights* of being anti-Sadat 'because it dealt with the open-door policy and the new parasitical commercial class'. His comment was 'Isn't Egypt suffering because of the influence of this class today?'[18] Alluding to the problems 'Ukasha had faced from the television censors, his article went on to condemn censorship in an age of increasing democracy.

State censorship is exercised in Egypt in the name of protecting the public from the morally, politically or religiously offensive. *Hilmiyya Nights* tested the limits of the more generous freedom of the press that has been President Mubarak's policy. The writer 'Ukasha clashed with the television censors who not only commented on the screenplay but also required cuts after the filming was complete. Many of the cuts requested by the censorship office were finally overridden on the personal authority of the Minister of Information and the head of the television sector responsible for the production of films and serials.

From the internal records of this clash about the third instalment, which covered the period of the 1970s, it is clear that most of the censors' objec-tions were political. They only asked that one sexually suggestive scene be cut but they wanted to cut lines in which President Nasser was praised or defended by sympathetic characters, lines in which lower-class good folk absolved Nasser by blaming those around him, those who 'isolated him from the people and built a wall around him higher than the Aswan Dam' so that 'the people couldn't reach him to tell him what was going on' and so that 'he did not trust the people in the street who loved him and could have protected him'. More tellingly, they objected to scenes suggesting criticism of President Sadat and his policies. For example, they requested more balance in the reaction of the characters to Sadat's visit to Israel in 1977. They asked 'Ukasha to add a scene showing people happy about the visit, a request he refused on budgetary grounds. They also asked him to change the timing of a scene in which the neighbour- hood coffee shop of a beloved patriotic character is sold; by having it coincide with Sadat's visit they felt he implied that it was Egypt being sold. Finally they asked that all dialogue be removed from a scene in a mosque, saying 'We don't want any discussion of religion and role of fundamentalists.' Ironically, the censors also objected to a scene in which a newspaper editor cuts part of a journalist's story as too dangerous. They insisted that this was inaccurate; there had been no censorship at the time of Sadat.

'Ukasha bitterly accused them in the press of 'destroying the work on grounds that to criticise the Sadat period is to be against the current regime in the country'. Turning the language of protection on its head, he argued that the state was not in need of protection by these unquali- fied censors.[19] Invoking his public mission he vowed that if he felt forced to produce Part 4 privately and it was banned from broadcast in Egypt, he would 'go around the streets with a video to show it to people in the coffee shops' so his words could reach the people.[20]

Hilmiyya Nights, a serial that showed how political events at the national level affected the lives of individuals and communities, a serial in which personal histories, fortunes and tragedies, were directly related to policies and events, battled with the censors. In contrast, several months into *The Bold and the Beautiful*, the director of censorship responsible for foreign films could still claim that there was very little to censor in the American serial. The characters are free-floating, their only real context being that created by the soap-opera world itself. This was read by many as making it 'human'. The censor, for example, defended the soap saying, 'The serial carries general human values and debates problems that are not place specific; they are close to many of the problems of Eastern society.'[21] Muna Hilmy, the daughter of the prominent Egyptian feminist Nawal El- Saadawi, defended the serial claiming that what the foreign serial offered that those 'serials irrigated by Nile water' didn't was a look inside people. Instead of external events – political, economic or social – one had people with feelings, desires, weaknesses, strengths, small wickednesses and good- ness. She defended the slowness of the serial as necessary to show the vastness of the human psyche and the politics of the serial as feminist.[22]

Critics of the American soap opera, on the other hand, deployed the discourse of protection – this time against bad art, immorality and American aid. 'Ukasha, the writer of *Hilmiyya Nights*, was provoked to analyse *The Bold and the Beautiful* when a major newspaper columnist praised the soap and invited Egyptian writers to watch it in order to learn the art of dramatic writing. Acknowledging its enormous success, 'Ukasha argued that like the earlier popular American imports this serial's popularity was not due to its artistic merit but rather to the fact that 'we in the nations of the Third World like to see the Western lifestyle which is forbidden to us because of the closed societies we live in. We like to watch pretty women in a range of abnormal sexual relationships that would be taboo in our Eastern societies.'[23] He took the moral high ground with his conclusion, 'God preserve us from what we watch on *The Bold and the Beautiful*: children encouraging their mother to get involved with a married man.'

Invoking the elitist discourse of 'art' 'Ukasha then contrasted the soap operas, 'targeted to housewives busy in their kitchens', to the high-quality imports such as *Roots* and *Upstairs Downstairs* so rarely shown on Egyptian television. Admiring the camera work and the casting, he nevertheless went on to criticise the techniques used in the soap opera; were any Egyptian writer to draw out stories over so many episodes or to have so many contradictions or shifts in character (classic criticisms of American soap operas), the critics would hang him. Instead of insulting Egyptian drama writers by asking them to learn from such programmes, he argued, columnists should request that censorship exercised on the work of Egyptian writers be lifted so that their full creativity could be enjoyed.

The final use of a discourse of protection hints that Egypt's inability to protect its citizens from American imperialism is at the root of the problem. 'Ukasha contrasted *Oshin*, the first Japanese serial to be broadcast in Egypt (a high-quality production that valorised honesty and simplicity and 'symbolized the triumph of the Japanese character over the tyranny of nature ... the character that built a civilization and achieved a high standard of technology and economy') to the American soap operas 'exported to poor Third World countries as part of American aid'.[24] Ahmad Bahgat, a traditionalist writer with Islamic leanings, complaining of the poor quality of *The Bold and the Beautiful* with its repetitions and the stupidity and immorality of its characters, sarcastically remarked in his column in the official government newspaper, 'Since the roulette wheel of the New World Order has stopped at the United States, we have to watch their silliest serials without the right to file a complaint.'[25]

UNENLIGHTENED SUBJECTS?

Thus, to justify television as more than entertainment, a socially concerned and politically conscious group of culture-industry professionals who came of age under Nasser have constructed as their object 'a public' in need of enlightenment. Their use of a discourse of protection is part of their patronisation of their public but it also serves to reinforce among the professional classes the faith that mass media have powerful effects.

But can we determine how the television serials produced for them affect these 'unenlightened subjects'? Although the answers to this are complex, on the basis of some ethnographic work in Egypt in the 1990s I will suggest how at least two groups who are the object of these professionals' efforts and discourse – poor working-class women in Cairo and villagers in Upper Egypt – seem to slip through their well-meaning nets.

'Ukasha might be relieved to discover that many of 'the uneducated' are protected from a pumpkin-seed serial like *The Bold and the Beautiful* by its timing and its language. A soap directed at America's subalterns – housewives (although watched by students and many others) – has in Egypt captured instead an elite, or at least middle-class, audience that includes as many men as women. To enjoy it one must know English or be able to read Arabic subtitles and one must not be too exhausted from a hard day's work to stay awake.

Likewise, he can be reassured that many of the Egyptian serials made by his less socially concerned colleagues are so far-fetched or of such poor quality that audiences ignore them.

He would be less happy to discover the ways some viewers resist the nourishing social messages of his *Hilmiyya Nights*, even as they acclaim it as the best serial ever made. An example will illustrate this. *Hilmiyya Nights* had numerous important women characters, most sympathetically portrayed and shown to be facing dilemmas shared by different generations of women. Morally good older women put up with mistreatment by husbands, including secret marriages and deceptions. Younger women struggled with the tensions between career and marriage. The serial glorified education, showing most of the daughters of working-class men going on to university, the daughter of a coffee shop owner and a singer becoming a university professor and the daughter of a factory worker and a dancer becoming a physician. In general the women were independent and able to take decisions on their own. The state feminism of Nasser's era was commended, one tough-minded wife of a factory worker counselling a friend to stand up for the rights 'Gamal' had given her.[26]

However, when asked what they liked about the serial, several poor women who work as domestic servants in Cairo volunteered not the serious political or social messages but the character of Nazik Hanem, the aristocratic, conniving, magnificently dressed *femme fatale* who plays the leading female role. One young woman whose husband had left her with two children to raise suggested, 'Nazik is the reason everyone watches *Hilmiyya Nights*. She's tough; she married four men. She wouldn't let anyone tell her what to do.' An older woman with a disabled husband explained why Nazik was so great: 'She's fickle, not satisfied with one type. She married many times. She represents what? What's it called? The aristocracy? She was strong-willed. And stubborn. Because of her desires she lost her fortune.' After a short silence she added, 'And Hamdiyya, the dancer, did you see her?' She laughed as she imitated a characteristic arrogant gesture of this belly-dancer turned cabaret-owner.

These were the two glamorous women characters with little nationalist sympathy who wrapped men around their fingers and wouldn't act like respectable ladies, despite the pleas of their children, their ex-husbands and their other relatives. These were also the two who took dramatic falls. The dancer became addicted to heroin after being strung along by a man she hoped to marry. By the time she was cured she had lost everything and had nowhere to go. Nazik Hanem's end was more complex but brilliantly played. She was someone who could not accept her age, even after being swindled out of her fortune by her fourth husband, a younger man who threw her aside. She became increasingly temperamental and then began dressing up like someone half her age, with a wig covering her grey hair, to flirt with a 20-year-old student. When scolded for this, she had a nervous breakdown.

None of the poor women who admired Nazik or the dancer ever mentioned the moral lesson of the fall; rather, they seemed to take vicarious pleasure in these women's defiance of the moral system that keeps good women quiet. These domestic workers were women whose respectability was threatened by their need to work outside the home and as servants. They struggled daily to claim and proclaim their respectability. They hid from their neighbours and sometimes even their relatives the actual sort of work they did and they had all adopted the *higab*, the head-covering of the new modest Islamic dress that, in Egypt, has come to be a sign of Islamic piety and middle-class respectability.

'Ukasha might have himself to blame for this resistance to his nationalist feminism and morality. For popular appeal and clarity in creating the righteous, modern, patriotic character, talented television drama producers often reach out to popular images, such as those purveyed in American soap operas, or introduce the debased 'other', usually parodied, for contrast. This can backfire as outrageous characters like Nazek Hanem, or the corrupt ignorant villainess of another successful serial by the same writer, *The White Flag*, steal the show from tiresomely earnest protagonists.[27]

Only one older woman commented on the more explicit national politics of the serial that had so exercised critics. She noted that *Hilmiyya Nights* was 'against Sadat' and that was why it showed what happened with the *infitah*, or open-door economic policy: people started importing all sorts of putrid goods, like canned meat that was actually cat food. Yet she felt free to disagree with 'Ukasha's basic position adding, 'In those days everyone was busy getting rich. There was lots of money around. For all of us.' Various political opinions circulate in Egypt and there is no reason to assume that the 'unenlightened' audiences of shows such as *Hilmiyya Night* are waiting passively to learn from the serials what to think.

Viewers were selective in their appreciation of the messages of these television dramas. They could disagree with the politics; they could marvel at and take pleasure in the defiant characters who lived as they could not. They accepted the moral stances presented only when they resonated with their worlds. This was clearest in poor women's positive responses to the moral conservatism about family and a mother's role promoted by Egyptian serials generally and *Hilmiyya Nights* in particular. As one admirer of Nazik Hanem noted, to explain why Nazik's daughter Zohra never found happiness, 'The poor thing. It was because her mother didn't take care of her. She abandoned her as a baby with her father. When the girl got sick and had a bad fever, his new wife brought her to Nazik saying, "Here take your daughter and hold her close." But she refused. So Zohra never knew the love of a mother. She had to depend on herself. So the man duped her [tricking her into a shameful secret marriage and a pregnancy]. Poor thing.'

The villagers of Upper Egypt with whom I have worked make no more pliable subjects for the enlightening messages of the serials than these working-class urban women. This is not because they are unfamiliar with television, however. Every household in the village near Luxor where I have been working had a television set. Many were simple black and white sets with poor reception balanced precariously on rickety shelves in corners of mudbrick rooms whose only other wall decorations might be a poster of a favourite soccer club or movie star. The wealthiest families in the village had large colour sets in their reception rooms – rooms that often also boasted padded couches and framed religious calligraphy. On every poor family's wish list, were they to sell a piece of land or somehow save enough for a down payment on the instalment plan, was a colour set.

Only on rare evenings would the television be silent; if there had been a death in the neighbourhood or among one's kin, if someone was ill at home and receiving visitors. The most common reason for televisions to be silent was loss of electricity, something that happened for a few minutes almost every day and occasionally for long frustrating hours. And precisely because electric power in the village was so weak, children often had to do their homework by the light of the television sets.

Rather, the impact of serials like *Hilmiyya Nights* is deflected by the ways villagers consume television. For one thing, like their urban counterparts, villagers I knew were capable of selective readings of dramas. This was often necessary since the distance between the 'realities' dramatised in the serials and the lives lived in the village was vast. The fashionable blonde stars of *The Bold and the Beautiful* in their plush offices and grand mansions are most obviously far from these hardworking people in mudbrick two-storey homes with blue-painted wooden doors wide enough to allow the donkeys, sheep and water buffaloes to pass through into the pens inside; but the characters portrayed in Egyptian serials like *Hilmiyya Nights* are hardly much closer. Most Egyptian serials are set in urban locations and deal with urban, often upper-class problems.[28]

An anecdote about watching television in a relatively poor household can illustrate the gulf between local and television lives and the selective ways women interpret what they watch. One evening, Yamna, the vivacious but exhausted mother of the family was preparing dinner with the help of her sister when the serial, *Love in a Diplomatic Pouch*, came on. Her sister had been there all day helping this overworked woman who had bread to bake and children to be watched when she went off to get fodder for the animals. The family was miserable that night – between the fever of the eldest son, the measles that had struck all four of the little girls, the three boys' end-of-year exams, the expenses and fatigue of a recent trip to a hospital in Assiut in search of a cure for the chain-smoking father's asthmatic cough, and the government's announcement the previous day that the price of flour was to be doubled, they wondered how they would cope. Yet the serial they watched centred on a wealthy diplomat's family and included characters like ballet teachers, woman doctors, journalists and radio personalities with career problems.

As Yamna cooked, her sister, wrapped in the black cloak women wear when they go visiting, shouted out a summary of the plot for her. She focused on the family dynamics that are the regular stuff of their own forms of telling life stories in the village. Divorces, arguments, absences, thwarted matches. She also picked up the moral message of the serial about women and family – the importance of the mother's role in raising her children and the ill consequences for their children of mothers who abandon them or put themselves or their marriages or careers first.

However, many of the 'women's issues' in this serial, written and directed by one of Egypt's few women directors, were constructed in psycho-social terms that were foreign to these women: 'psychological' problems like psychosomatic paralysis that love could heal, men unable to commit themselves to marry for fear of losing their freedom, mothers who cried because their children were not emotionally open with them, and psychiatrists treating drug addiction among the wealthy and educated. The women simply ignored in their discussions these aspects of the serial that were not part of their experience.

From my ethnographic work in the village, I would also suggest that the villagers make elusive targets for the cultural elite's modernising messages for a more complex reason: through the very ease with which they have incorporated television into their everyday lives. Although it is difficult to articulate how this happens, I would argue that television created its own world, one that was for the villagers only a part – albeit an exciting one – of their daily lives. What they experienced through television added to, but did not displace whatever else already existed. They treated the television world not as a fantasy escape but as a sphere unto itself with its familiar time slots and specific attitudes. It was a realm of knowledge about which people shared information: adolescents often had an encyclopaedic knowledge of Egyptian films and serials and people knew a staggering amount about the private lives and previous roles of actors and actresses who starred in the serials. The young people read magazines but everyone had access to this knowledge through hours of viewing and the glorification of stars promoted by Egyptian television itself through interview programmes and celebrity game shows.

In the villagers' attitudes toward the stars is a clue to the larger question of how television serials affect them. The villagers spoke about these stars as 'ours', somehow belonging to them as viewers, but not as 'us'. The same mix of entitlement and distance applied to the serials. They are for 'our' pleasure but they depict the lives of others who have different problems, follow different rules, and do not belong to the local moral community. What these others do, then, has little bearing on what we do or how we conduct our lives. The daily worries of trying to make ends meet, balancing a father's monthly salary of 130 LE (less than USA \$40) with work in the fields to grow clover for water buffaloes and sheep, of struggling to get families grown, through school, and married, of asserting rights to inheritances or extracting support from kin, of preserving one's moral reputation and standing in the face of in-laws and jealous neighbours with whom one has had disputes – these consume villagers. So do the pleasures of visits with friends and relatives, of meeting social obligations with generosity, of passing examinations, selling an animal, having a good harvest or wearing new clothes on the religious feasts.

Even when serials try to reflect village lives, as did a 1993 serial called *Harvest of Love* about Upper Egypt written by a politically concerned progressive woman writer, people reject the problems as not theirs. In this case people enjoyed the serial and recognised the dialect and occasional bits of clothing but alleged that its central issue – the problem of revenge killings – was something that happened elsewhere in Upper Egypt. Perhaps this happens in Sohag (a city to the north), some villagers offered, even though I had heard the vivid narratives about just such a revenge killing in their village only a decade earlier.

I was most struck by the suspension of judgment people applied to the compartmentalised television others because it was so different from their critical evaluations of neighbours and kin. This response resembled the villagers' curious but neutral discussions of the foreign tourists, archaeologists and researchers who were daily in their midst and had been since the early part of the century.

I am not arguing here that the villagers anxiously compartmentalise the 'modernity' television serials (or foreigners) present in order to preserve a static traditional community somehow untouched by the global or 'modernity'. On the contrary, while the village appears picturesque with its 'traditional' sights like mudbrick homes and swaying palm trees, donkeys and the occasional camel carrying loads of clover or sugar-cane leaves, men hoeing fields or walking barefoot along muddy irrigation canals, and women in long black robes balancing bundles on their heads, there is not an aspect of people's everyday lives that has not been shaped by 'the modern'.

The modern Egyptian state determined that sugar cane be grown in the region, decides on prices, requires permits and licences, conscripts all young men into its army, and runs the Antiquities Organisation that employs so many local men, prevents people from building in certain areas, and requires that they build in quaint mudbrick. It runs the schools that most children now attend, coming home weary from carrying the schoolbooks that teach about cleanliness, patriotism and religion.

People suffer from various health problems, the result of chemicals and pesticides, too much sugar in the diet, and waste – including plastic bottles, batteries, and Raid cans – thrown into the irrigation canals. The straight-backed men in their turbans and long pale robes are savvy about the difference between local physicians and specialists who are university professors and practice in Cairo, Mansura and Assiut. The women in black want 'television examinations' of their pregnancies and want to know if you had an ordinary delivery or a caesarian.

How well people eat and whether they decide to uproot cash crops to grow wheat is determined by such faraway organisations as the World Bank and the IMF. Whether the men are away looking for work depends on the state of the Saudi Arabian economy, the decisions of bourgeois investors in the Red Sea tourist developments, French archaeologists, and wealthy Lebanese refugees setting up chicken factories on the desert road to Alexandria, 600 kilometers away. Whether children who have learned to say 'Hello, baksheesh' come running home to give their mothers a few pounds, men who have developed pride in the art of carving pharaonic cats and Horus statuettes find buyers, and those who cook meals for the low-budget tourist groups visiting the tomb of King Tut on donkeys make enough to get new covers for their cushions all depends on whether the *New York Times* has reported 'terrorist' attacks in Cairo.

And contrary to the joke told in Cairo, everyone knows how to operate not just television sets but washing machines, refrigerators, fans and water pumps.

Television is, in this village, one part of a complex jumble of life and the dramatic experiences and visions it offers are surprisingly easily incor-porated as discrete – not overwhelming – elements in this jumble.

This is not to say that television in general has not transformed social life or imaginaries. There are at least three areas in which careful ethno-graphic work might reveal significant transformations. First, in social life: there is less visiting among households in the evenings since families stay home to watch television. More important, television may have increased the number of 'experiences' shared across generation and gender. Television brings families together in the evening and makes it more likely that men and women will socialise together as they sit around the single television set in the house. The focus of attention is the evening serial but families converse with each other while waiting for it, as when the start of the serial is delayed by government ministers droning on during the televised sessions of Parliament. Conflicts also arise, though, between generations and genders about which programmes to watch, just as exposure to television differs by generation.

Second, television may have changed the nature of experience itself. Some Egyptian professionals rationalised to me viewers' pleasures using a discourse of continuity, suggesting, for example, that the serials are like 'the stories a grandmother tells her grandchildren to send them to sleep', or 'like *The Thousand and One Nights*, where the story-teller would stop at the most exciting moment to attract the audience to listen to him the next day', or the North African tradition 'where the wandering poet who sings his poetry to the tune of the rababa stops every day at an exciting point in the story of 'Antar or Abu-Zeid al-Hilaly'.[29] But this ignores a distinctive feature of television drama, what Raymond Williams (1989) has called, referring to the frequency with which TV viewers are exposed to it, its possible role in dramatising consciousness itself.

The third area where television in general may be transforming experience is in its facilitation of new identifications and affiliations. Do the villagers feel part of an imagined community of citizens or consumers because they know they are watching the same programmes at the same time and being offered the same goods as people across the country?

To acknowledge or explore the general effects of television on experience is not, however, the same project as the one I've been pursuing in this paper, which is to track the effects of particular kinds of public-spirited programmes on their objects. Two factors conspire to undermine the impact of serials like *Hilmiyya Nights*. First, of course, the serials appear only as part of the flow (Williams 1975) of programming, sandwiched between films, pumpkin-seed serials, advertising, religious programmes, children's programmes, sports, news, nature programmes and countless talking-head shows. More important, their messages are evaluated from within, and hence often balanced or even contradicted by, the powerful everyday realities within which villagers, like poor working women in Cairo, move. These realities are both resolutely local and transnational.

Whereas *Hilmiyya Nights* and related serials condemn the consumerism and materialism encouraged in the 1970s with the renunciation of socialism and the turn to economic liberalisation, the proliferating television advertisements that precede the broadcast of evening serials and the middle-to upper-class lifestyles portrayed in most dramatic serials offer different messages. These are reinforced by local circumstances. At least among the schoolchildren, the availability of the goods in the nearby town of Luxor combines with these television messages to instil an insistent desire for specific brands of candy or running shoes (Amigo shoes with Ninja Turtles on them). For urban poor women, the availability of such goods is that much more persuasive.

Ukasha and the other enlightened professionals also exclude from their storylines any positive depiction of the various guises of the Islamic alternative being offered to Egypt's populace. Yet the Islamic identity and knowledge promoted by religious programmes on television interact positively with adults' experiences in the new or refurbished mosques that are being enthusiastically supported and children's experiences in schools, secular state institutions that are, somewhat ironically, the locus of religious pressure especially in rural areas. In the village where I worked, these children, the girls forced to wear the new Islamic headcovering and all subjected to the lectures of their aggressively religious schoolteachers, even discussed in class the significance of a television serial loosely based on the Koranic story of Joseph.

Furthermore, as for poor women in Cairo, there is little to reinforce the enlightening messages about culture, social responsibility and national unity the politically inspired culture-industry professionals are seeking to disseminate. *Hilmiyya Nights*, with its secular vision of a modern Egypt full of virtuous patriotic citizens, united across class by their love of country, sought to bring these subalterns into its modern fold.

But these subalterns are already folded into Egyptian modernity in a different way. The children who sing every morning the national anthem and memorise countless other nationalist songs from government schoolbooks may be somewhat receptive to the nationalist messages of television serials. Some, like a young village girl completing agricultural school, dream of impossible futures like being given a government plot of land in Sinai to develop. But their elders in Upper Egypt believe that their region has long been discriminated against and exploited by the north; they regularly experience the nation not through songs but through a formidable bureaucracy, a corrupt police force and army service (in which they are badly treated). The unity of rich and poor in national endeavours that *Hilmiyya Nights* idealises is undermined by their knowledge of how the wealthy buy their way out of the army and around all regulations. For urban women who are the exploited supports of a modern class system, solving the twin demands of work and respectability through 'Islamic' veiling, this vision of the nation must also find little corroboration.

The problem, finally, is that the kind of modernity these television serials depict as a vision for Egypt depends on class position and the availability of certain kinds of educational and career opportunity. The 'uneducated public' at whom these serials are directed participates in the more common form of modernity in the post-colonial world: the modernity of poverty, consumer desires, underemployment, ill health and religious nationalism.

ACKNOWLEDGEMENTS

I am grateful for funding support for research in Egypt in 1989–90 and 1993 from the American Research Centre in Egypt, the ACLS/SSRC Joint Committee on the Near and Middle East, and a Presidential Fellowship from New York University. I also want to thank Maha Mahfouz Abdel-Rahman and Hala Abu-Khatwa for research assistance; the participants of the SSRC conference on 'Questions of Modernity' for searching questions; and Daniel Miller for good suggestions and patience.

NOTES

1. Given the non-specialised readership for this paper, I have used an extremely simplified system of transliteration from the Arabic. To mark the letter *ayn* I use an apostrophe; otherwise all diacritics are absent as are distinctions between long and short vowels.
2. Interview with the author, 22 July 1990.
3. Interview with the author 15 April 1990.
4. Interview with the author, 15 April 1990.
5. Interview with the author, 22 July 1990.
6. So popular has it been internationally that its stars have been invited to act in Italian, Spanish and French films. They were treated as VIPs when invited to Egypt's Film Festival in December 1993, and thrilled audiences in India when they came on the air to wish Hindus well on a religious holiday. Many of these details were provided in a major magazine spread by Galal Al-Rashidy, 'The Stars of the Bold and the Beautiful Behind the Camera' (in Arabic), *Sabah al-Khayr*, 25 March 1993, pp. 46–50.
7. Ibrahim 'Issa, 'An American Researcher in an Important Book: Egypt Subsidises America!' [in Arabic], *Roz al-Yusuf* 3382, 5 April 1993.
8. It seems frequently the case that national productions are more widely popular than imports. For evidence from Europe, see Silj 1988.
9. Sayed Yassin, 'Cultural Papers: "Hilmiyya Nights" and Political Activity', *Al-Iqtisadi*, 9 July 1990, pp. 96–7.
10. With the increase in products available on the market, competition has become fierce and television advertising considered effective in a country where illiteracy runs high. According to Aida Nasr (*Cairo Today*, November 1992, p. 98), the television advertising industry grossed LE 50 million, gleaned from a 15–20 per cent commission.
11. For a stimulating discussion of the politics of television melodrama, see Joyrich (1992).
12. According to 'Abd al-Nur Khalil, 'The Ramadan of Television Captured People in a Bottle' (in Arabic), *Al-Musawwar* 3518, 13 March 1992, pp. 48–9, so wedded did the actors become to their roles that, after the conclusion of the serial, many of them complained that they felt trapped by their roles in *Hilmiyya Nights*. As in American soap operas, stars also quit the show before its conclusion and had to be replaced so audiences had to cope with the separation of character from actor.
13. According to Soha Abdel Kader (1985), based on a content analysis of television dramas and women's programmes in 1980, women are numerically under-represented in Egyptian television drama but often play significant roles (pp. 15–19). She argues, however, that women are 'always portrayed as more

morally "good" than men' (p. 61), something that was not true of *Hilmiyya Nights*.

14. The only exception in recent American television was the *Murphy Brown* situation comedy that attacked the Bush family-values campaign in retaliation for Vice President Dan Quayle's attack on the protagonist's decision to have a baby out of wedlock. The fact that it was a *cause célèbre*, reported in newspapers and thought worthy of a BBC documentary, indicates how unusual the explicit inclusion of politics was in American television entertainment.

15. For a discussion of the exclusion of the perspective of the Islamic movement from television serials, see Abu-Lughod (1993).

16. 10 June 1990, p. 10.

17. Articles entitled 'The Political Impact of Hilmiyya Nights' (in Arabic) (*Al-Wafd*, 14 May 1990, p. 5) and 'Historical Facts and Hilmiyya Nights' (in Arabic) (*Al-Wafd*, 21 May 1990, p. 5).

18. 'Hilmiyya Nights Between Nasser and Sadat', *Roz al-Yusuf* 3233, 28 May 1990, pp. 68–9.

19. Interview by Aynas Ibrahim (in Arabic), *Roz al-Yusuf*, 24 May 1990, p. 56.

20. Interview by Abla Al-Ruwayny (in Arabic), *Al-Ahaly*, 30 May 1990.

21. Dalal 'Abd Al-Fatah (in Arabic), *Roz al-Yusuf*, 3371, 18 January 1993, p. 10.

22. The men, she argued, are not macho and they don't dominate women. The women work and make money. They want to succeed and to make their own futures. They don't give in to fate or circumstances or gossip. They use their minds and all they've got. The pleasure viewers get from *The Bold and the Beautiful*, she continues, is in seeing confrontation and hope ('*The Bold and the Beautiful*: A Serial without Male Complexes' (in Arabic), *Sabah al-Khayr*, 11 February 1993, p. 59).

23. *Roz al-Yusuf*, 3371, 18 January 1993, p. 8.

24. The theme of protection even came up in this article 'Ukasha wrote about *Oshin*. Accusing Egyptian television authorities of conspiring to discourage viewing by placing it in an unusual time slot, he compared *Oshin* favorably to *Roots* and other high-quality serials of the sort they hated to import for fear that people might come to demand programmes that met intellectual standards. No doubt alluding to his battles with the censors, he accused them of perceiving these high-quality serials the way they perceived democracy – as something that Egyptians needed to be protected from and only given in small doses.

    Using a different food metaphor than Fadil's pumpkin-seed munching, 'Ukasha contrasted *Oshin*, a natural drama with no food preservatives or artificial flavours, to the 'hawawshy bread' of *The Bold and the Beautiful*. ('Hawawshy bread' is a kind of meat pie whose strong spices are known to cover poor-quality minced meat.) Instead of striking women showing off their bodies and male mannequins smiling promiscuously, *Oshin* told the profound story of an ordinary Japanese woman who overcomes great obstacles (Usama Anwar 'Ukasha, 'Pay Attention Gentlemen: "Oshin" Confronts the "Bold and the Beautiful"' (in Arabic), *Roz al-Yusuf*, 3385, 26 June 1993, pp. 52–3).

    Ironically, under public pressure, *The Bold and the Beautiful* was eventually reduced from nightly broadcasts and *Oshin* brought back on the air in late 1993. Only a few months later, however, *Oshin* had become the subject of tremendous criticism in the press because of its relentlessly depressing character.

25 *Al-Ahram*, 6 February 1993, p. 2.

26 On state feminism and its demise in Egypt, see Hatem (1992).

27 For more on *The White Flag*, see Abu-Lughod (1993).
28 Abdel Kader's (1985) study showed that there was a bias toward portraying the urban upper classes. Of fourteen serials and twelve short plays sampled during a 6-month period in 1980, none were set in rural areas (p. 36).
29 Nur Al-Sharif, interview with the author, 22 July 1990.

REFERENCES

Abdel Kader, Soha (1985) 'The Image of Women in Drama and Women's Programs in Egyptian Television'. Unpublished Report, Population Council.

Abu-Lughod, Lila (1993) 'Finding a Place for Islam: Egyptian Television Serials and the National Interest'. *Public Culture* 5 (3): 493–513.

Geraghty, Christine (1991) *Women and Soap Opera*. Cambridge: Polity Press.

Hatem, Mervat (1992) 'Economic and Political Liberalization in Egypt and the Demise of State Feminism'. *International Journal of Middle East Studies* 24: 231–51.

Hedges, Chris (1992) 'In Cairo Now a Coffee Shop is Just a Shop'. *New York Times*, 3 August.

Joyrich, Lynne (1992) 'All That Television Allows: TV Melodrama, Postmodernism, and Consumer Culture'. In L. Spigel and D. Mann, eds, *Private Screenings: Television and the Female Consumer*. Minneapolis: University of Minnesota Press, pp. 227–51.

Lerner, Daniel (1958) *The Passing of Traditional Society*. Glencoe, IL: The Free Press.

Miller, Daniel (1992) 'The Young and the Restless in Trinidad: A Case of the Local and the Global in Mass Consumption'. In R. Silverstone and E. Hirsch, eds, *Consuming Technologies: Media and Information in Domestic Spaces*. London and New York: Routledge, pp. 163–82.

Silj, Alessandro et al. (1988) *East of Dallas: The European Challenge to American Television*. London: British Film Institute.

Wilk, Richard (1993) ' "It's Destroying a Whole Generation": Television and Moral Discourse in Belize'. *Visual Anthropology* 5: 229–44.

Williams, Raymond (1975) *Television: Technology and Cultural Form*. New York: Schocken Books.

—— (1989). 'Drama in a Dramatised Society'. In A. O'Connor, ed., *Raymond Williams on Television: Selected Writings*. London and New York: Routledge, pp. 3–13.

10 Aboriginal art in a global context

Howard Morphy

INTRODUCTION: ART MARKETS, ART DISCOURSE

This chapter is concerned with the relationship between discourse on art and art markets. The particular focus is on Australian Aboriginal art in Western discourse about art, and the value and position of Aboriginal art in a global market. The dominant discourse in global art is centred on Western concerns, and the structure of the world art market is dominated by Western art products and objects defined according to the criteria of the Western art market. The dominance of the West influences art practice in that a global art, despite its great formal diversity, can be seen to be developing along the trajectory established by the recent history of Western art. Much modern Chinese art for example reflects Western formal traditions whereas little contemporary Western art is directly influenced by traditional Chinese painting, even though historically modernism was inspired, among other things, by Chinese art.[1]

However, despite its dominant position Western art discourse and the art market are in a constant state of change. The way in which art objects are conceived and their relative values can change radically without fundamentally altering the structure of the market. Often changes in the art market follow changes in artistic practice or reflect changes in the discourse about art. Such changes may come from within the Western tradition or may be generated indirectly from the periphery, from the articulation of one art world with another. Indeed it is in the nature of the Western category of art to expand anaconda-like by swallowing the products of its neighbours and its own and other people's pasts. Thus it changes not only its own criteria of existence but also transforms the meaning and value of the objects that it swallows up.[2]

The art market and art discourse are relatively autonomous. The market has constraints and properties that are to a degree common to all international markets and which operate independently of any intrinsic value of the objects that art discourse may be concerned with. Yet at the same time the one influences the other. Art criticism and art history may be used to sell work, authenticate objects and increase their value, and art history inevitably reflects the focus of and structure of interests within the art market by creating the resources for research and generating interest in particular areas. Nonetheless, discourse over art and art practice is often directed to changing the values and assumptions and definitions of the market, to bring it into line with current research or the self-definition of artists. One of the ways in which art discourse influences the art market is through the international 'blockbuster' exhibition which both challenges and supports existing values.[3]

International blockbuster exhibitions require the collaboration of national institutions – art galleries and government organisations, business corporations and academics, and art historians. They are enormously expensive to put on. In order to justify the expense a number of major galleries must be competing to show the exhibition, implying that they have anticipated the existence of a large potential audience. They must obtain sponsorship from international business corporations and they must obtain considerable government support both to help cover costs and to underwrite insurance. For all of these reasons blockbuster exhibitions are unlikely to be at the cutting edge of critical discourse, but they are a context which affects the impact of that discourse on public understandings and on market values and criteria of authenticity. They are exercises in persuasion and in the enhancement of prestige, aimed at increasing the cultural and often the commercial value of art, and as such might represent a variant of Appadurai and Leech's tournaments of value (Appadurai 1986: 21). Once they open they are already a battle won, they have gained the resources to exist and to compete for audiences on a global scale, to receive the attention of critics and reviewers, to be illustrated in magazines and newspapers and to have an extended life in the form of catalogues. Of course not all exhibitions succeed and many have conservative agendas that reinforce existing categories and values, giving new life to *The Impressionists*, *Tutankhamen* or *Andean Gold*. Nonetheless, the international exhibition remains one of the ways in which 'Western' categories of art change, and in which the established values of the art market are challenged and altered.

Aboriginal art had to wait until the late 1980s before it became the subject of a major international exhibition, and then two followed in quick succession: *Dreamings* and *Aratjara*. But before turning to these exhibitions I will consider briefly, from a historical perspective, the process of the creation of works of 'primitive' art, since it was as 'primitive' art that Australian Aboriginal art first entered both art discourse and the world art market. The agendas of the two international exhibitions were directed in part to changing the meaning of Aboriginal art, moving it out of the category of primitive art and freeing contemporary Aboriginal artists from the constraints that this definition imposed.

PRIMITIVE ART AND GLOBAL MARKETS

'Primitive' art – the art of the colonised peoples of the Fourth World (see Graburn 1976) – has to be created twice. It is first created to be used and valued in an indigenous context. Then it has to be created as a work of art in the Western sense, with a place in the Western history of art, a value in the art market, and a space reserved on the walls of an art gallery – in Maquet's terms it becomes art by metamorphosis (Maquet 1979). Until recently these two acts of creation were quite separate. The original producers of the work did not know of the existence of the second audience, and the Western re-creator of it as a work of 'primitive' art did not know (and often did not care) about its original meaning and was ignorant of the intentions of the person who produced it. This process of double creation involving spatially, temporally and conceptually separated acts depended on the existence of a strong Western/other opposition, and would seem to be contradicted by the development of global economic and cultural processes – world markets and a global discourse over art. It is not simply that the word 'primitive' is unacceptable (as many have argued) but that the very category exists in a time warp belonging to a short phase of world history that has now passed.

'Art', or rather those artefacts and activities that Europeans define as art, is an important component of Aboriginal culture. In 'traditionally oriented' Aboriginal society art is a system of communication, of encoding meanings about the ancestral past and a means of creating spiritual power (see, e.g., Morphy 1991). Art is integral to the process of passing knowledge from generation to generation. Art objects and designs are owned by groups of people, the rights to produce them are controlled, and sometimes access to them is restricted to people of a certain status. The production of art for ceremonial purposes is often an end in itself, with the producers being the only or main viewers. Until recently Aborigines did not make works to be bought and sold freely on an open market for display to an unknown and essentially foreign audience. The creation of Aboriginal art as 'art', as a commodity, has occurred through the process of European colonisation and has been an element of the incorporation of Aborigines into Australian society. In this respect Aboriginal art is no different from that of many other indigenous peoples.

The role that European artists played in the recognition of African art at the turn of the twentieth century is too well known to be discussed in detail here.[4] The process was one that arose out of the history of European art and colonialism. Although for several centuries works now classified as 'primitive' art had been collected and housed as ethnographic curios in museums of natural history, primitive art did not begin to find its way into art galleries and begin to be valued and marketed as fine art until European artists, breaking away from the perceived constraints of their own tradition, sought inspiration in exotic forms. This process of incorporation through European art ensured that when works of 'primitive' art were exhibited in their own right there would be an audience ready to appreciate them.[5] But it was likely that the audience would appreciate them not for what they were, but for how they inspired, or were related to, developments in European art (cf. Rubin 1984).[6] The value of the art in its indigenous context had been superseded by the intentions and perceptions of the European artist, critic and entrepreneur.

To the Western artist the value of 'primitive' art lay in its lack of contamination by the European tradition. It was thought pristine, primeval and, as such, liberating. As a consequence the work had to be pronounced free of European influence in order to be regarded as 'primitive fine art'. Once the artist became sophisticated in European ways, aware of the external market, and concerned to produce works directed towards it, then almost by definition he or she was no longer the producer of 'primitive fine art'. The primitive art market was concerned with the work of dead artists, or artists who soon would be dead and were in any case unknown, for younger artists were seen to be producing works contaminated by European contact. Although this attitude was generally less prevalent by the 1960s, it was still the attitude of many towards Aboriginal art. As Alan McCulloch wrote somewhat dismissively in his 1984 edition of the *Encyclopedia of Australian art*, 'Aboriginal art . . . has suffered from the fate of all primitive art after contamination with more sophisticated forms.'

This assumption that the quality of Aboriginal art is somehow diminished through contact with Europeans can clearly have a negative effect on contemporary Aboriginal artists whether or not the work they produce is in continuity with previous cultural forms. The effect of this can be seen in a letter written by the Australian Trade Commissioner in New York to the manager of Aboriginal Arts and Crafts limited in February 1977:

We thank you for your recent letter outlining your plans to penetrate the American Art and Craft market with the sale of your products. We have had extensive discussions with Museum directors, for example the Museum of Primitive Art, and leading importers of art objects from the Pacific in New York. From these conversations it has emerged that the market for your products in museums, private collections and so on would not be feasible. As per your catalogue it appears that you are prepared to manufacture for sale a wide variety of Aboriginal art objects. While these objects are 'Authentic' in the sense that they are made by traditional Aboriginal Craftsmen and painters use as media traditional materials and conform almost exactly to the genuine article, they would nonetheless not be considered 'Authentic' by museum curators. The criteria for an 'Authentic' item is that it must have been made for use and perhaps been used in traditional society and not made for sale. In your letter you mention for example the growth in sales of

African art in the United States. However, it must be realised that the items that are being sold are collected from traditional societies in Africa (and unfortunately sometimes stolen) and are not the objects of art that one can buy in the capital cities and major towns in Africa, which are made for sale to such people as tourists and so on.

And then here comes Catch 22 as far as the producers are concerned:

> ... We have ascertained from the Department of Aboriginal Affairs that exports of these authentic Aboriginal Artifacts such as objects of archaeological, ethnographical, historical, Sacred, ritual, or Ceremonial interest, are generally prohibited. They do of course say that artifacts made for sale can be readily exported.

The points to note here are that the authenticity of the art is clearly thought to be challenged by its commercial purpose and that the existence of authentic Aboriginal art is distanced not so much by its invisibility but by the fact that it must remain in an Aboriginal domain. Authentic Aboriginal art must remain in Australia under Aboriginal control. While on the surface this appears to be a recognition of Aboriginal rights it is an extremely muddled recognition, which results in work that Aborigines wish to produce for outsiders being labelled unauthentic or untraditional. It represents a classic example of Aborigines being disadvantaged by the European definition of them as other.

This primitive art market was an exploitative one. It was not the producer but the re-creator and later investors who stood to make money from the work. This left the Fourth World artist trying to produce for a European market with a particular problem: it was almost impossible to get a reasonable return for the work produced in his or her tradition (which was itself undergoing change), and have the work recognised and valued as primitive fine art. Such a market, built on 'uncontaminated' forms, could expand only by discovering 'uncontaminated' societies with cultural traditions that would soon be defined as dead. As far as the art market was concerned the 'recognised uncontaminated' traditions had an equivalent role to that of the 'recognised artist's oeuvre' in European art. Not all artists can achieve elevated status within the art market, because this would devalue the individual products. The market requires a limited resource, it requires that most artists' names fade, and it welcomes death as an end to production. As Michaels (1988: 60) notes: 'the artist's oeuvre provides a manageable limitation on the availability of the resource, which is the number of paintings produced in an individual's lifetime. Here the importance of the artist's death is related to the closure of the series.'

The logic underlying such a market is that there are a limited number of spaces available for allocation to marketable products. Any increase in the number of spaces is likely either to result in a decrease in the average price of the individual items or to require the creation of additional consumer demand which brings additional cash into the market. Art dealers have to be aware of both possibilities. They must be conscious of the need to maintain the value of the product through its uniqueness and at the same time they must be alive to the possibility of extending the market by persuading consumers of the value of new items or sets of items (artists' oeuvres and traditions of 'primitive art').

Until recently the spaces allocated to primitive art were filled with products labelled only by region and/or time. Other categories of art, for example, medieval or 'folk' art also shared this property of anonymity. In the case of post-Renaissance European art, the spaces have for long been filled by names of artists. The differences between the kinds of labels do not reflect underlying long-term differences in art practice or in the role of the artist in European and non-European society, though the art-historical traditions and bodies of expert opinion which provide the background support for the art market have sometimes represented the situation in this way. The diversity of both European and non-European art practice is so great that it is dangerous to make any grand generalisations. However it is pertinent to note that the status of the artist as an individual did not emerge in Europe until the Renaissance and later (Baudrillard 1981, Goehr 1992), and, conversely, that the anonymity of the 'traditional' artist in Africa, for example, has been greatly exaggerated (cf. D'Azevedo 1973). The differential labelling of the spaces is a reflection of European cultural and historical processes. Differences between European and primitive art were created through the process of colonialism and in association with twentieth-century developments in the art market (there was no high-value primitive art market in the nineteenth century).

The allocation of space to European art and primitive art according to different criteria clearly causes problems for those who succeed the producers of 'primitive art' in the contemporary world – the indigenous artists of the late twentieth century. The European artist is involved in a process of succession. Modern names replace the names of artists of the recent and distant past whose reputations are fading. At the same time art history and criticism resurrects names from the past to compete in value with present producers. Many artists may not wish to play any part in this competitive game and may reject the aesthetic and art-historical premises on which it is based. But as long as they manufacture products the market can carry on operating without their consent. The producers of indigenous art face a different problem. To gain recognition as individuals they more or less have to change category. The marketing of art as a product of an anonymous group works to the disadvantage of the producers. If they assert their individuality by pushing their own economic interests they become individualised and their art ceases to meet the criteria for occupying the anonymous spaces. The art market is not set up to accommodate easily joint title or corporate producer rights in artworks, unless those works can be taken to be anonymous artefacts whose significant reality is in the fictional world of the Western-defined other. In order to sell works to a global market producers have to make concessions to a Western definition of self; they must present themselves, or allow themselves to be presented, as individuals and thereby fit into a Western process of individuation in art. They have to become individuals who fit into art history and who have a place defined by the 'school' or regional style to which they belong, the exhibitions held of their work, the catalogues which document its development and the institutions which own it.

The contradictory position and the powerlessness of the indigenous artist should at once be apparent. The global art market which defines the difference between primitive and Western art, is Western in origin. It was set up primarily as a market for Western products and the spaces allocated for artworks were biased enormously in favour of Western art. The global art market reflects Western rankings of other traditions, giving highest rank and most space to those recognised as historically antecedent to Western traditions (Classical art) or to those which have been recognised as equivalent though lower-ranking civilisations (Oriental art). The art history industry that is part of the infrastructure for the market is similarly structured – as reflected in the relative number of entries in dictionaries of art and the number of lecturers in universities. To put it crudely, at any one point in time spaces for new entries are limited in number and there are far more gaps for European and American artists than for those of the indigenous world. The global art market simultaneously requires indigenous artists to change categories and makes it difficult for them to become members of the new category. There is a limit to the number of named indigenous artists that the market can accommodate.[7]

It is difficult to see how this contradiction can be resolved as long as Europe and America remain the centre of the global art market. It is possible to imagine decentred markets which create spaces for regional arts within their local arena. This already happens in countries such as Australia and Canada which have more complex internal markets for their own art than exist in the outside world. Many paintings by white Australian artists that have a high value within Australia are virtually unsaleable outside. However, an integrated world economy will always produce a market that transcends the local systems and which draws products from them. Often the role of the local market in its global context is to act as a filter, selecting out from the many those few artists who will operate on a global scale. However, as long as the global focus is in the West the flow from the local to the global will be limited by the spaces allocated within that market.[8] It might be argued that a truly decentred market could theoretically exist if a number of areas of equivalent concentration of wealth were dispersed globally, each of which reflected biases different from those exhibited by the Western art market. However, the historical priority of the Western market and the sheer weight of its tradition of art history would still have an effect on the categories and structure of these other markets.

DREAMINGS AND THE CREATION OF AN AUDIENCE FOR ABORIGINAL ART

When *Dreamings* opened in the Galleries of the Asia Society in New York, it was the culmination of a process that had been going on in Australia for a number of decades. There had been a number of travelling exhibitions of Aboriginal art before, but they had comparatively little impact at the time even though they undoubtedly contributed to the cumulative process that made *Dreamings* possible. Within Australia itself there had been two major travelling exhibitions. It had been intended that the second of these, *Aboriginal Australia*, which opened in 1981, would tour overseas (see Cooper et al. 1981). However, the organisers found it difficult to get venues outside Australia and eventually even the Australian tour had to end through bankruptcy. Less than a decade later, *Dreamings* was an overwhelming critical success both in terms of the publicity generated, the (largely positive) critical response and the impact it had on the commercial market for Aboriginal art.[9] As far as its audience size was concerned it was the most successful exhibition in the Asia Society's history. Before I consider the particular agenda of the exhibition organisers and the messages that they intended to get across, I will review the process of the acceptance of Aboriginal 'art' as art in Australia, since this provided the context for *Dreamings* and in a sense made it possible. *Dreamings* was the export of an Australian idea about Aboriginal art, which itself arose partly out of global discourse, and the promotion of that idea to a wider audience.

For most of the colonal history of Australia, Aboriginal material culture has been excluded from the art gallery and from the Western category of art. In order to be seen as 'art', in the conventional Western sense (cf. Tuckson 1964), a work has to be hung on an art gallery wall.[10] As recently as the 1960s Aboriginal art had hardly been allowed in the basement door of any art gallery in Australia and opportunities for its display were only just beginning to occur. Its present-day inclusion in the category has been the result of a historical process in which both Aborigines and non-Aborigines have been agents of persuasion (Morphy 1987, Jones 1988).

Until the late 1960s exhibitions of Aboriginal art were extremely rare in Australia (Morphy 1987, Jones 1988). The only paintings in art galleries as opposed to ethnographic museums consisted of a few bark paintings donated by the Commonwealth Government from Mountford's 1948 expedition to Arnhem Land, and the major collection made for the Art Gallery of New South Wales by Scougall and Tuckson. Interestingly, ethnographic museums themselves were purchasing less Aboriginal art in the 1950s and 1960s than they did in the earliest decades of the century (Morphy 1992). Outside Australia, exhibitions of Aboriginal art were virtually unheard of and, with a few notable exceptions (see Kupka 1965), collections were not being purchased by institutions. In America a few 'pioneer' private collections, notably those of Allan and Ruhe, had their beginnings around 1960, but again Aboriginal art was largely unknown. In the literature on primitive art Aboriginal art had the status of a footnote to the art of Oceania.

By the early 1980s the situation had changed so dramatically that it became increasingly hard to believe that the situation had ever been as it was in the past.[11] Aboriginal art had moved out of the ethnographic museums into the state and national art galleries, all of which began to compete with one another in building up their own collections. Considerable resources were being put into the purchase of Aboriginal art and the sponsorship of artists and craft centres in Aboriginal communities. Aboriginal art was being incorporated into the structure of national institutions and was literally built into the fabric of the New Parliament House in Canberra. Not only did the boomerang shape of the building signify Aboriginal Australia, but the forecourt was paved with a mosaic designed by the Western Desert artist Michael Nelson.

In the commercial arena galleries specialising in Aboriginal art, and exhibitions of Aboriginal art were opened, and exhibitions of the work of individual Aboriginal artists became routine. By 1993 there were twenty-eight galleries in Alice Springs alone specialising in Aboriginal art and craftwork. An indication of the economic significance of Aboriginal art and its growing international profile is provided by the results of a survey produced by the Australia Council in 1990: 'half the international visitors to Australia are interested in seeing and learning about Aboriginal culture, thirty percent of visitors in the questionnaire survey purchased Aboriginal arts or items related to Aboriginal culture, and the value of these purchases was estimated at A\$30 million for the current year' (Wild 1991: 1).

It is impossible to discuss in detail here how the changes came about. The essentialist argument would be that the richness of Aboriginal art became visible at last, whereas previously the evolutionary eye had been blind to it. However, the proponent of such an argument would have to take into account changing Western conceptions of art and would soon be drawn into debates about the political, economic and social dimensions of art. In part the increased interest resulted from a combination of Aboriginal political action and Australian political circumstance. Aborigines used art as an instrument in asserting their rights both to land and to cultural recognition. As Australian governments in the 1960s and 1970s became more sensitive to issues of Aboriginal rights they saw support of art as one of the least divisive ways of furthering Aboriginal interests. Political action also increased the visibility of Aborigines in Australian society, particularly in the southern states where the potential art market was, and at the same time communications between the north and south became easier. Aboriginal art also benefited from the movement of Australian nationalism away from its European roots, and from the opportunities presented by the Bicentennial celebrations in 1988 to dramatise issues of national identity.

In the 1980s Australian governments encouraged national arts institutions to fund Australian art as a means of establishing an Australian identity. Because of the structure of the Australian population, multiculturalism was projected as an integral part of that emerging identity. Although Aborigines were not clearly built into that agenda and indeed themselves rejected the position of being 'just another ethnic group in a multicultural society', the agenda in itself created spaces and resources that Aborigines were able to command. The National Gallery, when instructed to spend a substantial proportion of its budget on Australian art from the mid-1980s, was able to maintain its curatorial autonomy by spending much of it on Aboriginal as opposed to white Australian art.

The Australian Bicentennial reinforced this process. A celebration of Australia's two hundred years could only succeed if it came to terms with its colonial history and the Aboriginal holocaust on which it was built. Although Aborigines rejected the idea of celebrating the bicentenary, almost inevitably they used it as a context to assert their continued presence in Australian society by creating a counter theme of a National Year of Mourning. Many of the resources that were put aside for Aboriginal participation in the Bicentennial were used indirectly to fund events that were in many respects a subversion of the bicentenary. The National Gallery's purchase of two hundred hollow-log coffins as a memorial to the Aboriginal dead is one example. Because of widespread discomfort among sectors of the white Australian population and Aboriginal determination to make the events they organised a positive statement of their survival, many of the events that Aborigines organised and participated in became key public events of the year (see, e.g., Bell 1989).

It could be argued that the state, by channelling resources indirectly into Aboriginal events, which frequently took the form of cultural performances, subverted the Aboriginal protests and made them part of the ongoing development of Australian identity – in von Sturmer's (1989: 137) eloquent phrase driving 'one imagined community into the arms of another'.[12] Yet it is equally possible to reverse the argument and say that Aboriginal participation, on what they saw as their own terms, edged the trajectory of Australian cultural processes a little way in their direction. Certainly the Bicentennial gave an enormous boost to the sale of Aboriginal art and greatly increased its exposure overseas.

DREAMINGS EXPORTED

Although not officially so, *Dreamings* was another Bicentennial event. It opened in the Bicentennial year, capitalised on the interest generated about Australia and Aborigines by that event, and contributed to the way the Bicentennial was represented. The prime movers behind the exhibition were Peter Sutton, an anthropologist from the South Australian Museum, and Andrew Pekarik, Director of the Asia Society Gallery in New York. The exhibition developed themes that Sutton and his colleagues Chris Anderson and Philip Jones had been working on over a number of years and which had already resulted in one major exhibition *Art and Land* (Jones and Sutton 1986). The two main themes were firstly the presentation, and through that the acceptance, of certain works of Aboriginal material culture as fine art, and secondly the challenging of the criteria of authenticity used in the definition and valuation of Aboriginal art as primitive art. In essence the two themes were related since they could be said to involve the extinction of the category of primitive art and the inclusion of works previously included in that category within what could be considered the more general category of 'fine art'.

In the case of *Art and Land* the focus of the exhibition was on *toas*, relatively unknown objects from Central Australia which were said to have been manufactured as direction signs by the tribes of the Lake Eyre region of Central Australia and which had been collected at the beginning of the century by the missionary R.G. Reuther (see Jones and Sutton 1986, Morphy 1977). The exhibition was organised as a central component of the Adelaide Festival of Art; the agenda of exhibiting *toas* as art was quite explicit and became a focal point of debate in the media and in the arts press (see Sutton 1992). In the exhibition the functional aspects of the object were played down almost to the point of denial, and in the catalogue the *toas* were photographed in such a way as to enhance their aesthetic appeal to a Western audience. The objects were presented as the antithesis of primitive art, as something that had arisen out of the discourse between Aborigines and Europeans, emerging to an extent from Aboriginal understandings of European culture and aesthetics. Implicit in this approach is a rejection of Graburn's (1976) typological perspective on the arts of the Fourth World which, it could be argued, accepts the Western category of fine art in an unmodified way and assesses other works in relation to that category. It could be argued that by placing all works within the same Western category the category itself is subverted, or rather is expanded, by rejecting as irrelevant certain differences which at one time were thought to be integral to its existence – the difference for example between functional objects and artworks.

In *Dreamings* objects were selected on aesthetic grounds and were hung with minimal captions on well-lit gallery walls. The exhibition accepted the modernist premise that art was to be appreciated on the basis of its

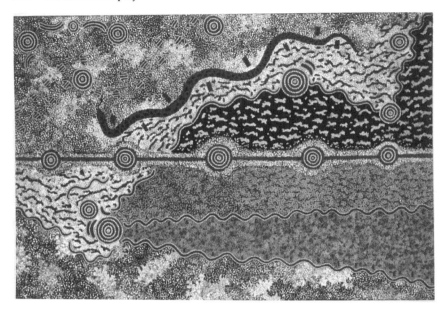

Figure 10.1 'Five Tjukurrpas (Dreamings)', Michael Nelson Tjakamarra (assisted by Marjorie Napaljarri), Papunya, 1984. This painting was shared in common between the *Dreamings* and *Aratjara* exhibitions and fitted the agenda of both exhibitions equally.

Source. Aboriginal Artists Agency Ltd. Courtesy of the Gabrielle Prizzi Gallery, Melbourne.

form but the catalogue, at least, added a cultural relativist codicil by showing how the objects could be approached from the basis of an Aboriginal rather than a European aesthetic. Since Aboriginal aesthetic considerations did not influence the way that the exhibition was hung, the accommodation of that perspective was only partial.

The second general theme was to challenge some of the criteria of the primitive art market by including work that had been made for sale to an outside market, work in an introduced medium, and work which was innovative, though it is important to note that work in these two categories selected for exhibition also showed strong continuity with pre-existing 'traditional' forms. The exhibition had a major section of Western Desert acrylics (see Figure 10.1), a tradition which originated in the early 1970s when Geoff Barden, a schoolteacher, encouraged some elders at Papunya, an Aboriginal settlement near Alice Springs, to paint 'traditional' designs on the schoolroom walls. Soon after, he encouraged them to paint on artist's board and by the end of the year several exhibitions of their paintings had been held in Alice Springs. The exhibition, rather than emphasising the uniqueness of the event and stressing its contemporary context as it might have done, for example, by setting up an opposition with earlier and more traditional Aboriginal art, implied instead that such events had been characteristic of the post-contact history of Aboriginal art. Among the earliest collected objects included in the exhibition were the *toas* which had previously been exhibited in *Art and Land* as examples of objects more or less invented for a European audience.[13] This emphasis on the dynamism of Aboriginal art, and by implication of Aborigines themselves in the post-colonial context, fitted in with a more general anthropological critique of the view of traditional societies as conservative and unchanging. An overall aim of the exhibition was to close the distance between Them and Us, Westerners and Aborigines. Andrew Pekarik revealed his assumptions and his agenda when he wrote: 'for Westerners beautiful objects are the accepted currency of cultural accomplishment' (cited in Myers 1991: 35).

Although the organisers' agenda was in part to close the distance between Aborigines and Westerners, some have argued that the way they chose to do it emphasised certain differences and exoticised and objectified Aboriginal Australians. Although the message of cultural diversity was quite in harmony with the inclusion of Aboriginal art within the European category, it could be argued that the exhibition reinforced a particular kind of view of Aboriginal society that was no longer representative of that diversity. The exhibition title, *Dreamings*, and the way it was advertised inevitably emphasised the religious dimension of Aboriginal art and the fact that it was the contemporary product of an ancient tradition. Although it was not presented as the 'oldest art' or the 'original art' or 'magical art' as it had been in earlier exhibitions, that was clearly part of its attraction to the audience, and one that it was difficult to counter without having a negative effect on the potential audience. The mystic nature of Aboriginal religion and its link to the land was one of the main things that the exhibition had going for it. In the catalogue and in their commentary on events that were organised the anthropologists tried to avoid presenting a stereotyped view. Moreover a large number of Aboriginal people participated in the opening symposium and hence were given the opportunity to provide a less mediated representation. However, by their selection of works, the exhibition organisers did reinforce a particular image of Aboriginal Australia that failed to reflect the diversity of contemporary Aboriginal Australians.

The exhibition excluded works that were painted by Aboriginal artists trained within the European tradition and whose works were indistinguishable on formal grounds from paintings produced by white Australian artists. It could be argued that by excluding a form of Aboriginal art that was most similar to that produced by contemporary Western artists and including works that were demonstrably in continuity with those independent of European genesis, the exhibition organisers were maintaining the difference of Aboriginal art and simultaneously creating differences between different kinds of Aborigines. This apparent contradiction with the overall aim of the exhibition, to include Aboriginal art within the more general category of art, explains much of the critical response to the exhibition.

The more conservative critics claimed that the exhibition as a whole was not art but ethnography – ethnography in this case being a mark of difference, a sign of otherness; and the more radical said that the exhibition, by failing to include contemporary art by Aborigines most influenced by European forms, had not gone far enough. It was partly in response to these latter critics that, four years later, *Aratjara* took the form it did.

PICTURES IN AN EXHIBITION

Aratjara opened its European tour in Düsseldorf before moving in August 1993 to the Hayward Gallery in London. The exhibition was organised by Bernard Lüthi, a Swiss/German artist, and Djon Mundine, an Aboriginal person from Sydney with a long-term involvement in the marketing and promotion of Aboriginal art. *Aratjara* shared with *Dreamings* the aims of achieving recognition for Aboriginal art and the critique of the conservative concept of primitive art. It differed in that it aimed to be more all-embracing and more representative of contemporary Aboriginal art. In order to achieve this the exhibition included a considerable number of paintings that were strongly influenced in formal terms by contemporary movements in Western art. These paintings were largely produced by people who had grown up in urban and rural communities in the southern part of Australia, and are often referred to under the general rubric of Koori art. This agenda reflected the perspectives of the organisers but it was also in harmony with the strong role of the Aboriginal Arts Board in the organisation and financing of the exhibition. In the Australia of the 1990s, government-funded bodies have a responsibility to treat all Aborigines equally. In addition there is political pressure from Aboriginal groups to ensure that they are all equally included within the category of Aborigines. Thus while considerable divisions may exist within the Aboriginal community, at least at an official level there is likely to be considerable pressure for international exhibitions of Aboriginal art to be as open as possible to the inclusion of art from all sectors.

As exhibitions, neither *Aratjara* nor *Dreamings* gave much away as to why particular works were included, since they followed the conventions of a Western fine art exhibition. Art in galleries is displayed for aesthetic contemplation, information is kept to a minimum. It is legitimate to ask why a painting is included or more generally why an object is present as an art object, but the works should speak for themselves. The function of the exhibition organiser is to choose which works to include, to decide on their juxtaposition and how they are to be hung. The intellectual process of creating an exhibition is surrounded by mystique, it centres on

Figure 10.2 'The white ibis called Godolba', artist unknown, Oenpelli, 1912. Collected by Paddy Cahill for Sir Baldwin Spencer

Source: Courtesy of the National Gallery of Victoria

the implicit meanings of exclusions and inclusions, and almost involves a system of secret knowledge. To understand the agenda of an exhibition it is necessary to know how it differs from previous ones on the same or related topics.

I will consider in detail only two of the paintings included in the *Aratjara* exhibition. The two are chosen to reveal the significant difference between the agenda of the *Aratjara* and that of *Dreamings* and in turn to reflect back on the historical processes that resulted in the exhibition. The life histories (Appadurai 1986: 17) of the paintings both show how they ended up in the same exhibition and provide the basis for challenging their inclusion.

The first painting is titled *The white ibis called Godolba* and was ascribed to an unknown Gagadju artist (see Figure 10.2). It was loaned by the National Museum of Victoria where it is part of the collection of paintings made in the second decade of this century, directly and indirectly, by Baldwin Spencer, the biologist and anthropologist. In June 1911 Spencer arrived at Oenpelli, a cattle property in Western Arnhem Land on the frontier of the European colonisation of Australia. As an academic, an administrator and a collector Spencer played a significant role in the institutional development of art in colonial Australia. He was a friend and sponsor of Arthur Streeton whose '*plein air*' landscapes revolutionised Australian painting and remain a continuing reference point. As Trustee of the Felton Bequest, Spencer was responsible for purchasing Australia's main collection of European Impressionist paintings for the National Gallery of Victoria. It was at Oenpelli that he saw for the first time paintings on bark produced by the Gagadju and other groups who lived there under the protection of Paddy Cahill, a buffalo shooter and rancher (Spencer 1912 and 1928). The main context of the paintings was on the walls of wet-season huts, though there is evidence that people also painted on separate sheets of bark. Certainly Spencer (1928: 793) encouraged them to do so since, as he wrote, 'collecting from their studios meant taking down the slabs on which they were drawn, that formed incidentally, the walls of their [huts]'.

Spencer viewed the Gagadju artists very positively and drew analogies between them and artists from other parts of the world. In contrast to his writing elsewhere about Aboriginal artefacts he wrote about Gagadju paintings as if they were art.

> Today I found a native who, apparently, had nothing better to do than sit quietly in camp, evidently enjoying himself, drawing a fish on a sheet of stringy bark . . . [he used] a primitive but quite effective paint-brush, made out of a short stick, six or eight inches long, frayed out with his teeth and then pressed out so as to form a disc . . . he held it just like a civilised artist . . . he did line work, often very fine and regular, with much the same freedom and precision as a Japanese or Chinese artist

Figure 10.3 'The nine ricochets (fall down black fella jump up white fella)', Gordon Bennett, Queensland, 1990

Source: Gordon Bennett

doing his more beautiful wash-work with his brush. They are so realistic, always expressing the characteristic features of the animal drawn ... there was relatively very much the same difference between them as between British artists.

The artists were paid for their paintings in sticks of tobacco, the number varying according to the size of the sheet of bark. When he left Oenpelli Spencer made arrangements for Cahill to send him further shipments of paintings and the *White ibis* was one that arrived the following year.

Spencer was clearly excited by Western Arnhem Land art and wrote about it in terms that could have been part of the discourse over primitive art that was occurring at the same time in Europe and was part of the development of modernism. However, Australia at the time was relatively isolated from Europe and it would be some decades before Aboriginal art would begin to have an impact on Australian art. Spencer's paintings remained in the National Museum of Victoria to be exhibited not as art but as ethnography and no more major collections from the region were made until after World War II. Indeed it was not until the 1970s that Aboriginal art began to gain widespread recognition and the flight of the *White ibis* to the Hayward gallery would doubtless have surprised both the artist and Spencer.

The second painting has a different kind of history. The painting by Gordon Bennett (Figure 10.3) is titled *The nine ricochets (fall down black fella jump up white fella)*. It was painted in 1990 and is owned by the Bellas Gallery in Brisbane. The painting is in highly complex postmodernist style, combining formal elements from many different traditions, mainly European and American but including in this case strong reference to Central Desert Aboriginal acrylics. The catalogue contains Bennett's (1993: 89) own analysis of his art which clearly positions it in a global context.

> I locate my aesthetic approach within the more conventional notions of Western aesthetic and iconographical traditions. My approach is however deconstructive in its orientation. I use strategies of quotation and appropriation to produce what I have 'called' history paintings. I draw on the iconographical paradigm of Australian and by extension European, art in a way that constitutes a kind of ethnographic investigation of a Euro-Australian system of representation in general, but which focuses on the representation of Aboriginal people in particular.

Earlier (p. 87) he writes 'I wish to reinstate a sense of Aboriginal people within the culturally dominant system of representation as human beings, rather than as a visual sign of the "primitive", the "noble savage" or some other European construct associated with black skin.'

The contrast between the life histories of the two paintings, one by the unknown artist the other by Gordon Bennett, and the questions that they pose about the category of Aboriginal art set the frame for this chapter. In some ways Bennett makes my argument for me both intellectually and by his artistic practice. His paintings are the outcome of his reflection on the relationship between local and global processes, the relationship between the appropriation of Aboriginal land and the creation of primitive art, on the relationship between art history and colonialism, between perspective and the definition of the other (Bennett 1993).[14] And, the themes of his paintings apart, as an artist trained in European traditions he could as easily belong to the art world of London or New York as Brisbane.

It could be argued, following Maquet's distinction, that in contrast to the unknown artist of the *White ibis* whose paintings undergo a meta-morphosis, Bennett is producing art by intention. Despite Spencer's obvious appreciation of Western Arnhem Land bark paintings he is clearly positioning them in a framework of opposition between primitive and civilised cultures. He is using the analogy with British, Japanese and Chinese art to elevate them into the category of artworks and is pointing out characteristics that they share in common with such works. He empha-sises the apparently unmotivated pleasure the artist gets from painting, and the skill and representational ability of the artist, characteristics that allowed the painting to be exhibited in the 1929 *Primitive Art* exhibition in the National Gallery of Victoria, Melbourne. Spencer was part of the process of creating Aboriginal art as an international art form – a process of which *Dreamings* and *Aratjara* are a later stage.

Bennett, in contrast, intends to produce a work of art, and exhibition in the Hayward Gallery as part of a blockbuster exhibition on Aboriginal art must make political as well as economic sense. Yet the distinction between the primitive artist defined by the other and the contem-porary artist is precisely the kind of distinction that Bennett's 'painted ethnography' is designed to uncover and that his paintings are constructed to challenge. His painting simultaneously challenges the category of tradi-tional Aboriginal art and defines him in relation to it. For much of the audience, *White ibis* provides the justification for the exhibition: the exhibition is the celebration of the art of the other, and into this Gordon Bennett's painting represents an apparent intrusion. For Gordon Bennett is avowedly not other but self and his inclusion as an Aboriginal artist adds confusion to what seemed to be the recognition of Aborig-inal art.[15]

The question that has to be answered and which the artist himself poses is why is Gordon Bennett, an art-school-trained, higher-educated contem-porary Australian producing self-consciously global art, categorised in the Hayward Gallery exhibition as an Aboriginal artist? What is an Aboriginal artist and does s/he exist as a local or a global concept and what processes operate to position Gordon Bennett and the painter of the *White ibis* as painters of Aboriginal art? What, in a global context, is the meaning of Aboriginal art?

These are questions clearly posed by the organisers *to* the audience, for they must have been aware that the inclusion of art that Westerners would see as coming from a fundamentally different tradition would be seen as a challenge to the more conservative critics.

The critic for the *Spectator*, Giles Auty (1993), for example, wrote that *White ibis* is 'one of the loveliest and most moving works in the whole exhibition ... [and it] ... bears out my contention that work by Aboriginal artists has generally declined in quality in direct proportion one suspects, to the amount of interested input from non-Aboriginals'. In contrast Gordon Bennett is more 'political than perceptual ... like his counter-parts hereabouts, Bennett is content to talk rather than paint a good picture'.

The reasons for the inclusion of Gordon Bennett and the painter of *White ibis* within the same category lie equally in Western art practice and art history and in the political position of Aborigines in post-colonial Australia. Aboriginal art is created by global processes but they are ones which involve Aboriginal agency and can to an extent accommodate Aboriginal political interests. There is an ultimate and almost irresolvable contradiction between the creation of value in Western art practice and Western art history (or more generally art writing) – a contradiction that appears to apply equally to modernist and postmodernist practice. Western art practice is in a continual process of change, in which newness and orig-inality is emphasised and valued highly in developing artists.

Art has a trajectory which contemporary artists are supposed to set, and work that falls behind that trajectory, which works over old themes or reproduces the characteristics of earlier styles, is considered dated, and tends to be negatively valued. However, in art writing and in the art market previous forms retain their value: they exist in a permanent state of being new, of having once been original. They are part of the corpus of Western art. Thus the retrospective view from art history includes a set of arts that were once produced – Renaissance art, Impressionism, Cubism – that have a relatively stable value and a position in a sequence of development, but which if produced today would have a different value and would most probably be unacceptable. A Renaissance painting produced in the 1990s is out of its time. Yesterday's paintings retain their value but yesterday's styles are unacceptable as models for today's prac-tice – though they may always be an inspiration and with the advent of postmodernism they can be a reference. Indeed it could be argued that it is necessary to keep works 'out of time' to provide a reference point. It is this that creates art history and avoids art chaos!

Over time, changing Western art practice and theory have altered the Western conception of other arts or of what other works are 'art', giving Oriental art, African art, folk art, a place in Western art history. Although some non-Western traditions, such as Chinese art, are given relative autonomy as traditions with trajectories of their own, there is a tendency for them to be treated in the same way as past schools of European art. They have a value established at their point of production by the West, in other words when they were recognised by the West or in Maquet's terms when they were metamorphosed. The essentially conservative nature of the concept of primitive art that I outlined earlier fits into this model. This is the reason why it is difficult to accept a work of 'traditional' Aboriginal art if it is painted today, since it is painted out of its time. Its Western art-historical time was at the point of its discovery by the West, which is what makes *White ibis* art, since it was part of the process of the discovery of Aboriginal art, but which makes a contemporary work in an identical form more problematic.

Produced in 1914, *White ibis* is easily acceptable as fine art even if some would still prefer to place it in the primitive or ethnographic subcategory. As fine art it belongs to its own tradition as well as to the history of Western art which discovered it. In exhibiting it the gallery director has a choice of which direction to go in, whether to exhibit it as a cultural artefact with its own history (which in the past would have meant exhibiting it in the ethnographic museum) or to exhibit it so that its formal properties can be admired (which in the past would have meant in the art gallery). However, an almost identical painting produced in the 1970s for sale would be more problematic since it represents a past discovery of Western art with a past influence on Western traditions that is contaminated by contact and produced out of time.

It would be wrong to accept such a state of affairs as inevitable, for as Fred Myers (1991: 28) has argued that would be to 'reify our own cultural concepts into a more stable form than they actually have'. The commercial success of the Western Desert acrylics and contemporary Western Arnhem Land bark paintings suggests that the criteria of the primitive art market have been challenged and that to an extent traditional Aboriginal art has been given a degree of autonomy as a tradition which has a duration beyond its incorporation into Western art history. Aboriginal art has maintained its value despite the commercial context of its contemporary production. At the same time Aboriginal art remains a potential external influence on white Australian contemporary art, and in that form, part of two strands of contemporary art practice: Aboriginal and European.

In contrast to Europe where primitive art had a strong influence on the development of art, Aboriginal art only minimally influenced the development of white Australian art until well into the twentieth century. Indeed until the 1950s Margaret Preston was almost alone among artists influenced by Aboriginal forms. However, since the 1950s the influence has grown stronger, in particular following the exposure to Western Desert art that occurred in the 1980s. The emphasis on change, which still characterises developments in Western art practice, does not of course mean that Aboriginal art cannot have a continuing impact on white Australian art, any more than it means that the influence of African art is restricted to its impact on the Fauvists or Die Brücke. It is in the nature of the Western creation of primitive art that it remains outside time as far as Western art is concerned, for it operates according to different rules.

Thus the inclusion of paintings by Gordon Bennett as Aboriginal art is seen as challenging because it poses fundamentally different questions about what art Aboriginal art is. Bennett fits firmly into the Western category of artist working explicitly in a postmodernist tradition. Yet he identifies with the artist of the *White ibis* as a fellow Aboriginal artist and when he uses Western Desert motifs he is using art which, in the post-modern context in which he operates, is integral to his conception of self.[16] The Western creation of Aboriginal art as a category ironically parallels the contemporary Aboriginal creation of a pan-Aboriginal identity which includes all Aborigines within the same category. It is this pan-Aboriginality that means that a white Australian artist producing similar paintings to Gordon Bennett and also using Aboriginal themes could be accused of appropriating the other in contrast to Gordon Bennett's appropriation of self! This contradictory situation which arises out of the colonial process and the development of a Western-centred art history is brought into the open by the inclusion of paintings such as *White ibis* and *The nine ricochets* in the same exhibition. This in part explains on the one hand the divergent critical reaction to the exhibitions and the diverse views of it among different Aboriginal groups on the other.

There are critics who, like Giles Auty, argue that Gordon Bennett is not producing Aboriginal art at all but (an inferior) version of Western art, in contrast to the artist of the *White ibis*. On the other hand there are critics such as John MacDonald, the editor of the influential journal *Modern Painters*, who drew the opposite conclusion and found the whole distinction between Aboriginal and other art untenable. He begins his review of *Aratjara* (MacDonald 1993) by reflecting on some recent exhibitions of white Australian art and asserts that 'a single Aboriginal painting in either exhibition might have put Australian art in proper perspective'. He goes on to comment favourably on the variety and complexity of the art in the exhibition and then interestingly argues that in acknowledging the diversity of the category Aboriginal art through the exhibition: 'the boundaries of this term have been so far expanded as to be on the verge of disappearing', and concludes with: 'this is in some ways, an attempt to normalise Aboriginal art, but it might be that only by first breaking down the aura of the exotic will we arrive at a clearer understanding of these extraordinary works and the human beings who make them'.

On the Aboriginal side there is certainly a view from some of the artists from the more remote communities that the work of Koori artists is not Aboriginal in the sense they understand their paintings to be, and indeed there is sometimes an expression of sorrow that the artists have lost their traditions which echoes the response of the more conservative art critics. On the other hand there are many Aboriginal people who are angry at the suggestion that they are categorically distinct and see attempts to distinguish between different traditions of art on the basis of their degree of Aboriginality as being offensive. Indeed, despite its almost wholly positive tone, MacDonald's review was castigated by one of the artists on the basis of his use of the term 'urban Aboriginal' which has acquired many of the connotations of not being a real Aborigine.

Myers sees Aboriginal art as simultaneously 'our' product and 'their' product. 'Our' product in that it is accepted by the Western art market partly on its own terms. 'Their' product in that Aboriginal motivations and histories are the major determinants of the form it takes. The local–global relationship is in fact mediated through the intervening structure of the Australian state which influences the way in which Aboriginal art is received by global audiences. Aboriginal artworks that are received on a world market or by a global audience are generated in part by local Australian circumstances. Aboriginal art is influenced both by the motivations of the Australian political establishment and by the political actions of Aborigines in the context of the existence of the state.

As Myers (1991: 53) has argued, Aboriginal culture has been part of the way Australia has created a global identity that transcends the particular colonial circumstances of its recent history.

> The Aboriginal and the Outback are, increasingly, the source of Australia's self marketing for the international tourist industry, the 'difference' they have to offer. These constitute an important dialectical dimension of emerging formulations of Australian national identity: something essentially outside and before the nation that lies also at its heart, central to its identity.

As far as Aborigines are concerned art is an expression of their political identity. In the case of 'traditionally oriented' groups it is a means of asserting their particular values and arguing for their rights to be respected, initially on a national and subsequently on an international stage. In the case of Aborigines from urban communities art frequently provides a political commentary on the history of their repression and the circumstances of their post-colonial existence. Indeed it is this dimension of the art – the themes that are taken up and the position of the artist – that creates the difference from contemporary white Australian art, as well as perhaps the choice of formal influence. Koori art is more likely to include references to traditional Aboriginal art than are paintings by contemporary white Australians.

CONCLUSION

In Australia the changing position of Aboriginal art has resulted in its incorporation in discourse on Australian art in general. It tends now to be collected by the same institutions, exhibited within the same gallery structure, written about in the same journals as other Australian art. And in many respects this has come about because, over many years, Aboriginal people have been struggling to make Aboriginal art part of the agenda of Australian society. It could be interpreted as the appropriation of

Aboriginal art by a white Australian institutional structure; the reality has been a much more equal relationship. Issues such as the alienation of art from the producer, the protection of intellectual property, the role of the government in the marketing and production of art, the autonomy of tradition, the relationship between representation and abstraction, have developed as critical foci in Australian art precisely because of the inclusion of Aboriginal art within the debate. The breakdown of simple dichotomies has emphasised rather than reduced the diversity of Aboriginal art, and has enabled the distinctions within the category to emerge in a non-prescriptive way.

Outside Australia there has been an exponential increase of interest in Aboriginal art, in particular since the mid-1980s. A sign of the growing interest in and marketability of Aboriginal art is its movement from a footnote on Pacific art to occupation of a Thames & Hudson 'World of Art' space of its own (Caruana 1992). However, the danger of the move out of Australia is that it will result in a re-pigeonholing of Aboriginal art and artists. Many of the movements that resulted in change in Australia have had their effect elsewhere in the world but, with the possible exception of North-West Coast America, the inclusion of indigenous art within the mainstream has not occurred in such a significant manner. Overseas, it is almost inevitable that the case to establish the authenticity of Aboriginal art in the contemporary world will have to be re-argued and there is always the danger of the art being repositioned in some lumpen category. A recent article in the *Guardian* by Waldamar Januszczak provides an example of both of these processes.

> Just as you can walk into any supermarket these days and buy nibblets from every corner of the world, so you can walk into an art gallery and sample the cultural drupelets [sic] of a thousand far flung races. Most of this produce is fake rubbish. Certainly this is true of Aborigine art, a huge exhibition of which is on the way to the Hayward Gallery. Aborigines neither painted on canvas nor showed in Bond Street until a bunch of Aussie crocodile dealers realised that 20,000 years worth of sand pictures had already blown into the billabong: now vaguely Aboriginal artists with vaguely Aboriginal names like Peter Possum or Cliff Koala are Dreaming on – on canvas – all the way to the bank. The same process of cultural franchising has given us the Shona sculpture of Zimbabwe or the Inuit carving of the Canadian arctic. What all these fake international art forms have in common is a desire to give us white folks what we want – what we expect from an exotic culture.

Whereas white Australian art is likely to be included in the mainstream European or American traditions because of its ancestry (though with limited spaces for named artists!), Aboriginal art is likely to be re-pigeon-holed as 'ethnic' art, and to occupy a slot in a programme or a space in a gallery that is otherwise filled by Makonde art or Inuit art or contemporary Papua New Guinea prints – and people will try to draw analogies across those categories. Aboriginal art entered New York through the galleries of the Asian Society and in the Hayward Gallery in London it will occupy a programming space allocated to ethnic art. As a curator I have been told: 'I like Aboriginal art, I have a collection of Eskimo carvings', and 'the Bushmen are doing the same as the Aborigines'. I am not sure why such comments make me feel so uncomfortable. Perhaps I am afraid that the category of 'primitive art' is being born again in another guise.

In Australia, Aboriginal art is on the verge of incorporation within the process of individuation that is characteristic of the marketing of European art. It has entered the process actively and, from a conservative perspective, can be seen to be challenging established canons. If ever there was a battle to respect the anonymity of Aboriginal art which, some have argued, characterised its use in indigenous contexts, then that battle has been lost. However, Aboriginal artists have maintained a considerable degree of control over the exhibition of their work and the use of their names. Aborigines are consulted before their work is exhibited in Australia and the names of dead artists are not used until their families consider that an appropriate time has elapsed since their death. The major Aboriginal art prize has become known as the 'Son of Mawalan Prize' since the death of the artist it commemorates. There are many examples of ways in which Aboriginal etiquette and systems of rights in paintings do influence the Australian 'art world', in addition to any effect the form and content of the art may have. In Europe and America so far Aboriginal art tends to be exhibited as a category, although the names of the artists are recorded where known and background information is made available through accompanying catalogues. Moreover unless an exhibition originates in Australia it is unlikely that Aboriginal political action will intervene to constrain the way in which the art is presented. Whereas in Australia the death of Aboriginal artists is respected by the silencing of their names, in Europe, were their names known, it is unlikely that the wishes of their kin would be respected.

Such a re-incorporation into gross categories is not inevitable. The art world is becoming more willing to acknowledge complexity and to recognise that although the Western category of art in its greed can swallow the products of all other cultures, it can also respect their variety and difference. It is here that Australian Aboriginal art may have an important role to play. In Australia the impetus that has moved Aboriginal art into the public eye has been in part the conscious political action of Aboriginal people. The debates that have been part of its public emergence in Australia, the breaking down of categories that was a consequence of its movement into the art galleries, have to an extent followed it to Europe and America. The inclusion of Koori art with art from Arnhem

Land and Central Australia, the complex two-way relationship between Aboriginal art and painting by Australians of European descent, all these things confront overseas audiences with the issues that lie behind developments in contemporary Australian art. And these issues are relevant to understanding art on a global scale.

NOTES

1. For a discussion of contemporary Chinese art see *China Avant-Garde*, the catalogue of a major exhibition organised in 1993 by the Haus der Kultures, West Berlin and The Museum of Modern Art, Oxford.
2. Hence James Clifford's (1988: 213) plea for an 'influx of truly indigestible artifacts' – though I would not underestimate the capacity of the Western category of art to absorb anything that an anthropologist could find to feed it with! For a discussion of an anthropological concept of art see Morphy (1994).
3. Although blockbuster exhibitions ought to be a great resource for anthropological research since they are one of the West's main forms of cultural representation, they have been comparatively little researched (though see Myers 1991). However, relevant work has been done on the related topics of Great Exhibitions (Benedict 1983), museum exhibitions (Karp and Levine 1991) and cultural festivals (Appadurai and Breckenbridge 1992).
4. The classic account remains Goldwater 1986 [1938].
5. This view was represented by Frank Whitford in his review of the *Aratjara* exhibition in the *Sunday Times*, 1 August 1993: 9.13. 'If we are unable to see such paintings through Aboriginal eyes we are equally unable to view them as though for the first time. Their qualities are shared by other kinds of primitive art that we have been educated to admire by Western painters who have incorporated such conventions in their work. This may be regrettable since it prevents us from perceiving the true nature of "primitive" art, but it is a fact that we are as conditioned by our culture as an Aborigine is by his.'
6. Indeed Aboriginal art was initially incorporated in the Australian art exhibitions of the Australian National Gallery on precisely this basis, in that selected works of Aboriginal art were displayed in appropriate relationship to works in the European tradition that could have been thought to be influenced by them. Since until recently Aboriginal art had not been a dominant influence in the development of white Australian art this formula for exhibition was not a particularly successful one.
7. The New York art dealer John Weber sees the accommodation of the art market to Aboriginal art as being a technical problem 'as Australia has not previously generated an art movement of international significance, the art power structure is at a loss to deal professionally with the fast emerging Aboriginal scene' (Weber 1989, cited in Myers 1991: 41). I would argue that the power structure is integral to the creation of the structure of the international art market.
8. The world art market has the characteristics of a world system as defined by Friedman following Frank (see Chapter 7, this volume) as an integrated, partly hierarchical structure of relations which has determining consequences on the ways in which components from the periphery are incorporated.
9. Myers (1991) provides a detailed analysis of some of the reviews of *Dreamings* and of the critical discourse surrounding the exhibition.
10. Myers (1991:27), referring to an exhibition of Western Desert paintings as art in the Weber gallery in New York observes 'the acrylics are hung to emphasise that role as defined by the West. No information is presented about specific

content: only the name of the painter, date and title are given, although an accompanying catalogue traces some of the general historical tradition relating to the production of the images.'

11. For the general history of European attitudes to Aboriginal art see Jones (1988) and Morphy (1987). For the commercialisation of Aboriginal art see Loveday and Cook (1983), Altman (1989) and Altman and Taylor (1991).

12. As Kapferer (1989: 142) notes, 'Aboriginals have come to represent a system intimately engaged in their destruction.' Lattas (1991: 312) provides an interesting example of the way in which the Aboriginal theme of mourning for the dead of the colonial holocaust, that was so central to their response to the Bicentennial, can in effect be appropriated in the interests of a wider Australian identity. The process involves the interpretation of Aboriginal themes to convey common messages about the human condition. Because those common messages are themselves part of a Christian heritage and relate most directly to white Australian concerns, Aboriginal interests are in effect subordinated to a Western version of the human condition. Aborigines are inevitably caught up in a struggle with other Australians and with institutional interests to exercise some control over the fixing of the meaning of their own history and cultural practices.

13. For a number of reasons I do not in fact accept the argument that *toas* were innovative to anything like the extent that Jones argues. For example while *toas* were certainly influenced by the context of their collection, on the whole I think it is probable that they were functionally direction signs. However, in the context of the exhibition they were presented as objects innovated in response to European contact.

14. Writing of his paintings Bennett (1993: 89) explains that they problematise perspective, since he associates perspective with a particular way of classifying the world that gives priority to the position of the viewer, 'Aborigines caught in this system of representation remain frozen as objects within the mapped territory of a European perceptual grid.'

15. 'There came a time in my life, in my sense of self and identity as an Australian, when I became aware of my Aboriginal heritage. This may seem of no consequence to the subject at hand, but when the weight of European representation of Aboriginal people as the quintessentially primitive "other" is realised, and perhaps understood as a certain level of abstraction involving a discourse of self and other with which we become familiar in our books and our classrooms but which we rarely feel on our pulses; then it may be seen that such an awareness was problematic for my sense of identity. The conceptual gap between self and other collapsed and I was thrown into turmoil' (Gordon Bennett 1993: 87).

16. Bennett's own explanation of his use of Western Desert concepts is worth quoting: 'It has been said of Aboriginal art of the Western Desert that it produces a finite design by subtraction – even quotation – from a potentially infinite grid of connected places/Dreamings/people, in which the real spatial relationships are literally rectified and represented. My approach to quotation within the European tradition is to select images from Euro-Australian art history which have accumulated certain meaning over time, placing them in new relationships to other images ... by recontextualising images [I attempt to show] ... new possibilities of meaning and identification' (Bennett 1993: 89).

REFERENCES

Altman, J. (1989) *The Aboriginal arts and crafts industry*. Canberra: The Australian Government Publishing Service.

Altman, J. and L. Taylor (1991) *Marketing Aboriginal art in the 1990s*. Canberra: Aboriginal Studies Press.

Appadurai, A. (ed.) (1986) *The social life of things*. Cambridge: Cambridge University Press.

Appadurai, A. and C.A. Breckenbridge (1992) Museums are good to think: heritage on view in India. In I. Karp, C. Mullen Kreamer and S.D. Lavine (eds), *Museums and communities: the politics of public culture*. Washington: Smithsonian Institution Press, pp. 34–55

Auty, Giles (1993) *Spectator*, 7 August, XX.

Baudrillard, J. (1981) Gesture and signature: semiurgy in contemporary art. In *For a political economy of the sign*. St Louis: Telos.

Bell, S. (producer/director) (1989) *88.9 Radio Redfern*. Sydney: Film Australia.

Benedict, B. (ed.) (1983) *The anthropology of World Fairs*. Berkeley: Scolar.

Bennett, G. (1993) Aesthetics and iconography: an artist's approach. In B. Lüthi (ed.), *Aratjara: art of the first Australians*. Düsseldorf: Kuntsammlung Nordrhein-Westfalen, pp. 85–91.

Caruana, W. (1992) *Aboriginal art*. London: Thames & Hudson.

Clifford, J. (1988) *The predicament of culture*. Cambridge MA: Harvard University Press.

Cooper, C., H. Morphy, D. Mulvaney and N. Peterson (1981) *Aboriginal Australia*. Sydney: Australian Gallery Directors Council.

D'Azevedo, W.L. (1973) *The traditional artist in African society*. Bloomington: Indiana University Press.

Goehr, L. (1992) *The imaginary museum of musical works: an essay in the philosophy of music*. Oxford: Oxford University Press.

Goldwater, R. (1986) [1938] *Primitivism in modern art* (enlarged edition). Cambridge, MA: Belknap Press.

Graburn, N.H.H. (1976) *Ethnic and tourist arts: cultural expressions of the Fourth World*. Berkeley: University of California Press.

Jones, P. (1988) Perceptions of Aboriginal art: a history. In P.J. Sutton (ed.), *Dreamings: the art of Aboriginal Australia*. Ringwood: Viking/Penguin, pp. 143–79.

Jones, P. and P. Sutton (1986) *Art and land: Aboriginal sculptures of the Lake Eyre region*. Adelaide: South Australian Museum.

Kapferer, B. (1989) *Legends of people, myths of state: violence, intolerance and political culture in Sri Lanka and Australia*. Washington: Smithsonian Institution Press.

Karp, I. and S.A. Levine (1991) *Exhibiting cultures: the poetics and politics of museum display*. Washington: Smithsonian Institution Press.

Kupka, K. (1965) *The dawn of art*. New York: Viking Press.

Lattas, A. (1991) Nationalism, aesthetic redemption and Aboriginality. *The Australian Journal of Anthropology* 2/3: 307–24.

Lüthi, B. (1993) *Aratjara: art of the first Australians*. Düsseldorf: Kuntsammlung Nordrhein-Westfalen.

Loveday, P. and P. Cook. (1983) *Aboriginal arts and crafts and the market*. Darwin: North Australian Research Unit.

McCulloch, A. (1984) *Encyclopedia of Australian art*. Melbourne: Hutchinson.

Maquet, J. (1979) *Introduction to Aesthetic Anthropology* (2nd edn). Malibu CA: Udena Publications.

Michaels, E. (1988) Bad Aboriginal art. *Art and Text* 28: 59–73.

Morphy, H. (1977) Schematisation, communication and meaning in *toas*. In P.J. Ucko (ed.), *Form in indigenous art: schematisation in the art of Aboriginal Australia and prehistoric Europe*. Canberra: Australian Institute of Aboriginal Studies.

—— (1987) Audiences for art. In A. Curthoys, A. Martin and T. Rowse (eds), *Australians: a historical library*. Sydney: Fairfax, Syme & Weldon Associates, pp. 167–75.

—— (1991) *Ancestral connections: art and an Aboriginal system of knowledge*. Chicago: University of Chicago Press.

—— (1992) Gaps in collections and spaces for exhibition – reflections on the acceptance of Aboriginal 'art' in Europe and Australia. *Art Monthly Australia Supplement – Aboriginal art in the public eye*, pp. 10–13.

—— (1994) The anthropology of art. In T. Ingold (ed.), *Companion encyclopedia of anthropology*. London: Routledge, pp. 648–85.

Myers, F.R. (1991) Representing culture: the production of discourse(s) for Aboriginal acrylic paintings. *Cultural Anthropology* 6(1): 26–62.

Rowlinson, M. (1980) Introduction. In C. Cooper et al. *Aboriginal Australia*. Sydney: Australian Gallery Directors Council.

Rubin, W. (1984) 'Modernist Primitivism, an introduction'. In W. Rubin (ed.), *Primitivism in twentieth century art*, Vol. 1. New York: Museum of Modern Art.

Spencer, W.B. (1912) *The native tribes of Northern Australia*. London: Macmillan.

—— (1928) *Wanderings in wild Australia* (2 vols). London: Macmillan.

Stirling, E.C. and E.R. Waite (1919) Description of toas or direction signs. *Records of the South Australian Museum* 1: 101–55

Sutton, P.J. (ed.) (1988) *Dreamings: the art of Aboriginal Australia*. Ringwood: Viking/Penguin, pp. 143–79.

—— (1992) 'Reading Aboriginal art'. In D. Walker, J. Horne and M. Lyons (eds), 'Books, readers, reading', *Australian Cultural History* 11: 28–38.

Tuckson, J.A. (1964) Aboriginal art and the Western World. In R.M. Berndt (ed.), *Australian Aboriginal art*. Sydney: Ure Smith.

von Sturmer, J.R. (1989). Aborigines, representation, necrophilia. *Art and Text* 32 (Autumn): 127–39.

Wild, S. (1991) Introduction. In J. Altman and L. Taylor, *Marketing Aboriginal art in the 1990s*. Canberra: Aboriginal Studies Press.

11 Traversing the global and the local: fújì music and praise poetry in the production of contemporary Yorùbá popular culture

Karin Barber and Christopher Waterman

EXTENSION, DOMESTICATION, INTENSIFICATION

The widespread perception of globalisation as a tide of mainly American shlock, swamping authentic cultures and imposing a diluted and homogeneous plastic culture of Coca Cola and McDonalds over the entire earth's surface is, as Ulf Hannerz has pointed out, more an exercise in metropolitan self-criticism than an informed account of what is happening in the periphery (Hannerz 1991). An attractive alternative is the view that locals selectively 'appropriate' elements from metropolitan cultures in order to 'construct' their own hybrid medium in which to articulate their own, historically and socially specific, experience. Hannerz gives this discussion a helpful push by working on the assumption that this is a generally shared condition – 'we are all being creolised' – and that there is a continuum of creolisation, stretching from the metropolitan centres to the rural backwoods. As with creole languages, culture which is created from a fusion of disparate elements becomes a self-reproducing expressive medium into which people are born and which provides them with their perspective on the world. Rather than one global, homogeneous, mass culture, what we will find is a continuum of innumerable different, local, creoles (Hannerz 1987, 1991).

The advantages of the creolisation model are apparent. First, it stresses the active, creative role of people as culture producers, rather than representing them as passive victims of global gangrene. Second, it draws attention to the fact that in colonial and post-colonial African cultures we witness the creation of something qualitatively new, with its own dynamics, rather than just a dilution or corruption of something formerly authentic. And third, this new thing is represented as a language-like generative system; the function and significance of the heterogeneous elements are determined by their place in this system and not by the meaning they had formerly in their source culture. This gives us some leverage on the question of the repositioning and transformation of cultural elements, so obvious in modern African popular cultures.

However, the creolisation model also has a tendency to encourage an analytic binarisation of the field of culture, into 'indigenous' (traditional, local) and 'imported' (modern, global) elements. Even though the product of creolisation is represented as a qualitatively new system with its own inner dynamics, the model does take as its starting point two or more separate prior cultures, recognisable elements which are then fused to form a new whole. An inadvertent by-product of this tends to be the simplification and reification of both halves, but especially the 'indigenous' half, which is usually taken as the baseline. Hannerz himself is careful to avoid this, and his use of the idea of creolisation is correspondingly flexible and productive; but in many writings on hybridity in African popular culture there is a tendency to assume that the 'indigenous' can easily be identified as such and distinguished from the 'imported'.[1]

In this paper we investigate Yorùbá *fújì* – a contemporary popular music style – in relation to *oríkì*, an oral poetic genre of much longer standing, in order to propose an alternative to the endogenous/exogenous model as applied to Yorùbá culture. *Oríkì* ('praise poetry' or attributive epithets) have long been a master discourse in the constitution of individual and collective identities in the Yorùbá-speaking area.[2] They are still widely performed at life-cycle ceremonies, religious rituals and festivals and at celebrations of individual wealth and achievement. Addressed vocatively and dialogically to a listening subject – the 'owner' of the *oríkì* – the performance enhances and intensifies the subject's presence by accessing an extensive constellation of memories and emblems, often evoking the powers of ancestors or other persons. *Fújì* music is a popular modern commercial genre which is disseminated live, through records and cassettes, and through video.

An analysis which sought to investigate *fújì* in terms of hybridity would easily identify apparently 'indigenous', 'traditional' elements: the use of the Yorùbá language; the incorporation of long-established verbal genres such as proverbs and *oríkì*; the philosophy expressed in some of the lyrics; and the patron–client networks which are the socioeconomic *raison d'être* of *fújì* performance. Features which look and sound 'exogenous', drawn from the repertoires of a global, electronically disseminated mass culture, are even more strikingly apparent. The texts contain sections in English, including African-American English; the bands use imported musical technology; musical styles include themes culled from European and American media; in the videos, the visual imagery includes a continual flow of representations of imported commodities. Moreover, the style itself seems at first sight the obvious outcome of transnational culture flows. *Fújì* is a highly eclectic and incorporative genre, juxtaposing textual, musical and (in the videos) visual fragments in a shifting and unstable flow of pastiche and allusion. *Fújì* seems to have most of the characteristics attributed to postmodernist art: heterogeneity, inter-textuality, the decentring of narrative authority, the unmooring of signs from their customary referents

(Jameson 1984), the prevalence of quotation (Hutcheon 1989)[3] and the mixing of genres which denies ultimate authority to *any* generic perspective (Collins 1989).

But those characteristics that appear most typical of postmodern Western mass consumer culture – fragmentation, heterogeneity, decentring, suspension of judgment, mixing of genres – are, as we shall show, to be found in even more concentrated form in *oríkì*. There is no reason to believe that these features of *oríkì* performances are the outcome of a recent process of globalisation. This is not to say that *oríkì* were postmodernist all along – indeed, such a claim would be meaningless – but rather to suggest that some of the features unhesitatingly identified by social science as typical of Western modernity may be produced by other processes and have other meanings (cf. Strathern 1992).[4] On the one hand, Europe continues unhesitatingly to put down to 'Western influence' everything that fits its own paradigm of modernity; on the other hand, particular developments in European philosophy, such as deconstructive and postmodernist criticism, make partly visible particular, hitherto unperceived, dimensions of certain African cultures. This suggests that the 'endogenous' and the 'exogenous' should not be too hastily identified on formal grounds and from an external perspective.

If we ask instead how locals perceive and define the foreign, it becomes apparent that we have little information on the subject. Commentators have simply taken it for granted that the distinction is self-evident. But in the trading cultures of West Africa, long attuned to the incorporation of novelty (see Collins and Richards 1982), it is clear that certain imported elements have been assimilated into local 'strategies of selfhood and identity' (Friedman 1991: 161). Syncretic music in West Africa goes back at least to the early eighteenth century (Coplan 1978). In some cases imported technology has facilitated the self-conscious 'indigenisation' of musical practice, as when Yorùbá *jùjú* musicians adopted electronic amplification after World War II, a shift in acoustical balance which allowed them to incorporate a wider range of 'traditional' percussion instruments (actually a mixture of Yorùbá and Afro-Cuban drums) and dance rhythms (Waterman 1990a). It is true that the words 'imported' and 'genuine' are often used synonymously, and 'local-made' is a term of disparagement. But the question is whether what is imported is necessarily seen as *foreign* just because it is manufactured outside the country. A Yorùbá woman of Barber's acquaintance said 'The oyinbos [Europeans] know how to make lace, but they don't know how to use it. They hang it at their windows – imagine!' It seemed to be her view that lace was really meant for Yorùbás, or Nigerians, for they knew its function and value better than the mere manufacturers. In an Ìbàdàn nightclub, Waterman observed *jùjú* musicians poking holes in the speakers of their imported PA systems, so as to maximise the dense textures and buzzing timbres favoured in Yorùbá evaluations of musical sound.

If the notion of the 'foreign' needs qualification, so does the notion of the 'indigenous'. This is a situation where not just the elite, but also masses of the urban poor and intermediate classes, self-consciously valorise local practices as 'our traditional heritage' – seeing them simultaneously (as it were) from within and from without, with sincerity but also with ironical self-consciousness. While most of the time life undoubtedly just goes on, following habit, experience, and rules of thumb, it is clear that some activities of daily life are now recognised by their practitioners as part of 'traditional culture', a recognition initiated and fostered by outsiders. Considerations like these lead to ever more complicated elaborations and qualifications of the base distinction between endogenous and exogenous, to a point where it becomes almost too cumbersome to be useful.

Instead, we propose a view of Yorùbá genres as involving a process of *extension*, *domestication* and *intensification*. *Fújì* music, *oríkì*, and other Yorùbá performance genres *extend* from a local point and traverse what lies beyond the immediate locality. Their practitioners *domesticate* difference by incorporating fragments from a multiplicity of sources into local stylistic configurations and social strategies. The ultimate goal of any performance is to *intensify* the presence, image and prospects of local actors. But the 'local actors' themselves are not seen as stable, fully constituted givens; rather, the process of performing oral genres is one of creating and consolidating personae out of diverse, multifarious, overlapping materials, materials often borrowed from other people – a process that suggests a highly sophisticated conception of personality as an assemblage of traits, fused together by social interaction and attention. This perspective does not erase the striking differences between *oríkì* and *fújì*, which are grounded in different processes of production, dissemination and consumption. On the contrary, it provides a more sensitive means of assessing such differences. Nor does it seek to claim that the two genres are really in perfect continuity with each other and with pre-colonial 'Yorùbá' culture. On the contrary, extreme ruptures, shifts of perspective and deliberate differentiations are evident. But if Yorùbá cultural forms are inherently incorporative and porous – as numerous Yorùbá genres seem to be (Ọlatunji 1984, Akinnasọ 1993) – and if their *point* is the traversal, dissolution or non-recognition of many kinds of boundaries, then they are not easily apprehended through a paradigm based on an endogenous/exogenous distinction.[5]

FÚJÌ MUSIC

The Yorùbá term *fújì* refers to a cluster of popular music and dance styles, produced and patronised mostly by Muslims, and performed live at parties and life-cycle celebrations – naming ceremonies, weddings, funerals and business launchings – in cities and towns throughout southwestern Nigeria. *Fújì* music is also distributed in mass-reproduced form on LPs and cassettes. The superstars of the genre, Alhaji Dr Sikiru Ayinde Barrister and Alhaji Professor Ayinla Kollington, and their lesser competitors appear on federal and state government television every day, and their music, played in taxis, buses, bars and market stalls, is a ubiquitous feature of the soundscape of Yorùbá towns. In recent years, *fújì* has outstripped its major competitor, *jùjú* music, in terms of record and cassette sales and the vigour of the genres' respective segments of the live music economy. An average LP release by Alhajis Barrister or Kollington sells 100,000 to 200,000 legitimate copies, and five to ten times as many bootleg cassette copies, distributed through informal networks.

Fújì is an outgrowth of *ajísáàrì* music, customarily performed at around 3 a.m. during the Ramadan fast by groups of young men associated with neighbourhood mosques. *Ajísáàrì* groups, generally led by a singer who is accompanied by a chorus and drummers, walk though the neighbourhood, stopping at compounds to wake the faithful for their early morning meal (*sáàrì*). *Fújì* emerged as a named genre and a marketing label in the late 1960s, when former *ajísáàrì* singers Barrister and Kollington were released from active duty in the Nigerian Army, made their first recordings, and began their periodically bitter rivalry. Although the genre has been partially detached from the sacred calendar of Islam, almost all *fújì* musicians and the majority of fans are Muslims, and the record companies are careful to release special *fújì* LPs on the major holy days (e.g. Id-el-Fitr, Id-el-Kebir, Ramadan).

The production of Yorùbá popular music is a complex and multiply situated social process. *Fújì* bands are hierarchically organised, and are often led by a praise-singer who has acquired his skills by moving up through the ranks of other groups. This individual, the 'band captain', reaps the lion's share of profits generated by the band. Live performances at Yorùbá naming, wedding and funeral ceremonies, in which participants 'spray' cash onto the foreheads of the musicians, are the most reliable source of remuneration for most bands, since royalty arrangements are not generous and profits are undercut by a highly dynamic and productive market in bootleg recordings.[6] Competition for live engagements is fierce, particularly among non-superstar groups. Only the biggest stars with the best connections are able to secure overseas tours and distribution arrangements. Unlike musicians such as Fẹlá Aníkúlápó-Kútì and King Sunny Adé, *fújì* musicians have not built up a big non-Nigerian following overseas. When on tour in England, Germany, and the United States, Barrister and Kollington perform mainly for Nigerian expatriate communities. These tours serve primarily as an opportunity to accumulate symbolic capital, including luxury items (prominently displayed on LP jackets and in music videos) and new forms of musical technology.

An investigation of competing etymologies for the term *fújì* suggests a keen appreciation of the interpenetration of 'global' and 'local' patterns. Barrister himself claims to have coined the term after seeing a poster of

Mount Fuji in a travel bureau office, thinking that it would lend his music (and personality) an aura of magnificent spirituality. Other informants linked the term to Fuji camera film – an expensive commodity and index of cosmopolitanism – and to the European term 'fugue', connoting complexity, refinement and authorial control. There are popular recordings from the 1950s in a proto-*fújì* style which bear the stylistic designation *fààjì*, meaning 'enjoyment' or 'sensual pleasure'. When presented with a range of etymological alternatives, *fújì* fans seem generally to allow, even to savour, the possibility of multiple origins. Musicians constantly fashion new genre names, and this is a source of interpretive pleasure for fans.[7]

Contemporary *fújì* music bears the traces of successive stylistic appropriations by practitioners, who attempt to create broad patronage networks that overlap boundaries between the elite and the masses, Islam and Christianity, and the ideological force-fields of cosmopolitanism and *ijìnlè* ('deep') Yorùbá tradition. *Fújì* performances, which at all-night celebrations of various sorts may run for 4 or 5 hours without a break, and on recordings are limited to about 22 minutes by the major studio's practice of recycling old 2-inch master tapes run at 30 ips, are long sequences of discursive themes strung together along dance grooves. The poetic discourse of *fújì* unfolds like a series of meandering paths, contingently joined, undergirded by 'rolling' rhythms and dense sonic textures, with changes of direction marked by the occasional authoritative signal from the band captain. Themes range from philosophical ruminations about the inevitability of death and the importance of good behaviour to frank sexual commentary and vivid evocations of the band's experiences abroad.

Fújì performance practice typically involves both serial juxtapositioning and simultaneous layering of diverse motifs, textures, styles and gestures. In an introduction to one of his videos, Alhaji Barrister describes his *Fújì Extravaganza* as 'a series of musics, artistically composed: one style, another style, one style after the other. *Fújì*', he continues, 'is an artistic composition whereby styles are utilised as the structure of the music.' Alhaji Professor Kollington, the other big *fújì* star, calls his style *Fújì Rópòpò*; the term *rópòpò* refers to the stirring together of diverse ingredients into a satisfying soup. Both metaphors – style as structure, and style as stew – suggest a compositional process in which exotic images, styles and technologies are subjected to the control of the band captain, and Yorùbá tradition itself becomes a self-consciously manipulated category.

In recordings produced by Lagos-based labels for the market in southwestern Nigeria and among migrant Yorùbá populations elsewhere in Nigeria and in other countries, the concept of *the song* as a minimal unit of production and consumption coexists somewhat awkwardly with the fluid and socially contingent patterns of Yorùbá popular performance practice. LPs and cassettes of *fújì* music usually carry four to twelve discrete song titles on their covers, usually the names of individuals or groups who have patronised the band captain or who, by virtue of their general popularity, deserve praise (e.g. Nelson Mandela). Other titles refer to dance fads or to place names, rather like pins stuck into a schematic map of the singer's transnational networks (e.g. 'America Wonder', 'Destiny World', or the ubiquitous references to London, where the big *fújì* stars perform semi-annually for Nigerian expatriate audiences). But there is no attempt to squeeze the slippery stuff of performance into the discrete 3 to 5 minute chunks that are the basic production units of the global music industry. Titles refer not to internally unified blocks of musical expression, but rather to transitory performative strategies. The 'songs' supposedly indexed by titles on the jackets of LPs are in fact loose and shifting clusters of expressive materials, stitched together with a few thematic threads, and hung on hooks comprised of a distinctive bit of melody, and a dance rhythm with an accompanying constellation of bodily movements.[8]

Another layer of shifting juxtapositions was added with the recent emergence of *fújì* videos, bankrolled by the major Lagos-based record labels (Orikun Ibusun, Decca WA, EMI), and produced by entrepreneurs who gain technical experience working for the Nigerian Television Authority and taping naming, marriage and funeral ceremonies on private commission. In these videos the sound recording is produced first, and the visual images are synchronised with the rhythmic flow and shifting stylistic and rhetorical patterns of performance.[9]

The flow of juxtaposed and heterogeneous fragments, alluded to by both Barrister and Kollington, can be identified at every level of performance. At the level of *musical styles*, Muslim chant, church hymns, highlife classics, sections of *jùjú* music, Indian film themes, popular songs (such as Abéòkúta's 'national anthem', *Àwa lomo Abéòkúta*) and talking drums and drum machines are serially juxtaposed. Shifting from a sequence of Islamic-style singing or an old highlife song from the 1950s to a sequence of praise for a wealthy patron, the leader might sing the line 'Now I turn and go to the house of X'. This sort of formula serves as a signal to the musicians, who in response might perform a unison rhythmic cadence, and then shift from a 16/8 pattern to a 12/8 pattern (maintaining the basic underlying dance pulse), while negotiating a sudden drop in volume and intensity.

At the level of *language* there are shifts from the predominant Yorùbá to sequences of English and Pidgin. Syncretism occurs even at the level of the individual lexeme, as in Barrister's neologism fanimorous – 'My *fújì* music is fanimorous' – which attaches an adjectival suffix (*-ous*) to the Yorùbá expression *fani móra* ('to attract people to you'). *Linguistic registers* range from highly regarded traditional idioms characteristic of Yorùbá poetry to slang, including expressions coined and put into circulation by the band itself. Not only linguistic registers, but entire textual genres are layered and juxtaposed. *Òwe* (proverbs) and *ofò* (incantations), as well as *oríkì*, are frequently quoted, and bits of Qur'anic texts are often added. Barrister's 1990 album and video *Fújì Extravaganza* opens with a self-announcing 'signature tune' characteristic of traditional oral artists and couched in imagery drawn straight from their repertoires:

> A gbéré wa dé
> Àwa ló lódù orin tuntun
> Báwòko bá ń ṣeré
> Kéyẹkéyẹ má fohùn lẹyẹ oko
> Àròyé niṣẹ ìbakà o
> Igbe kíké niṣẹ ẹyẹ
> Bólógbùró ṣe lóhùn tó
> Ó ṣì ń foríbalẹ́ fóba orin
> Àtàròyé ìbakà o
> Àtigbe kíké iṣẹ́ ẹyẹ
> Báwòko ò mórin wá
> Àròyé kí nìbakà máa rí wí?
> Igbe kí lẹyẹ ó wulẹ̀ ké lásán-lásán?
> Kí lológbùró óò fi ohùn orin kọ?

> We bring our show
> We own the secret of new songs.
> If the *awòko* bird is singing
> Let no other lesser bird make a sound
> Babbling is the work of the canary
> Chattering is the work of birds
> However beautiful the voice of the *ológbùró* bird
> She must still bow down before the King of Songs.
> With the babbling of the canary
> And the chattering, the work of birds,
> If the *awòko* doesn't bring songs
> What kind of babbling will the canary manage to produce?
> What kind of chattering would the birds bother to do?
> What song would the *ológbùró* bird use her voice to sing?[10]

Frequently, the vertical metaphoric axis of 'deep Yorùbá' texts is cross-cut by the horizontal plane of transnational musical allusions. The lyric presented above is sung to the melody of 'Malaika', probably composed in the 1950s by the Kenyan musician Fadhili William, 'collected' and copyrighted by Pete Seeger while on an African tour in 1963, and later covered by Seeger, Miriam Makeba, Harry Belafonte, the Brothers Four and other figures in the so-called 'urban folk revival' of the 1950s.[11]

Such Yorùbá texts, drawn from long-established oral repertoires, are juxtaposed with passages in English and Pidgin; and the English texts are themselves deliberately heterogeneous. They range from schematic representations of the romantic lyrics of mainstream Western pop (as when Barrister sings 'Don't doubt my love, my sweetie/I love you') to approximations to African-American speech, as in the 1982 recording *Fújì*

Americano where Alhaji Barrister, singing in the nasal, melismatic style associated with Islam, takes his fans to an American dance party:

> Hi, ladies and gentlemen!
> Now listen
> I'm now giving you our new *Fújì* Americano
> If you want to dance to *Fújì* Americano
> All you need to do is stroll along with your babe, dress
> properly, watch your step, and dance very beautifully,
> because:

> *Fújì sound is beautiful, so nice, beautiful*
> Now listen again
> If you don't come wit' your babe
> Make sure you don't fuck around with another man's babe
> That man may be a mother-fucker
> Because a man with a .45 [handgun]
> Is a man with an argument
> And sure, *Fújì* sound is now internationally accepted
> And is being carried to Great Britain by the Supreme *Fújì*
>   Commander

These shifts between linguistic registers and genres, and between the contrasting commentary of musical styles, are constant.

In *fújì* music videos, visual images and styles of representation are similarly juxtaposed, producing a texture of pastiche and allusion. There is only room for a few examples. A brief clip of the Cameroonian football star Roja Mila, shown kicking a goal and shaking his buttocks in celebration, becomes the basis for a dance step called 'The Roja Mila', the verbal directions for which are sung in Islamicised vocal style while Barrister is shown demonstrating it; a high-fashion model's nylon-clad legs are caressed by the camera's gaze as the band captain approvingly compares them to Mila's legs, and to the legs of the Argentinian footballer Maradona; newsclips of Nelson Mandela's release from prison shift into close-ups of hairstyles (the 'Mandela', the 'Burkina Faso', the 'Santana') and footage of the band captain in military uniform leading an exuberant crowd down a Lagos street; a proverb about the power of the lion over subordinate animals is visually overlaid with images of lions (*National Geographic*-style footage and rampant heraldic lions supporting the British crown); oneiric glimpses of mosques, sunsets, bottoms, aquariums, talking drums and plastic flowers adumbrate a series of interpretive fields around the multi-dimensional persona of the band captain (as pious Muslim, as good-timing ruffian, as Yorùbá bard, as millionaire entrepreneur).

Long stretches of the videos are home-movie style shots of the band performing at parties, but with the band captain and chorus girls in constantly changing costumes; these sequences are interspersed with scenes of the band captain in a domestic setting, surrounded by the emblems of bourgeois success (gilt wall lamps, large shiny sofas, coffee tables). There are also frequent evocations of glamour, in the style of American Grade B movies, but filmed locally on the Lagos Marina or in luxury hotel sites. Newsreel, home-movie and glamour sequences do not exhaust the videos' styles of representation, however. In *Fújì Extravaganza*, an extended reflection on the inescapability of death is illustrated by a dramatic portrayal of Death approaching and overthrowing his victims one by one. The costumes, and the stylised yet lively comic acting, make this sequence indistinguishable from Yorùbá popular theatre, which has itself recently moved into the video market in a big way.

The multiple 'texts' of the *fújì* performance, then, unroll in a leisurely flow of heterogeneous and eclectically assembled styles, themes and motifs, at the level of the music, the words and the visual images. The *extensibility* of the genre seems limitless; the images traverse geographical and social distances, bringing into the audience's field of experience the emblems of local upward mobility (e.g. the motor launch that carries the Ray-banned band captain and his fashion-model companion) and overseas journeys (e.g. the song describing a visit to 'Destiny World', where American technology is evoked with the words 'We all entered a big lift; suddenly the lights went out, and all the whites screamed "Oh my mother!"').

This style seems to fit perfectly into the picture of a globalised post-modernism. However, traditional Yorùbá oral genres do not make themselves heard in *fújì* only through explicit quotations of chunks of text or the use of particular kinds of imagery. In a larger sense, *fújì* can be seen to be working well within the parameters of *oríkì* chanting; indeed, in most respects, *oríkì* can be shown to go further in the direction of textual fragmentation, juxtaposition, heterogeneity and decentredness.

ORÍKÌ

Oríkì are a poetic genre that almost all Yorùbá-speakers know (even if sketchily), identify with and value greatly. Even today, *oríkì* are performed at all significant events in Yorùbá collective life – festivals, naming ceremonies, chieftaincy installations, weddings, funerals – as well as more casually as a form of commendation or greeting. They are performed by both men and women, and by ordinary members of households as well as by professional entertainers. They constitute the basis of innumerable localised or specialised chants, often treated in academic literature as distinct genres. Some professional *oríkì* chanters have made records and appeared on television, and it is not uncommon for rich people to hire *oríkì* singers as well as a *jùjú* or *fújì* band to entertain their guests at a big celebration. The continued ubiquity of *oríkì* performance, and the space it shares with more 'modern' performance genres, means that *fújì* musicians have ample opportunity to absorb and borrow from its repertoires.

Oríkì are often quoted in recognisable form in *fújì* texts. In *Fújì Extravaganza*, Barrister includes a well-known opening formula drawn from the repertoire of *oríkì* chanters (cf. Babalọla 1966b: 58):

> Mo dé wẹ́rẹ́wẹ́rẹ́ bí eji alẹ́
> Mo dé kùtùkùtù bí eji òwúrọ̀
> Mo dé wàràwàrà bí eji ìyálẹ̀ta

> I arrive gently like the evening rain
> I arrive at dawn like the morning rain
> I arrive in torrents like the noon-time rain

In his 1982 album *Ọmọ Araiye*, Kollington hails himself with his own. *oríkì orílè* the '*oríkì* of origin' with which people most profoundly identify:

> Èmi lọmọ 'Bá ò rígún
> A à gbọdọ̀ ṣẹbọ
> Bá ò rákalà
> A ò gbọdọ̀ ṣorọ̀
> Bá ò bá rí wọléwòde
> A ò gbọdọ̀ wọlé tọba . . .'

> I am the child of 'If we haven't got a vulture
> We must not make sacrifice
> If we haven't got a hornbill
> We must not conduct the ritual
> If we don't first see the guard
> We must not go into the palace to look for the *ọba* . . .'

But though much of the text of *fújì* performances is directed to enhancing the band and the band captain's image, it more often takes the form of hyperbolically flattering comments and far-fetched narratives peppered with slang, rather than actual *oríkì*. When they set out to praise a prominent patron, the words are often no more than a string of nicknames and titles, or unvarnished commendations sounding like commercial advertisements:

> Bí Toyota lẹ́ fẹ́ o
> Ẹ rí Múùfutáù
> Bí Volkswagen lẹ fẹ́
> Ẹ rí Múùfutáù

> If it's a Toyota you want
> See Mufutau
> If it's a Volkswagen you want
> See Mufutau . . .

It is in their form, in the way they use fragmentation to project them-selves out from their local site of performance, that *fújì* songs seem to be constituted within the parameters of the *oríkì* mode.

Oríkì are like names, which are felt to encapsulate the essential quali-ties of the subject they belong to, and in being addressed to that subject, to activate its powers. Persons, lineages, towns, deities and other entities accumulate these name-like formulations over time, as their qualities and propensities are revealed. A person might thus accumulate, over a life-time, a corpus of twenty *oríkì* each composed by a different person, at a different time, to commemorate a different facet of his or her life. An *oríkì*-formulation may be brief or extensive, condensed or elaborated. But like names belonging to the same person, *oríkì*-formulations, what-ever their form, have no intrinsic syntagmatic connection with each other: each epithet is potentially autonomous, indicating often in a cryptic or incomplete way its own separate hinterland of meaning. A performance of *oríkì* strings together large numbers of such inherently disjunctive materials, in an order and combination that can be varied at will. Furthermore, the performer can and often does produce supplementary disjunctions to an inherently fissured text, by breaking off before she has completed an item, leaving it as a mere allusion which the knowing audience will be able to complete.

This highly fluid and shifting textual environment is hospitable to borrowings and interpolations of all kinds. Since the utterance of *oríkì* empowers the subject to whom it is addressed, profusion is valued, and this gives rise to ingenious appropriations of material from a wide range of sources: from other bodies of *oríkì* attributed originally to other subjects; and from other genres, such as *òwe* (proverbs), *ęsę Ifá* (Ifá divina-tion verses) and even *àló àpamò* (riddles). The singer also intersperses her chant with prayers and philosophical utterances, commentary on the context and on her own performance, and songs, where a distinct rhythm and melody signal a transition from the prevailing speech-like chanting mode. The result can be a labile tissue of fragments, an assemblage of quotations, which nonetheless amounts, for the addressee, to a satisfying, 'filling', emotional and social experience of enhancement.

Through their disjunctiveness, *oríkì* make connections. They enhance the addressee – the owner of those *oríkì* – partly by citing a profusion of relations with other people. *Oríkì orílè* link a subject to a wide category of quasi-kin who claim common identity through origin in an ancient, named town. Subjects are also linked to numerous specific, named persons, living and dead, through salutations of the form 'child of . . .', 'father of . . .', 'husband of . . .', 'friend of . . .'. Very often, a subject's father, mother, grandparents and earlier forebears are evoked in *oríkì* chants. Their powers and attributes are in this way accessed to enhance the aura of their living descendant. The 'people' who are the basis of a successful man's status are repeatedly invoked in *oríkì* until the recipient of the performance seems like the centre of a constellation with innumerable lines of connection radiating out from him.

The following text is an excerpt from the transcription of a performance of *oríkì* that was addressed by an Òkukù woman, Bólátitó, to her husband's late father Ọmọníjẹ́, a great figure in Òkukù in the 1950s.[12] The utterance, overall, is an act of 'homage', an invocation of the powers of the ancestor, and an evocation of his personality. But it is made up of a variety of materials of different styles, forms and provenance. It opens with Ọmọníjẹ́'s personal *oríkì* evoking his outrageous behaviour (lines 2–5). These may have been originally formulated as *àkìjà* ('provocative epithets') designed to attack rather than flatter, by pointing to scandalous behaviour. They are incorporated into the *oríkì* because they signal something distinctive and memorable about his persona, as well as suggesting his power to break the rules and get away with it. The performer then comments in general terms on the importance of the mother (lines 6–8), and cites some of Ọmọníjẹ́'s mother's *oríkì orílè* (lines 9–11). She turns to of Ọmọníjẹ́'s own *oríkì orílè*, i.e. those of his agnatic descent group (lines 12–14); she adds the personal *oríkì* of one of Ọmọníjẹ́'s royal ancestors, the nineteenth-century *ọba* Oyèékàknbi, celebrating his unassailability (lines 15–18). She concludes this passage with a formula stating that she has travelled far enough down the road to Ọmọníjẹ́'s *ilé* ('house', lineage, compound) and will turn back there (lines 19–20) – a signal of a change of theme which, as we have seen, has been borrowed by *fújì* singers. She then comments philosophically on the importance of *oríkì* as accumulated 'nicknames' that testify to a life well-lived, thus simultaneously validating Ọmọníjẹ́'s reputation and her own activity in enhancing it (lines 21–4). Then – after migrating through the *oríkì orílè* of a number of other people associated with Ọmọníjẹ́, texts which are not included here – she adds a popular local song commenting on Ọmọníjẹ́'s excessive love of feasting during his life-time (lines 25–7), before closing with a resounding affirmation of her own worth, in defiance of detractors and ill-wishers who belittle her (lines 28–34).

Ọmọníjẹ́ Ajítòní mo ríbà baba ọkọ̀ mi	1
Akélépo ó tà ń gbígbóná, ọkọ Oyèbọ́lá	2
Asòrò-àná-di-bá-mìín	3
Ọnà tí yóò jẹ mà ní ń yán, Babaa Pópóọlá	4
Ọmọníjẹ́ Ajítòní mo ríbà baba ọkọ̀ mi	5
Ilé ìyá làgbà	6
Gbádéjọbí Ajídé, ilée baba lakúsùn ẹ́ni	7
Ìpàkọ́ nilé ìyá, iwájú tọ́ ọ rí nilée baba	8
Ọmọ Olúpo, Ọkòmòjè	9
Á ìí dúró tọlójà ká a pòsé owó	10
Ahá sékété tọ́ o rí ni wọn fi ń yọwo fáyaba	11

Ìṣèsú mo kọwẹ̀ n ò kójó   12
Mo kójó tán, ijó ń yọ mí lẹ́nu   13
Ìṣèsú ará odò Ọ̀rọ   14
Ọmọ adòyì kápá   15
Ápá ò kápá   16
Ọmọ adòyì kósè, osè ràmú jìgì   17
Adòyì kà kànga, kànga ò ṣe é kó sí . . .   18
. . . Bíbẹ̀ yẹn ò ṣọ̀nà, bíbẹ̀ yẹn ò ní í jọlé   19
Bàbáà mi mo padà níbẹ un . . .   20
Aì í dàgbà òjẹ̀   21
Ọmọníjẹ́, ká má mà lálàjẹ́   22
Níjọ tá a bá gbó   23
Tá a bá tọ́ ni ọmọ ẹni í ń fi kini . . .   24

Orin: Ọmọ Gbàǹgùnlùbọ́   25
 Abélébọ ṣégùúsí   26
 Gbàǹgùnlùbọ   27
 . . . Èyin ò rásínwín tí ò gbọ́n   28
Asièrè tí ò yànńyàn bí ọ̀pẹ̀lẹ̀   29
Àyánfúnnkẹ́ Àbíkẹ́ wọ́n á ní meè lọ́ba kan   30
Béníwá yóó mà sì wí   31
Mobọ́látitó Àbíkẹ wọ́n á ní me è níbi kan   32
Mo lè bọṣọọlè n fènìyàn ró   33
Ọmọ Orí-olówó Bọ́látitó Àbíkẹ́ aráà mi pọ̀ jomi lọ.   34

Ọmọníjẹ́ Ajítòní, I pay homage to my husband's father   1
One who makes the palm-oil seller sell while it's still hot   2
One who resurrects yesterday's problem to make a new one
  today   3
He's preparing the ground for the raking-in of bribes, father of
  Pópóọlá   4
Ọmọníjẹ́ Ajítòní I pay homage to my husband's father   5
The mother's house is senior   6
Gbádéjọ́bí Ajídé, the father's house is one's final resting place   7
The mother's house is the crown of the head, the father's house
  is the forehead   8
Child of Olúpo Àláelú, Ọkòmòjẹ́   9
No-one supports an *oba* only to sigh for want of money   10
They use a little gourd to dole out money to the royal wives   11
Ìṣèsú I learnt to swim, I didn't learn to dance   12
I finished learning to dance, dancing became a nuisance   13
Ìṣèsú native of river Ọ̀rọ   14
Child of 'They tried to surround [and overthrow] the *apá* tree   15
The *apá* tree cannot be overthrown'   16
Child of 'They gang up on the *osè* tree, the *osè* tree flourishes
  more than before'   17

'They conspire around the well, but can't throw themselves
    into it' ...   18
If that isn't the way, if that doesn't seem like the house   19
My father, I will turn back at that point ...   20
... We don't grow to a ripe old age   21
Ọmọníjẹ́ Ajídé, without acquiring some nicknames   22
When we grow old   23
In righteous old age, our children will use them to praise us   24

Song: Child of 'Busybody'   25
One who helps the celebrant shell melon-seeds for the feast   26
'Busybody'   27
Don't you see the crazy fellows with no sense in their heads   28
Mad people who don't make sense, like divination that doesn't
    come out right   29
Àyánfúnnkẹ́ Àbíkẹ́, they'll say I have no half-brothers   30
When other people talk about me   31
Mobọ́látitó Àbíkẹ́, they'll say I have no family   32
I could take off my clothes and wrap myself in people   33
Child of Orí-Olówó, Bọ́látitó Àbíkẹ́, my people are more
    copious than water.   34

Even this short excerpt from a much longer performance gives some sense
of the range of materials which an accomplished performer can incorporate. Each of the component segments of this text is entirely discrete;
many come from larger bodies of material to which they gesture back.
For example, the *oríkì orílẹ̀* of the Òkukù royal family, Ọmọníjẹ́'s
patrilineage, is a very extensive corpus revolving around the themes of
the ancient city of Kóòkin, the rivers that mark the royal land, the cults
which belong to the royal family, their wealth, their taboos and so on. In
the passage above, there is a brief 'quotation' of this corpus:

      I learnt to swim, I didn't learn to dance
      I finished learning to dance, dancing became a nuisance

Cited in isolation, as it is here, this sounds highly cryptic. To an informed
listener, however, these lines will immediately evoke a memory of the
River Ọ̀tin – Òkukù's principal river – and the large body of *oríkí* which
celebrate the royal history associated with it. The informed listener will
'read' these lines as a double claim: first, that members of the royal family
are so strongly associated with the royal river that they 'swim' before they
'dance'; second, that when they do dance, they become such a centre of
attraction that their popularity actually becomes burdensome to them. The
fragment of text relates not so much to the other fragments which
surround it in the performance, as to the extensive (and also itself internally disjunctive) corpus from which it is taken. Note how the syntax of
this short statement deliberately heightens the sense of fragmentation:

there are no connective words to explain the relationship between its four constitutive clauses, which are simply placed in juxtaposition for the audience to connect up for themselves.

Disjunction, then, is the principle of constitution of *oríkì* chants. Items of different form, provenance and reference are strung together in order to achieve the intense impact of contrast. The excitement of listening to *oríkì* lies partly in a performer's skill in leaping over the gaps between the textual elements of her performance. No segment is complete in itself. Each segment may speak in a different 'voice' and from a different point of view from the others assembled within the same performance. There is apparently no controlling authorial voice; when the performer speaks *in propria persona*, her interventions constitute just one element in the assemblage.

This disjunctive and labile textuality is thrown out like a net to draw in points of concentrated personality, and establish channels between beings through which power can flow. First of all, a strong dialogic bond is set up between the performer and the recipient, the addressee, of the *oríkì*. It is no accident that Bólátitó includes forceful affirmations of her own social worth, her wealth in 'people', for she and the addressee are two poles between which a current of empowerment flows. The performer establishes her own identity, as one pole, in the act of enhancing the identity of her subject as the other. The greater her own charisma as a performer, the greater the intensity of this enhancement. The reciprocity of the relationship is foregrounded in the text itself. Second, she enhances her addressee by opening channels between him and other individuals and bodies of people: his illustrious royal ancestor Oyèékànbi; his mother and the whole scattered network of people (the Olúpo people from Àjàsé) with whom she shares an *orílè* or common origin; his own Ìsèsú people of Koòkin, the great eighteenth-century town which preceded Òkukù and which is the origin and source of identity for the Òkukù royal family. A longer excerpt from Bólátitó's performance would have yielded many more connections with bodies of paternal, maternal and affinal relations. Citing the *oríkí* evokes not only the subject's compound in Òkukù but a wide network of known and unknown 'kin' scattered in clumps throughout Yorùbáland.

The fragmented, essentially allusive and uncompleted form of *oríkì* performances, then, intensifies the addressee's presence by drawing in a multitude of points of reference – to people and places, past and present. The process of saluting someone with *oríkì* is seen as a journey, the performer travelling into one *orílè* after another and returning, so that origin and identity are envisaged as metaphysical 'places' or destinations.[13] Omoníjé – the great, jovial, outrageous cousin of the *oba* – is at the centre of the chant upon which all these lines of connection converge. His intensely compacted magnificence is irradiated by the evocation of his royal ancestors, his origin, and his innumerable networks of 'people' leading out in all directions.

THE ENDS OF PERFORMANCE: FÚJÌ AND ORÍKÌ COMPARED

Both *fújì* and *oríkì* chants, then, are flowing concatenations of fragments which, through their very fragmentedness – through their juxtaposition of heterogeneous references, their prevalent mode of quotation and allusion – effect transcendence of the here-and-now. *Fújì* maps out a constellation of points beyond the immediate experience of the band's audience. This includes London, America, Japan (suggested in the very name of the genre), the high life symbolised by the Federal Palace Hotel and the yacht in the Marina. But it also reaches 'downward' into a hypostatised 'deep Yorùbá tradition', evoked by frequent quotations of *oríkì* and proverbs, and philosophising couched in the idiom of older oral genres. Just as it extends out into transnational popular culture and down into local traditions – thereby shaping people's interpretations of the global and the local – so, too, *fújì* draws heavily upon other contemporary Yorùbá popular genres, such as urban topical songs, televised situation comedy, the itinerant popular theatre, hairstyles and football. Like other forms of popular music in West Africa, *fújì* reaches out from the immediate, local grounds of its production and consumption in order to capture and domesticate difference.

Oríkì extend through a profusion of cryptic allusions back to the originary moment of present-day social groups and to their networks of forebears, as well as to the children, wives and other associates of the present-day addressees. *Oríkì* depend, much more than *fújì*, on intensely charged and detailed local knowledge to make their full impact; but, like *fújì* texts, they move constantly beyond the immediacy of the local, linking huge swathes of scattered and shadowy quasi-kin through an untraceably distant expanse of time. If *fújì* traverse space, *oríkì* chants traverse time embodied in space, memory embedded in places. Both genres, then, operate in a field where the boundaries of the 'local' fade into invisibility, but where the point of the performance is to charge with energy the aura of the key personalities immediately engaged in it. The purpose of transcendence of the local is to open channels through which enhancement flows to the performer or the recipient of the performance.

However, there are obvious and striking differences between *fújì* and *oríkì* chants. *Fújì* music is produced as a commodity for sale – in the form of cassettes, records and videos – as well as a performance. It is aimed at a mass public; and it inhabits a cultural sphere defined in part by the consumption of objects of glamour. Though professional *oríkì* chanters do inhabit the margins of this sphere of commercial entertainment, the centre of the *oríkì* tradition is local and domestic, sustained by talented but nonprofessional performers, often 'women of the household' (Barber 1991). *Oríkì* are performed in specific social and ritual contexts and addressed to known, specific subjects; they are not beamed to a mass audience defined by its participation in a sphere of consumer electronics.

From this underlying difference in production and consumption patterns flow differences in the texture and orientation of the two performance genres. *Fújì* music spreads its range of references more widely and more thinly than *oríkì*. It encompasses several languages; genres as diverse as cinema, popular theatre and oral poetry; and allusions to at least three other continents – and it distributes its effects through several channels, for the dance music and the spectacle of the band in action are at least as important as the words. It is more readily consumable. There are quotations from 'deep Yorùbá' registers, but the intense acts of recognition and interpretation that *oríkì* demand from the listener are unlikely to be called forth on the dance floor by *fújì*. Rather, the pleasure of 'reading' *fújì* lies in the listener's ability to recognise references scattered across several media: not only linguistic registers and textual quotations, but also sonic textures, rhythm patterns, melodic paraphrases and, in the videos, dance movements and sartorial styles. As Collins and Richards have suggested, 'an important part of the appeal of "popular" music in West Africa is the range of references upon which it is based, and the delight an audience takes in decoding these influences and quotations. Listeners are reminded of the way they have come and the route they may hope to travel' (Collins and Richards 1982: 131).

At the heart of the difference between *fújì* singing and *oríkì* chanting is the relationship between the performer and the recipient(s) of the performance. *Oríkì* chants open an intense reciprocal and dialogic relationship between singer and subject, in which both poles are consolidated through salutations, but where the subject – the recipient of the utterance – is the main focus. The disjunctive materials cohere around the addressee. The subject is built up through the process of heaping a profusion of name-like epithets upon his or her head. Far from implying a unitary notion of human and social identity, however, this process suggests that creation of social personality is the outcome of work: prolonged and vigorous attention from others is what constitutes a salient social personality. And the elements out of which the social persona is constituted speak with a multiplicity of voices. The 'self' appears highly concentrated – almost magnetic in its compact radiance – but at the same time internally highly diverse, assembled from networks of past and present personalities.

In *fújì* music, on the other hand, the central subject is unquestionably the band captain. *Fújì* celebrates, as it produces, celebrity; rather than a dialogic exchange stretched between two poles, all attention has slid to the performer's end. Like *oríkì* and like other genres of modern Yorùbá popular music, *fújì* may be sung in honour of a prominent big man – often the patron of the band, or someone whose patronage the band captain hopes to secure. But while the big man may provide the occasion for the performance, its real subject is the band captain. In some of the videos, the big man appears at the band captain's side, as his friend – a demonstration of the band captain's status, not the big man's. Much of the content of *fújì* songs deals with the captain, the band's musical style, the styles of dancing they inaugurated, their adventures abroad, their popularity, the categories of people who enjoy dancing to their music and so on. The advent of video in the mid-1980s only enhanced tendencies that were already evident in the songs. *Fújì* is above all a representation of the multiple alternative personae of the singer, a striking of attitudes, an advertisement of styles. If *oríkì* work to constitute a single, intense personal presence out of a multiplicity of migrating and borrowed elements, thus tapping into the powers of others, *fújì* seems to evoke the power and freedom enjoyed by a single person to occupy alternating, stylistically distinct roles or manifestations.

While *oríkì* chants name their subjects in a way that is felt to evoke their essential being, the naming that takes place in *fújì* is the opposite of Adamic. It is a naming that quite patently makes claims that cannot be substantiated. The band captains' own self-citation as 'General', 'Professor', and 'Dr' is only the starting point. Kollington opens the *Kasabubu* video with a sequence of citations of his own honours and titles, purportedly conferred on him by universities and government bodies all over the world: 'African *Fújì* Cradle Expander (OAU); Grand Order of Havana (UI); Professor and Master in *Fújì* Music (USA); Best Traditional Musician (1989 London) ... Best Dressed Artiste (1992); Grand Commander of Nigeria Youths; General of Music (FGN); Nwanne di Namba of Igboland.' The big claims are often put in English and the vocabulary chosen for its impressive sound: 'Africa International Music Ambassadors', 'Artistic Composition', 'Distinction Sounds'. In his *Fújì Extravaganza*, Barrister sings 'My type of *fújì* music is genuine'. But 'genuine', of course, is synonymous with 'imported', and what is imported is consumable commodities. While *oríkì* performances assemble the diverse materials out of which social being is constituted, and direct them intensively at the addressee, *fújì* singers multiply, spread and imprint their own image on everything. In doing so, *fújì* stars advertise themselves both as consumers of the good life, and as the central instance of an assemblage of objects of consumption.

'TRADITION' AND ETHNIC IDENTITIES

Both *oríkì* and *fújì*, then, are eclectic and incorporative, drawing on a range of materials to assemble a heterogenous flow of juxtapositions. The texts, we have suggested, stretch away from the point of performance to constellations of points beyond it, in an extended network of allusion which is felt to enhance the status or well-being of the focal personality (in *oríkì*, mainly the subject/addressee; in *fújì*, mainly the band captain).

But while *oríkì*, in this process, consolidate the identities of individuals, lineages and extended categories of kin/townspeople, *fújì* – like most contemporary Yorùbá popular genres – consolidates a category that did not exist before the mid-nineteenth century and is still not fully established: the category of 'the Yorùbá' as a whole (cf. Waterman 1990b).

One of the registers or repertoires on which *fújì* draws is traditional Yorùbá oratory. When *fújì* singers quote proverbs or include passages of *oríkì*, they are doing what *oríkì* chanters do, drawing on available materials from a variety of registers; but they are also citing 'tradition' as a category. The whole field of 'tradition' becomes one component in an eclectic soup of textuality. Not only specific textual references, but the idea of 'tradition' itself is being evoked. This self-conscious identification of tradition as a value as well as a source and resource is a feature of many other popular Yorùbá genres: the travelling theatre, Yorùbá-language films, fiction, neo-traditional oral poetry. All maintain simultaneously a subterranean, internal continuity with older forms of expression and a conscious external relation to them as 'tradition' (the fact that they refer to them *àṣà ìbílẹ̀* ('indigenous/native customs') shows this). *Àṣà ìbílẹ̀* are almost always associated with a pan-Yorùbá identity and, to a lesser extent, with Nigerian nationalism.

In the many *oríkì* Barber recorded in Òkukù, there was not one single reference to 'the Yorùbá', let alone to Nigeria. Rather, references were to the so-called 'Yorùbá sub-groups' – the Ìjẹ̀ṣà Ègbá, Ọ̀yọ́, and so forth – and, even more frequently, to ancient 'towns of origin' such as Ọ̀fà, Àrán-Ọ̀rin, Ìlá. In all contemporary genres of Yorùbá popular culture, by contrast, the audience implicitly or explicitly addressed is one made up of 'Yorùbás'.

In *Arẹwà*, Kollington sings:

> Ọrọ̀ kan ń dùn mí lọ́kàn
> Láàrin àwa Yorùbá . . .
> Ẹ jé ká ronú ìjìnlẹ̀ gidigidi
> Ká má dẹni ẹ̀hìn o . . .
>
> There's one thing that pains me a lot
> Amongst us Yorùbás
> Let's think deeply about it
> So that we don't fall behind [in the race for progress].

He goes on to say that among the Yorùbá, husbands and wives disagree, brothers and sisters fall out, instead of helping each other. He urges his audience 'Let us be more like the Hausa and the Igbo who don't destroy themselves.' This passage is an explicit allusion to Hubert Ogunde's famous play *Yorùbá Ronú!* (Yorùbá, Think!), staged in response to the Action Group crisis which threatened to destroy the Western Region with internecine strife after the split between Awólọ́wọ̀ and Akíntọ́lá in 1962.

Ogunde was one of the foremost spokesmen of Yorùbá cultural nationalism, and an agent of the process by which local and regional identities were politicised by the Action Group in the 1950s and thereafter. Kollington's explicit tribute to him, and assumption (however temporary and unconvincing) of his mantle, shows that ethnic consciousness has not just 'filtered down' from the politicians and leaders; it has been taken up and vigorously disseminated by popular musicians and popular theatre leaders. The very institutions that were crucial in the promotion of a transethnic and transnational 'creolisation' – schools, churches, the press, the media – were the means by which the notion of a pan-Yorùbá identity was established and made visible. Thus while *fújì* has a much wider range of fields to span with its net of disjunctive allusions than *oríkì*, it has also been instrumental in drawing new boundaries.

ACKNOWLEDGEMENTS

We are grateful to Kọla Oyesiku, Toyin Ajayi, Bayọ Ogundijọ and Andy Frankel for their help with the transcription and interpretation of some of the *fújì* texts used in this paper. We would also like to thank Keith Breckenridge and Helen Verran for their invaluable comments.

NOTES

1. Fredrik Barth has recently warned against a view of 'societies' as unitary, bounded units, and urged that we reject the idea that 'certain processes are endogenous to these isolates and should be understood in terms of internally shared cultural features, while others are exogenous and should be linked to culture contact, change and modernisation' (1992: 21).
2. Personal *oríkì* – that is, collections of epithets commemorating the actions and qualities of named individuals – are usually composed during the lifetime of the person concerned, and there are *oríkì* remembered today that are said to have belonged to historical figures going back as far as the seventeenth century. The fullest and richest corpora belong to figures from the nineteenth and early twentieth centuries. *Oríkì-orílè* – the *oríkì* by which large groups of people claim common origin in an ancient, named town – are more difficult to place historically. There are scholars who believe that some *oríkì-orílè* originated as early as the thirteenth century (see Babalọla 1966: 12).
3. 'Quotation', in *fújì*, is artful and deliberate and often involves a certain kind of suspension of judgment. It cannot, however, be said to be ironical in the manner that Hutcheon identifies as characteristic of postmodern texts.
4. In Yorùbá culture, this goes for other features commonly associated with, or attributed directly to, Western modernity too – individualism, highly developed notions of the autonomous self, commercial exchange and money as fundamental social metaphors, among others.
5. We want clearly to differentiate approaches that rely upon the imposition of a putative distinction between the exogenous and the endogenous, which we are critiquing, from Jonathan Friedman's useful notion of 'endo-sociality' (see Chapter 7, in this volume). Friedman's analysis impresses upon us the importance of a comparative anthropology of consumption, grounded in a detailed understanding of local colonial and post-colonial histories.

6. While many band captains have attempted to gain some degree of control over the production and distribution of recordings, they are still at the mercy of Nigerian entrepreneurs who have developed connections with transnational conglomerates, and bootleggers, who make music available on a mass scale for a fraction of the cost of the 'genuine' product.

7. Articles in popular tabloids devoted to the nightlife of Lagos and Ìbàdàn often discuss the implications of new genre terms and slang phrases coined by *fújì* musicians.

8. The advent of long-playing 33⅓ rpm microgroove discs allowed Yorùbá musicians to begin recording extended performances that more closely captured the macro-temporal flow of live performances. This could be taken as another example of the 'indigenisation' of musical practice via imported technology.

9. In the video version of his 1992 album *Kasabubu*, Kollington closes a long sequence with the remark 'That is the end of the first side; I hope you enjoyed it.'

10. Note the tripartite image structure, in which three lexical items from the same semantic field are placed in parallel with each other and one of the three is highlighted: in this case, the *awòko* bird, noted as the most melodious of all singing birds. The *ìbáàkà*, a small canary-like bird, has a high, thin, tuneful song. The *ológbùró*, a larger bird, has a powerful voice but is not as tuneful. This method of attributing excellence is highly typical of Yorùbá oral poetry, and of *oríkì* in particular. The self-praise, as a performer's opening gambit, is also highly typical of professional *oríkì* performers, who often have a 'signature' by which they hail themselves as they begin a performance.

11. A 1968 recording of 'Malaika' by a Swedish band called the Hep Stars (later ABBA) was covered in 1981 by the German-based disco band Boney M (Wallis and Malm 1984: 182–6), and it is this last version which is most familiar to Barrister's fans in Lagos.

12. Òkukù is a smallish town in the Òsun area, and the place where the research on *oríkì* used in this paper was conducted. For a full account see Barber (1991).

13. For more discussion of the idea of 'place' and identity in Yorùbá texts, see Barber (1994).

REFERENCES

Akinnaso, F. Niyi (1993) 'Bourdieu and the Diviner: knowledge and symbolic power in Yorùbá Divination'. Paper presented at the Fourth Decennial Conference of the ASA, Oxford.

Babalola, Adeboye [S. A.] (1966) *The Content and Form of Yorùbá Ìjálá*. Oxford University Press.

Barber, Karin (1991) *I Could Speak Until Tomorrow: Oríkì, Women and the Past in a Yorùbá Town*. Edinburgh University Press.

—— (1994) 'The Secretion of Oríkì in the Material World', *Passages* (Northwestern University) 4 (7) (passim).

Barth, Fredrik (1992) 'Towards greater naturalism in conceptualizing societies', in Adam Kuper (ed.), *Conceptualizing Society*, European Association of Social Anthropologists, London: Routledge.

Collins, Jim (1989) *Uncommon Cultures: Popular Culture and Post-Modernism*. London: Routledge.

Collins, John and Paul Richards (1982) 'Popular music in West Africa – suggestions for an interpretative framework', in David Horn and Philip Tagg (eds), *Popular Music Perspectives*, vol. 1. Goteborg and Exeter: International Association for the Study of Popular Music.

Coplan, David (1978) 'Go to my town, Cape Coast! The social history of Ghanaian highlife', in Bruno Nettl (ed.), *Eight Urban Musical Cultures*. Urbana IL: University of Illinois Press.

Friedman, Jonathan (1991) 'Consuming desires: strategies of selfhood and appropriation', *Cultural Anthropology* 6 (2): 154–63.

Hannerz, Ulf (1987) 'The world in creolisation', *Africa* 57 (4): 546–59.

—— (1991) 'Scenarios for peripheral cultures', in Anthony D. King (ed.), *Culture, Globalization and the World-system*. London: Macmillan.

Hutcheon, Linda (1989) *The Politics of Postmodernism*. London: Routledge.

Jameson, Frederic (1984) 'Postmodernism, or the cultural logic of late capitalism', *New Left Review* 146: 53–92.

Olatunji, O. O. (1984) *Features of Yorùbá Oral Poetry*. Ibadan: Ibadan University Press.

Strathern, Marilyn (1992) 'Parts and wholes: refiguring relationships in a post-plural world', in Adam Kuper (ed.), *Conceptualizing Society*. London: Routledge.

Wallis, Roger and Krister Malm (1984) *Big Sounds from Small Peoples: The Music Industry in Small Countries*. London: Constable.

Waterman, Christopher A. (1990a) *Jùjú: A Social History and Ethnography of an African Popular Music*. Chicago University Press.

—— (1990b) 'Our tradition is a very modern tradition: popular music and the construction of a pan-Yorùbá identity', *Ethnomusicology* 34 (3): 367–79.

Name index

Subject index